André Thevet's
North America
A Sixteenth-Century View

An edition-translation,
with notes and introduction,
by Roger Schlesinger and
Arthur P. Stabler

McGill-Queen's University Press
Kingston and Montreal

Thevet's name written on the second folio of the *Codex Mendoza*
Courtesy Bodleian Library, Oxford University

RS: For my parents,
Pauline and Edward, with love

APS: For my wife, Nancy H. Stabler,
for her patience and moral support

Contents

Illustrations

Maps

Following Page xliii

Preface

The main purpose of this book is to present an annotated edition–translation of the North American portions of the work of André Thevet (1504–1592), the Royal Cosmographer of France during the second half of the sixteenth century. In a sense, then, it is intended to complement the excellent editions and studies of Thevet's writing on South America, and especially Brazil, by Suzanne Lussagnet and Frank Lestringant. The need for an edition–translation such as this was clearly recognized early in this century by William F. Ganong, and more recently by Bernard G. Hoffman. The latter, together with Marcel Trudel and the late Samuel Eliot Morison, personally encouraged the authors to undertake this task and supported our efforts to obtain funding for the project from the National Endowment for the Humanities.

Scholars have had difficulty in gaining access to Thevet's materials on North America. His only complete work involving this area to be edited is the *Singularitez de la France antarctique* (see Bibliography). An English translation (with no annotations and a number of errors) was made by Thomas Hacket in 1568. Thevet's second major work containing North American material, the *Cosmographie universelle* (1575), has never been translated or annotated, while the third text presented here, the *Grand Insulaire*, has remained in almost illegible manuscript and presents many problems of sixteenth-century French vocabulary, spelling, and grammar. Since the original of this work has not been published, except for a few brief extracts, we include here the French text of the Canadian section of the *Grand Insulaire*, which appears to have the most interesting and original material. In addition, we have collated the relevant portions of three other Thevet manuscripts which are for the most part extracts of earlier works: the *Histoire de deux voyages*, *Second Voyage d'André*

Thevet, and the *Description de plusieurs isles.* While the publication of our texts involves some repetition of material, we felt that any attempt to delete the repeated portions destroyed the continuity of the individual texts. In annotations, our aim was to be reasonably complete, but since the information derives from many different fields of knowledge it is probable that some items have escaped identification or explanation. In any case, we have not tried to exhaust the field of Thevet research, but chiefly to make the texts available in translation for further investigation.

Arthur P. Stabler has established the texts and translated them, while Roger Schlesinger has been primarily responsible for the historical annotation. Both collaborated on the introduction. Thevet's manuscript texts, as well as his *Cosmographie universelle*, were obtained on microfilm from the Bibliothèque Nationale in Paris, and are now available to scholars at the Holland Library of Washington State University.

RS Pullman, Washington
AS Pacific Grove, California

Arthur Stabler passed away just as this book was going to press. I will miss him – he was a fine scholar and a good friend. RS

Acknowledgments

To thank all of the individuals who helped answer difficult questions or contributed bits of information would require several pages, but we would like to make special acknowledgment of the assistance of the following institutions: the Bibliothèque Nationale of France, the British Library, the John Carter Brown Library at Brown University, and the McHenry Library of the University of California at Santa Cruz. At Washington State University we thank the staff of Holland Library and particularly that of the Interlibrary Loan Department; Dean Lois B. DeFleur, who provided funds for the preparation of our manuscript; David H. Stratton, former chairman of the Department of History; and Jean-Charles Seigneuret and John Brewer, former and present chairmen of the Department of Foreign Languages, for their support and encouragement; Fredric C. Bohm, managing editor of the Washington State University Press, for his help with maps and illustrations; and Thomas C. Faulkner, director of the Humanities Research Center, who provided the technical expertise for phototypesetting this book. Among the staff of McGill-Queen's University Press we want to thank editors David Norton, Joan McGilvray, and Rosemary Shipton for friendly and expert help. We are particularly indebted to the works of the scholars mentioned in the Preface—Ganong, Hoffman, Lussagnet, Lestringant, Trudel, Morison—and also to that of H.P. Biggar, whose edition of Cartier's *Voyages* proved invaluable. Finally, we especially thank Meg Grimaldi for endless typing and many helpful suggestions about the editing of this book.

Terre
Mer
D'André Theuet fut telle l'apparence
Qui le premier cheminant l'vniuers
Courut Europe, Afrique, Asie jmmense
Premieres pars de ce Monde diuers
Et vid encor l'autre terre quembrasse
Le Ciel vouté sous l'Antarctique Gond
Et le feist voir ainsi qu'il se compaße
Descrit et peint dedans son Globe rond
T. D. L. fe.
Antuerpiæ.

Figure 1 Portrait of André Thevet
Courtesy Bibliothèque Nationale, Paris

Introduction

André Thevet once wrote that "It is impossible for any living man, never having left a place, however good a rhetorician he may be, to describe foreign countries unless he wishes impudently to lie."[1] It is somewhat ironic, therefore, that although he had indeed traveled widely, Thevet was nevertheless regarded by the majority of his contemporaries as an impudent liar. One of the first French writers to describe North America, his claims to have done so from first-hand experience in the New World have been met with a good deal of skepticism. Not only did Thevet receive some of the harshest criticisms of any literary figure of his day—involving rare agreement among Catholic and Protestant writers—but his poor reputation as a scholar has continued until recent times.

Modern scholars, however, have developed a more positive assessment of Thevet's value as a source for sixteenth-century North America, and for Canada in particular. Marcel Trudel, for example, although describing him as "a bogus scholar and a naïve compiler of facts," also notes that some of Thevet's information, resting on no known written sources, is absolutely correct.[2] Apparently Thevet obtained much of this original data from interviews with explorers and pilots, with Canadian natives who were brought back to France, and with fishermen who had returned from the Gulf of St. Lawrence.

The identification of Thevet's original contributions to our knowledge of sixteenth-century North America is difficult for at least two reasons.

1 André Thevet, *Cosmographie universelle*, 2 vols. (Paris, 1575), fol. 991v. All references are to the second volume of Thevet's *Cosmographie* unless otherwise noted.

2 See Marcel Trudel, "André Thevet," in *Dictionary of Canadian Biography/Dictionnaire biographique du Canada*, 1: *1000 to 1700*, ed. George W. Brown and Marcel Trudel (Toronto, 1966), pp. 679–80. Thevet is listed in the *Dictionary* only in an Appendix of "Persons whose identity is uncertain or who may never have come to what is now Canada." A similar, balanced assessment of the potential value of Thevet's work on North America has been offered by D.B. Quinn, who declared: "Thevet's memory was always bad, and he had what almost amounted to genius in confusing his information, but it may just be worth while to put his opinions on record." *England and the Discovery of America, 1481–1620* (New York, 1974), p. 140.

First, the fields of knowledge represented in his works are so disparate that it would take a battery of experts to be sure of identifying his original materials. Second, Thevet complicated matters by frequently transferring data from one part of the world to another: for example, the figure of Cudragni, a Canadian deity, reappears in the Mexican section as a prophet of the Spanish conquest. For Canada, however, Thevet's works provide valuable information on the clothing, marriage customs, religious practices, hunting methods, tactics of war, habitations, and dietary habits of the natives.[3] He gave one of the earliest descriptions of snowshoes, and he wrote several interesting paragraphs praising the healthy lives and good customs of some of the natives, passages which certainly contributed to the developing concept of the Noble Savage.[4] Thevet also was the first to use several place names, including Anticosti, Tadoussac, Miramichi, and Gaspé. For Mexico, Thevet's use of manuscript sources allowed him to present material on Aztec creation myths and religious

3 It is difficult to identify the specific group of natives that Thevet is describing at any given time. A judicious attempt to do so is D.B. Quinn, *Sources for the Ethnography of Northeastern North America to 1611*, National Museum of Man Mercury Series, Canadian Ethnology Service Paper No. 76 (Ottawa, 1981), pp. 29–36; see also map 18 for the general location of native groups in eastern Canada. For further information on the ethnography of these peoples see *Handbook of North American Indians*, gen. ed. William C. Sturtevant, 15: *Northeast*, ed. Bruce G. Trigger (Washington, D.C., 1978); and Alfred G. Bailey, *The Conflict of European and Eastern Algonkian Cultures, 1504-1700* (St. John, 1937; second ed., Toronto, 1969).

4 The concept of the Noble Savage is explored in Hoxie Fairchild, *The Noble Savage: A Study in Romantic Naturalism* (New York, 1928), and Hayden White, "The Noble Savage Theme as Fetish," in *First Images of America: The Impact of the New World on the Old*, ed. Fredi Chiappelli, 2 vols. (Berkeley, 1976), 1: 121–35. For more on conceptual frameworks used by European authors, including Thevet, in an attempt to understand and explain American native life see Henry S. Bausum, "Edenic Images of the Western World: A Reappraisal," *South Atlantic Quarterly* 67 (1968): 672–87; and three studies by Cornelius J. Jaenen: "Conceptual Frameworks for French Views of America and Amerindians," *French Colonial Studies* 2 (1978): 1–22; "French Attitudes toward Native Society," in *Old Trails and New Directions: Papers of the Third North American Fur Trade Conference*, ed. Carol Judd and Arthur Ray (Toronto, 1980), pp. 59–72; and "France's America and Amerindians: Image and Reality," *History of European Ideas* 6 (1985): 405–20. Related to the concept of the Noble Savage is the idea of The New and Infant World, where Amerindians were "living counterparts of European ancestral tribes" (Jaenen, "Conceptual Frameworks," pp. 6–8). In *Singularitez*, for example, Thevet compared Canadian Indian agricultural practices with those of the ancients. That some of these comparisons may be the work of a collaborator of Thevet's, Mathurin Héret, is indicated by Frank Lestringant in the introduction to his 1983 edition of the South American section of the *Singularitez* (see Bibliography), pp. 18–25. See also the Canadian section of *Singularitez*, chap. 82: "On the Country Called New[found]land," note 54.

beliefs that were not found in other contemporary works; his use of Laudonnière's narrative about the French colony at Fort Caroline, while it was still in manuscript, enabled him to pose as an expert on Florida as well. Specific remarks about Thevet's contributions are annotated in the relevant texts.

In addition to Thevet's original contributions to our knowledge of sixteenth-century North America, his works are interesting because they reveal the mentality of the author – a man of modest birth who eventually became prominent in court circles and an "authority" on foreign lands; a man eager to preserve his prestige whenever it was attacked. His opinions about and descriptions of sixteenth-century North American lands and cultures reveal him as possessing an essentially medieval religious outlook, but with a strong Renaissance curiosity about natural phenomena, human nature, and foreign places. Finally, Thevet is a fascinating author simply because of some of the tales he has to tell, including the well-known story of the exiled damsel Marguerite de Roberval.

Life and Works

Historians know very little about Thevet's early life. A native of Angoulême, he was until recently believed to have been born either in 1502 or 1504;[5] however, Frank Lestringant makes a convincing case for a birthdate of 1516 or 1517, based on an unequivocal statement by Thevet himself in his *Cosmographie universelle*, fol. 319: ". . . which happened in the year of our salvation one thousand five hundred seventeen, just fourteen months after the day of my birth: which was when Martin Luther began to oppose the Roman Church."[6] Later, with the support of the powerful La Rochefoucauld family, he obtained a university education (at Poitiers and Paris) and then secured an appointment as private secretary to the Cardinal of Amboise. Perhaps inspired by the books

5 Although almost all authorities agree that Thevet was eighty-eight years old when he died, there is disagreement over the dates of his birth and death. See Marcel Destombes, "André Thevet (1504-1592) et sa contribution à la cartographie et à l'océanographie," *Proceedings of The Royal Society of Edinburgh*, sec. B, 72 (1971-2): 123–31, esp. 123 and 129n.

6 André Thevet, *Cosmographie de Levant: Edition critique par Frank Lestringant* (Geneva, 1985), p. xiii and n1. From the same note we learn that "Thevet had been placed at the age of ten years in the Franciscan monastery of Angoulême 'against his will.'" Recent studies have been discovering interesting, if minor, details of Thevet's later life. In addition to this edition of the *Cosmographie de Levant*, see Lestringant's edition of the *Singularitez* (Paris, 1983). Also see Jean Baudry's edition of the *Singularitez* (Paris, 1982) and *Documents inédits sur André Thevet, cosmographe du roi* (Paris, 1983).

in the cardinal's library at Gaillon, Thevet developed a strong interest in travel, and made several journeys to Italy, Switzerland, Naples, and Africa in the 1540s. Indeed, he eventually became one of the most widely traveled Frenchmen of his day, and claimed to have spent seventeen years of his life in foreign places.[7]

Thevet's career as an author of geographical literature began with a journey to the Middle East. In June 1549, under the patronage of the Cardinal of Lorraine, Thevet sailed from Venice to the Levant, where he remained for four years.[8] He toured Constantinople with the Genoese ambassador in November 1549, and accompanied the naturalist Pierre Gilles to Chalcedonia, Rhodes, Athens, and Alexandria in a search for antiquities in 1550. He also visited Lebanon, Arabia, and Malta.[9] Shortly after his return to France, Thevet published an account of his travels in the East under the title *Cosmographie de Levant* (Lyon, 1554), which he dedicated to his former patron, François de la Rochefoucauld.

In the following year, 1555, Thevet obtained the position of *aumonier* (chaplain) for the expedition to Brazil of Nicholas Durand, Chevalier de Villegagnon.[10] Villegagnon landed at Guanabara (Rio de Janeiro) on 10 November 1555, but Thevet apparently fell ill soon thereafter and returned to France about ten weeks later (late January 1556) on the first available ship. Thevet claimed to have made this return journey by a more northerly route, one which took him past Haiti, Cuba, Florida, and "very close to Canada."[11] By this latter phrase Thevet apparently meant that he had traveled to the region north of the Carolinas, but historians have been uncertain about this claim. George Dexter, for example, writing in

7 See the Dedication to King Henri II in Thevet's *Cosmographie universelle*, 1: fol. 1v.

8 There is almost complete agreement in the sources that Thevet departed for the Levant in 1549. For unspecified reasons, however, Marcel Trudel gives 1537 for the approximate date of departure. According to Trudel, Thevet's trip lasted five or six years (see his "André Thevet," p. 679). Other accounts place Thevet's return to France between 1552 and 1554.

9 See Louis Moreri, *Le Grand Dictionnaire historique* (Paris, 1759), 10: 138. Pierre Gilles (1490-1555) was a French humanist, whose study of Aristotle and other ancient writers led him to study zoology and ichthyology. For more information see E.T. Hamy, "Le Père de la zoölogie française: Pierre Gilles d'Albi," *Revue des Pyrénées* 12 (1900): 561–88; see also the edition of the *Singularitez* by Jean Baudry, p. 16.

10 On Villegagnon see Arthur Heulhard, *Villegagnon, roi d'Amérique, un homme de mer au XVIe siècle (1510-1572)* (Paris, 1897), and Manuel Tomaz Alves Nogueira, *Der Moenschritter Nikolaus Durand von Villegaignon* (Leipzig, 1887).

11 See *Singularitez*, chap. 14: "On the Peninsula of Florida."

the fourth volume of the *Narrative and Critical History of America*, edited by Justin Winsor (Boston, 1884), evaluated Thevet's description of his return trip to France as follows: "No satisfactory information can be obtained from his story; and indeed his reputation for truth-telling is so poor that many historians are inclined to reject altogether his recital of the voyage along our coast. It may be that Thevet invented the whole of it as a thread upon which to hang the particulars about Florida, Norumbega, and other countries which he gathered from books."[12] Dexter's case is strengthened by the fact that Thevet himself wrote very little about the country between Florida and the forty-third parallel.

Upon his return to France, Thevet published an account of his experiences in "Antarctic France": *Les Singularitez de la France antarctique* (Paris, 1557).[13] This work, one of the earliest illustrated French books about the New World,[14] discussed the fate of the Villegagnon expedition and contributed valuable ethnographic information on the Tupinamba Indians. It also included Thevet's account of his alleged experiences in other parts of the Western Hemisphere including Newfoundland, Canada, Florida, and Mexico.

Although the account of Jacques Cartier's second voyage to the Gulf of St. Lawrence (*Brief Récit & succincte narration, de la navigation faicte es ysles de Canada* . . . [Paris, 1545]) had already been published, Thevet declared that he had decided to write about Canada because no one else had yet done so, and because he had obtained a knowledge of the region from Cartier himself. Indeed, Thevet's discussion of Canada and its inhabitants is particularly interesting for its descriptions of native war customs and hunting methods, medicinal practices, clothing styles, and religious beliefs.

The *Singularitez* enjoyed a favorable reception. Other French editions appeared in Paris and Antwerp in the following year, 1558, and in 1561 and 1568 Italian and English translations were published in Venice and London respectively (see Bibliography). As a result of the success of this work, and of his *Cosmographie de Levant* (1554, 1556), Thevet obtained

12 See George Dexter, "Cortereal, Verrazano, Gomez, Thevet," in *Narrative and Critical History of America*, ed. Justin Winsor, 8 vols. (Boston, 1884; reprinted New York, 1967), 4: 1–32, esp. 12.

13 North America is covered in fols. 144–64 (pp. 382–444 of Gaffarel's 1878 edition). For other editions and translations see the Bibliography.

14 The Paris editions of the *Singularitez* of 1557 and 1558 have illustrations printed from the same blocks, but the illustrations of the 1558 Antwerp edition are laterally reversed derivatives of those in the Paris editions. See William C. Sturtevant, "First Visual Images of Native America," in Chiappelli, ed., *First Images of America*, 1: 417–54, esp. 451n40.

a number of official positions at court and in the church. He became *aumonier* to Catherine dei Medici,[15] Royal Cosmographer to four French kings (Henri II, François II, Charles IX, and Henri III), canon of the Cathedral of Angoulême, abbot of Notre Dame de Masdion in Saintonge, and overseer of the Royal Collection of Curiosities at Fontainebleau. About his duties in this latter position Thevet wrote: "As for rare, good, and inquiring minds, I can confirm that he [Charles IX] esteemed them very much. I confess having received many courtesies, bounties, and liberalities from him, and he often sent for me to clear up the problems he had with respect to maps and foreign countries."[16]

Although Thevet made no subsequent journeys to America after the publication of the *Singularitez*, he did write several additional travel accounts. In 1575 he published his most extensive work, *La Cosmographie universelle d'André Thevet, cosmographe du roy*.[17] Here he attempted to convey an entirely different impression about his voyage to the New World. In the *Singularitez* Thevet said that he had been "very close to Canada," but now, almost twenty years later, he asserted not only that he landed in Canada, but that he had spent twenty days there examining the country and talking to the natives.[18] Indeed, many of Thevet's descriptions of Canada in the *Cosmographie* were written as if he were relating his own personal experiences, and he even included (fictitious) conversations with the natives.[19]

A good deal of the data on the style of life of the inhabitants of Canada is more elaborate and detailed than that found in the *Singularitez*, and Thevet added new material on how the natives hunted bears and about the discovery by the French of sugar maple sap. The latter story, Thevet said, was told to him by Cartier himself. Thevet also added to the *Cosmographie* the interesting tale of the ill-fated *damoiselle* Marguerite, allegedly marooned on an island by her uncle Jean François de la Roque, Sieur de Roberval. Although he claimed to have heard this story from the heroine

15 Catherine dei Medici (d. 1589) was Queen of France and wife of Henri II. For Thevet's remarks about obtaining this position see *Vrais Pourtraicts et vies des hommes illustres* . . . 2 vols. (Paris, 1584), 1: fol. 223r.

16 *Vrais Pourtraicts*, 1: fol. 228v.

17 North America is described in the second volume, fols. 984 to 1020.

18 See *Cosmographie*, chap. 3: "On the Land of Canada and Baccaleos."

19 Bernard G. Hoffman, who examined these conversations to look for words not found in Cartier, concluded that all but two of Thevet's phrases seem to derive from the 1545 edition of the *Brief Récit*. See his *Cabot to Cartier: Sources for a Historical Ethnography of Northeastern North America, 1497-1550* (Toronto, 1961), pp. 178 (table 7) and 179.

herself, there are reasons for doubt. First, Thevet said that Marguerite was Roberval's niece. If this were true, then he most likely would have heard the story in 1543 or 1544 from Roberval (Thevet's "familiar"),[20] yet he made no mention of this episode in the *Singularitez*.[21] Also, by the time that Thevet wrote the *Cosmographie*, two published versions of the story of Marguerite were already in existence. In 1558 Queen Marguerite of Navarre had published the first version in her *Heptaméron*, and a second account of the exiled *damoiselle* appeared in the fifth volume of François de Belleforest's *Histoires tragiques* (first edition, 1570). A comparison of Thevet's story with these other published accounts shows clearly that he knew them.[22]

Both Florida and Mexico also received more attention in the *Cosmographie* than in any of Thevet's other works. For Florida, he concentrated on the colonizing activities of the French at Fort Caroline. It is obvious that Thevet knew and used the account written by the leader of the colony, René de Laudonnière (see "Sources" section of this introduction). Thevet's account of Mexico is important for its descriptions of creation myths, history, and folklore. One modern scholar of Aztec civilization has called Thevet's survey "in some respects the most original and valuable of all those written outside Spain and the Indies."[23]

Unlike the *Singularitez*, the *Cosmographie* was not well received. Strong attacks on Thevet's faulty scholarship were made by the Calvinist minister Jean de Léry, and by a rival cosmographer, François de Belleforest (see "Reputation" section of this introduction). The celebrated English compiler of travel literature, Richard Hakluyt, referred to the Cosmographies of Thevet and Belleforest, both published in 1575, as "wearie volumes bearing the titles of universall Cosmographie which some men that I could name have published as their owne, beyng in deed most untruly and unprofitablie ramassed and hurled together . . . "[24] Modern

20 See *Cosmographie*, chap. 6: "History of Three French Persons Being in New-Land."

21 Later, in his *Grand Insulaire*, Thevet claimed to have told the Marguerite story in the *Singularitez*. See chap. "Isle de la Damoiselle."

22 The historic validity of this incident rests on the naming of some islands in the Gulf of St. Lawrence the Isles à la Damoiselle by Jean Alfonse de Saintonge, Roberval's chief pilot, in 1542, and on these three sixteenth-century accounts. For more information see Arthur P. Stabler, *The Legend of Marguerite de Roberval* (Pullman, Washington, 1972), and Robert La Roque de Roquebrune, "Marguerite de La Roque et l'ile de la Demoiselle au Canada," *Nova Francia* 6 (1931): 131–42.

23 Benjamin Keen, *The Aztec Image in Western Thought* (New Brunswick, N.J., 1971), p. 152.

24 See the preface "To the Reader," *Principal Navigations* (1589), in *The Original Writ-*

scholars have treated the *Cosmographie* little better. Complaining about folio 1008 in particular, "the outstanding case of Thevet's mendacity," William F. Ganong suggested that the author, "faced on the Atlantic coast by a great paucity of material, invented what he thought needful to give human interest, and the semblance of exclusive new knowledge, to this part of his book."[25]

Thevet's third major geographical work, *Le Grand Insulaire et pilotage d'André Thevet angoumoisin* (Paris, 1586), remains unpublished.[26] Although this is ostensibly a description of the most important islands of the world, Thevet's organization of material on North America here is no more systematic than in his published books. The *Grand Insulaire*, however, did add some new material for Canada. Specifically, Thevet provided for the first time a native vocabulary list, based indirectly on Cartier's, and he also gave a lengthy addendum of sailing directions from the *Routier* of Jean Alfonse (see "Sources" section of this introduction).

In the *Grand Insulaire* Thevet corrected the "errors" of others and defended himself from his critics. In particular, he complained about the faulty scholarship of his rival Belleforest on issues ranging from the extent of the "new lands" to errors in statements about whales and hake. The *Grand Insulaire* was also more political in tone, and Thevet frequently objected to the activities of the Spaniards in the New World while he enthusiastically promoted the idea of French colonization.

The portions of the *Grand Insulaire* on Florida and Mexico were much smaller than those in the *Cosmographie*. Thevet said that he was describing the way of life of the natives of Florida because no one else had really done so, but a good deal of his material here consisted of arguments with Girolamo Benzoni and Jean de Léry for making false statements of fact, and with Richard Hakluyt and Martin Basanier for publishing Laudonnière's narrative, which he claimed they had borrowed from him. For Mexico, Thevet provided more religious folklore and

---

ings and Correspondence of the Two Richard Hakluyts, with an Introduction and Notes by E.G.R. Taylor, 2 vols. (London, 1935), 2: 402. For the relationship between Hakluyt and Thevet see "Sources" section of this introduction.

25 William F. Ganong, *Crucial Maps in the Early Cartography and Place-Nomenclature of the Atlantic Coast of Canada*, with an Introduction, Commentary, and Map Notes by Theodore E. Layng (Toronto, 1964), pp. 434–5.

26 North America is covered in fols. 143–59, 176–7, 180–3, and 403–7 of this manuscript, BN MS fr. 15452. Suzanne Lussagnet has published extracts of the Brazilian portions of Thevet's *Cosmographie*, his *Histoire de deux voyages*, and his *Grand Insulaire* in her *Les Français en Amérique pendant la deuxième moitié du XVIe siècle: Le Brésil et les Brésiliens par André Thevet*, Introduction par Ch.-A. Julien (Paris, 1953).

history.

Thevet's last published work, the *Vrais Pourtraicts et vies des hommes illustres . . .* (Paris, 1584), was a collection of over two hundred biographies.[27] Although many classical personalities are represented, the originality of the work lies in its depiction of contemporary figures, including several from the New World: among these are Montezuma, Atabalipa, Paracoussi ("Roy du Platte"), and Paraousti Satouriona ("Roy de La Floride") [figs. 10 and 14].[28]

Among the other manuscripts that Thevet left are *Histoire de deux voyages* (1588), *Second Voyage d'André Thevet* (1587-8), and *Description de plusieurs isles* (1588). In the *Histoire de deux voyages*, Thevet tried to convince his readers that he had made two separate voyages to the New World. In addition to his "second" voyage of 1555 – the one with Villegagnon – Thevet now claimed to have made an earlier voyage in 1550 with the French pilot and cartographer Guillaume Le Testu;[29] the authenticity of this "first" voyage remains doubtful because of Thevet's failure to mention it in his *Singularitez*. Furthermore, this expedition was supposed to have taken place at the same time (circa 1550) that Thevet claimed also to have been in the Holy Land and at Cartier's house in Saint-Malo.[30]

27 For a list of editions and translations see Bibliography.

28 The biographies of these New World figures are in the second volume of the *Vrais Pourtraits* as follows: Montezuma, fols. 644–5; Atabalipa, fols. 641–3; Paracoussi, fol. 656; and Paraousti Satouriona, fols. 663–4. The *Vrais Pourtraits* also contributed to the popularity of copperplate engravings. Indeed, Thevet may have been one of the first to foresee the esthetic advantages of engraving for book illustration. For more on this subject see the introductory remarks by Rouben C. Cholakian in *Les Vrais Pourtraits et vies des hommes illustres. A Facsimile Re-edition*, 2 vols. (Delmar, New York, 1973), 1: ix–xi.

29 On Testu see Albert Anthiaume, "Un pilote et cartographe Havrais au XVIe siècle, Guillaume Le Testu," *Bulletin de Géographie Historique et Descriptive* (1911), pp. 135–202. For Thevet's claim in the *Grand Insulaire* to have made a first voyage to the New World see chap. "Isle of the Assumption," fol. 151r.

30 The disputed question of Thevet's alleged "first voyage" to the New World must for the time being remain open. Most commentators, including ourselves, have been very skeptical, primarily on the basis that (1) Thevet says nothing about any such voyage in the *Singularitez*, and (2) that in the years 1550-1, which he alleges as the date of the voyage, there is virtually incontrovertible evidence that Thevet was traveling in the Levant – a fact which also casts grave doubt on his claim to have conferred with Jacques Cartier and Sebastian Cabot at Saint-Malo in the same year (1550). Lestringant, however, has discovered a probably independent reference to *two* voyages made by Thevet to the "Antarctic countries," in the *Secrets de la Lune* by the physician Antoine Mizauld (Paris, 1571). See Lestringant, "La Conférence de Saint-Malo (1552-1553)," in *La Renaissance et le Nouveau Monde*, ed. A. Parent, et al. (Quebec, 1984), pp. 37–44: this article gives the

The *Second Voyage d'André Thevet*, also an account of Thevet's "two" voyages, included a vocabulary of Canadian native languages which is identical to that given in the *Grand Insulaire*. Here Thevet elaborated on the discussion of his voyage with Villegagnon, and claimed to have been in the New World for several years rather than for a period of months, as he had stated in the *Singularitez*. The *Description de plusieurs isles*, Thevet's last work (which ends abruptly in mid-sentence), appears to have been largely copied from the *Grand Insulaire*. Nevertheless, the manuscript is very useful in elucidating difficult passages in the latter because it contains the best penmanship among Thevet's manuscripts. Unfortunately the geographical data here are very confused, and the lapses of memory of an elderly man are evident. At one point Thevet even repeated a section of the same manuscript.

Thevet died in Paris on 23 November 1592 and was buried at the Grand Convent of the Franciscans in a tomb he had earlier made to order. It is said that Thevet, feeling his end to be near, visited the convent daily while the tomb was under construction, to make sure that it would be ready when needed.

Sources

It is difficult to determine precisely how Thevet obtained the information that he put into his works because he never acknowledged the use of any written sources. However, an analysis of the North American sections of his work reveals that he made extensive use of the third volume of Giovanni Battista Ramusio's *Delle navigationi et viaggi*.[31] This three-volume compilation of travel literature was published in Venice in 1550, 1556, and 1559. The *Terzo volume* (third volume), covering the New World, was actually the second to appear, in 1556, and its dedication is dated 1553.

---

most up-to-date discussion of the questions of both the "first voyage" and the "conference" of Saint-Malo. See also Lestringant's review of the edition of Thevet's *Singularitez* by Jean Baudry (who defends the thesis of the "first voyage," but in essence bases his opinion on nothing but Thevet's own assertions) in *Bibliothèque d'Humanisme et Renaissance* 44 (1982): 693–5. For Thevet's itinerary in the Holy Land see Jean Adhémar, *Frère André Thevet, grand voyageur et cosmographe des rois de France au XVIe siècle* (Paris, 1947), pp. 23–30; and for his statements about being Cartier's houseguest see *Grand Insulaire*, chap. "Isle of Cedars in Florida."

31 On Ramusio see George B. Parks, "Ramusio's Literary History," *Studies in Philology* 52 (1955): 127–48; his "The Contents and Sources of Ramusio's *Navigazioni*," in *New York Public Library Bulletin* 49 (1955): 279–313; and Antonio del Piero, "Della vita e degli studi di Giovanni Battista Ramusio," *Nuovo Archivo Veneto* n.s. 4 (1902): 5–112. We have used the 1606 edition of Ramusio's work.

If this date represents the year that the work was completed, it is possible that Thevet knew the contents of this volume before the publication of his first book on the New World, the *Singularitez*. Certainly Thevet made ample use of Ramusio's accounts of New France (the letter of Giovanni da Verrazzano, the first and second relations of Jacques Cartier, and the discourse of Jean Parmentier) in this work. Thevet also used the *Terzo volume* later in the *Cosmographie* and *Grand Insulaire*, where he copied Ramusio's Italianate spellings and even his infrequent errors. In particular, Thevet's native vocabulary lists in the *Grand Insulaire* are obviously based on Ramusio's version of the Cartier word lists.[32] We have seen no evidence that Thevet used either the manuscript or the published French versions of the relations of Cartier's first two Canadian voyages.

In addition to the accounts printed in Ramusio's *Terzo volume*, there is a strong probability that Thevet possessed or had access to three important manuscript sources on Canada: the accounts of Cartier's third voyage (1541), the voyage of the Sieur de Roberval to discover the Kingdom of Saguenay (1542-3), and the *Routier* of Roberval's pilot, Jean Alfonse de Saintonge (1544).[33] Thevet borrowed material from Cartier's narrative in both the *Singularitez* and *Cosmographie*, and he made extensive use of the Roberval account and Alfonse's *Routier* in the *Grand Insulaire*.[34] Indeed, the portion of that manuscript following folio 403 is

32 See "Language of the Inhabitants of the New Lands," in *Grand Insulaire*, chap. "Isles des Demons." Marius Barbeau has argued that Cartier did not compile the vocabularies himself, but that they were "the fruit of prolonged and expert home work," and perhaps put into final form by Rabelais. See his "Cartier Inspired Rabelais," *Canadian Geographical Journal* 9 (1934): 113–25; "How the Huron-Wyandot Language was Saved from Oblivion," *Proceedings of the American Philosophical Society* 93 (1949): 226–32; and "The Language of Canada in the Voyages of Jacques Cartier (1534-1538)," *Bulletin of the National Museum of Canada* no. 173 (1961): 108–229. Also see Percy J. Robinson, "The Huron Equivalents of Cartier's Second Vocabulary," *Transactions of the Royal Society of Canada*, 3rd ser., 42, sec. 2 (1948): 127–46.

33 These three accounts can be consulted in H.P. Biggar, *The Voyages of Jacques Cartier* (Ottawa, 1924): Cartier, pp. 249–59; Roberval, pp. 263–70; and Alfonse, pp. 278–303; see also notes 36 and 37.

34 Compare the Cartier passage given by Biggar in *Voyages*, pp. 254–5, with Thevet's *Singularitez*, chap. 80: "On the Ores, Precious Stones, and other Singularities found in Canada," and his *Cosmographie*, chap. 4: "On the Utility of the Said Country of Canada." For a second example, compare the Cartier account in Biggar, *Voyages*, p. 251, with Thevet's *Cosmographie*, chap. 6: "History of Three French Persons Being in New-Land" (fol. 1019r), in which Roberval, now viceroy of Canada, authorizes Cartier to depart and go before him to the New World. Also compare the text of the *Grand Insulaire*, chap. "Isle of Orleans," with that of Roberval in Biggar, *Voyages*, pp. 263–70. Biggar refers to passages in Thevet's *Cosmographie*, passim, but without suggesting any derivation from

almost entirely based on Alfonse (perhaps the "Portuguese pilot" referred to in the *Singularitez).*[35] Today, the narrative of Roberval's voyage and that of Cartier's third voyage are known to us only from the English translations in the third volume of Richard Hakluyt's *Principal Navigations*, published in 1600.[36] For three centuries, Alfonse's *Routier* was also known only in English translation in Hakluyt; however, the original, a part of Alfonse's own *Cosmographie*, was rediscovered and published by Georges Musset in 1904.[37]

Thevet's knowledge of these sources, long before Hakluyt published them, raises questions about the possible transmission of materials from Thevet to Hakluyt. We know that Hakluyt did acquire two other manuscript sources from Thevet, the *Codex Mendoza* and René de Laudonnière's *l'Histoire notable de la Floride*. It is therefore not unlikely that Hakluyt obtained these additional narratives from Thevet as well. He certainly had the opportunity to do so during the period 1583-8 when he resided in Paris as chaplain to the English ambassador, Sir Edward Stafford.[38] That Thevet was Hakluyt's source for Alfonse's *Routier* be-

---

Cartier.

35 Alfonse was sometimes referred to as a Portuguese because he married a Portuguese woman. See H.P. Biggar, *The Early Trading Companies of New France* (Toronto, 1901; reprinted St. Clair Shores, Michigan, 1972), p. 223; also *Singularitez*, chap. 77: "The Religion and Style of Life of These Poor Canadians."

36 See Richard Hakluyt, *The Principal Navigations Voyages Traffiques & Discoveries of the English Nation,* second ed., 3 vols. (London, 1598–1600; reprinted in 12 vols., Glasgow, 1903–5; New York, 1965), 8: Cartier, pp. 263–72; Roberval, pp. 283–9.

37 Alfonse's *Routier* was published in Hakluyt, *Principal Navigations*, 8: 275–83. The original, BN MS fr. 676, was published as *La Cosmographie avec l'espère et régime du soleil et du nord par Jean Fonteneau dit Alfonse de Saintonge, Capitaine-pilote de François Ier, publiée et annotée par Georges Musset* (Paris, 1904), pp. 475–503. Evaluations of Alfonse's work are in Auguste Pawloski, "Les plus anciens hydrographes français (XVI siècle). Jean Fonteneau, dit Alfonce. Ses collaborateurs: La science de l'hydrographie et de la cosmographie au milieu de XVIe siècle," *Bulletin de Géographie Historique et Descriptive* (1905): 237–51; and Lazare Sainéan, "La Cosmographie de Jean-Alfonse Saintongeais," *Revue des Etudes Rabelaisiennes* 10 (1912): 19–67. Thevet also had access to Alfonse's *Les Voyages avantureux du capitaine Jean Alfonce Saintongeois*, which was published after his death (circa 1549). Thevet's name appears in this work, above the *Tables de la déclinaison* (Musset, *Cosmographie*, p. 28). See also note 39.

38 See Arthur P. Stabler, "En Marge des récits de voyage: André Thevet, Hakluyt, Roberval, Jean Alfonse et Jacques Cartier," *Etudes Canadiennes/Canadian Studies*, 17 (1984): 69–72. Quinn believes that Hakluyt acquired the accounts of Cartier's third voyage, the Roberval expedition, and Alfonse's *Routier* while in France. See D.B. Quinn, ed., *The Hakluyt Handbook*, 2 vols. (London, 1974), 2: 438–9. Other mentions of Hakluyt's contacts with Thevet are in vol. 1: 281, 288, 292, and 294. For more information on

comes a virtual certainty when it is noted that the versions of both these writers present numerous variants in common when compared with the presumed original published by Musset.[39]

For his descriptions of Aztec civilization, Thevet relied primarily on written sources. Among these accounts are two important manuscripts, the *Codex Mendoza* and the *Histoire du Méchique*. Much of Thevet's data on the creation myths and religious folklore of the Aztecs came from this latter source, which has been tentatively assigned to the sixteenth-century Franciscan Andrés de Olmos.[40] This manuscript also contained a French translation of the *Historia general y natural de las Indias* of Gonzalo Fernández de Oviedo y Valdés (Seville, 1535). Antonio de Mendoza, first viceroy of New Spain, commissioned the *Codex Mendoza* (circa 1541-50) in order to portray the history and culture of the natives of Mexico to his sovereign, the Emperor Charles V.[41] This beautifully illustrated document traced the history of the Aztecs from the establishment of Tenochtitlan in 1324 to the Spanish conquest by Cortés in the early sixteenth century, and also gave an account of the daily life and customs of the natives. The *Codex* apparently came into Thevet's possession when French ships intercepted the Spanish vessel carrying it to Europe.[42] Thevet inscribed his name several times on the document

---

Hakluyt's activities in France see George B. Parks, "Hakluyt's Mission in France, 1583-1588," *Washington University Studies* 9 (1922): 165–84.

39 For a comparison of Hakluyt's text with that of Alfonse see Biggar, *Voyages*, pp. 278–303.

40 The *Histoire du Méchique* was published by Edouard de Jonghe in *Journal de la Société des Américanistes de Paris*, n.s. 2 (1905): 1–41. See Ángel María Garibay Kintana, *Historia de la literatura náhuatl*, 2 vols. (Mexico City, 1953–4), 2: 33, 48–9. For more on Olmos, the author of *Arte de la lengua mexicana* (1547), see Jeffrey K. Wilkerson, "The Ethnographic Works of Andrés de Olmos, Precursor and Contemporary of Sahagún," in *Sixteenth Century Mexico: The Work of Sahagún*, ed. Munro S. Edmonson (Albuquerque, 1974), pp. 27–77; and Garibay Kintana, *Teogonía e historia de los Mexicanos: tres opúsculos del siglo XVI* (Mexico, 1965).

41 The best modern edition is that of James Cooper Clark, *The Mexican Manuscript known as the Collection of Mendoza and Preserved in the Bodleian Library Oxford*, 3 vols. (London, 1938). A discussion of the artistic and technical aspects of this and related codices can be found in Donald Robertson, *Mexican Manuscript Painting of the Early Colonial Period: The Metropolitan Schools* (New Haven, 1959); also see Robertson, "Mexican Indian Art and the Atlantic Filter: Sixteenth to Eighteenth Centuries," in Chiappelli, ed., *First Images of America*, 1: 483–94.

42 See Samuel Purchas, *Hakluytus posthumus, or, Purchas his pilgrimes. Contayning a History of the World in Sea Voyages and Land Travells by Englishmen and Others*, 5 vols. (London, 1624–6; reprinted in 20 vols. Glasgow, 1905–7), 15 (1906): 413, for an

and added the date 1553 [frontispiece]. In 1587, when he was in Paris, Richard Hakluyt purchased the *Codex* from Thevet for twenty French crowns.[43] Later, Samuel Purchas published it, claiming the *Codex* to be "the choisest of my Jewels."[44]

Thevet's descriptions of Mexico and of Aztec society were also based on two printed sources. The first, Ramusio's *Terzo volume*, contained Italian translations of Peter Martyr's first three *Decades*, the 1535 edition of Gonzalo Fernández de Oviedo y Valdés's *La Historia general y natural de las Indias*, the Second, Third, and Fourth *Letters* of Cortés, and the relations of Pedro de Álvarado, Diego Godoy, the "Anonymous Conqueror,"[45] Cabeza de Vaca, Nuño de Guzmán, Coronado, and Fray Marcos de Nizza. Indeed, Thevet mentions, in his *Cosmographie*, the narratives of those who had written about New Spain in virtually the same order as they appear in the table of contents of the *Terzo volume*: "I well know that Christofle Coulon, Americ Vespuce, Pierre Martir Milannois, Gonzale de Ouiedo, Fernand Cortez, Pierre Dauarre, Diego Godoy, Aluare Nunes, Nuane de Gusman, Françoys Vlloa, Fernand Alarcone, & Françoys Vasques, most of them Spanish Captains, have described them, their narrations being published at Paris, Lyons, and Venice . . . "[46] Thevet also relied very heavily on Francisco López de Gómara's *Hist-*

---

account of how Thevet came to possess this document. Purchas's account of the *Codex* is on pp. 412–504. See also Thevet's description in his *Vrais Pourtraicts*, 2: fol. 515r.

43 D.B. Quinn, *Hakluyt Handbook*, 1: 294. Samuel Purchas, apparently in error, said that Hakluyt bought the *Codex* after Thevet's death (*Hakluytus Posthumus*, 15: 413).

44 *Hakluytus Posthumus*, 15: 412.

45 The account of the "Anonymous Conqueror" appeared in Ramusio's *Terzo volume* as "D'un gentil'huomo del Signor Fernando Cortese, Relatione della gran Città del Temistitan Messico, & d'altre cose della Nuova Spagna." We have used the English translation of Marshall H. Saville, *Narrative of Some Things of New Spain and of the Great City of Temestitan Mexico: Written by the Anonymous Conqueror, A Companion of Hernan Cortes* (New York, 1917). Examples of Thevet's use of the "Anonymous Conqueror" are indicated in the notes to the text.

46 *Cosmographie*, fol. 1025. Thevet is referring to Christopher Columbus, Amerigo Vespucci, Pietro Martire d'Anghiera, Gonzalo Fernández de Oviedo y Valdés, Hernando Cortés, Pedro Arias de Ávila, Diego Godoy, Álvar Núñez Cabeza de Vaca, Nuño de Guzmán, Francisco de Ulloa, Hernando de Alarcón, and Francisco Vásques de Coronado. Ramusio's table of contents lists the authors in this order: Don Pietro Martire Milanese, Gonzalo Fernando d'Ouiedo, Fernando Cortese, Pietro d'Aluardo, Diego Godoi, un gentil'huomo del Signor Fernando Cortese, Aluaro Nunez detto Capo di Vacca, Nunno di Gusman, Francesco d'Vlloa, Francesco Vasquez di Coronado, and Fernando Alarchon. Thevet's attempts to Gallicize these names accord with his typical reluctance to have his written sources identified.

oria general de las Indias (Saragossa, 1552) for information about the customs and institutions of Aztec society. Gómara, who had served Cortés as private secretary and chaplain from 1541 to 1547, obtained much of his material on Aztec history, society, and religion from Motolinia's *Memoriales* (composed circa 1542).[47]

Thevet's work on North America also provided a detailed account of the customs and way of life of the native Timucuans of Florida, and a description of the French settlement at Fort Caroline. Thevet said that the leader of the colony, René de Laudonnière, gave him this information.[48] In fact, Thevet's description of Florida at times follows Laudonnière's *l'Histoire notable de la Floride* almost verbatim. Apparently Thevet possessed Laudonnière's narrative, which he suppressed in order to pose as an authority on Florida. He complained bitterly, for example, that when he loaned his copy of the manuscript to his colleague Richard Hakluyt, the latter (together with the French mathematician Martin Basanier) published it without his permission. Hakluyt only said that the history "had bene concealed many yeeres."[49] In addition to Laudonnière's account, Thevet may have had access to the illustrations of Jacques Le Moyne, the Huguenot artist who accompanied the Laudonnière expedition to Florida, and to the account of Nicholas Le Challeux.[50]

47 Gómara's *Historia general* was translated into French by Martin Fumée in 1578. We have used the two-volume edition of Gómara's work published in Barcelona in 1954. Examples of Thevet's reliance on Gómara are indicated in the notes to the text.

48 René Goulaine de Laudonnière's *l'Histoire notable de la Floride* (Paris, 1586) was also published in London in the following year under the title *A Notable Historie Containing Foure Voyages Made by Certaine French Captaines into Florida*, and was reprinted in Hakluyt's *Principal Navigations*, 8: 439–86; 9: 1–100. For a new English translation see *Three Voyages*, edited and translated by Charles E. Bennett (Gainesville, Fla., 1975).

49 Hakluyt, *Principal Navigations*, 8: 439. On the relationship of the Florida accounts of Thevet and Laudonnière see Frank Lestringant, "Les Séquelles littéraires de la Floride française: Laudonnière, Hakluyt, Thevet, Chauveton," *Bibliothèque d'Humanisme et Renaissance* 44 (1982): 7–36. For Thevet's complaint see the Florida section of the *Grand Insulaire*.

50 Le Moyne's work, as well as that of Laudonnière, was published by Theodore de Bry as *Brevis narratio eorum quae in Florida . . . Gallis acciderunt . . .* (Frankfurt, 1591). For a new translation of Le Moyne, with a critical commentary on his drawings, see *The Work of Jacques Le Moyne de Morgues: A Huguenot Artist in France, Florida, and England.* Foreword, Catalogue, and Introductory Studies by Paul Hulton, with contributions by D.B. Quinn, R.A. Skelton, William C. Sturtevant, and William T. Stearn, 2 vols. (London, 1977). Lestringant, in his review of this book, says that several of the engravings by Le Moyne were taken from Thevet, and were based on the *Codex Mendoza*. He suggests that Le Moyne consulted the *Codex* in London after Hakluyt acquired it from Thevet. See his review in the *Bibliothèque d'Humanisme et Renaissance* 42 (1980): 776–8.

Thevet also obtained information from a wide correspondence with other geographers,[51] and he certainly used maps of the period, many of which are no longer in existence.[52] Thevet's own maps—originally he used some three hundred in the *Grand Insulaire*—are characterized by one modern scholar as "pioneering in intent but flawed in execution. In brief, they mingle, often carelessly, material derived from earlier sources with genuine new information; and when a factual basis is not available, Thevet is tempted to invent."[53] Indeed, Thevet's maps provide a good illustration of the problems presented generally by his works. Marcel Destombes has pointed out that the coordinates of Thevet's maps match those of Mercator's 1569 world map, but that often the detail is incorrect. An example is his map of Newfoundland [map 6], which is inverted so that the St. Lawrence is to the east. In addition, to take advantage of an open space in the northeast, Thevet added the "Isle of Thevet" off the coast of Newfoundland. He had also placed another "Isle of Thevet" off the coast of Brazil [map 4].[54]

While Thevet was silent about his written sources, he boasted that his information on Canada (and elsewhere) came from first-hand experience and eyewitness accounts. Indeed, he repeatedly claimed to have inter-

---

See also R. Joppien, "Etude de quelques portraits ethnologiques dans l'oeuvre d'André Thevet," *Gazette des Beaux-Arts* (April, 1978): 125–36. Le Challeux, an elderly carpenter, was one of those who escaped from Fort Caroline. His account, *Discours de l'histoire de la Floride, contenant la cruauté des Espagnols contre les subjets du Roy, en l'an mil cinq cens soixante cinq* (1566), is translated in Stefan Lorant, *The New World: The First Pictures of America* (New York, 1946), pp. 88–116.

51 See Thevet's letter to Abraham Ortelius in J.H. Hessels, *Abrahami Ortelii Epistulæ* (Cambridge, Eng. 1887), pp. 329–30. Karl Burmeister, *Briefe Sebastian Münsters* (Frankfurt, 1964), p. 9, suggests that Thevet corresponded with Sebastian Münster. See also *Cosmographie*, chap. 15: "The Province of Mexico," fol. 990r.

52 For evidence of the existence of Cartier's maps see H.P. Biggar, *A Collection of Documents Relating to Jacques Cartier and the Sieur de Roberval* (Ottawa, 1930), pp. 74–7; Biggar, *Voyages*, pp. 260, 314–15; and Ganong, *Crucial Maps*, pp. 255–6.

53 P.E.H. Hair, "A Note on Thevet's Unpublished Maps of Overseas Islands," *Terrae Incognitae* 14 (1982): 105–16, esp. 105–6, 105n3, 107n11. For the best information on the maps of the *Grand Insulaire*, both extant and missing, see the contribution of Frank Lestringant to Mireille Pastoureau, *Les Atlas français, XVIe–XVIIe sìcles* . . . (Paris, 1984), pp. 481–95.

54 Destombes, "André Thevet," p. 128; Hair, "Thevet's Maps," pp. 108, 112n28, and 114 and n37; and Lestringant, "Nouvelle-France et fiction cosmographique dans l'oeuvre d'André Thevet," *Etudes Littéraires* (April-Aug., 1977): 161–73. Hair suggests that the Isle of Thevet in South America is perhaps an island in Rio Massiambu, near Santa Catarina Island, Brazil.

viewed Jacques Cartier, his "great and particular friend," at his home in Saint-Malo. During his visit with Cartier, Thevet said that he also met Sebastian Cabot, with whom he conversed for "nine whole days."[55] In addition to Cartier and Sebastian Cabot, Thevet said that he had interviewed Donnacona, the chief of Stadacona, who was captured by Cartier and taken to France, where he lived for four years. Donnacona learned to speak French well and, according to Thevet, gave him information about native religious beliefs.[56] Of course, Thevet's insistence that he had access to eyewitnesses served his own interests. It allowed him, as Frank Lestringant has pointed out, to exercise his imagination freely and "fictionalize" his geography.[57] These claims also gave his work the appearance of presenting information which could not be found in other contemporary written sources.

Reputation

During his lifetime Thevet did not enjoy a good reputation as a scholar. His contemporaries, particularly Jean de Léry and François de Belleforest, ridiculed his work and vilified his character. Léry, one of the ministers sent by Jean Calvin to participate in the establishment of Villegagnon's ill-fated colony in Brazil, charged Thevet with making false and misleading accusations concerning the role of the Protestants in the eventual failure of the enterprise. According to Léry, Thevet was little more than an impudent liar and his works were "second-hand rags and tatters."[58] Belleforest, who had written one of the liminal odes honoring Thevet in the *Singularitez*, edited a French version of Sebastian

55 See the Florida section of the *Grand Insulaire*; see also Lestringant, "La Conférence de Saint-Malo (1552-1553)," p. 39.

56 See *Singularitez*, chap. 75: "On the Country of Canada;" *Cosmographie*, chap. 4: "On the Utility of the Said Country of Canada."

57 For more on this thesis see Frank Lestringant, "Nouvelle-France et fiction cosmographique," 145–73. The importance accorded by Renaissance and earlier historians to *autopsie*, or "things seen with one's own eyes," is also emphasized by Lestringant in his edition of Thevet's *Cosmographie de Levant* (see Bibliography), pp. xlix–li, and in his edition of Agrippa d'Aubigné's *Les Tragiques* (Paris, 1986), p. 56.

58 Original text: "vieux haillons et Fripperies." See Léry's preface to his *Histoire d'un voyage fait en la terre du Bresil, autrement dit Amerique* (La Rochelle, 1578). Modern editions include *Histoire d'un voyage fait en la Terre du Brésil, autrement dite Amérique*: Etablissement du texte et glossaire de Michel Contat. Postface de Jean-Claude Wagnières (Lausanne, 1972); and *Indiens de la Renaissance: histoire d'un voyage fait en la terre du Brésil, 1557*: Présentation par Anne-Marie Chartier (Paris, 1972).

Münster's *Cosmographia universalis*[59] which appeared in two volumes in 1575, several months before the publication of Thevet's own *Cosmographie*. Perhaps because of their competing Cosmographies, the two authors resented each other bitterly and neither missed an opportunity to attack the integrity and credibility of his rival. Belleforest, for example, accused Thevet of stealing material from his book,[60] and Thevet repeatedly pointed out that Belleforest, who had never traveled to the New World, of necessity had to rely upon the descriptions of others.[61]

Perhaps the French historian Jacques-Auguste de Thou offered the most critical description of Thevet's personality and reputation in his *Histoire universelle*:

[He] applied himself to writing books, which he sold to miserable publishers: after having compiled extracts of different authors, he added to them everything he could find in road guides and other such books, which are in popular hands. In fact, more ignorant than you could possibly conceive and having no acquaintanceship with literature, nor antiquity, nor chronology, he put in his books the uncertain for the certain, the false for the true, with an astonishing assurance. I remember that some of my friends, clever people with a keen wit, having gone one day to see him to amuse themselves, made him believe in my presence ridiculous and absurd things, which children even would have trouble swallowing; which made me laugh a lot. I can therefore not keep from pitying some people, who,

59 Among Münster's more important works are a Latin edition of Ptolemy's *Geographia* (1540), illustrated with twenty-seven woodcut maps after Ptolemy and twenty-one of his own design, and his own *Cosmographia universalis* (1544), reworked and enlarged by Belleforest in 1575. The literature on Münster is large. A valuable modern study is Karl Burmeister, *Sebastian Münster: Versuch eines biographischen Gesamtbildes* (Basel and Stuttgart, 1963).

60 Belleforest noted that a "certain author of Singularitez Antarctiques" stole from other authors and accepted rumor as truth. See François de Belleforest, *La Cosmographie universelle de tout le monde: Auteur en partie Munster* . . . 2 vols. (Paris, 1575), 2: cols. 2039–40. Adhémar has shown that Thevet in fact had seen Belleforest's *Cosmographie* before his own was published and that he had taken, almost verbatim, entire passages from Belleforest. See his *André Thevet*, p. 76.

61 According to Thevet, Belleforest, on his deathbed, begged forgiveness for the attacks he had made upon Thevet's scholarly reputation. See *Vrais Pourtraits*, 2: fol. 560r. In a letter to the cartographer Abraham Ortelius, Thevet also complained about Belleforest and Sebastian Münster as follows: "During the lifetime of the good father Seb. Munster I recall that having written me familiarly, he took in good part some remarks I had made to him and which he did not find superfluous touching foreign countries. He did not mention my name nor did Belleforest, although it is no lie that they greatly profited from me in remedying their inexperience. Sometimes they sought me out, they made many mistakes, and did not always show me the gratitude they owed me." Hessels, *Epistolæ*, pp. 329–30.

although well-versed in the sciences not only do not perceive his stupidities of a charlatan, but cite him every day with honor in their writings. I have often been astonished that a man so easily fooled, has himself fooled persons of such great reputation. I therefore warn them now to no longer in the future dishonor their works by citing an author so ignorant and contemptible.[62]

De Thou's judgment of Thevet was supported by Henri Lancelot du Voisin, Sieur de La Popelinière, who claimed that both Thevet and Belleforest wrote not for the public interest, but for their own profit, "which they obtained by the miserable work of their unbridled pens."[63]

In the following centuries Thevet's reputation did not improve very much. The brief, critical accounts that appeared in the eighteenth century, for example those of Jacob Le Duchat and J.-P. Nicéron, noted the typical accusations of Thevet's ignorance and mendacity.[64] By the mid-nineteenth century the *Nouvelle Biographie générale* concluded that Thevet's works had fallen into a well-deserved oblivion.[65] At the turn of the twentieth century Henry Harrisse described the North American portions of the *Cosmographie* as a "tissue of lies,"[66] and in the following year H.P. Biggar bluntly expressed the prevailing opinion of the value of the Canadian sections of Thevet's best-known work, the *Singularitez*, when he wrote: "With the exception of a few facts about snowshoes, hunting and the medicinal preparations of savages, he tells us absolutely nothing new."[67] More recent criticism of Thevet is exemplified by the remarks of Geoffroy Atkinson in his *Les Nouveaux Horizons de la Renaissance française* (Paris, 1935). In his section on "Critical Sense,"

62 See J.-A. De Thou, *Histoire universelle*, 2 vols. (London, 1734), 2: 651.

63 See *Histoire des histoires* (Paris, 1599), pp. 455–8, for La Popelinière's assessment of Thevet and Belleforest. These remarks are also found in Pierre Bayle, *An Historical and Critical Dictionary*, trans. Jacob Tonson, 4 vols. (London, 1710), 1: 568. The tenor of the criticisms of both La Popelinière and De Thou would appear to betray their own personal biases.

64 Jacob Le Duchat, *Satyre Menippée de la vertu du catholicon d'Espagne*, 3 vols. (Regensburg, 1711), 2: 285; *Les Bibliothèques françoises de La Croix du Maine et de Du Verdier*, nouvelle éd., 6 vols. (Paris, 1772–3; reprinted Graz, Austria, 1969), 1: 21–2; and J.-P. Nicéron, *Mémoires pour servir à l'histoire des hommes illustres dans la république des lettres*, 43 vols. (Paris, 1729–45), 23 (1733): 74–83.

65 *Nouvelle Biographie générale*, ed. Jean C.F. Hoefer (Paris, 1853), 45 (1866): 127.

66 Henry Harrisse, *Découverte et évolution cartographique de Terre Neuve et des pays circonvoisins 1497-1501-1769* (Paris, 1900), p. 156.

67 Biggar, *Early Trading Companies*, p. 233. Biggar offers a critical estimate of Thevet's works on Canada on pp. 231–42.

Atkinson characterized Thevet as ignorant, pretentious, stupid, a plagiarist, and an *attardé*. No one, Atkinson stated, would have criticized Thevet's work had it appeared a half-century earlier, but by the second half of the sixteenth century the "geographical marvelous" was already a dead genre, and real scholars with a critical sense had appeared.[68]

At the same time that Atkinson was writing these words, William F. Ganong began to rehabilitate Thevet's reputation as a source for sixteenth-century Canada. In particular, Ganong emphasized two main points: that Thevet's text contained important, original, and correct geographic and ethnographic information, and that these data derived from oral sources. For example, Ganong suggested that the Canadian chapters in the *Singularitez* may well have been developed from notes taken down during Thevet conversations with Jacques Cartier at Saint-Malo. "Thevet," according to Ganong, "would thus play the role of a reporter seeking material for his own writings, but with all of a reporter's limitations in dealing with unfamiliar events, scenes, and objects, plus others inherent in the indifference to correct detail prevalent in his age." Further, Ganong declared that the *Singularitez* appeared to be "a sincere attempt to set down his [Thevet's] information as he understood it; and it certainly does contain some items of real information which should be taken into account by future students of the Cartier voyages and of Canadian aboriginal customs."[69]

Bernard G. Hoffman followed Ganong in exploring the value of Thevet's Canadian data. In an intensive study of early ethnographic sources for North America, *Cabot to Cartier* (1961), Hoffman observed that among French cosmographers contemporary with Cartier, "the most im-

68 *Nouveaux Horizons*, pp. 289–97, 428–9.

69 See Ganong, *Crucial Maps*, p. 386. One item of particular interest in the *Singularitez* is Thevet's description of the use of tobacco by the natives of America (North and South). Whether credit for the introduction of tobacco into France should go to Thevet rather than to Jean Nicot, the French ambassador in Lisbon (1558-60), is a point of controversy. Thevet claimed that he brought back tobacco seed from Brazil and cultivated it at Angoulême before Nicot sent the seed to François II. Although supporters of Nicot, whose name survives in the word nicotine, deny Thevet's claim, it is interesting to note that Thevet brought *Nicotiana tabacum*, the type of tobacco used almost universally today, back from Brazil. Nicot's seed—which originally came from Florida—is *Nicotiana rustica*, and is primarily grown in Turkey. See Earl J. Hamilton, "What the New World Gave the Economy of the Old," in Chiappelli, ed., *First Images of America*, 2: 853–84. Another point in favor of Thevet's priority is that it was the Tupinamba word for tobacco, *petun*, mentioned by Thevet in *Singularitez*, fol. 60r, and *Cosmographie*, fol. 1014r, which became the original word in French, Portuguese, and English. One may note also that later another a genus of plants, *Thevetiana*, was named for our traveler.

portant, the most misread, and the most condemned is André Thevet." For this opinion Hoffman blamed not only "Thevet's somewhat unfortunate attempts at historical fiction, possibly an attempt to enlarge the marketing possibilities of his book," but also "careless, hasty, biased scholarship on the part of various students." He concluded that "whether we consider his voyage accounts as valid, or as being fictional adventure, we must give him credit for having used the best factual materials available. Specifically, Thevet's description of Canada contains original information obtained verbally from Cartier himself, which could not have been invented by any stretch of the imagination and which is subject to check."[70] Thus, for Hoffman, Thevet's works are invaluable sources for the early ethnography of eastern Canada. More recently, Olive P. Dickason not only ranked Thevet with Léry and Hans Staden as the period's leading sources of New World ethnographic material, but, she wrote, he "casts his net wider than the other two, who confined their attentions to Brazilians. Thevet not only added flesh to the bare bones of Cartier's published observations, but also pondered entrepreneurial prospects of New France that Cartier must have considered but did not record."[71]

These opinions are supported by a particularly significant part of the *Grand Insulaire*. On folio 154 Thevet gave three native place names in the Gulf of St. Lawrence region: *Thadoyzeau*, *Naticousti*, and *Mechsameht*. This is the earliest known record of the surviving names Tadoussac, Anticosti, and Miramichi, and historians know of no written sources through which Thevet could have obtained these toponyms. Perhaps they derive from his conversations with eyewitnesses, or from an account of Cartier's third voyage no longer extant. Whatever their origin, however, they offer evidence for the authenticity of some of Thevet's Canadian data. Later, in his *Description de plusieurs isles*, Thevet also became the first to record the name Gaspé (in the form *Gaspay)*.[72]

In addition to ethnohistorians, French scholars have found much of interest in Thevet's works because they reveal so clearly his psychological and intellectual characteristics. His first champion, no doubt, was his nineteenth-century editor Paul Gaffarel, who lamented Thevet's lack of

70 Hoffman, *Cabot to Cartier*, pp. 171–2.

71 Olive P. Dickason, *The Myth of the Savage and the Beginnings of French Colonialism in the Americas* (Edmonton, 1984), p. 178.

72 See our extract of the *Description de plusieurs isles*. Ganong traced the earliest known use of *Gaspay* only back to Hakluyt in 1600. See *Crucial Maps*, p. 374, and *Principal Navigations*, 8: 277.

organization and his tendency to exaggerate, but Gaffarel also pointed out that Thevet's works had preserved for future generations curious details about the New World which otherwise might have been lost. For Gaffarel, Thevet's most important characteristics were his insatiable curiosity and his desire to acquire and disseminate as much knowledge as possible.[73]

Among twentieth-century authors, Gilbert Chinard has one of the best assessments of Thevet in his *L'Exotisme américain*:

> There is in all these works which treat America such an accent of truth, or if one prefers, such ingenuousness, that I for my part cannot condemn [Thevet] so severely. Poor monk, full of good will and thirst for knowledge, he had traveled too long in the marvelous regions of the Orient, and had read too many compilations and accounts of adventurous voyages for his feeble brain to be able to resist them. He seems to have been a victim of a sort of mirage, and clearly shows this curious psychological characteristic of the traveler who, before setting out, studies too much without always choosing his authors well, the country where he wishes to go, and afterwards is not able to throw off the obsessive recollections of his readings.[74]

Charles-André Julien, in his introduction to Suzanne Lussagnet's *Le Brésil et les Brésiliens par André Thevet* (1953), took up many of the same themes and compared Thevet to a "commentator who wanders over the world on the trail of unpublished and picturesque materials." He thought that Thevet's main qualities were "a passion for traveling that made monastery life unbearable for him, a scorn for danger which caused him to face the perils of the sea and forays into 'strange' countries, an insatiable curiosity which led him to continually refresh and complete his knowledge, and finally the art of interviewing those in the know and extracting information from them."[75] Other recent favorable opinions of Thevet include those of Jean Céard and Jean Baudry. Céard, in his masterly *La Nature et les prodiges . . .* (Geneva, 1977), gives Thevet his due, citing his "curiosity"(his spirit of scientific inquiry), his concept of the infinite variety of nature, and his reverence for God as the creator of such marvels. According to Céard, Thevet repeatedly declined to

73 Paul Gaffarel, "André Thevet," *Bulletin de Géographie Historique et Descriptive* (1888), pp. 166–201.

74 G. Chinard, *L'Exotisme américain dans la littérature française au XVIe siècle* (Paris, 1911), pp. 89–90.

75 Lussagnet, *Brésil et les Brésiliens*, p. v.

believe in "monstrous" races of man and other genera of nature, ascribing natural "singularities" rather to the diversity of natural creation and adaptations to climate and other features of the habitat. As for the contemporary detractors of Thevet cited by Atkinson, Céard has these pertinent observations:

Moreover, what basis is there for lending credence to Belleforest, Léry and Chauveton? It is well known that their motives for criticizing Thevet were not pure; and if they had been so, the haughtiness, even the peevishness with which Thevet constantly rebukes any author who dared to treat the same subjects as he did were sufficient to irritate anyone: four centuries later his self-conceit is still irritating. His enemies revenged themselves upon him by giving him a bad name which he still has not got over! However, if the authors cited reproach him for his pretensions, his offhand manner and his errors, they do not seem to accuse him of lacking critical sense [cf. Atkinson]. Finally, we have difficulty believing that a man of "medieval ignorance" (so says Atkinson) could have won the esteem of Jean Cinquarbres, Genebrard, Dorat, Ronsard, Du Bellay, Baïf, Jodelle, Guy de la Broderie, and obtain the important post of the King's Cosmographer. Let us besides remember that, if some specialists could criticize his *Cosmographie universelle*, nevertheless it awoke general interest.[76]

Baudry's opinion of Thevet is expressed in the introduction to a facsimile edition of Thevet's *Singularitez de la France antarctique* (Paris, 1981). In addition to reinforcing the positive judgments of scholars such as Chinard, Julien, and Céard, Baudry even defends Thevet's veracity, and in particular his claim to have made a "first voyage" to the Americas around 1550 with Guillaume Le Testu – a claim which the present authors have reasons to doubt.

Perspicacious and entertaining discussions of Thevet from both literary and psychological standpoints are found in the recent works of Frank Lestringant, by far the most prolific of all Thevet specialists. Above all, Lestringant emphasizes the idea that Thevet, although pretending to be a savant, is really a writer of fiction – which may be taken as a diplomatic way of calling Thevet a liar. Lestringant also notes Thevet's jealousy of his "authority and credit," and demonstrates that his works were generally disorganized and confused, thereby agreeing with many of Thevet's previous critics. However, Lestringant also has favorable things to say on Thevet's behalf. For example, he emphasizes Thevet's

76 Jean Céard, *La Nature et les prodiges . . .* (Geneva, 1977), p. 283n39.

recommendations of vigorous efforts of colonization in Canada[77] and remarks that "definitely, the Thevetian project appears to exhibit an extreme coherence, one is even tempted to say, clairvoyance . . . . The lesson of the Canadian prospective according to Thevet is that, at the outset, a political will suffices to give birth to a country and a nation."[78]

In sum, judgments of Thevet's worth vary, perhaps in some cases for partisan reasons, but more particularly according to what the reader expects to find in his works. Certainly Thevet cannot be taken at face value—as a fountain of learning on virtually all subjects, and especially on geography and ethnohistory. Besides, his tiresome criticisms of the authors who dared to infringe upon "his" territory, his pretensions to infallibility, and his occasional "impudent lies" and clumsily concealed plagiarisms, executed in the same breath as his repeated claims that he had "refused to publish anything other than that which I have seen with my own eyes or heard when I was in the countries about which I have often spoken to you,"[79] do not do him honor. However, if we consider Thevet as a product of his somewhat faulty education, his class, his era, and his monastic profession, and if his works are considered variously as travelogues, sources for natural history, anthropology, ethnography, and even romance, there is much of interest in him. It is clear that if it were not for his "insatiable curiosity" and his not inconsiderable courage as a Renaissance tourist, a good many "singularities" of the period would not be available to us today.

A Note on the Translation. Thevet himself said, "I have not much concerned myself with the niceties of language—which you have to learn in the labors of those whose profession that is."[80] This translation attempts to render Thevet's French in a manner that makes his work readable, but neither destroys nor improves the character of the original. Among the more important changes that have been made are the creation of paragraphs in Thevet's text, the inclusion of conjunctions and prepositions and, on a few occasions, the repositioning of a clause within a sentence to clarify confused references. Capitalization has been regularized, but

77 *Grand Insulaire*, fol. 150v.

78 Frank Lestringant, "L'Avenir des terres nouvelles," in *La Renaissance et le Nouveau Monde*, ed. Alain Parent et al. (Quebec, 1984), pp. 50–1. Also remarking on this prophetic side of Thevet is Gilles Lapouge, who terms Thevet "a rustic futurologist,"even comparing him to Leonardo da Vinci. See Gilles Lapouge, *Equinoxiales* (Paris, 1979), pp. 50–4.

79 *Cosmographie*, f. 1025v.

80 Ibid.

Thevet's spelling of proper nouns and his use of italics and accent marks have been left as in the original as much as possible. Translations of quotations are our own unless otherwise noted. Numbers within brackets in the texts refer to the folios of the originals: the Paris, 1558, edition of the *Singularitez*; the Paris, 1575, edition of the *Cosmographie*; and the manuscript of the *Grand Insulaire* (in the text, the titles of Thevet's unpublished manuscripts have been italicized). Full references to works cited, if not found in the text or notes, appear in the Bibliography.

In editing these works we have not located all of Thevet's references to things he has written "elsewhere." Nor have we sought to provide explanations for all place names mentioned by Thevet, having limited our annotations to those of special interest. Also, notes are usually given only for the first mention of an item. Additional references to items in the text can be found in the Index.

The Maps

MER DESPAIGNE:
MER DE FRAN CE:
TERRE NEUVE:
Grande baye
Terre du Laborador:
ours sur les glaces

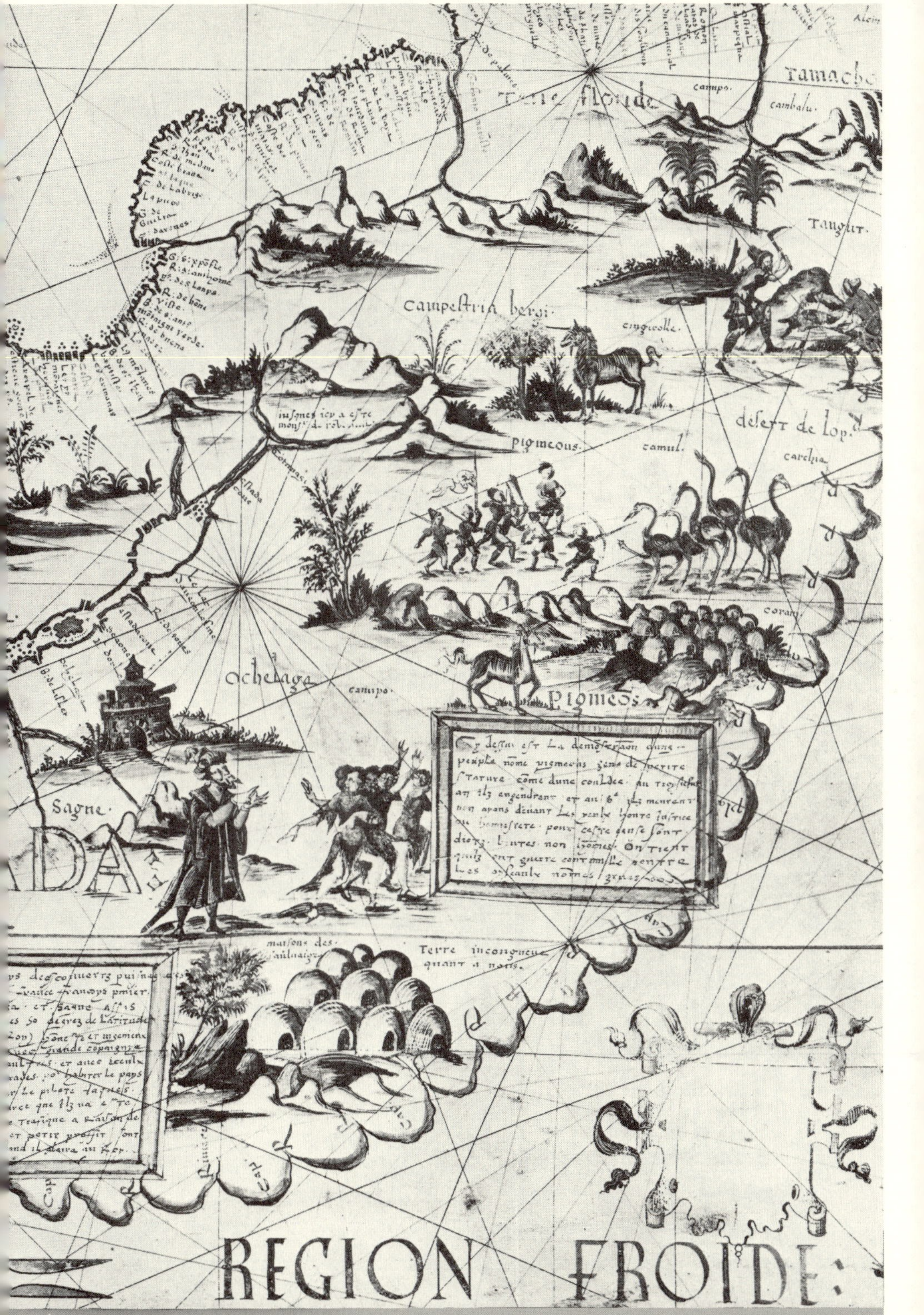

Map 1 1550 map of Pierre Desceliers
H.P. Biggar, *The Voyages of Jacques Cartier* (Ottawa, 1924)

Map 2 1569 map of Mercator (redrawn), northern extension
D.G.G. Kerr, *A Historical Atlas of Canada* (Toronto, 1960)

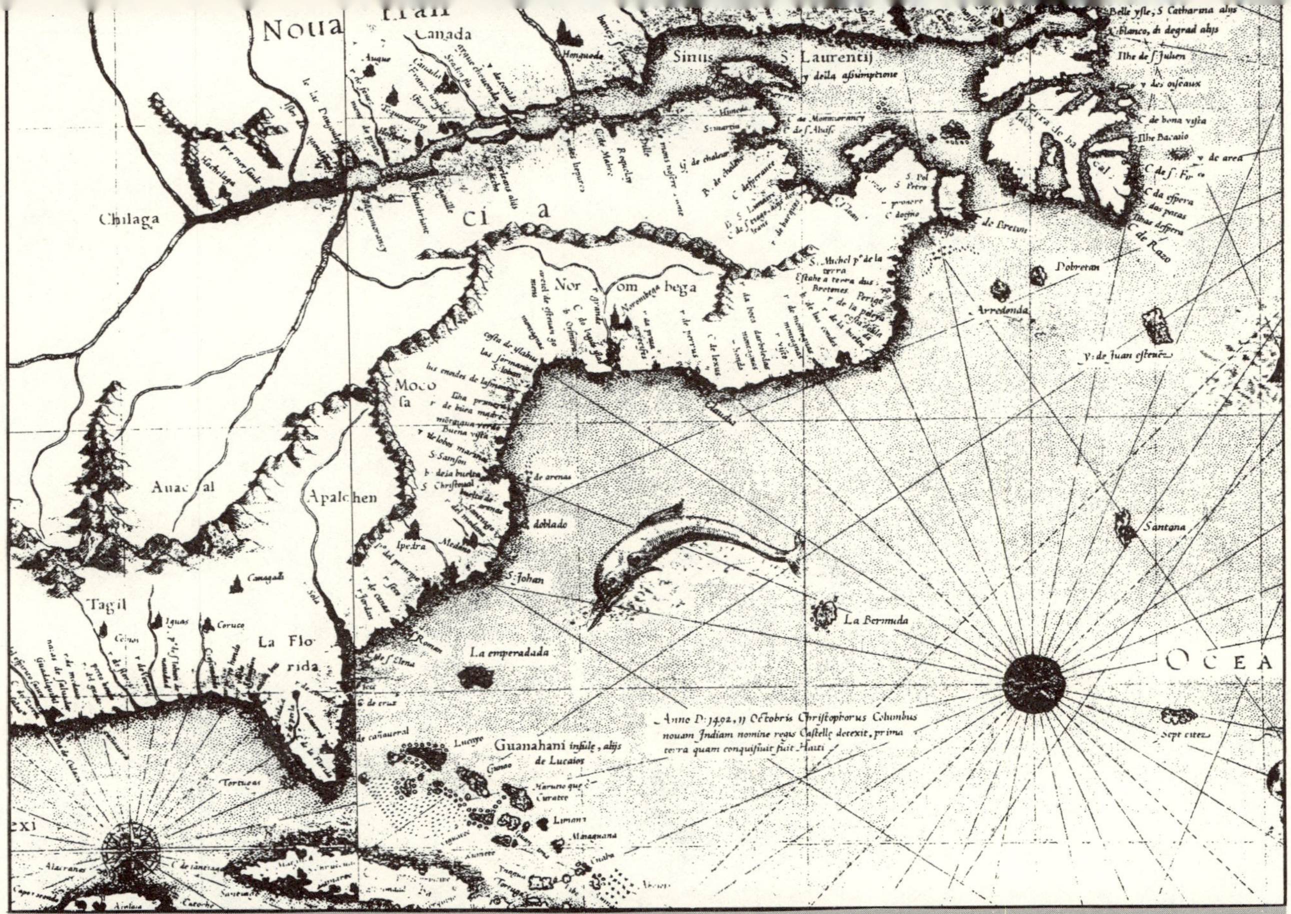

Map 3 1569 map of Mercator, with southern detail
M. Trudel, *Atlas of New France* (Quebec, 1968)

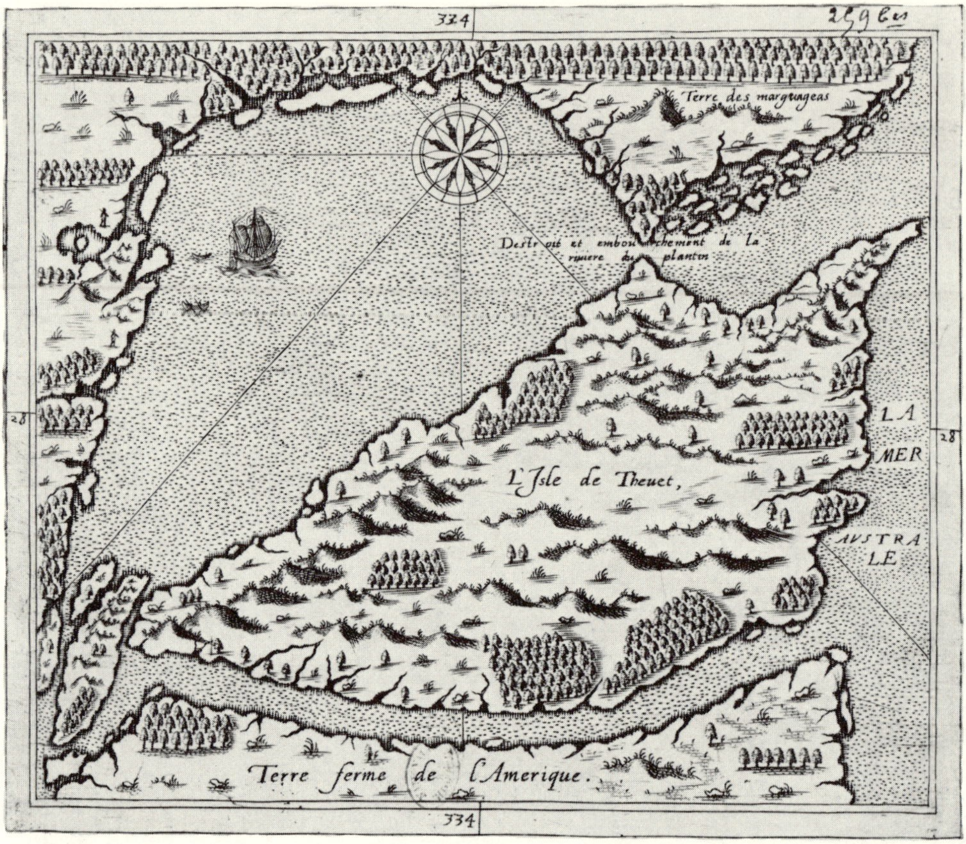
334
Terre des marguageas
Destroit et embouchement de la riuiere des plantin
LA MER AVSTRALE
L'Isle de Theuet,
Terre ferme de l'Amerique.
28
28
334

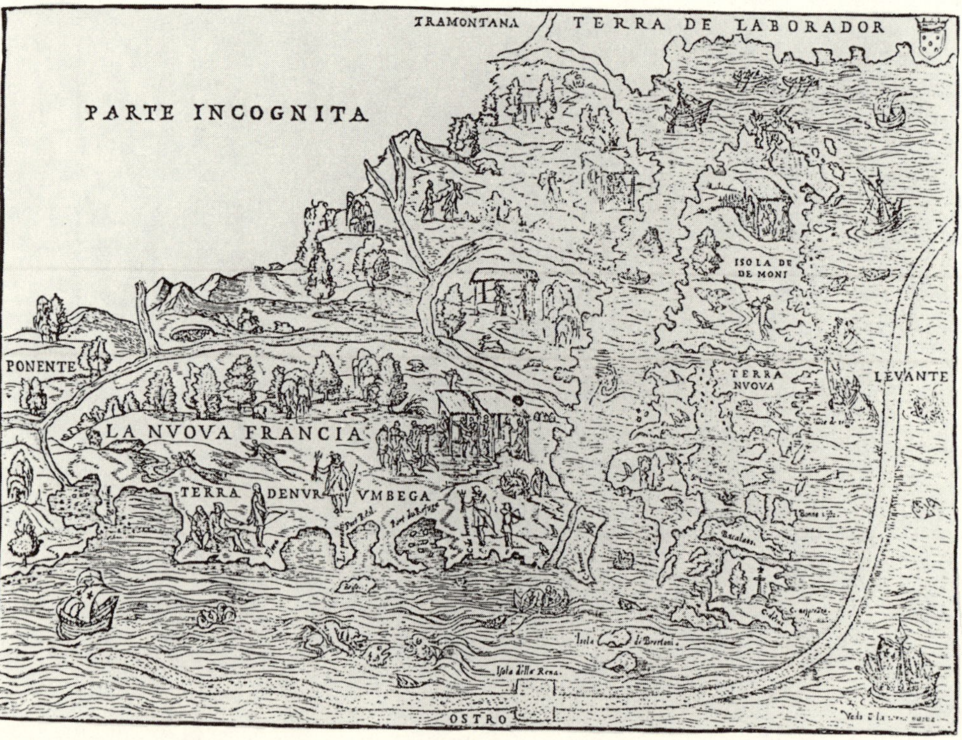
TRAMONTANA
TERRA DE LABORADOR
PARTE INCOGNITA
ISOLA DE DE MONI
PONENTE
TERRA NVOVA
LEVANTE
LA NVOVA FRANCIA
TERRA DENVR VMBEGA
OSTRO

Map 4 (opposite top) Isle of Thevet in South America
Thevet's *Grand Insulaire*, fol. 260 *bis*.
Courtesy Bibliothèque Nationale, Paris

Map 5 (opposite below) Ramusio's map of New France
Ramusio's *Terzo volume*, fol. 353r.
Courtesy E.O. Holland Library at Washington State University

Map 6 (above) Isles des Terres Neuves. Note the reversal of Newfoundland, with the St. Lawrence River to the east, and the North American "Isle of Thevet"
Thevet's *Grand Insulaire*, fol. 143 bis.
Courtesy Bibliothèque Nationale, Paris

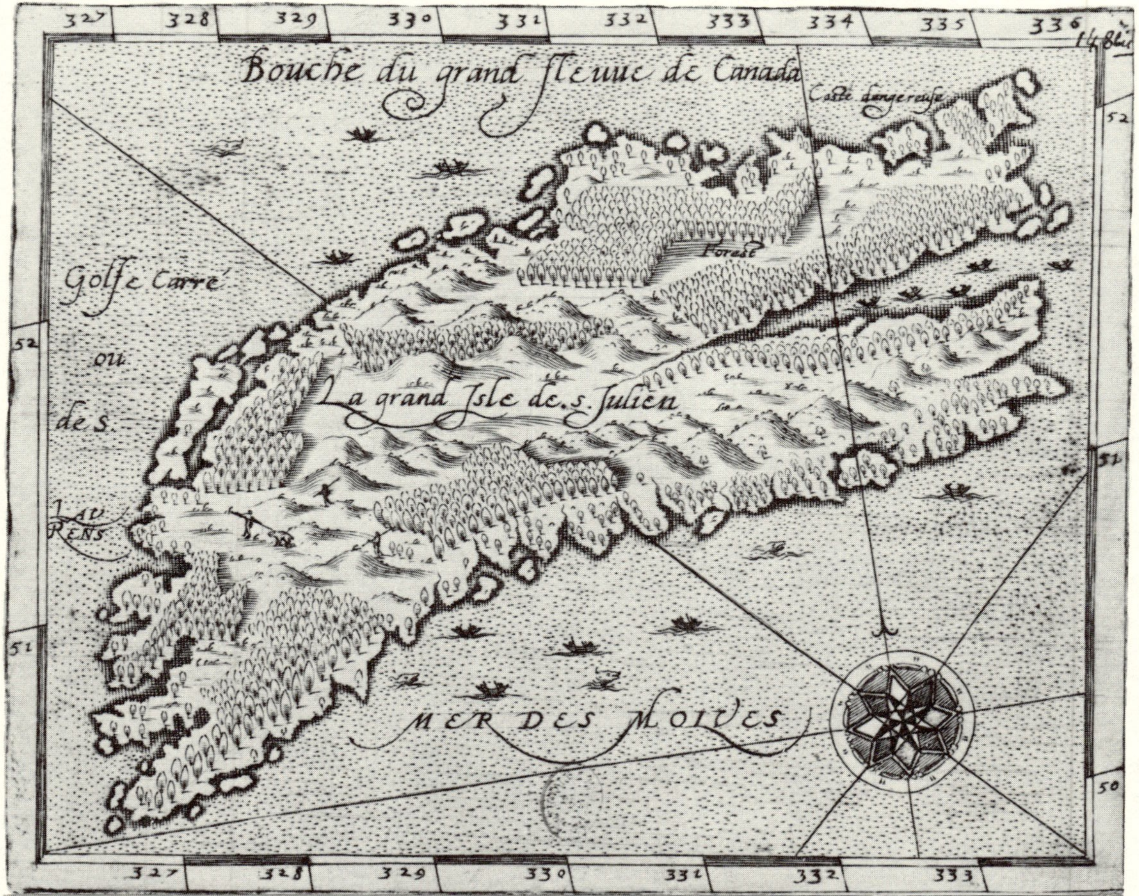

Map 7 Isle of St. Julien, Thevet's *Grand Insulaire*, fol. 149r.
Courtesy Bibliothèque Nationale, Paris

Map 8   Florida shown as an island
D.B. Quinn, *New American World* 1 (New York, 1979)

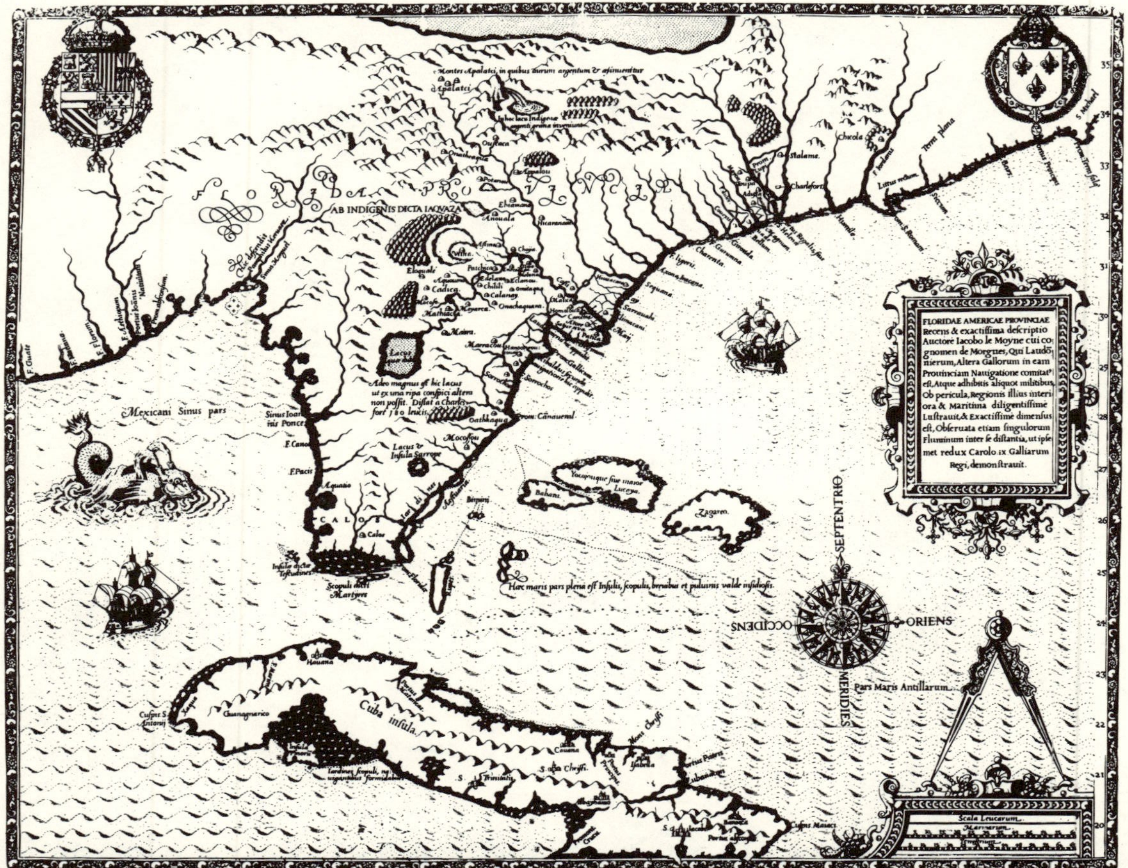

Map 9 Jacques Le Moyne's map of Florida
A. Johnson, *America Explored* (New York, 1974)

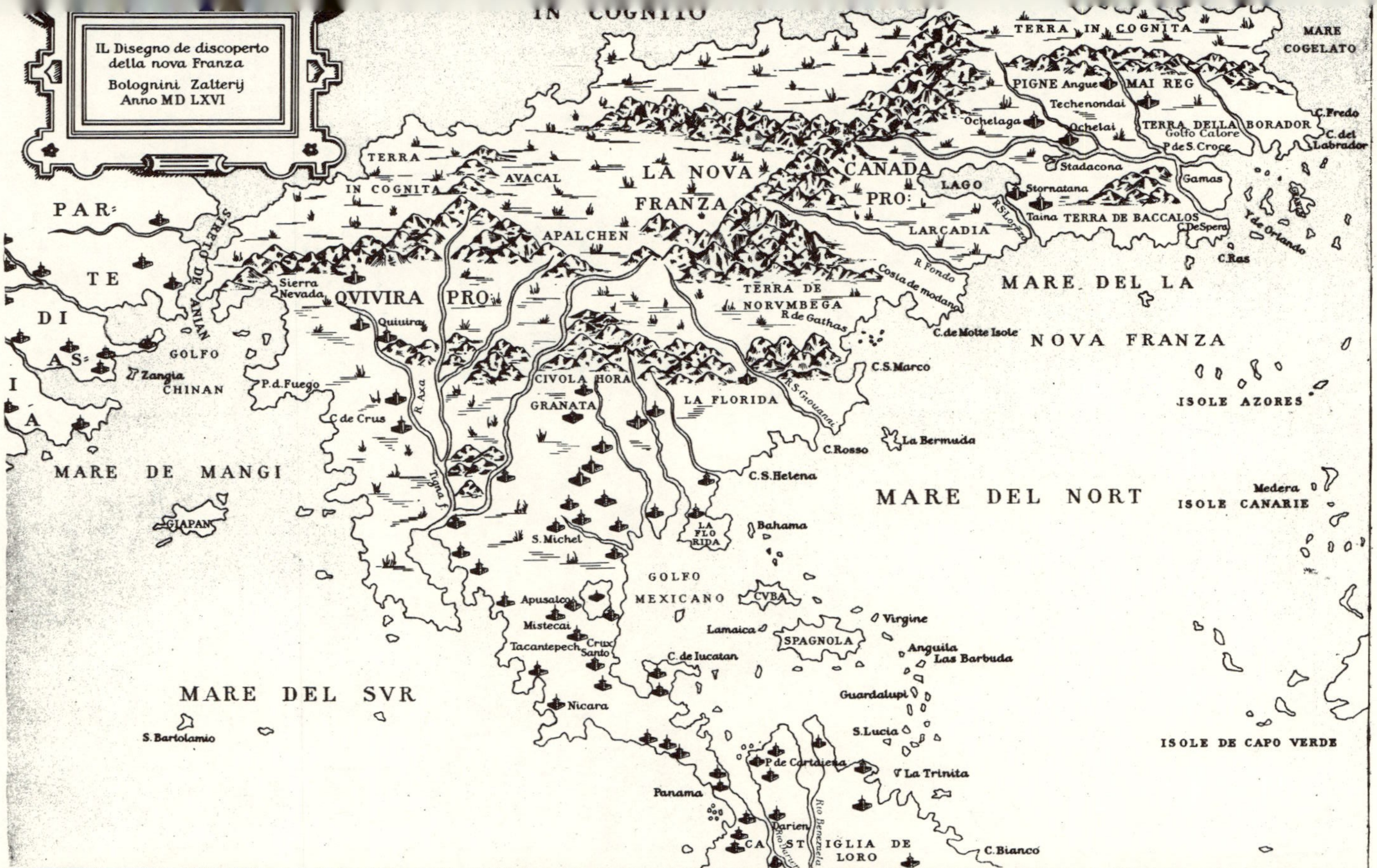

Map 10 1566 map of B. Zaltieri (redrawn) showing the Strait of Anian
D.G.G. Kerr, *A Historical Atlas of Canada* (Toronto, 1960)

Map 11 Thevet's map in the *Cosmographie universelle*, based on Mercator's 1569 map

Thevet's *Cosmographie universelle. Courtesy John Carter Brown Library at Brown University*

Map 12 Ramusio's map
of Themistitan
Ramusio's *Terzo volume*,
fol. 250r.
Courtesy E.O. Holland
Library at
Washington State
University

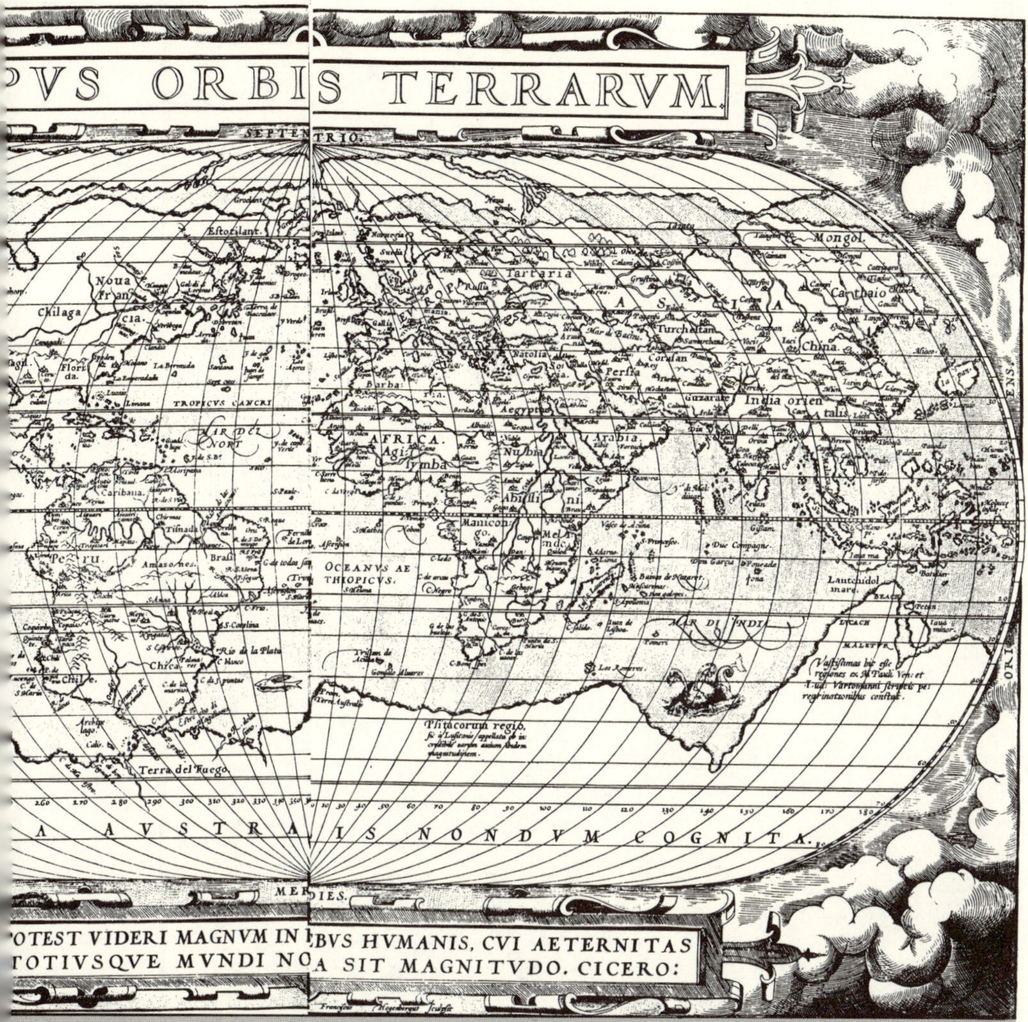

Map 13 1570 map of Abraham Ortelius
A.E. Nordenskiöld, *Facsimile Atlas* (Dover, 1973)

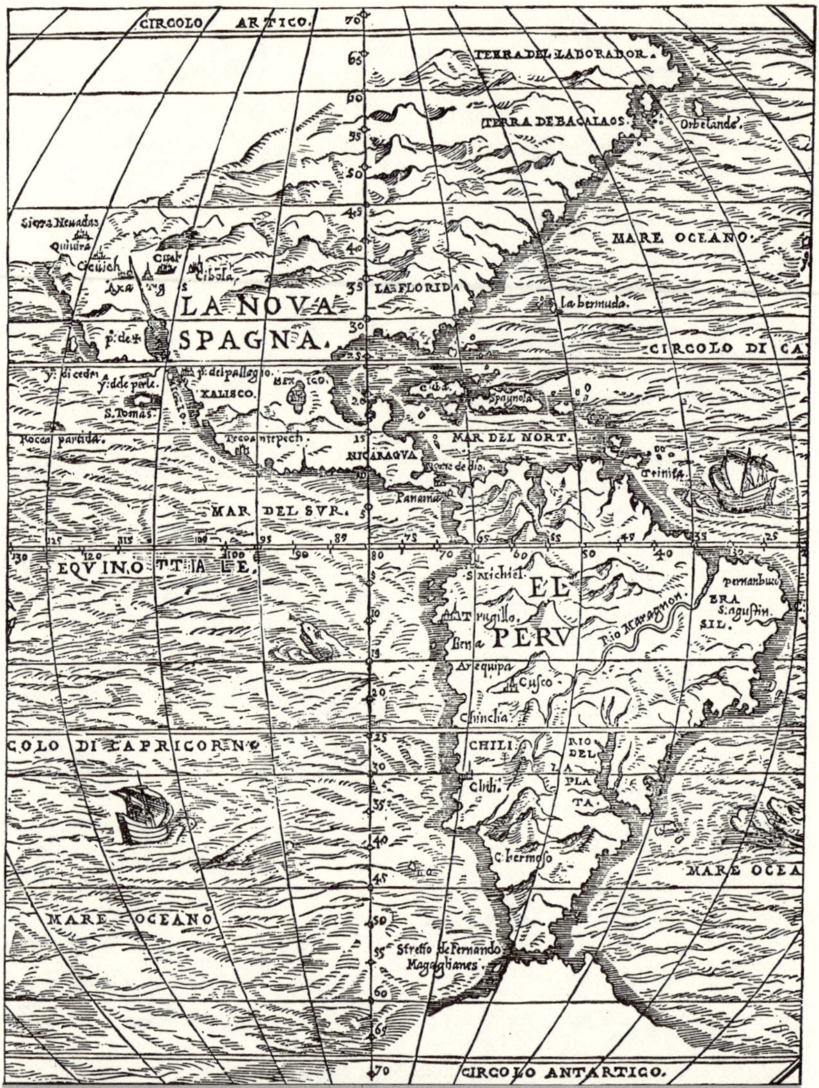

Map 14 Ramusio's 1556 map
J. Winsor, ed., *Narrative and Critical History of America* 2 (New York, 1967)

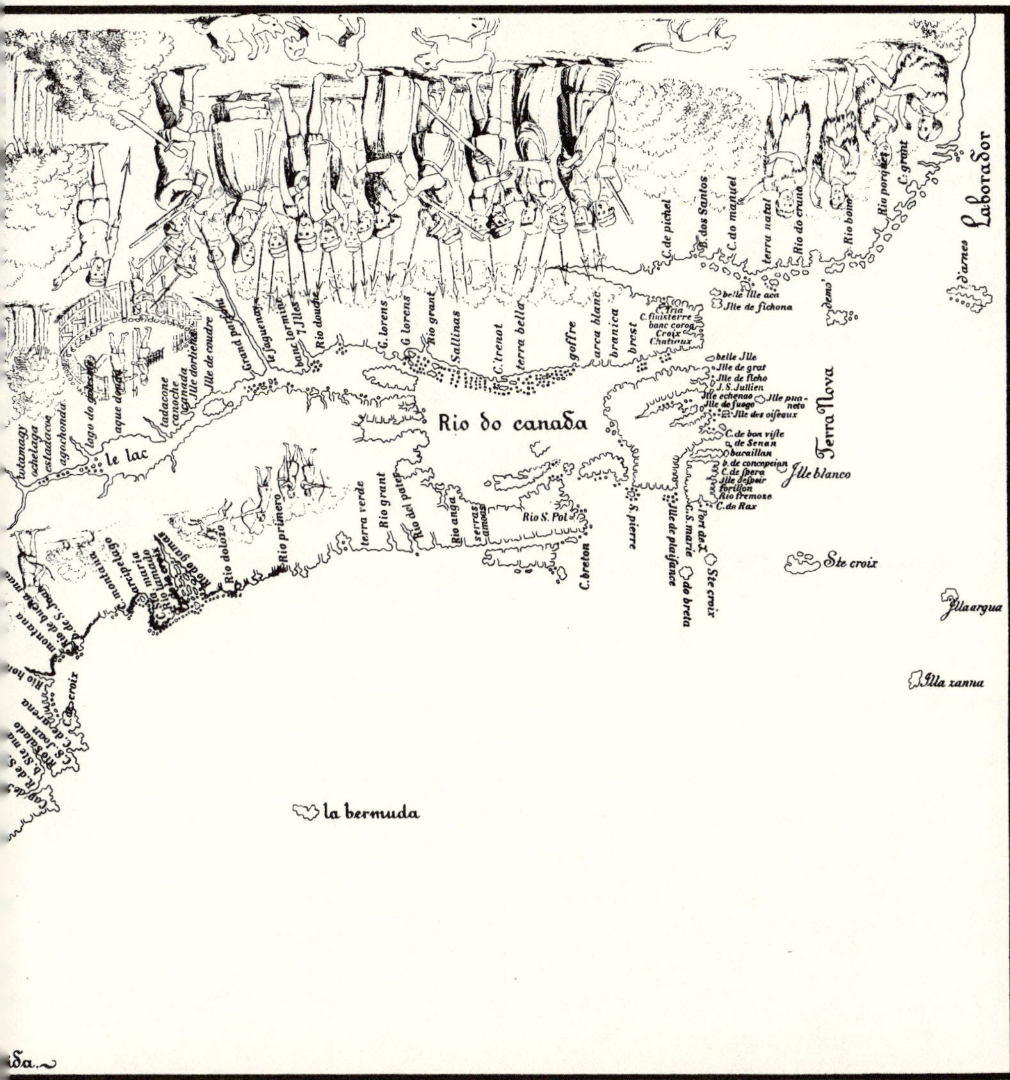

Map 15 1547 map by Nicholas Vallard (redrawn) showing France-Roy
M. Trudel, *Atlas of New France* (Quebec, 1968)

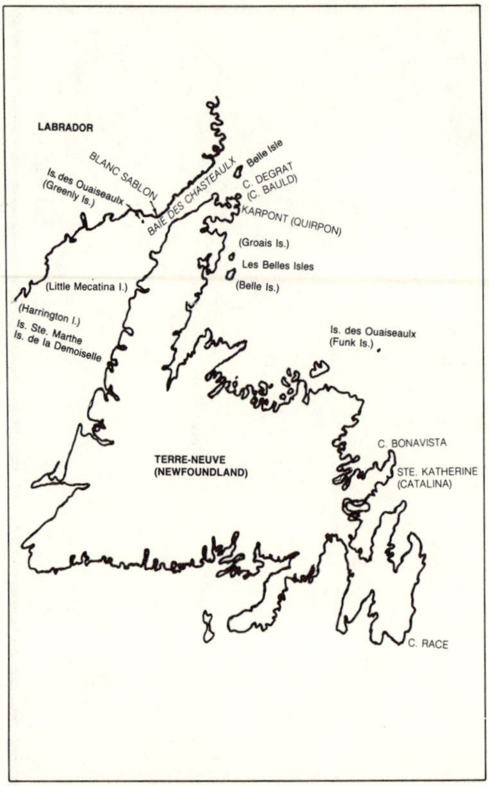

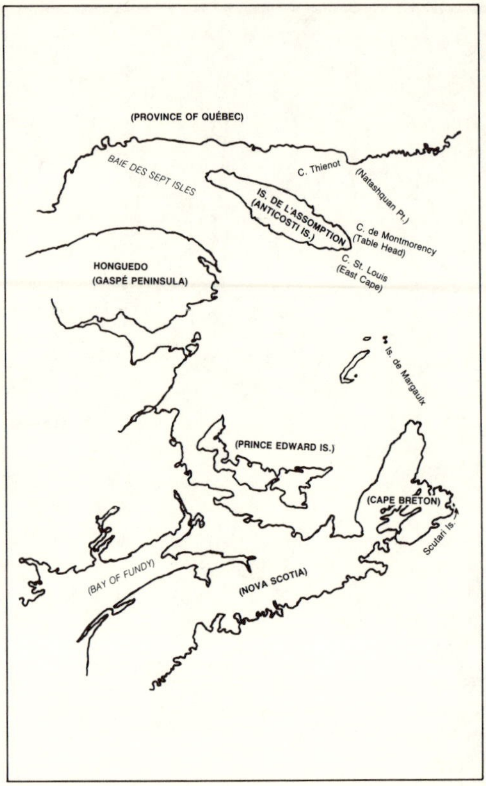

Map 16 Sixteenth-century and modern Canadian place names
Map by Fredric C. Bohm, managing editor, Washington State University Press

Map 17 Sixteenth-century and modern Canadian place names
Map by Fredric C. Bohm

Map 18 General location of native Canadian tribes
Map by Fredric C. Bohm

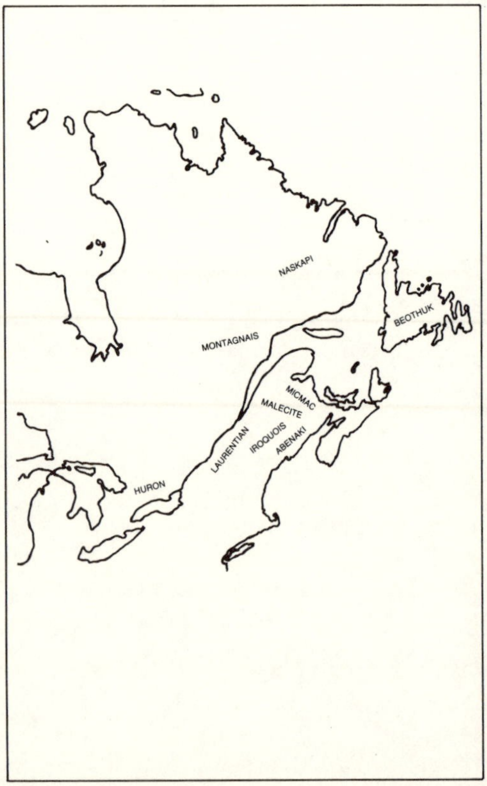

PART 1

Canada

Singularitez de la France antarctique

[149r] On the Country of Canada, Hitherto Called Baccalos, Discovered in Our Time, and the Style of Life of the Inhabitants

CHAPTER 75

Since this country in the north was discovered in our time by a certain Jacques Cartier, Breton, master pilot and captain, a man expert and well-versed in the sea, and this by command of the late King François I, whom God may absolve; I decided to write briefly in this place what seems to me worthy of being written, although according to the order of our return voyage it should have preceded the next chapter.[1] What motivated me even more to do this was that I have not seen that anyone else has treated it, although the matter in my opinion is not without merit and I had certain knowledge of it from the said Quartier who discovered it.[2]

This land being almost beneath the zenithal Arctic pole is joined on the west to Florida and to the islands of Peru [South America] and from there runs along the Atlantic coast to the Baccales, of which we have spoken. This place I believe to be the same as those who have made recent discovery have called Canada (as it often happens that we name as we please something which [149v] others know nothing about), being bounded to the east by a sea extending from the glacial or hyperborean

1 This chapter, of course, does precede the next one. Obviously Thevet meant "followed" rather than "preceded."

2 Although Thevet implies that this "certain knowledge" is oral, he is in fact taking much of his information from Cartier's *Brief Récit & succincte narration, de la navigation faicte es yseles de Canada, Hochelage & Saguenay & autres* . . . (Paris, 1545). Thevet apparently knew Cartier's work only from the Italian translation in Giovanni Battista Ramusio's *Terzo volume delle navigationi et viaggi nel quale si contengono le navigationi al mondo nuovo* . . . (Venice, 1556).

one; and on the other side by a mainland called Campestre de Berge, contiguous with this region to the southeast.[3]

There is a cape called Lorraine,[4] or by those who discovered it called the Land of the Bretons, next to the New Lands where today the cod are caught [with] a space of ten or twelve leagues[5] between them, [and] the said New Land [is] attached to this high land which we have called Cape Lorraine. To the northeast there lies a quite large and long isle between the two, which has about four leagues circumference. The said land begins right near the said cape to the south, where it runs east-northeast, and west-southwest, the larger part of it going to the land of Florida arranged in the form of a semi-circle towards Themistitan [Mexico City].

Now to return to Cape Lorraine which we were discussing. It is located on the land to the north, which is bordered by a mediterranean sea (as we have said) just as is Italy between the Adriatic and Ligurian seas. And from the said cape going west and west-southwest there are approximately two hundred leagues, all sand and gravel without any port or harbor. This region is inhabited by a number of people of quite large stature, very tricky, who usually wear masks and are disguised by lineaments of red and blue, which colors they get from certain fruits.[6] The said land was

3 Compare Thevet's description of the location of Canada here with those in the *Cosmographie*, chap. 3: "On the Land of Canada and Baccaleos," and in the *Grand Insulaire*, chap. "Isle of the Assumption." Cartier used the term Canada both as a synonym for the village of Stadacona and for the region between the Saguenay River and Quebec. See W.F. Ganong, *Crucial Maps in the Early Cartography and Place-Nomenclature of the Atlantic Coast of Canada* (Toronto, 1964), pp. 308–9; and Samuel Eliot Morison, *The European Discovery of America: The Northern Voyages A.D. 500–1600* (New York, 1971), p. 429. In the ancient Greek religion the Hyperboreans were a mythical people living in a paradise beyond the north wind. *Campestre de Berge* (mountainous region) and *mare glacial* appear on several maps and globes of the period [map 1].

4 A land or coast of Lorraine is mentioned by Giovanni da Verrazzano. See Lawrence C. Wroth, *The Voyages of Giovanni da Verrazzano* (New Haven, 1970), p. 137n10. Cartier, however, claimed that he had named Cape Lorraine on his second voyage (see H.P. Biggar, *The Voyages of Jacques Cartier* [Ottawa, 1924], pp. 237–8 and 238n2). See also Thevet's other mentions of Cape Lorraine in the *Cosmographie*, chap. 3: "On the Land of Canada and Baccaleos," and the *Grand Insulaire*, chap. "Isle of the Assumption."

5 Cartier used the *petit mille marin*, three of which made the *petite lieue marine*, or 2.31 nautical miles according to Morison, *European Discovery*, p. 387, "Cartier's Mile and League."

6 See also *Cosmographie*, chap. 3: "On the Land of Canada and Baccaleos." The description of these natives probably derives from Jean Parmentier's account of native facial markings and Verrazzano's red and blue ornaments—both accounts were available to Thevet in Ramusio's *Terzo volume* (Parmentier, fol. 359r; Verrazzano., fols. 350–2). Cf. Bernard G. Hoffman's translation of Parmentier's narrative, "Account of a Voyage

discovered from within the said sea [the Gulf of St. Lawrence] in 1535 by seigneur Quartier, as we have said a native of St. Malo. So besides the vessels he used for his voyage, [he had] some boats carrying fifty to eighty [150r] men [with which] he explored the hitherto unknown country up to a large spacious river which they named the Abbey of Warmth,[7] where very good fish are found in abundance, chiefly salmon. Then they traded in several neighboring localities, that is, our men giving axes, knives, fishhooks, and other implements for pelts of deer, otter, and other fur-bearing animals which they have in abundance. The barbarians of this country gave them a good welcome, showing good will to them, and happy at their coming and acquaintanceship. A mutual friendship was conceived and practiced between them.

After doing this and passing on they found other peoples almost the opposite of the first both in language and in way of life, and they said they had descended the great Chelogua [Hochelaga] River to go make war on the first neighbors; which Captain Quartier later heard and found out from one of their boats which he captured with seven men, of which he kept two whom he took to France to the king.[8] These he brought back on his second voyage, and [Cartier] having once again brought them [to France], they embraced Christianity and died as such in France. The way of life of these first barbarians has never been learned nor what there is in their region, because it has not been frequented nor otherwise trafficked.

[150v] On Another Region of Canada
CHAPTER 76

As for the other part of this region of Canada, where these last savages live and frequent, it has since been explored up the said Chelogua

Conducted in 1529 to the New World, Africa, Madagascar, and Sumatra, Translated from the Italian, with Notes and Comments," *Ethnohistory* 10 (1963): 1–79, esp. 13, and Wroth, *Verrazzano*, p. 138. The description of Girolamo Benzoni, however, is also similar to Thevet's: "They stain their bodies with the juice of herbs, and other red and black colours. . . " See his *History of the New World* [Venice, 1565], trans. and ed. W.H. Smyth (London, 1857), p. 10. A more recent edition is *La Historia del Mundo Nuevo*, traducción y notas de Marisa Vannini de Gerulewicz. Estudio Preliminar Leon Croizat (Caracas, 1967).

7 Thevet apparently misread La Baye de Chaleur as l'Abaye de Chaleur.

8 Hochelaga is the name given by Cartier to the St. Lawrence River on his second voyage. See Biggar, *Voyages*, pp. 106–7 and 106n86. The village of Hochelaga itself was situated on the site of present-day Montreal. See James F. Pendergast and Bruce G. Trigger, *Cartier's Hochelaga and the Dawson Site* (Montreal, 1972). This mention of a second group of natives and of Cartier's capture of two of them is clearly based on Cartier's account of his first voyage. However, contrary to his usual practice, Thevet has greatly abbreviated this material. See also *Cosmographie*, chap. 3: "On the Land of Canada and Baccaleos."

[Hochelaga] river for more than three to four hundred leagues by the said Quartier, by command of the king, where he found a well-populated country in his second as well as his first navigation. The people are as obedient and friendly as possible and just as familiar as if they had been brought up with us forever, without any sign of ill will or other severity. And there the said Quartier built a small fort and a building for himself and his men to winter over and to defend themselves against the rigors of such cold and biting air.[9] He was quite well treated for the country and the season, for the inhabitants brought him each day their skiffs loaded with fish such as eels, lampreys, and others—also wild meat, which they take in large quantity.

Indeed they are great hunters, summer or winter, with devices or otherwise. They use a kind of rackets woven with cords like a sieve, two and one-half feet long and one foot wide, as I represent for you in the picture below [fig. 2]. They wear them under their feet in the cold and snow, especially when they go hunt wild beasts, so as not to sink in the snow as they pursue their hunt.[10] These people dress in deerskins cured and prepared in their fashion. [151r] To capture these animals, ten or twelve of them get together armed with long lances or pikes fifteen to sixteen feet long, armed at the end with some bone of a stag or other beast a foot long or more, instead of iron, carrying [also] bows and arrows armed the same way. They then go through the snows which are around all year long, tracking the stags through the said very deep snows and uncover the trail, which having been uncovered they set up cedar branches, which are green in all seasons, in the form of a net under which they hide themselves, armed as I said. And as soon as the stag arrives, attracted by the pleasure of this greenery and the path beaten down, they hurl themselves on him with thrusts of the pikes and arrows so that they force him to leave the path and get into the deep [151v] snow up to the belly, where being unable to make headway he is struck by blows until dead. He is skinned on the spot and cut into pieces which are wrapped in his skin and dragged through the snow to their houses. And thus they were brought to the fort of the Frenchmen, meat and skins, to

9 The reference here is to Cartier's fort at the harbor of Ste Croix. See Biggar, *Voyages*, p. 174.

10 For Thevet's other descriptions of snowshoes, see *Cosmographie*, chap. 3: "On the Land of Canada and Baccaleos," and *Grand Insulaire*, chap. "Isle of the Assumption." There is also an illustration of an American native on snowshoes on the 1555 map of North America by Guillaume Le Testu. See William C. Sturtevant, "First Visual Images of Native America," in *First Images of America: The Impact of the New World on the Old*, ed. Fredi Chiappelli, 2 vols. (Berkeley, 1976), 1: 417–54, esp. fig. 19.

Figure 2 Thevet's illustration of snowshoes being worn by natives while hunting
Thevet's *Cosmographie universelle*, fol. 1011r.
Courtesy John Carter Brown Library at Brown University

exchange for something, i. e. some little metal tools and other things.[11] And I would not want to omit this, which is remarkable: that when the said savages are ill with fever or persecuted by some other internal ailment, they take the leaves of a tree which is very similar to the cedars which are found around Mt. Tarare in the Lyons region, and they make a juice of it which they drink. And without a doubt there is no illness, however entrenched it may be in the body, which this beverage will not cure in twenty-four hours, as the Christians often experienced; and they brought the plant back here.[12]

The Religion and Style of Life of These Poor Canadians, and How They Resist the Cold
CHAPTER 77

These people in their way of life and government are rather close to the laws of nature. Their marriage [custom] is that a man will take two or three wives without other solemnity, like the Americans of whom we have already spoken.[13] In their religion they have no other method or ceremony of worshipping or praying to God than to contemplate the new moon, [152r] called in their language *Osannaha*, saying that *Andouagni* calls it so and sends it little by little so that it advances or retards the waters.[14] Further, they do believe that there is a creator greater than the

11 Thevet may be relying here on an oral source, as this information on hunting does not appear in the written accounts he is known to have consulted.

12 Compare Cartier's account of the *Annedda* tree in Biggar, *Voyages*, pp. 212–15. Jacques Rousseau has identified this tree as *Thuja occidentalis* (*Arbor vitæ* or White Cedar). See his "L'Annedda et l'Arbre de Vie," *Revue d'Histoire de l'Amérique Française* 8 (1954): 171–213. See also *Cosmographie*, chap. 5: "On the Country Called New[found]land," and *Grand Insulaire*, chap. "Isles of the New Lands."

13 Thevet uses the word Americans to refer to the natives of Brazil. He gives a more elaborate account of the marriage customs of the Canadians in *Singularitez*, chap. 78: "On the Apparel of the Canadians," and *Cosmographie*, chap. 4: "On the Utility of the Said Country of Canada."

14 In his *Cosmographie*, chap. 3: "On the Land of Canada and Baccaleos," Thevet gives the correct native words for moon and god: *Assomaha* and *Cudragny*. Thevet's variant spelling here may be either the result of oral transmission (he claims in the next paragraph to have received his information from Donnacona) or careless transcription from a written source. Regarding the term *Cudragny*, it is interesting to note that Guillaume Postel, in his *De Orbis terrae concordia* (1543), wrote: "Those lands to be found near those of Francis King of the French in the north, are accustomed to be marvelously disturbed by these demons, to the point that they can in no wise be quieted. They call this kind [of demon] *Cudiague* . . . " Cf. Arthur P. Stabler, "Rabelais, Thevet, l'Isle des Démons et les paroles

sun, the moon, or the stars, and who holds everything in his power: and that is the one whom they call *Andouagni*, however without having any form or method of praying to him.

There are, however, in some regions of Canada some who adore idols and sometimes have forty or fifty of them in their dwellings, as was truly told me by a Portuguese pilot[15] who visited two or three villages and the lodges in which the natives live. They believe that the soul is immortal and that if a man behaves badly, after his death a great bird takes his soul and carries it off. If one behaves well the soul goes to a place adorned by many beautiful trees and birds singing melodiously. This was explained to us by the lord of the country, named *Donnacona Aguanna*, who died in France a good Christian, speaking French, for having been kept there four years.[16]

And to avoid prolixity in the story of our Canadians, note that these poor people are afflicted with a perpetual cold, from the absence of the sun as you will understand. They live in villages and hamlets in certain houses constructed in the form of a semi-circle twenty to thirty paces long and ten wide, covered with tree bark or reeds. And God knows how the cold penetrates them, so badly built, badly covered, and badly supported so that often the pillars and rafters fall under the weight of the snow on top.[17]

Notwithstanding this excessive cold they are powerful [152v] and war-like and insatiable workers. It would seem that all these northern peoples are thus courageous, some more some less, just as those toward the other pole, especially in the tropics and around the equator are the contrary, because the excessive heat of the air draws their natural warmth out and dissipates it so they are only hot on the outside and cold on the inside. The [northerners] have their body heat closed and kept inside them by

---

gelées," *Etudes Rabelaisiennes* 11 (1974): 57–62, esp. 59.

15 Possibly Jean Alfonse. See Introduction.

16 For Cartier's capture of Donnacona see Biggar, *Voyages*, p. 227.

17 See also *Cosmographie*, chap. 3: "On the Land of Canada and Baccaleos," and *Grand Insulaire*, chap. "Isle of the Assumption." This description of the native village is similar to Cartier's account of Hochelaga, which, he says, is circular. See Biggar, *Voyages*, pp. 155–7. A plan of Hochelaga appeared in Ramusio's *Terzo volume*, and is reproduced in fig. 9. For a critique of this diagram see W.D. Lighthall, "The False Plan of Hochelaga," *Transactions of the Royal Society of Canada*, 3rd ser., 26, sec. 2 (1932): 181–92. This article also appears in Pendergast and Trigger, *Cartier's Hochelaga*, pp. 374–80. See also Verrazzano's description of native houses: "When we went farther inland we saw their houses, which are circular in shape, about XIIII to XV paces across, made of bent saplings. . . . " (Wroth, *Verrazzano*, p. 139).

the external cold, which therefore renders them robust and valiant: for the strength and virtue of all parts of the body depend on this natural warmth. So the sea around this country is frozen in the northern areas, and this is because it is too distant from the sun which, as it goes from east to west, passes by the middle of the universe although obliquely. And the greater the natural body heat, the better the processing and digestion of foods in the stomach. The appetite is also greater. So this northern people eat much more than those of the opposite side, which is why there is often famine in Canada, plus the fact that their roots and other fruits on which they must sustain and nourish themselves all year are frozen, [and] their rivers likewise for the space of three or four months. We have said that they cover their houses with tree bark; they also make boats from it to fish in fresh and salt water.

Those of the country of Labrador, their neighbors (who were discovered by the Spaniards, who thought they would find here a strait to go to the island of the Moluccas where the spices are), are equally subject to the cold, and cover their little lodges with skins of fish and of wild animals, as do many of the other [153r] Canadians. Furthermore the said Canadians live communally like the Americans [Brazilians], each one working at what he knows how to do. Some make earthenware pots, others platters, dishes, and wooden spoons, others bows and arrows, baskets, and articles of clothing from pelts with which they cover themselves against the cold. The women till the soil and turn it up with certain instruments made of long stones and sow the seed, especially millet, large peas [corn?] of various colors like we plant vegetables over here. The stem grows like sugar cane bearing two or three ears, of which one is always larger than the others like our artichokes. They also plant beans that are flat and white as snow which are very good. This species is found in America [Brazil] and Peru [South America]. There are also many gourds [pumpkins] and squash, which they eat cooked in the coals as we do over here.

There is besides a very fine little seed resembling seed of marjoram, which produces quite a large plant. This plant is highly prized and they dry it in the sun after collecting heaps of it. They wear it around their neck in little pouches of the skin of some animal in a kind of cylinder with a hole in the end in which they stick a piece of this dried plant which, having rolled it between their hands, they set fire to it and take the smoke of it into their mouth by the other end of the cylinder. And they take it in such quantities that it comes out of their eyes and nose. Thus they perfume themselves at all hours of the day.[18] Our Americans [Brazilians] have another way of perfuming themselves, as we said above.

[153v] On the Apparel of the Canadians, How They Wear Their Hair, and Their Treatment of Their Children
CHAPTER 78

The Canadians, more advanced than the natives of America [Brazil], know how to cover themselves with skins of wild beasts [and] with the fur, prepared in their manner (as we have already touched upon), perhaps forced to by the cold and for no other reason. This motivation was not present for the others [Brazilians], so that they remained totally nude without any shame before each other. These, however (I mean the men), are not completely clothed but rather wrapped in a furry skin in the manner of an apron, to cover the front and shameful parts, having them pass between the two legs fastened with buttons on the two thighs. Then they put on a large belt which strengthens the whole body, with the arms and legs bare. But over the whole thing they wear a big coat of pelts woven together as well as if the most skillful furrier had done it. The coats are made of otter, bear, marten, panther, fox, hare, rats [muskrats?], coneys, and other skins, cured with the fur, which in my opinion is the source of the statement of certain ignoramuses that the savages had fur.[19]

Some have written that Hercules of Libya, coming to France, found the people living almost in the manner of the savages both of the East Indies and America [Brazil], completely uncivilized, and both the men and the women went almost [154r] naked. The others were clothed in the skins of divers kinds of beasts. Such was the first condition of the human race, at the beginning being rough and barbarous, until through the passage of time necessity forced men to invent a number of things for the preservation and maintenance of their lives.

18 Thevet's difficulty in describing the smoking of tobacco is surprising since he had seen it in Brazil. For a more detailed account see *Cosmographie*, chap. 4: "On the Utility of the Said Country of Canada." Also compare Cartier's statement that "We made a trial of this smoke. When it is in one's mouth, one would think one had taken powdered pepper, it is so hot." See Biggar, *Voyages*, pp. 184–5.

19 See also *Cosmographie*, chap. 3: "On the Land of Canada and Baccaleos." For more information on the concept of the wild man as applied by Europeans to native peoples in America see, for example, Olive Dickason, "The Concept of *l'homme sauvage* and Early French Colonialism in the Americas," *Revue Française d'Histoire d'Outre-Mer* 64 (1977): 5–32, and Richard Bernheimer, *Wild Men in the Middle Ages* (New York, 1970), esp. 96–101. In Antiquity, Hercules was frequently shown wearing an animal skin, and in the Middle Ages was sometimes shown as hairy.

So out of their rough barbarity these poor savages admired our clothing, the fabric and how it was made, and in America [Brazil] they asked us on what kind of tree this fabric grew, believing that wool grew on trees like their cotton. The use of [wool] has long been ignored and it was invented, according to some, by the Athenians and put to use. Others have attributed it to Pallas, because wools were in use before the Athenians had built their city. That is why the Athenians so greatly honored and reverenced it, from having received this great boon from her. And so it is probable that the said Athenians and other peoples of Greece used to dress in skins like our Canadians: and likewise the first man, as Saint Jerome says, thus giving an example to posterity to do likewise and not to go around all naked; in which we cannot sufficiently praise and be grateful to God, who by special affection above all other parts of the world must have uniquely favored our Europe.

It remains to say how they wear their hair: that is, differently from the Americans [Brazilians]. Both men and women wear their hair black, very long, and there is only this difference: that the men have the hair piled up [154v] on the head like a horse's tail with wooden needles through it and on top a skin of tiger, bear, or other beast, so that to see them accoutered in this way, you would suppose them to be disguised thus to go on stage looking more like the portraits of Hercules which the ancient Romans made to amuse themselves (as we still depict him today) than anything else. Others wrap and envelop the head with sable martens, so called from the name of a religion [error for region] in the north where this animal is plentiful. These we esteem here for their rarity, and thus such furs are reserved for the ornaments of princes and great lords, having both beauty and rarity. These men do not wear beards any more than do the Americans [Brazilians] because they pull it out as soon as it grows.[20]

As for the women, they dress in deerskins prepared in their manner, which is very good and better than what we have in France, without losing one hair of it. And so enveloped they wrap the entire body with a long belt with three or four turns around the body, with one arm and one

20 See also Thevet's description of native hairstyles in *Cosmographie*, chap. 3: "On the Land of Canada and Baccaleos." These details are similar to those given by Cartier: "They wear their hair tied up at the top of their heads like a handful of twisted hay, with a nail or something of the sort passed through the middle . . . "; also, in speaking of the chieftain of the natives of Hochelaga, Cartier notes that he wore on his head a "red band made of hedgehog's skin" (see Biggar, *Voyages*, pp. 22, 61, 164). Verrazzano also described natives with hair tied behind the head "like a small tail." See Wroth, *Verrazzano*, p. 134. Also see Parmentier's description in Hoffman, "Account of a Voyage," pp. 13–14. As mentioned, these sources were available to Thevet in Ramusio.

breast outside this skin which is attached to one shoulder like a pilgrim's scarf. To continue our discussion, the Canadian women wear breeches of tanned leather and very well made in their mode, adorned with some dye made of plants and fruits or else of mineral dye, of which there are several kinds. The shoes are made of the same material and fancy work.[21]

They observe marriage with all fidelity eschewing adultery above all, although it is true that each man has two or three wives as we already mentioned elsewhere. The lord of the place, named [155r] *Agahanna*, can have as many of them as he wishes.[22] The girls are not scorned for having served for several young men before being married, just as in America [Brazil]. And for this there are certain lodges in their village where they meet, the men having intercourse with the women, separated from the young people, boys and girls.[23] Widows never remarry however many there are of them after the death of their husband, but remain in mourning the rest of their lives, having their faces all blackened with powdered coals [mixed] with fish oil. Their hair always hangs over their faces without being tied or put up at the back, as the others do, and they keep this up till their death.[24]

As to the treatment of babies, they bind them and wrap them up in four or five marten skins sewed together. Then they attach and tie them to a piece or plank of wood with a hole through it at the behind so there is always an unimpeded opening, and between the legs [is] a sort of little funnel or spout made of soft bark where they can make water without touching or soiling their body in front or behind, nor the furs in which they are wrapped. If this people were closer to Turkey, I would guess that they learned this from the Turks, or else taught it to them. Not that I want to imply that these savages believe it to be a sin that babies should get wet in their own urine, like that superstitious nation of the Turks. It [is] rather a more civilized [custom] which they have, because you can

21 See *Cosmographie*, chap. 3: "On the Land of Canada and Baccaleos," for a more detailed account of the clothing of native women.

22 The term *Agahanna* means chief. Cartier used *Agouhanna*: the old Mohawk word for chief is *Aguayanderen*. See Biggar, *Voyages*, p. 121 and n59.

23 Cartier wrote: "We saw this with our own eyes; for we discovered wigwams as full of these girls as is a boys' school with boys in France." See Biggar, *Voyages*, p. 182. But see also J.F. Lafitau, *Customs of the American Indians Compared with the Customs of Primitive Times*, ed. and trans. William F. Fenton and Elizabeth L. Moore, 2 vols. (Toronto, 1974, 1977), 1: 129–30, where Cartier is interpreted to refer to virgins, not whores, who were soon debauched by alcohol.

24 All of this material on native customs, including marriage, is also furnished by Cartier, and is, undoubtedly, Thevet's source. See Biggar, *Voyages*, pp. 181–2.

understand how much the poor brutes surpass them in culture. They set up this plank, sharpened [155v] point in the ground, with the baby at the lower end, who thus sleeps erect with its head hanging down.[25]

Their Style of Making War

CHAPTER 79

As this people seems to have almost the same customs as other savage barbarians, so none are found more prompt and accustomed to make war on each other than they are, and they have the same kind of war with a few exceptions. The Tontanians, the Guadalpes, and the Chicorins constantly war against the Canadians and divers other peoples who come down this big river of Ochelaga and Saguenay.[26] These rivers are extraordinarily beautiful and large, having very good fish in great quantity; also by these they can penetrate three hundred good leagues into the country and into the lands of their enemies, without using larger ships because of the danger of the rocks. And the ancients of the country say that he who follows these two rivers in a few moons (which is their way of measuring time) will find a diversity of people and an abundance of gold and silver. Also these two rivers, separated from one another, meet and join at a certain spot just like the Rhone and the Saone at Lyon, and thus joined go far into New Spain for they border on each other like France and Italy.

And therefore when it is a question of war their great *Agahanna* (which means like king or lord) commands his vassal [156r] lords, as each village to its superior, that they resolve to come and be before him with good and sufficient equipage of men, provisions, and other supplies as it is their custom to do. These then, each in his area, immediately prepares to do his duty and obey the command of his lord without failing or any kind of opposition. And so they come by water in their little skiffs of small

25 For a similar description of the treatment of infants see *Cosmographie*, chap. 4: "On the Utility of the Said Country of Canada." The cradle prevalent among the Algonquian and Iroquoian natives of the region was made of a thin rectangular board, frequently carved and painted, with a projecting footrest for the infant. See *Handbook of North American Indians*, gen. ed. William C. Sturtevant, 15: *Northeast*, ed. Bruce G. Trigger (Washington, D.C., 1978), p. 317, fig. 22 "cradleboards."

26 This is the first mention of the Tontaniens and Chicorins, according to Ganong, who identifies the Toutaneans (Cartier's Toudamans) as the Micmacs, the Chicorins as the Montaignais, and guesses that Guadalpes is a Huron-Iroquois name for the Esquimaux (see his *Crucial Maps*, pp. 432–3). Also see Biggar, *Voyages*, pp. 177–8, for Cartier's account. Thevet also mentions the Tontanians (or Toutaneans), Guadalpes, and Chicorins in *Cosmographie*, chap. 3: "On the Land of Canada and Baccaleos."

length and width, made of tree bark, as in America [Brazil] and other surrounding places. The assembly then made, they go seek their enemy. When they know they are about to meet them they place themselves in the best order possible to fight and give assault, with an infinity of ruses and stratagems according to their way. The [156v] defenders fortify their lodges and cabins with pieces of wood, faggots, and branches soaked in a certain oil of the seal or other fish. This [is done] to poison their enemies if they approach, setting them on fire, from which is given off a thick black smoke dangerous to smell for the stink is so terrible that it kills those who smell it. Besides which it blinds the enemies, who cannot see one another. And they know how to direct and arrange this smoke so that the wind blows it away from them and toward the enemy. They also use poisons made from certain tree leaves, plants, and fruits, which substances [having] dried in the sun they mix up with these faggots and branches, then set fire to them from a distance when they see the enemy approaching. In this way they tried to defend themselves against the first to discover their country, trying with fat and oils to set fire at night to the ships of those people anchored near the seashore. At which our people, informed about this plan, took steps so as not to be at all discommoded by it.[27]

Anyhow, I have heard that these poor savages had only cooked up this plan justly and reasonably, considering the wrongs they had suffered from the others. The fact is that our people having landed, some young fools for amusement (vicious and unreasonable, however, like some kind of tyranny) cut off the arms and legs of some of these poor people just to see if their swords were cutting well, they said, notwithstanding the fact that these poor barbarians had received them humanely [157r] with all gentleness and friendship. And so afterwards they have not allowed any Christians to approach and set foot on the ground on their shores and boundaries, nor do any business with them as we have since found out from experience.[28]

Now so as not to draw out our discussion these Canadians march to war four by four, uttering when they see each other or approach one another astounding and frightful cries and shouts (as we have said about the Amazons) to terrorize and frighten their enemies.[29] They carry many

27 For Thevet's other accounts of native war tactics see *Cosmographie*, chap. 3: "On the Land of Canada and Baccaleos," and fig. 3.

28 For a more detailed account of the cruelty which the French practiced upon the natives see *Cosmographie*, chap. 3: "On the Land of Canada and Baccaleos."

29 Apparently this is an early reference to "war-whoops."

ensigns made of birch branches, adorned with feathers and plumages of swans. Their drums are of certain skins stretched and tied as on the frame on which one makes parchment, carried by two men on each side, and [an]other being behind striking with two sticks as energetically as he can. Their flutes are made of the bones of legs of the stag or other wild animal.

So these Canadians fight with arrow-shots, round clubs, square clubs, lances, and wooden pikes with a bone point at the end instead of iron. Their shields are panaches, which they wear on the neck, turning them to the front or the back as they wish. Others wear a sort of helmet made of very thick bear skin to protect the head. So did the ancients like the savages: they fought with fist blows, kicks, biting, grabbed each other by the hair and other such actions. Later they used stones to fight, which they threw at each other, as you can read in the Holy Bible. Further, Herodotus, in his fourth book, speaks [157v] of a certain people who fought with sticks and clubs. He also says that the virgins of this country used to fight with one another every year with stones and sticks in honor of the goddess Minerva on her birthday. And Diodorus[30] recounts in his first book that clubs and lion skins were used by Hercules to fight—for in the past no other arms were in use. Whoever wants to look into Plutarch and Justinian and other authors will find that the ancient Romans fought completely naked.[31] The Thebans and Lacedemonians revenged themselves on their enemies with blows of crowbars and huge wooden clubs. And you must not think that back then this poor people was not as hardy as the ones today, from having been all naked and with no clothes, such as our Canadians have now of large skins, or that they were similarly devoid of arms and tricks of war which these savages have nowadays. I could cite you several authors telling of the manner in which the ancients conducted warfare but for the present what I have said will suffice.

To return to the people of Canada, which is our principal subject: this people does not treat war prisoners in the same way they do in all of America [Brazil]; that is, they do not eat them as the others do, which is much more tolerable. True, if they capture some of their enemies or are otherwise victorious, they skin their head and face and lay them out in

30 Thevet's reference is to Diodorus Siculus, the author of a universal history in forty books, *Bibliotheca historia*. Only fifteen books survive.

31 Plutarch, a Greek biographer, is best remembered for his *The Parallel Lives*. The Byzantine emperor Justinian (d. 565) was responsible for codifying Roman law.

a circle to dry.[32] Then they carry them to their country, showing them proudly as a symbol of victory to their friends, wives, and old men, who in their weak old age can no longer carry [158r] the burden.[33] Moreover, they are not as bellicose as the Peruvians [South Americans] and those of America [Brazil], perhaps because of the difficulty caused by the snows and other incommodities which they have over there.

On the Ores, Precious Stones, and Other Singularities Found in Canada
CHAPTER 80

The country and territory of Canada is beautiful and well situated and very good in itself, except for the intemperate weather which is against it as you may well suppose. It has several trees and fruits which we do not know over here. Among others there is a tree of the size and shape of a large walnut tree of ours, which remained a long time useless and unknown until someone wishing to cut one down, there came out of it a sap which was found to have as good a taste and delicate as the good wine of Orleans or of Beaune [according to] the opinion of our people who then tried it—that is the captain [Cartier] and other gentlemen of his company; and right away they collected four or five large pots of this juice. You can image that since then these Canadians, enamored of this liquor, carefully guard this tree for their beverage since it is so excellent. This tree in their language is called *Couton*.[34]

Another thing is almost incredible to one who has not seen it: there is in Canada a number of places and regions where very beautiful grapevines [158v] grow all by themselves naturally in the earth without cultivation,

32 The custom of scalping is also mentioned by Cartier who, on his second expedition in 1535, saw "the scalps of five Indians, stretched on hoops like parchment." See Biggar, *Voyages*, p. 177. For more on scalping see James Axtell, *The European and the Indian: Essays in the Ethnohistory of Colonial North America* (Oxford, 1981), esp. 16–35, "The Unkindest Cut, or Who Invented Scalping? A Case Study," and pp. 207–41 "Scalping: The Ethnohistory of a Moral Question." See also *Cosmographie*, chap. 3: "On the Land of Canada and Baccaleos." Thevet also describes scalping in his *Singularitez*, chap. 64: "On the Peninsula of Florida."

33 Thomas Hacket, in his 1568 English translation of the *Singularitez* has "cannot go to the warres . . . " which may be what Thevet means. See his *The New Found Worlde* . . . (London, 1568), fol. 130r.

34 Thevet tells a much more elaborate and miraculous story about the discovery of maple sap by the French in his *Cosmographie*, chap. 4: "On the Utility of the Said Country of Canada." Also see Crestien Le Clerq, *New Relation of Gaspesia*, ed. and trans. W.F. Ganong (Toronto, 1910), pp. 122–3, and Ganong's *Crucial Maps*, p. 433.

with a large quantity of grapes, large, well-formed, and very good to eat (however there is no mention that the wine of them is equally good). Undoubtedly those who first discovered this found it most strange and admirable.[35]

This country is well furnished with mountains and plains.[36] In these high mountains are found certain rocks similar in weight and color to gold ore; but when they assayed it, to find out if it were genuine, it could not withstand fire and was dissipated and changed into ashes. It is not impossible that here is to be found ore as good as that of the Isles of Peru [South America] which might be mined further inland. As for iron and copper desposits they are also to be found, also little stones with diamond-shaped points, some of which come from the plains others from the mountains. Those who first found them thought to have instant riches, thinking they were real diamonds, of which they brought back an abundance. From this is derived the proverb known to all today: it is a diamond of Canada.[37] Actually it resembles a Calcutta or an East Indian diamond. Some say it is a type of fine crystal—to which [question] I can give no other solution than to follow Pliny, who says that crystal comes from snow and hard-frozen water, and thus concretized.[38] So in places subject to ice and snow it is possible [that] some part of them through the passage of time dry out and concretize into a body as shining and transparent as crystal. Solinus[39] deems this opinion to be false, that crystal comes entirely from snow: for if this were true it would be found only in cold places [159r] like in Canada and similar cold regions—but experience shows us the contrary, as in the isles of Cyprus and Rhodes and in several places in Egypt and Greece (as I myself have seen in the time that I was there), where an abundance of crystal was and

35 Thevet's account of grapevines growing wild is again more elaborate in his *Cosmographie*, chap. 4: "On the Utility of the Said Country of Canada." Verrazzano had also noticed grapevines growing wild and climbing up trees. He observed that "they would doubtless produce excellent wines if they were properly cultivated." See Wroth, *Verrazzano*, p. 136. Cartier had also mentioned the wild grapevines, as for example in the account of his third voyage. Biggar, *Voyages*, p. 254.

36 *Plauures*, a misprint for *planures*.

37 For the same story see *Cosmographie*, chap. 4: "On the Utility of the Said Country of Canada."

38 Pliny, a Roman author of the first century A.D., wrote *Historia naturalis*. This work was a revered authority on science throughout the Middle Ages and into the sixteenth century.

39 Solinus (fl. 200 A.D.) wrote *Collectanea rerum memorabilium*, a geographical summary of parts of the known world based on Pliny and Pomponius Mela.

today still is found; which is a true argument for judging that crystal is not congealed water, since in these countries of which we are speaking the heat is incomparably greater and more frequent than in Canada, a country afflicted with perpetual cold. Diodorus says that crystal is concretized from pure water, not congealed by cold but rather dried out by great heat. Nevertheless, that of Canada is more brilliant, and in every way shows itself to be a finer stone than those of Cyprus and other places.

The ancient emperors of Rome greatly prized fine crystal and had vessels made from it from which they ate. Others made statuettes of it which they kept in their cabinets and treasuries. Likewise the kings of Egypt, in the days when Thebes the great flourished, adorned their sepulchers with fine crystal which was brought from Armenia Major and the coast of Syria. And from this crystal the kings were represented by portraits from life to remain (they thought) as a perpetual memory. That is how the ancients esteemed crystal and how they used it. Today it is used to make drinking vessels and goblets, a thing much prized if it were not too fragile. Also in this country is found much jasper and chalcedony.

[159v] On the Earthquakes and Hail to Which This Country of Canada Is Very Subject

CHAPTER 81

This region of Canada is extremely subject to earthquakes and hail, from which this poor people, ignorant about natural things and even more about heavenly things, fall into extreme fear, even though such things are frequent and familiar to them.[40] They think this proves that this comes from their gods because they have irritated and angered them. However, natural earthquakes are simply caused by winds bottled up in cavities in the earth, which through great turbulence cause it to move, as on the earth they cause trees and other things to tremble, as Aristotle argues very well in his *Meteors*.[41] As for hail, it is no wonder that it is frequent there, from the intemperance and inclemency of the air, [the country being] just as cold in its middle region as in its lowest because of the distance from the sun, which never gets close to it except when it comes to our tropic.

40 We have found no specific source for Thevet's idea that Canada is subject to earthquakes. It may be pure invention, but it is interesting to note that there was a minor tremor in New Brunswick as recently as October 5, 1985. See also *Cosmographie*, chap. 4: "On the Utility of the Said Country of Canada."

41 Thevet is here referring to Aristotle's *Meteorologica*, a work in four books on meteorology.

This is why the water falling from the sky (the air being perpetually cold) is always frozen, which is nothing more than snow or hail.

Now when these savages feel such disturbances, they retire into their huts from the vexation it causes them, [taking] along with them some of their domestic animals that they raise, and there honor their idols whose form differs little from the fabulous Melusine of Lusignan, half-serpent, half-woman, since the head with the hair [160r] represents roughly (according to their savage mind) a woman. Now the rest of the body [is] in the form of a serpent, which could furnish a pretext for the poets to pretend that Melusine was their goddess, since she flees by flying according to the yarns of some who tell the said romance.[42] [This idol] they usually have in their homes.

Earthquakes are dangerous even though their cause is known. Since we are on this subject we will say a word about them, citing the natural philosophers, and the damages they cause. Thales of Miletus, one of the seven sages of Greece, said that water was the origin of everything and that the earth, floating in the middle of this water like a ship on the open sea, was in a perpetual quaking, sometimes greater sometimes smaller. Democritus was of the same opinion, and he said further that the water underground, augmented by the rain, being too plentiful to be contained in the veins and capacities of the earth due to its excessive quantity, caused this quaking, and this was the source of the springs and fountains which we have. Anaxagoras said it was fire which, seeking (as is its nature) to rise and unite with the elemental fire, caused not only this quaking but various openings, chasms, and such like on earth, as we see in various places. He buttressed this opinion by the fact that the earth is burning in various spots. Anaximenes was sure that the earth itself was the sole cause of this quaking, which cracking open from the excessive heat of the sun the air entered in in great quantity and with violence. Afterwards, the earth having reunited and rejoined itself together again, [the air] finding no exit [160v] moved here and there in the bowels of the earth, and from that came this quaking— which seems to me more reasonable and close to the truth, according to what we have cited from Aristotle; also wind is nothing more than extremely agitated air.

But these opinions expressed on the natural causes of earthquakes can very well be incorrect, because the wish and will of the Supreme [Being

42 On the fabled Melusine of Lusignan see Algernon Tudor-Craig, *The Romance of Melusine and de Lusignan* (London, 1932). Again, the use by Canadian natives of a Melusine-like idol would appear to be a Thevet invention. See, however, Thevet's assertion, *Cosmographie*, chap. 4: "On the Utility of the Said Country of Canada," that such an idol had been presented by Roberval to Henry VIII of England.

is] unknown to us. The damages which follow them are destruction of towns and cities, as happened in Asia with the seven cities of the time of Tiberius Caesar, and of the capital city of Bithnia during the reign of Constantine. Some have also been swallowed up in the earth, others submerged in water, as were Elice and Bura at the ports of Corinthia. And to speak briefly, these quakes occur sometimes with such vehemence that besides the aforesaid damages, they make islands of land like it did with Sicily and some places in Syria and others. They sometimes unite islands to the continent, as Pliny says of those of Doromisce and Perne in Miletus. They have even made lakes out of plains and fields in old Africa. Seneca also relates that a flock of five hundred sheep and other animals and birds were once swallowed up and lost by an earthquake. For this reason they stay (for the most part) near the shores to avoid the earthquakes, knowing from experience and not from reason that swampy places are not as subject to earthquakes as firm land. The reason for this is obvious to one who understands the cause of the quakes as set forth above. This is why the very rich [161r] and famed Temple of Diana in Ephesus, which lasted more than two hundred years, so sumptuously built that it deserved to be numbered among the spectacles of the world, was set on piles in a swampy place to escape earthquakes, until the time when a certain madman named Helvidius, or as some claim Eratosthenes, to get himself notoriety and be talked about, set fire to it and burned it to ashes. For this same reason the Romans had built an excellent temple to Hercules near the Tiber and there made sacrifices and prayers.

Now the earthquakes in Canada are sometimes so violent that from five or six leagues from their houses into the country there will be found more than two thousand trees (sometimes more, sometimes less) fallen to the ground, in the mountains as well as in the flat country; rocks piled on top of one another, lands sunken down and swallowed up and all that comes from nothing else but this shaking of the earth. This can happen to any regions subject to earthquakes. So much for earthquakes, without further digression from our route.

On the Country Called New[found]land

CHAPTER 82

After having left the latitude of the Gulf of Canada, we passed on beyond taking our direct route to the north, leaving the land of Labrador, the islands they call the Isles of the Devils, and Cape Marco, fifty-six [161v] degrees distant from the line.[43] We sailed along to the right of this region they call New Land. [It is] extremely cold, which is why those who first discovered it did not stay there long, nor [do] those who go there occasionally for trade. This New Land forms one of the extremities of Canada, and it is in a river which for its size and width almost seems to be a sea. It is called the River of the Three Brothers, distant from the Isles of the Azores four hundred leagues, and nine hundred from our France. It separates the province of Canada from the one we call New Land. Some moderns have believed it to be a strait of the sea, like that of Magellan, through which one might go from the Atlantic to the South or Pacific Sea; and in fact Gemma Frisius (even though he was an expert in mathematics) nevertheless erred in trying to persuade us that this river about which we are talking is a strait, which he calls the northern, and has shown it thus in his atlas.[44] If what he had written were true, the Spaniards and the Portuguese would have been wasting their time seeking another strait three thousand leagues distant from this one to get into the Pacific and go to the islands of the Moluccas where the spices are.

This country is inhabited by barbarians clothed in wild animal skins like those of Canada, very inhumane and intractable, as those who go there to fish for the cod we eat over here have indeed experienced. These maritime people live almost exclusively on fish which they take in great quantity, especially seals, whose flesh, which is very good, they eat. They make a [162r] certain oil from the fat of this fish, which after being melted has a reddish color, and they drink it with their meals as we here would drink wine or water.[45]

43 The Isle of the Devils is, of course, the celebrated Isle of Demons which Thevet will later make the island on which Marguerite was exiled by her uncle Roberval. Had he known this story in 1557-8 Thevet certainly would have mentioned it here. The tradition of an Isle of Demons in the Labrador-Newfoundland area antedated this account by many years. See map 11 for Thevet's own map giving an *I. des diables*. Cape Marco also appears on several maps of the period. See Henry Harrisse, *The Discovery of North America: A Critical, Documentary, and Historic Investigation* (London and Paris, 1892; reprinted Amsterdam, 1961), p. 178. See also *Grand Insulaire*, chap. "Isle of Demons."

44 Thevet may well be relying here on the Gemma Frisius map of 1537, for on this map the northern strait is designated *fretum arcticum sive triũ fratrũ*. According to Ganong, the three brothers were the Corte-Reals. See *Crucial Maps*, p. 200 and fig. 62. The Strait of the Three Brothers is also mentioned by Francisco López de Gómara in his *Historia general de las Indias* (Saragossa, 1552; reprinted 2 vols. Barcelona, 1954), 1: 22, and by Jehan Sheyfue in 1553. For the latter see D.B. Quinn, ed., *The New American World*, 5 vols. (New York, 1979), 1: 220.

45 See also *Cosmographie*, chap. 5: "On the Country Called New[found]land," and *Grand Insulaire*, chap. "Isle of Demons." Thevet may have developed his description of

From the skin of this big strong fish, like that of some land animal, they make coats and clothing after their fashion. [It is] a remarkable thing that in an element so humid as this, which is humidity itself, there can be an animal which has a tough dry skin like the terrestrial ones. They have also other fish clothed in rather hard leather, like porpoises and dogfish, and others covered with hard shells, such as tortoises, oysters, and mussels. Besides they have an abundance of all kinds of fish, large and small, off which they usually live. I am amazed that the Turks, Greeks, Jews, and divers other nations of the Levant do not eat dolphins or certain other fish with no scales, both of salt and fresh water, which makes me believe that these [natives of Newfoundland] are smarter and more intelligent [since] they find the taste of this meat more delicate than do the Turks, Arabs, or other such packets of superstitious people.

In this place [Newfoundland] whales are found (I mean in the open sea, for such fish never approach the shore) who live only on very small fish. Indeed the fish which whales usually eat is no larger than our carp, an almost impossible thing considering its size and largeness. The reason is, according to some, that the whale, having a very narrow throat in proportion to the body, cannot devour anything larger; which is still a remarkable secret which the ancients did not know, nor indeed the moderns, although [162v] they have written treatises on fish.[46] The female never has more than one young at a time, to which she gives birth like a terrestrial animal without eggs as do the oviparous fish. And what is even more remarkable, she gives milk to her baby after its birth, and for this she has breasts on her stomach under the navel. No other salt or fresh-water fish does [this], except the seal—to which Pliny bears witness. This whale is very dangerous on the sea if you meet one, as those of Bayonne well know from experience, for they are accustomed to take them. On this topic, when we were in America [Brazil], the ship of some merchant passing from one country to another on business or other errand was turned over and destroyed with everything in it, from meeting a whale which struck it with its tail.[47]

---

this drink from Roberval's mention that the natives drink seal oil at their great feasts. See Biggar, *Voyages*, p. 269.

46 There are several works on fish to which Thevet may be referring here: Guillaume Rondelet, *Libri de Piscibus Marinis* (Lyon, 1554-5); Conrad Gesner, *De piscibus et aquatilibus omnibus libelli III novi* (Zurich? 1556?); and two works by Pierre Belon, *De aquatilibus libri duo cum iconibus* (Paris, 1553), and *La nature & diversité des poissons, avec leurs pourtraicts . . . au naturel* (Paris, 1555).

47 For Thevet's discussion of whales, see *Cosmographie*, chap. 5: "On the Country Called New[found]land," and *Grand Insulaire*, chap. "Isle of Demons."

In the same area in which whales are found there is often a fish which is its perpetual enemy. Upon meeting one [this fish] invariably stabs it in the stomach (which is its softest part) with its sharp, cutting tongue, like a barber's lancet. [A whale] thus attacked is hard put to escape and avoid death, according to the natives of New Land and solitary fishermen. In this sea of New Land there is another kind of fish which the barbarians of the country call *Hehec*, having a beak like a "sea-parrot."[48]

There are also many dolphins which often show themselves above the waves and on the surface, leaping and tumbling in the air.[49] Some take this to be a presage of storms and tempests, with strong winds [163r] from the direction from which they come, as Pliny says, and [also] Isidore[50] in his *Etymologies*. Experience has made me more certain of this than the authority of Pliny or others of the ancients. On the same subject, some have written that there are five kinds of presages and prognostications of future storms in the sea, as Polybius [when he was] with Scipion Æmilian in Africa says.[51] Also there are plenty of very large mussels.

As for land animals, you will find many of them there, and very wild and dangerous beasts, such as large bears, who almost all of them are white. And what I say of the beasts goes for the birds, whose plumage is nearly white, which I think occurs because of the excessive cold of the country. These bears are a nuisance night and day in the cabins of the savages, eating their oils and fish when they have a reserve of them. As for the bears, as we have fully discussed in our *Cosmographie de Levant* [fols. 19r–21r], we will say in passing that the natives of the country, persecuted by their importunities, capture them. For this they dig deep

48 Ganong believes that Thevet's *hehec* may be a giant octopus. He also says that the term "sea- parrot" was applied by the French to the common puffin. Quinn, however, thinks that Thevet is describing a swordfish. See respectively, Ganong, *Crucial Maps*, p. 433, and "The Identity of the Animals and Plants Mentioned by the Early Voyagers to Eastern Canada and Newfoundland," *Transactions of the Royal Society of Canada*, 3rd ser., 3, sec. 2 (1909): 197–242, esp. 231; and D.B. Quinn, *Sources for the Ethnohistory of Northeastern North America to 1611*, National Museum of Man, Mercury Series, Canadian Ethnology Service Paper No. 76 (Ottawa, 1981), p. 33. Actually, it appears that Thevet is describing two "fish"; the first, with the "cutting tongue like a . . . lancet" would be a swordfish, and the second (the *hehec*), with the parrot-like beak, an octopus. See also *Cosmographie*, chap. 5: "On the Country Called New[found]land."

49 Compare Thevet's account here with that given in his *Cosmographie*, chap. 5: "On the Country Called New[found]land," where he refers to porpoises "incorrectly called dolphins . . . "

50 Bishop of Seville (d. 636).

51 Scipio Aemilianus, a Roman general, destroyed Carthage during the third Punic War. The historian Polybius was his close associate and mentor.

[holes] in the ground near trees or rocks, then cover them cleverly with branches or foliage of trees. [These holes are dug] near where some swarm of honey bees is located, which bears seek out and persistently follow and are very fond of, not I think so much to satiate themselves with as for curing their eyes, which are naturally weak, as well as the whole skull, so that even being stung by these bees to the point of bleeding from the head, this brings them some relief.[52] There too one sees a kind of animal large as the wild ox,[53] having rather wide horns and greyish skin, [163v] from which they make clothing, and several other beasts whose skins are rich and noteworthy. The country moreover is mountainous and infertile because of the climate and also the kind of land [which is] thinly inhabited and badly cultivated.

Of birds you do not find so many as in America [Brazil] or Peru [South America], nor as beautiful. There are two kinds of eagles, of which one frequents the waters and lives almost exclusively on fish, even those which are covered with large scales or shells; these they carry up into the air and then let drop to the ground, thus breaking them in order to eat what is inside. This eagle nests in large trees on the seashore.

The natives desire nothing but what is necessary to their natural needs, so that they are not gourmets and do not go seek them [exotic foods] in distant lands; and their nourishment is healthy, with the result that they do not know what it is to be sick. Rather, they live in continual health and peace and have no occasion to be envious of one another because of their property or patrimony—for they are all almost equal in possessions and are all rich in mutual contentment and degree of poverty. They also have no place designated for administering justice because they do no wrong to each other. They have no laws, any more than our Americans [Brazilians] and other peoples of the mainland, other than that of nature.[54]

52 Thevet's "bear remedy" is an obvious transference of the current bleeding therapy used for humans. For more on bleeding therapy see *Cosmographie*, chap. 1: "On the Peninsula of Florida."

53 Thevet refers to this animal as the Buttol in *Cosmographie*, chap. 2: "On the Beverages Used by the Floridians." See fig. 11 for Thevet's illustration of the animal.

54 This description of the natives as happy, healthy children of nature, living communally, without individual property, and at peace with one another, of course presages the concept of the Noble Savage, which was to find its culmination, perhaps, in the works of Rousseau (cf. Introduction, note 4). Compare Thevet's description with that offered in a letter written in 1502 by Amerigo Vespucci to Lorenzo di Pier Francesco de' Medici: "Having no laws and no religious faith, they live according to nature. They understand nothing of the immortality of the soul. There is no possession of private property among them, for everything is in common. They have no boundaries of kingdom or province.

The maritime people usually eat fish as we have said. The others content themselves with the fruits of the earth, which it produces for the most part without cultivation or being worked. The ancients had a similar life as Pliny tells us. We see even today that the earth produces by itself without [164r] cultivation. On this Virgil relates that [in] the forest of Dodona, beginning to dwindle either from its great age or from being unable to support the population which was increasing, men were obliged to work the earth and depend upon it for the necessities of life.[55] So much for their agriculture.

This people has little inclination to make war unless attacked by their enemies. Then they go on the defensive in the style and manner of the Canadians. Their instruments for inciting one to battle are animal skins stretched in a circle which they use as [164v] drums, with animal-bone flutes like the Canadians. If they perceive their enemy coming from afar, they prepare their arms (which are bows and arrows). On beginning the combat their chief (whom they treat as a king) will go first, clothed in beautiful skins and plumages, seated on the shoulders of two strong savages, so that everyone will know him and be prompt to obey all his commands. And when they obtain victory God knows how they honor him! They they return joyously to their lodges with their banners (which are tree branches adorned with swan feathers swirling in the air) unfurled, and bearing the scalps of their enemies stretched on little hoops (as I have tried to picture in the preceding illustration) [fig. 4].

They have no king, nor do they obey anyone. Each one is his own master. There is no administration of justice, which is unnecessary to them, because in their code no one rules." Vespucci's letter is in J.H. Parry, ed., *The European Reconnaissance: Selected Documents* (New York, 1968), p. 187.

55 The forest of Dodona was the ancient sanctuary of Zeus, in Epirus.

Cosmographie universelle (Book 23)

[1008v] On the Land of Canada and Baccaleos, and on Several Rivers of the Coast of Norumbega
CHAPTER 3

Having left Florida on the left hand, with a great number of isles, islets, gulfs and promontories, you see one of the most beautiful rivers on earth, named by us Norombegue and by the Barbarians *Aggoncy*, and marked as "big river" on some marine maps.[1] Several other beautiful rivers enter into this one, and upon it in the past the French had built a little fort some ten or twelve leagues upstream, which was surrounded by the fresh water which empties into it [the river]: and this place was named Fort Norombega. Several pilots who think themselves the most knowledgeable of Europe, speaking of pilotage, tried to make me believe that this Norumbegian country was Canada proper. But this is not so, as I told them, since this country is at forty-three degrees and that of Canada at fifty-one degrees and fifty-two degrees. This is what it is to lack experience, mistress of all things.[2]

1 Although the first appearance of the name *Norumbega* (in the form *oranbega*) is on the 1529 map of Girolamo Verrazzano, Thevet may simply be reading from the Mercator map of 1569 where there is a Fort Norumbega located near a *r. grande* [map 3]. Cf. W.F. Ganong, *Crucial Maps in the Early Cartography and Place-Nomenclature of the Atlantic Coast of Canada* (Toronto, 1964), pp. 130–2; and D.R. McManis, *European Impressions of the New England Coast 1497-1620* (Chicago, 1972), chap. 2: "Gilbert's Norembega: The Elizabethan Image," pp. 49–67. In *Cosmographie*, chap. 5: "On the Country Called New[found]land," Thevet says that *Aggonzi* means head. For more information see "The Glorious Kingdom of Norumbega," in Samuel Eliot Morison, *The European Discovery of America: The Northern Voyages A.D. 500–1600* (New York, 1971), pp. 464–70, 488–91.

2 This favorite expression of Thevet's is taken from Aristotle, *Metaphysics*, 1: 4. The phrase was also used by Cartier (H.P. Biggar, *The Voyages of Jacques Cartier* [Ottawa, 1924], p. 87).

Before approaching this river an isle surrounded by eight very small islets appears before you, which are near the land of green mountains and the Cape of Isles.[3] From there you continue to sail along the coast to the mouth of the river, whose entry is dangerous because of the great number of large, high rocks, and many reefs; and its mouth is marvelously wide. Some three leagues up the said river a beautiful isle presents itself before you, which has about four leagues circumference, inhabited solely by some fishermen and various kinds of birds. [It is] called by them *Aiayascon* because it has the form of an arm which they call thus.[4] Its length is north and south and it could easily be populated; likewise several other islets which are at some distance, and [one could] make a very fine fortress on it to control the entire coast.

Having set foot on land in the surrounding country, we perceived a large number of people who were coming straight to us from all directions, and in such a multitude that you would have said [that they looked like] a flock of starlings. Those who walked in front were the men, whom they call *Aquehuns*; afterwards the women, whom they call *Peragruastas*, then the *Adegestas*, who are the children; and last were the girls, named *Anias-gestas*. All these [1009r] people were clothed in pelts (which they call *Rabatatz*) of wild beasts. So observing their appearance and actions, we had some distrust of them and therefore we retired to our ship. However, seeing our fear they raised their hands into the air, signing that we were not to doubt them, and to render us more assured they sent to our ship four of their chiefs who brought us food. In recompense for which we gave them a few cheap trinkets, for which they were as happy as possible.

The following morning I was commissioned with several others to go to them to find out if they would aid us with food, of which we had a great shortage. Having entered the house (which they call *Canoque*)[5] of a certain kinglet whose name was *Peramich*, we saw several dead beasts hanging on the posts of the said house, which they had prepared (as they told us) to send to us.[6] This king gave us a very good welcome, and

3 In the *Grand Insulaire*, chap. "Isle of St. Julien," Thevet's Cape of Isles has become the "Cape of the Turtles."

4 See *Cosmographie*, chap. 5: "On the Country Called New[found]land," and the *Grand Insulaire*, chap. "Isle of St. Julien," where Thevet says that the island is square.

5 The words *Aquehuns*, *Peragruastas*, *Adegestas*, *Anias-gestas*, *Rabatatz*, and *Canoque* derive from Cartier's vocabulary. Thevet's source, however, was not Cartier himself but Ramusio, as is shown by variant spellings and definitions. See Introduction.

6 For the same account, but without mention of the name Peramich, see *Grand*

to show us the good will he bore us he had a good fire made (which they call *Azista*) on which he had meat and fish placed to roast. At this juncture appeared several rogues bringing to the king the heads of six men whom they had taken and massacred in war. This frightened us, fearing that they would do the same to us, so toward evening we stole off to our ship without saying goodbye to our host. At this he was greatly irritated, and so he came to us the next morning accompanied by three of his children, showing a sad countenance because he felt that we had come away discontent. Then he said to us in his language *Cazigno, Cazigno, Casnoüy danga addagrin*: which is to say, Come, come ashore my brothers and friends. *Coaquoca Ame Couascon, Kazaconny*: come drink of what we have. *Arca-somioppach, Quenchia dangua ysmay assomaha*: we swear to you by the heaven, the earth, the moon, and the stars: you shall have no more harm than ourselves.[7]

Seeing the good will and attitude of this old man, a score of our men set foot on land, each provided with his arms; and then went with him to his lodge where we were treated with what he had. Meanwhile a great number of people arrived who made over us and offered to do our pleasure, saying that they were our friends. But the climax of this was in the evening when we wished to retire and take leave of the company, giving thanks. This they did not want us to do: the men and the women as well as the children implored us to remain, using these words—*Cazigno agnyda-hoa*: my friends, do not budge from here, you shall sleep with us tonight. However, they harangued and begged in vain; they could not induce us to sleep with them. Rather we retired to our ship, and having remained there five whole days we hoisted anchor and left them with great satisfaction on both sides.

Because of the sandbanks and reefs we made for the open sea. But we had not sailed fifteen leagues out when the east wind was so contrary to us and the sea so swollen that we all thought we would perish. However, finally the tempest blew us some fifty leagues from there to the mouth of the Arnodie river between [the] Juvid river and the Right Cape, where we were forced to anchor and go upriver about half a league to avoid the tempests and storms of the sea.[8]

Insulaire, chap. "Isle of St. Julien." Thevet's source for this name is unknown to us.

7 The dialogue here and in the next paragraph has been patched together by Thevet from Cartier's vocabulary via Ramusio.

8 As Ganong points out, the Arnodie and Juvide rivers appear in no other records, and he adds: "Evidently our author, faced on the Atlantic Coast by a great paucity of material, invented what he thought needful to give human interest, and the semblance of

The people of this country gave us no less of a welcome than the first. To be sure they did not have as much venison, but in fresh and salt water fish they surpassed them, and especially in salmon, which they name *Ondacon*, and in lampreys, which they call *Zistoz*.[9] Of such fish they [1009v] brought us once a whole boatload full, of which we salted down about half a *muid*,[10] which served us well to complete our voyage. Leaving this river and sailing straight for Baccaleos you cross and sail the sea to the Isle of Thevet,[11] then to the Isles of Sainte Croix,[12] Isles of the Bretons, [Isle] of the Savages, up to the level of Cape Breton, so named because the Bretons discovered that land in the year 1504.[13]

---

exclusive new knowledge, to this part of his book." See *Crucial Maps*, p. 435. However, *Arnodie* may well be a misreading of *Arcadie*, a Verrazzano place name appearing on early maps. *Juvide* may derive from the *Promontorium Jovium* of the Verrazzano letter and 1529 map of Girolamo Verrazzano (cf. Lawrence C. Wroth, *The Voyages of Giovanni da Verrazzano*, [New Haven, 1970], pp. 140n15, plates 20 and 22). *Cap droit* is evidently an error for *coste droicte* (right coast) which appears on several early maps, including the Desceliers map of 1546. See *Grand Insulaire*, chap. "Isle of Demons," for another mention of the river of Arnodie "and that of Juvide, which you leave to the right."

9 *Ondacon* and *Zistoz* are from the Cartier-Ramusio vocabulary.

10 According to Emile Littré, *Dictionnaire de la langue française*, 4 vols. (Paris, 1863–9), a *muid* was a dry or liquid measure containing approximately 268 liters, or a barrel to contain this amount.

11 Frank Lestringant appears to be the first to notice that Thevet has named two islands after himself—one in the region of Canada and the other near Brazil. See his "Nouvelle-France et fiction cosmographique dans l'oeuvre d'André Thevet," *Etudes Littéraires* (April-Aug., 1977), pp. 161–73. See *Cosmographie*, chap. 4: "On the Utility of the Said Country of Canada," where Thevet says that the isle is "on the other side" of the equator, which for him is always the southern hemisphere. See also the discussion of the other Isle of Thevet in *Les Français en Amérique pendant la deuxième moitié du XVI siècle: Le Brésil et les Brésiliens par André Thevet* (Paris, 1953), ed. Suzanne Lussagnet, pp. 313–20; and map 4.

12 The Isle of Ste Croix is mentioned by Jean Alfonse, see Biggar, *Voyages*, p. 303 and n1, and is shown on the Vallard map of 1547 [map 15].

13 Jean Parmentier, in his "Discorso d'un gran Capitano di Mare Francese" (1539), writes that Newfoundland "was discovered 35 years ago [that is, in 1504] by the Bretons and Normans, for which reason it is called Capo di Brettoni." The "Discorso" was published in Giovanni Battista Ramusio's *Terzo volume delle navigationi et viaggi nel quale si contengono le navigationi al mondo nuovo . . .* (Venice, 1556). The quotation above is from Bernard G. Hoffman's translation, "Account of a Voyage Conducted in 1529 to the New World, Africa, Madagascar, and Sumatra, Translated from the Italian, with Notes and Comments," *Ethnohistory* 10 (1963): 14. See also the Mercator map of 1569, which bears the inscription: *"Anno 1504 Britones primi inuenerunt litora nove Francie circa ostia Sinus S. Laurentii."* [map 2]. It has been suggested, however, that the "alleged presence of Bretons in that region so early has no historical support, and rests in confusion of French Bretons with English Britons,—who were John Cabot and his Bristol crew." See Ganong,

Having designated for you the course to the north, from the point of Florida to that of Baccaleos, which lies at forty-eight degrees thirty minutes of latitude and 327 degrees longitude,[14] there only remains for me to describe the mainland, after having briefly discussed some islands whose approach is dangerous: into which [the mainland] we entered, having been blown there by the winds where we experienced the rigors of the cold which tormented us for more than twenty days. During this time I had the leisure to walk around and seek out what was rare and singular in this country. [It] extends into the sea in the north for a good two hundred leagues.

The neighboring isles are extremely numerous and very large: [for example] those in the gulf between Arcadia and the Promontory called and named by me Angoulesme for my birthplace; those which are near Flora and Paradise; or those which are enclosed in the port of refuge [Refugio]; or those which afterwards extend along the ocean more northwards near those which are called Bonne veuë[15] (which are close to the isle which bears the name of the country of Baccaleos). Some believe that these islands are continental and joined to the mainland because of their great extent: but I, who have seen them in person, I have seen and recognized that there is a good distance and extent of sea from these isles to the mainland. This country is so named because of a large fish named Baccaleos.[16]

Crucial Maps, pp. 275, 418.

14 In the early sixteenth century the only known method of ascertaining longitude was by timing an eclipse, often with extremely inaccurate results. For more information see Samuel Eliot Morison, *Admiral of the Ocean Sea*, 2 vols. (Boston, 1942), 1: 243.

15 Angoulesme [modern Angoulême] (named not by Thevet by but Verrazzano), Flora, Paradise, Refugio, and Arcadia are place names deriving from Verrazzano. See Wroth, *Verrazzano*, pp. 82–4, 137, nn9, 11; and map 5. Giovanni da Verrazzano appears to have named the area Arcadia because of its trees and its resemblance to the Arcadia of Ancient Greece. E.H. Wilkins, however, believes that Thevet's *Arcadie* is based on the world map prepared by Giacomo Gastaldi for the first Italian translation of Ptolemy's *Geographia* (Venice, 1548). He further states that Thevet's *Arcadie* is the first use of this form of the name, but that the "cap de l'Arcadie" mentioned here is a product of Thevet's confusion or imagination. See his "Arcadia in America," *Proceedings of the American Philosophical Society* 101 (1957): 4–30, esp. 14. For more information see Stefano Grande, *Le Carte d'America di Giacomo Gastaldi* (Turin, 1905); Ganong, *Crucial Maps*, pp. 132–3, 434. Thevet also mentions Arcadia in the *Cosmographie*, chap. 5: "On the Country Called New[found]land," and chap. 2: "On the Beverages Used by the Floridians, " and in the *Grand Insulaire*, chap. "Isles of the New Lands." *Bonavista* is a common name on early maps.

16 Peter Martyr first identified Sebastian Cabot as the author of the name "Land of the Bacallaos": "Cabotto calls these lands Terra de Bacallaos, because the neighboring waters

Canada is the country which is bordered on the south by the mountains of Florida, on the north by Baccaleos, on the east by the Atlantic Ocean, and to the south again faces the point of Florida and the Isles of Cuba; and the point of Baccaleos extends to the port of refuge [Refugio]. I am sure that the land there [Baccaleos] is even better than that of Canada, and there are very fine rivers which enter one hundred leagues into the middle of the country and are navigable, such as the *Barad*, which word in the Indian language means country.[17] And in my judgment I believe that it would be better to live in this country of Baccaleos, either on the mainland or on the neighboring isles, since the land is not so cold as that of Canada: also the people there are much more approachable and the sea more fertile in fish. Not that I wish to give here a fable, as did a venerable Spaniard in a little history of the Indies of Peru, where he relates that this sea so swarms with fish that they hinder the course of great ships.[18] You might as well lend credence to this as to what Thomas Porcachi from Arrezzo, an Italian, says in a certain booklet on islands:[19] that what we call the New World (which is properly this coast to Peru [South America]) is the Antarctic country. Poorly considered on his part, seeing as there is more than sixteen hundred leagues distance of coast between them. Also the country of Canada is not the one they call Nurumberg [sic],[20] containing a great extent of mainland which several have tried to explore: but not one has so well succeeded as Jacques Cartier, Breton, one of my best friends, from whom I have obtained bits of information since he has explored the country from one end to the other.

---

swarm with fish similar to tunnies, which the natives call by this name." See *De Orbe Novo: The Eight Decades of Peter Martyr D'Anghera*, trans. from the Latin with Notes and Introduction by Francis A. MacNutt, 2 vols. (New York, 1912), decade 3, book 6, 1: 348. Since Martyr writes only a few lines further on, "Cabotto frequents my house, and I have him sometimes at my table," it has been assumed that Martyr took this statement directly from Cabot himself. For more on *Baccaleos* see *Grand Insulaire*, chap. "Isles of New Lands." Thevet, like Martyr, also claimed that he interviewed Cabot. See *Grand Insulaire*, chap. "Isle of Cedars in Florida."

17 This name may derive from the *r. de Barques* of Mercator's 1569 map.

18 This story, told by Sebastian Cabot, was reported by Peter Martyr. Martyr, of course, was not a native Spaniard.

19 This reference is to Tommaso Porcacchi, *L'isole piv famose del mondo descritte da Thomaso Porcacchi da Castiglione Arretino* . . . (Venice, 1572).

20 Although the geographical limits of Canada and Norumbega were different to each cartographer of this period, Canada was chiefly confined to the region north of the St. Lawrence, and Norumbega to the south—i.e., the present northeastern United States.

Here before passing on I cannot remain silent about those who play the entrepreneur, and promise mountains of gold to the princes and great lords, proposing the subjection of the barbarians, which would be a good thing to do, and [speak of] the great [1010r] riches which are to be found in the said countries. But even if all that were true, you have to attend to what I have already said to several of them, that if they were not well-advised, wise, and wily in their enterprises, they would get no more profit out of them than some others have who have lost their lives and their capital in them. Although the kings of Spain and Portugal are friends and allies of our own Sovereign Prince, the sea pilots, sailors, and captains pay no attention to such alliances, or whether there is peace or war on land. So once you leave Europe and go into Africa or in some part of the land of Guinea, the sailors no longer know each other, so that the Spaniard makes a slave of the Portuguese even though their kings may be relatives, neighbors, and good friends. The Frenchman, the Scotsman, and the Englishman scarcely pardon one another in these distant countries. And you cannot blame the princes and princesses, seeing as it is done without their knowledge. I have seen this going on in Africa, chiefly around Cape Verde and the Manicongre river, and on both sides of the Equator, under both tropics, even in Florida and on this northern coast. As for what they try to tell our European princes, that there is on this mainland an abundance of gold, silver, and [precious] stones – this is deceiving them, since most of the riches and treasure which can be got out of Florida, Canada, and Baccaleos is in furs and the cod and whale fishery. I think one could find gold and silver deposits just as well as you might find in France: but what kind of deposits? inferior, and more full of sulphur than of good gold, and which would cost more to doubly refine than any profit you would get out of it. I say the same with regard to gems, which I know from experience.

This country was discovered by our people in the time of the great King François I, regarding which I shall give a brief summary, and I shall speak in the least possible number of words that I am able, although I know that few men other than myself have written about it. This country then extends far northwards, and approaches that which is under the Arctic circle, which we call one of the poles or pivots supporting the sphere. Consequently you can imagine how cold the land must be, and yet not uninhabitable. Now Canada is the equivalent of land, and this name came from the first to land there. For when someone asked them what they were looking for in this place, they answered that they were *Segnada Canada*, men seeking land, and since then the name has stuck like a nickname, and also to most of the isles and provinces newly discovered.[21] To the north it extends to the arctic or hyperborean sea. Therefore all this country is included, with Baccaleos and Labrador as well, under the name of Canada. And on the other side there is a mainland called *Campestre de Berge* which extends to the southeast.

In this province to the east lies Cape Lorraine, so named by us, and others call it Cape Breton because it is there that the Bretons, Biscayans, and Normans go and sail, going to the New Land to fish for cod. Near this cape is situated an isle named Heuree to the northeast, four or five leagues in circumference and quite close to the mainland, and another in triangular form named *Carbassa* by the natives and by us Isle of the Virgins.[22] And this land begins at the said cape towards the south, where it lies east-northeast and west-southwest. The majority of it facing Florida is in the form of a half circle, as if looking to the kingdom of Themistitan. The coast of Canada from Cape Lorraine southwards extends into the sea as does Italy into the Adriatic and Ligurian seas, forming a peninsula.

[1010v] In the region then closest to Florida (which some call French land, and the natives *Norombegue*) the land is quite fertile in various kinds of fruits, as for example mandourles, which is a fruit like a pumpkin, the juice of which is very good and the flesh delicate.[23] The inhabitants of the country are friendly, easy to handle, and pleasant in their conversation. Their range and principal habitat extends westward on the great river of *Hochelaga*, quite close to the promontory called Angoulême. That is where their king, whom they call in their jargon

21 This is the earliest known attempt to interpret a native Canadian place-name, according to Ganong's *Crucial Maps*, p. 429. The name Canada derives from the Iroquois-Huron word *Cannata*, meaning a collection of buildings or a town. See Biggar, *Voyages*, pp. 245, 309; Morison, *European Discovery*, p. 429; and *Grand Insulaire*, chap. "Isle of the Assumption." This anecdote is absurd, as it has the Europeans using native vocabulary.

22 *Heuree* is probably the modern St. Paul Island, which lies in Cabot Strait north of Cape Breton and which Cartier saw. The Vallard map of 1547 has an *I. de Plaisance* (pleasure) in the appropriate region, and it is possible that this is the source of Thevet's *Heuree* [sixteenth-century French: *heuree*—pleasant or fortunate]. See map 15. Ganong also suggests that *Carbassa*—perhaps Thevet's misreading of *Cabo Rassa* (Cape Race)—may be Scatari Island off the eastern point of Cape Breton about twenty leagues from St. Paul Island. The Isle of Virgins probably derives from the Isle of Eleven Thousand Virgins on several early maps. See Ganong, *Crucial Maps*, p. 429; and Bernard G. Hoffman, *Cabot to Cartier: Sources for a Historical Ethnography of Northeastern North America 1497-1550* (Toronto, 1961), p. 173.

23 Thevet here is close to the account of Parmentier. See Hoffman, "Account of a Voyage," p. 15.

Agouhanna, usually resides, who is quite pleasant to foreigners who come there.

Quite the contrary are those who dwell more inland towards Baccaleos: for they are wicked, deceitful, and cruel, and they mask their faces, not with masks or cloths, but by painting their faces with divers colors, especially with blue and red, so to render themselves more hideous to those who approach them. These men are big and strong and go around clothed in skins, and pluck out all the hair they have on their body except that of the head, which they draw up in a top-knot just like we tie and bind up our horses' tails over here. And they make their laces and bands from the tendons of wild beasts they kill (and so do all their neighbors, which I had forgotten to tell you). The colors with which they paint their faces are extracted from certain herbs and flowers of which they press out the juice; and so their paints are just as vivid as you would make here with Azure or the finest Lac that they bring you from Oriental countries. They have millet for food and make flour from it. They have melons also, but not as good as ours; and eat much more fish than meat, and especially eels very large and tasty.

If you go farther you will turn towards another great river, which our people have called Chaleur Bay, where there is a great quantity of salmon, larger and meatier than ours. In that country the only trade materials are deer skins, which they call *Aiomesta*,[24] otters, and other furs, for of gold and silver they know little. The inhabitants of this river [Chaleur Bay] usually wage war with those who live on the great *Hochelaga* river, and are different from them in language, customs, and style of life. The Hochelaga ones are those who have been best-known to the French. Indeed our people took two of them [to] King François I, who [later] returned [them] to their own country. [They were] favored and well-treated by all the barbarians who for this reason were more friendly than ever to our people, saying that *Cudragny*,[25] who is their god, was a liar who had told them that their men had been killed by the bearded foreigners. As for the savages who are on the other river [Chaleur Bay], we have not been able to find out what kind of people they are because, having heard that the river got narrower and that it was congealed with ice,[26] Captain Cartier told me that he did not have enough small boats

24 Ramusio gives *aionnesta* for cerf. Cartier has *Ajonuesta*.

25 *Cudouagny* is mentioned by Cartier in his second vocabulary list. Ramusio gives *Cudragny*. See Biggar, *Voyages*, pp. 139, 179–80, 243.

26 At Quebec the St. Lawrence River (Hochelaga River) is only 3230 feet wide, hence *kebec* – "where the stream is obstructed." This passage about the "other river" which became

and so put off exploring it for another voyage. As for the other region [the western] and part of Canada, it is situated more than two hundred leagues beyond the Hochelaga River; nevertheless [it was] discovered by our men, although it extends far north and borders the country which is called "unknown."

The country [Canada] is well populated, the inhabitants peaceful and friendly and the most obliging you could see. It was in their country that the French built long ago a fort near a mountain they named Mont-Royal,[27] so as to winter there and rest [upon] coming into these lands; plus the fact that the place is in itself pretty. This fort was built [here] because of a fresh-water river, named *Stadin*[28] which neighbors it, and another of salt water named *Islee* ["full of isles"]. These are not so large as those of Fauve, nor that of Daconie,[29] so named by the barbarians of the country.

[1011r] As for the great river of Hochelaga, there are very beautiful islands in it, e. g. that of Laisple,[30] which is right at its mouth, and that of Orleans, so named in honor of the late Duke of Orleans.[31] One could easily fortify oneself on these and populate and cultivate them. Our people lived quite well there because the inhabitants of the country brought them more fish than they wanted and also much venison, to which they are accustomed, using the bow and catching the animals with many clever ruses. Among other things they use a kind of rackets, woven and constructed with animal tendons, square, and whose holes are very

---

narrower and traversed "the other region and part of Canada" also derives from Cartier's second voyage. See Cartier's account in Biggar, *Voyages*, pp. 107 and n88, 172–5, 194–5.

27 For Cartier at Montreal see Biggar, *Voyages*, pp. 155, 168.

28 Cartier gives *stadin* as the name of a village near that of *Stadacona*, the seat of Donnacona. A *stadin flu* appears on the Mercator map of 1569, emptying into the St. Lawrence at the Isle d'Orleans [map 3].

29 Ganong believes that the names *Islee*, *Fauve*, and *Daconie* may derive from Cartier's third voyage. See his *Crucial Maps*, pp. 433–4. However, *Fauve* may be a misreading of Mercator's *r. de fouez*, and *Daconie* of *(lac) Dangoulesme* – both of which appear close to the *stadin flu* on Mercator's 1569 map. See map 3.

30 In the *Grand Insulaire*, chap. "Isle of the Assumption," *Laisple* becomes *Jaisple*. It is likely that Jaisple, and the Isle of Siplos on other maps, may derive from a misreading of Assumption – lasa(m)ptio(n). See Ganong, *Crucial Maps*, pp. 300–1, 428, 462–3.

31 The Isle of Orleans was discovered by Cartier on his second voyage, and he named it the Isle of Bacchus because it was covered with grapevines. Later the name was changed, perhaps by Cartier himself, to honor Charles, Duke of Orleans, a son of François I. The Mercator map of 1569 has a *y. d'orleans aliis de Baccho*. See Biggar, *Voyages*, pp. 126, 127n73, 232; and map 3.

small like those of a sieve. They are in the proportion of two and a half feet [long] and almost as wide, as the present illustration portrays and represents to you [fig. 2]. And they use these, tying them to their feet, as much against cold as to keep them from sinking into the snow when they are hunting wild beasts, and also so as not to slip on the ice. They clothe themselves with pelts cured and prepared in their fashion, in winter the fur side inside against the flesh, and in summer the leather touching their flesh with the fur on the outside.[32]

So to take these animals you will see ten or twelve of them armed and furnished with long staves, like stakes and partisans [truncheons], lances or pikes, some of them twelve, others fifteen feet long, armed at the end not with iron or other metal but with some good bone of a deer or other beast, a good foot long and moreover pointed, and carrying bows and arrows armed in the same manner. Thus provided they go out into the snow all year long, this [snow] being very familiar to them. When hunting deer, wild boars, wild asses, and reindeer in the depths of these snows they prepare their blinks [trail markers] just as our hunters do, so as not to get lost.[33] [1011v] And sometimes when the stag has come out, whether to feed or otherwise, knowing the route he has taken they make shelters of cedars (which are abundant in this country), and they hide under these green shelters waiting for the stag to come. As soon as the animal approaches they emerge from their ambush and run upon him with their pikes and bows; and with their hue and cries make him lose the beaten path and get into the deep snow up to his belly so that the poor

32 This information on the use of pelts is corroborated by Lorenzo Pasqualigo, a Venetian living in England at the end of the fifteenth century. His account is reproduced, in part, by Henry Harrisse, *The Discovery of North America: A Critical, Documentary, and Historic Investigation* (London and Paris, 1892; reprinted Amsterdam, 1961), pp. 66–73, esp. p. 71.

33 D.B. Quinn, *Sources for the Ethnography of Northeastern North America to 1611*, National Museum of Man Mercury Series, Canadian Ethnology Service Paper No. 76 (Ottawa, 1981), p. 28, points out that Thevet's assertion that there were wild boars in Canada may derive from the account of the Roberval voyage. When the latter is examined (cf. Biggar, *Voyages*, p. 268), it is clear that the present passage of Thevet is even closer to the Roberval account than Quinn has noted. Roberval: "They feede also of Stagges, wild bores [!], Bugles, Porkespynes, and other store of wilde beastes." Thevet: ". . . deer, wild boars, wild asses, and reindeer. . . . " Biggar notes that "bugles" were "no doubt the moose" (most English dictionaries define the word as "sort of a wild ox"), but Hakluyt most likely used it to translate the word *alce*—Fr. "wild ass." Thus Thevet, who as we have shown knew the original of the account of the Roberval voyage (see Introduction), duplicates the first two and probably the first three items of Roberval's list, and incidentally furnishes the French originals for the words used by Hakluyt: *cerfs, sangliers, alces*.

beast cannot get away— partly because of the snow which hinders it and also because by then they usually are hit and mortally wounded by the bows or lances.

After the massacre is over they skin it and cut it into pieces and drag it in its skin to their retreats. These are small villages and tawdry hamlets of a few houses arranged in the form and figure of a semi-circle, which the people call *Canocas*, large and about twenty-five or thirty paces long and ten paces wide with some covered with tree bark others with skins and with reeds. God knows how piercing the cold is in their houses, seeing as how the wind comes in from all sides; and they are so poorly covered and supported that often the pillars and beams either break or give way under the weight of the snow on top, which they call *Camsa*, so that in their sleep they have this dew and refreshment on their covers.

Since all this barbaric people cannot live without this way of doing things, because civilization and literature do not wean them from it, these Canadians, who are the fiercest known people and who have no arts or trades whatever, are always occupied in warring with some of their neighbors. Now those with whom these savages are angry and whom they often fight, are the *Toutaneans*, *Guadalpes*, *Chicorins*, and others. These are located along the two great rivers of the *Saguene* [Saguenay] and *Hochelaga*, which are of such marvelous extent that each enters more than four hundred leagues into the land. On them one can navigate [only] some fifty leagues with large vessels because of the rocks which are very numerous; and the savages travel on them from place to place. The natives of Baccaleos, closer to Canada than to anywhere else, are their allies and march with them in war.

The natives say that if you would sail up the said rivers, that *Assomaha*,[34] which is in a few moons (that is how they count and reckon time), you would find masses of gold and silver and a great diversity of peoples. And these two rivers finally join between Florida and the Cape of the Three Brothers, making a crescent as they unite in those regions and flow into the sea, since these regions embrace each other and are neighbors just as are France and Italy. The Hochelaga River, which is the wider, has its first source in the Prat and the Gadate mountains.[35]

34 The word *Assomaha* (moon) comes from the Cartier-Ramusio word list.

35 On the Mercator map of 1569 *Mont de Prato* is just west of *r. de fouez*. The name may go back to Cartier's Cape Prato, identified by Biggar as Cap d'Espoir on the Gaspé Peninsula and by Ganong as Cape Percé. For a discussion of the relevant evidence see Morison, *European Discovery*, p. 386. Ganong believes that *Gadate* derives from *Gotin*, a term which Thevet used in the *Grand Insulaire*, chap. "Isle of Demons." See Biggar, *Voyages*, p. 58n2 and 235n83; and Ganong, *Crucial Maps*, pp. 263, 434.

Then it makes you a lake—which is at least twenty leagues wide—of fresh water of the rivers named Estendue, which comes from the north, the Corry, Tortimage, and the Passer (named by the first to discover it the Montmorency): all these rivers make a beautiful promontory surrounded by a great number of little islets.[36] This lake bears the name of Angoulême as does the promontory I have just mentioned, in honor of one of the late royal children, son of the great King François, duke of that city.[37] As for the said Saguene River, the entrance is marvelously beautiful and good too and is to the north. And some twenty leagues from its mouth on the right hand is seen a mountain named Honguade,[38] at the foot of which was built another fort for greater security against the fury of these people.

When therefore it is a question of war in Canada, their great [1012r] *Agahanna*, which means king or lord, commands each of his people to come to him in such numbers as he specifies and to bring with them their arms and food for their subsistence during the time in which he intends to make war. The king does not pay anyone (since they have no use or knowledge of gold, silver, or other metal proper for money, no more than the other barbarians of all this country from one pole to the other),

36 Cf. *Grand Insulaire*, chaps. "Isle of Demons," and "Isle of Orleans." *Estendue* (Fr. "extended") may be a confused version of *Estadacone* [Stadacona] which appears on many of the "Portuguese–Cartier" maps; or it may derive from the Stadin river of the Mercator map of 1569. According to Hoffman, *Cabot to Cartier*, pp. 175–6, the name may refer to the Ottawa River, and Tortimage (which also appears on the "Portuguese-Cartier" maps but not on Mercator) to the hills bordering it. Mercator places the names Montmorency and Chambriant on the south shore of the St. Lawrence between Montreal and Quebec on his 1569 map [map 3]. Passer is also found on contemporary maps, including that of Le Testu of 1555. Corry may derive from a misreading of Secrories, which also appears on several of the "Portuguese-Cartier" maps (see the list of toponyms given by Ganong, *Crucial Maps*, p. 332.)

37 Verrazzano's letter states that the Lake of Angoulême was named for the Province of Angoulême, not after a son of François I as Thevet says. See Wroth, *Verrazzano*, p. 137n11.

38 The name Honguedo appears in the narrative of Cartier's second voyage (Biggar, *Voyages*, pp. 103 and n68). The name appears on many maps of the period. Both Biggar and Ganong give it as the native name for the Gaspé. Ganong guesses that this place name, the Huron-Iroquois name for the Gaspé basin and surrounding region, may derive from *Conguedo*, (throat)—a term descriptive of the shape of the Gaspé (Ganong, *Crucial Maps*, pp. 286, 300; and Biggar, *Voyages*, pp. 103, 178, 193, 235). On most of the "Portuguese-Cartier" maps Honguedo is placed correctly on the south shore of the St. Lawrence. Thevet, however, places it on the north shore and states that a fort was built there. It thus again becomes clear that Thevet was probably using the Mercator map of 1569 which erroneously locates Honguedo some distance up the Saguenay and shows a fort adjacent to it [map 3].

rather they are obliged to march according to his will. Most of their combats are waged on rivers, in their little [canoes] which are long and narrow made of tree bark, as savages do in many places.[39]

As soon as the assembly and general muster are made they go find the enemy, and know where he is, being informed by their spies. At the hour of the encounter they deploy so skillfully their squadrons and show themselves so clever in either attacking or defending, and making use of ruses and stratagems according to their styles of warring, that it proves that it is nature which makes the good soldier and captain. These people deploy no less than fifteen thousand combatants,[40] fortifying themselves in their lodges and cabins.

Now to fortify themselves without loss of their people they have a lot of faggots, bundles, pieces, and branches of cedar wood, all greased with the fat of the sea-bass and other fish and some poisonous compound. Seeing their enemies, they try to turn themselves against the wind and get their adversaries facing it. And then they set fire to these faggots, from which emerges a smoke so thick, black, and dangerous to smell, from the stench of the materials and the poisons mixed into these faggots, that some are suffocated. And even if they do not die from it, since they are blinded by the smoke, the others who are in the clearness of the daylight without hindrance of the smoke fall on them and make such carnage of them as they wish. Which I have tried to picture for you in the present portrait [fig. 3].

They also have trees which are very tall and large, which they use only for this purpose because they are so poisonous that the mere smell of their smoke will kill a man. If anyone falls asleep under one he feels such a stunning in his head that if he does not take immediate measures he risks losing his life. [1012v] This tree is called *Hoga Athau*, which means "cold tree."[41] I have seen such trees in Stony Arabia: and the Arabs will

39 Thevet here appears to be paraphrasing the incident in Cartier's narrative when Donnacona, whose title was Agouhanna, came to Cartier with men in twelve canoes. Biggar, *Voyages*, p. 121.

40 This number, no doubt an exaggeration, does not appear in Thevet's account in the *Singularitez*.

41 The vocabulary of Cartier's second voyage gives *Hoga* meaning leaves and *Athau* meaning cold (see "Second Dictionary," in *Grand Insulaire*, chap. "Isle of Demons"). Although this lethal tree does not exist in Canada, there is such a tree—the Manchineel—which grows in tropical America and is so poisonous that people are warned not to stand under it in a rain. This may be the same tree that Peter Martyr described thus: "Most of all is the shade of this tree noxious, for whoever sleeps for any length of time beneath its branches, wakens with a swollen head, and almost blind, though this blindness abates

Figure 3 Canadian natives at war
Thevet's *Cosmographie universelle*, fol. 1012r.
Courtesy John Carter Brown Library at Brown University

not let their horses and camels sleep in the shade of these trees, which they name in their language *Alaos* or *Alhalih*, giving it the name of an almond-tree because it has similar leaves. These trees, when the leaves and branches are cut into pieces, produce a certain yellowish milk which they rub on their arrows to make them poisonous. It is this juice which the Canadians use in their wars to kill those whom they wish. They attempted to use this trick against our men when they traveled there, but they were foiled: for our men having been warned about this, and that they planned to set fire to the ships, surprised them before they had time to do it.

I have heard that these poor people had good and just cause to do this because some fools and madmen (more cruel than is the nature of Frenchmen) were killing these savages as a pastime and were cutting off their arms and legs as if they had been no more than tree-trunks or animals. This notwithstanding the fact that these poor people had received them with all kindness, saying to them *Aignah Adagrim Casigno Cazahoaquea*: Good day, brother, let us go have a drink together. And then being a bit more familiarized, said to them *azaca, Agoheda*: give us some knives. And so they began to try to prevent the Christians from landing, thinking they would get the same treatment as they had had from these madmen. This people rejoiced exceedingly seeing foreigners: and to attract them to them and have them land, they made a fire for them, which they name *Agista*. Having cast anchor, you see around you thousands of these poor people, rejoicing at your coming, bringing their little skiffs to the ships, shouting and constantly repeating these words *Cassigno Casnouydanga*, which mean: come into our skiffs, brothers and friends, to see our beautiful country so greatly desired by you.[42] And you must not go trade there except in good numbers since they still remember this outrage, and once offended it is impossible to conciliate them.

But let us come back to our discussion. When these Canadians go into battle they march four by four and utter frightful howls when they approach (just as we have said about the women who are falsely called Amazons) in order to intimidate their enemies. Do not think that they go in disorder, for they have ensigns of branches of birch or other trees, adorned with large plumes of swans and other birds, which are carried

---

within a few days." (see *De Orbe Novo*, decade 2, book 1, 1: 191). Thevet also spells *Athau* as *Athan*. See *Cosmographie*, chap. 4: "On the Utility of the Said Country of Canada." The effects are suggestive of poison oak.

42 Again, these "quotations" from the natives are knitted together by Thevet from the Cartier-Ramusio word lists.

by those with the greatest reputation for valiance. Moreover, they use tambourines made of certain skins stretched and laced, like on a frame on which you stretch parchment, which two men on each side carry, and another behind striking this skin with two batons with as much vim as possible. Their flutes are made of the bones of high-striding wild beasts, which they make correspond to the sound of the drum rather skillfully.

Their combats are so furious that once they have attacked each other they must conquer or die or flee; and they do not take prisoners, but kill all those they can. They fight with arrows, with large round clubs, and with [ordinary] clubs. They have shields made of skins and covered with plumes which they use very skillfully when the occasion requires. Some have head-covers difficult to pierce which are made of the skins of the sea-wolf[43] and of beavers. These Canadians, although they are definitely not cannibals, i. e. eaters of human flesh, still [1013r] having taken an enemy, they kill him then throw his body to the animals to eat. They skin the face and the head and they set aside these skins out in a circle to dry, then carry it to their houses to show it to their *Aquehum*, *Peragruasta*, *Addegesta*, *Agniagesta*, i.e. the old men, women, children, and girls (for this is what they call them in these lands), by whom they are praised, with glory to their name and family, and they incite them to carry on proposing the examples of their predecessors. They carry their king (having obtained victory over their enemies) seated on the shoulders of two of the biggest and strongest of the troop, which they call *Cabata*,[44] so that everyone can recognize and honor him in the manner that you will see in the present illustration [fig. 4]. Now although they are great warriors, still they do not like bloodshed as much as the natives of Peru [South America] and America [Brazil], since the others attack their enemies just for pleasure and to chase them out of their territory. These Canadians do not do so, only making war to avenge a wrong received; otherwise they do not make war on anyone.

The skins from which they make their clothes are of beavers, bears, panthers, foxes, hares, rats, wild asses, reindeer and other beasts, and they prepare the leather with the fur. This has given rise to the statement of some (too simple in my opinion) who say that the savages are hairy.

43 Thevet is referring here to the *loup marin*, a term applied by early voyagers generally to seals. See William F. Ganong, "The Identity of the Animals and Plants Mentioned by the EarlyVoyagers to Eastern Canada and Newfoundland," *Transactions of the Royal Society of Canada*, 3rd ser., 3, sec. 2 (1909): 223.

44 It is unclear whether Thevet means that *Cabata* refers to "the biggest and strongest of the troop," or to the "troop" itself. In any case, Cartier and Ramusio give *Cabata* as the word for a dress.

Figure 4 Thevet's illustration of scalps, drums, and drumsticks made of animal bones
Thevet's *Cosmographie universelle*, fol. 1013r.
Courtesy John Carter Brown Library at Brown University

The great Hercules, coming to France, found the people living almost like these savages do today. They in their simplicity on seeing our clothing are astonished and ask what kind of trees they grow on, thinking that wool grows on trees just as cotton grows on little bushes. The men and women have very long black hair which the men wear in a top-knot. The women sometimes have their hair loose on their shoulders, and others bind it like the men without putting any pelt on top of it such as the men do. They dress in deer skin prepared in their way so that not a hair falls out of it, and thus enveloped they cover their whole body with it and fasten it with a belt using three or four turns, having always outside this costume one arm and one breast just like a pilgrim's scarf. These *Peragruasta*, or women, do not go bare-legged but have shoes made of tanned and well-worked leather, enriched with divers colors which they make [1013v] from herbs and fruits.

These northern peoples are great eaters. That is why in Canada they often suffer famine in the regions which I have described above, since being great gluttons their provisions are soon consumed. Very often the freezes spoil the fruits and roots on which they live. And they cannot fish either, because for three or four months of the year the rivers are frozen with ice, on which they also run just like the Russians and Muscovites on the sea. As for their drink, water suffices when other beverages fail for the lack of plants and fruits.

On the Utility of the Said Country of Canada, and on the Grapevines that the Land Produces Naturally
CHAPTER 4

All of this Canadian people from Florida to the land of Labor [Labrador], including Baccaleos and the neighboring isles (as many of them as are habitable), is without any law or religion whatever, living as guided by the instinct of nature, since they have no ceremonies or form of praying to God, whom they have the fantasy of calling *Cudragny*. Thus this degenerate people believe that there is some divinity in the moon, whose crescent when they see it they contemplate with admiration, saying that *Andouagni* (which is the same as *Cudragny*) sends them *Assomaha*, which is the moon (for such is the name they have given it), and makes it come out and appear little by little, so that it advances or retards the waters—showing that they clearly understand the effect of this star with respect to the tides. It would be incorrect to judge from that that they worship either the sun or the moon. They admit indeed that Cudragny, or Andouagni (the two are one), is the creator of everything and that he is much greater than the sun (which they call *Ysmay*) or the moon or other stars, and say that it is he who holds everything under his power and who sends them what is necessary.

Further, they believe in the immortality of the soul. And these good people say that when a man dies who has been wicked, a great bird comes with very sharp and cutting claws and beak and carries off his soul. If on the contrary he has been good, his soul goes off of its own accord to a place embellished with many sorts of trees and where there are birds which sing the most melodious songs in the world night and day.[45] I have this from a king of the country, who was chief over all others, who was called *Dona coua* [sic], *Aguanna*, who died in France in the time of the great King François, who spoke our language very well and having lived there four or five years died a good Christian. I saw and spoke with him to be more certain of the singularities of his country, and he told me that his seniors had told him that when a man (whom they call in their language *Aguelhum*) came to earth, the sky, (which they call *Quemhia*) formed a new star called *Siquehoham* which appeared in the sky to be the guide of this man. Whereas on the contrary when an *Aquelhum*, *Peragruastu*, *addegesta*, *aquiaquesta* (which are man, woman, son, or daughter, as they say), came to pass away and leave Canada, then a star was lost in the sky never to be seen again.[46]

They greatly rejoice to see the sun and the moon, taking pleasure in their brightness and especially that of the sun because it melts the ice and warms the earth, albeit rather pitifully since the *Athan*, or cold, is very severe there, as the moon because of its humor and natural coldness freezes and cools the season more than they would like. And in any case they have great fires day and night, which they call *Arista*, and the [1014r] smoke *Quea*, in their lodges or *Canoques*, by means of which they protect themselves against the rigors of the winters and cold, which

45 Compare Cartier's account during his second voyage in Biggar, *Voyages*, p. 179. Thevet is here corroborated by a later account of Nicolas Perrot, who writes: "All the savages who are not converted believe that the soul is immortal; but they maintain that when it is separated from the body it goes to a beautiful and fertile land, where the climate is neither cold nor hot, but agreeably temperate. They say that the land abounds with animals and birds of every kind. . . . " See *The Indian Tribes of the Upper Missippi Valley and the Region of the Great Lakes As Described by Nicholas Perrot, French Commander in the Northwest; Bacqueville de la Potherie, French Royal Commissioner to Canada; Morrell Marston, American Army Officer; and Thomas Forsythe, United States Agent at Fort Armstrong*, ed. and trans. Emma H. Blair, 2 vols. (Cleveland, 1911), 1: 89.

46 This vocabulary is taken from the Cartier-Ramusio word lists.

are almost perpetual with them, and more vehement than is the heat of the sun under the equinoctial line.

These barbarians each take two or three wives without any other ceremony, and yet adultery is much detested by these poor people. The Lord *Aguahama*, who is the king, because of his rank, can have as many of them as he wishes. The girls are no less prized if during their period of liberty they have given themselves to the young men, so long as they [the men] are not married: for everyone must be satisfied with the provision of his house.[47] Now by the same token that the girls are free and dissolute, on the contrary the honor and chastity of the widows is admirable, since in the first place they never remarry, mourning over their dead husband, rubbing their face black with ashes or grease or fish oil, the ashes being powdered.

As for the treatment of their children by married women, it is as follows: they bind them and swaddle them in four or five marten skins sewn together, which serve them as baby's clothes. Then they attach them to little wooden planks which are pierced at the spot of the place where one voids the excrements of nature so that this opening is always free. And between the legs, right at the penis of the baby, there is a sort of little spout made of tree-bark, very soft and tender, through which he voids his water without soiling his body either in front or behind, or even the pelts with which he is wrapped. If these people were closer to Turkey, I would guess that they had learned this from the Turks or that the Turks had been apprentices of these savages. In this however I praise the savages more than the Turks, since the disciples of Mahometh prevent their children from soiling themselves with any excrement believing it to be a sin, while the Canadians do it for the health of their children and because it seems to them more civilized and proper.

In this country are found many pumpkins and gourds (which they name *Casconda*), which they eat roasted in the coals as we do pears. They also use a certain fine seed, like that of marjoram, which however comes from a quite large plant named *Theniot*.[48] This plant is much esteemed among them; they gather it in piles and dry it in the sun, and then when it is dry they pulverize it and put it in little leather sacks. It is with this powder that they often perfume themselves all day, placing

47 This apparently means that married men had to be satisfied with whatever wife (or wives) they had taken.

48 In his account in the *Singularitez*, chap. 77: "The Religion and Style of Life of these Poor Canadians," Thevet does not give the name *Theniot* for tobacco, which he has already described and called *petun*–an authentic Tupi term–in his material on Brazil.

it in a cornet; and lighting the other end they inhale its smoke so that it comes out of their eyes and all the other conduits of their face, saying it lengthens their life. Differing from their use of this powder our natives of the Antarctic [Brazil] take *Petun* in a Palm-leaf, for the pleasure they obtain from smelling a good odor: and I can assure you from having tried it, how good it is for purging the heart.

Moreover the country of Canada is beautiful in itself, well situated and very pleasant. There are many trees and of many kinds which we do not know in France and which have great properties: and several plants and bushes were brought back from there which today are to be seen in the royal garden at Fontainebleau. Among others there is one called *Cotony*, which is of the size of one of our large walnut trees.[49] This tree was [considered] for a long time as useless and without profit until one of our people wanted to cut one. As soon as it was cut to the quick a liquor came out of it in quantity. This being tasted, was found to be of such good taste that some thought it to be equal to the goodness of wine—so that some people collected an abundance of this liquor and helped refresh our people. And to see and experiment on the source of this drink, [1014v] the said tree was sawed down and its trunk being on the ground a miraculous thing was discovered in the heart of the tree: a Fleur-de-lys well pictured, which was admired by all. About this some said that it was a very good presage for the French nation, which in the passage of time through the diligence and zeal of our kings could conquer and some day bring to Christianity this poor barbarous people. Captain Jacques Cartier with whom I stayed five months in his house in St. Malo in Brittany, and other captains and gentlemen worthy of faith (even a canon of the city of Angers who was present at the embarkment)[50] assured me that the thing was very true. The Canadians will not forget the excellence of this liquor and will remember always those who discovered use of it, considering the excellence of this beverage—better certainly than that which they and their neighbors had used previously.

Besides this [tree] another grows there which they call *Auzuba*,[51] which is big and tall and the leaves are like those of our pear-trees but much thicker. The fruit is indeed among the most delicate you could eat, being

49 In the *Singularitez*, chap. 80: "On the Ores, Precious Stones, and other Singularities," Thevet spelled the word *Couton*. In this account Thevet specifically claims for the French of Cartier's expedition what he had only implied in the *Singularitez*, credit for the accidental discovery of the sap of the Sugar Maple. He has also expanded the story considerably.

50 For details see Biggar, *Voyages*, p. 92n11.

51 We have been unable to find a reference for this word.

just like the musk pear, which formerly I ate on the Island of Negrepont and in the region of Athens. But if you do not put this fruit into water to control a certain milk it produces, just like that which comes out of a still-green fig, it will be impossible for you to eat it, it is so sticky: but as soon as it is soaked in water a bit all this milk and viscosity washes off and you can eat it easily.

I will tell you of another case which would seem almost incredible, and to myself also if I had not seen it in several places in Baccaleos. In Canada in several of the coastal regions you see beautiful grapevines growing there without tending or cultivation by a living soul, and which bear grapes which the savages call *Orobà*,[52] and are good to eat: but I do not know whether the wine is any good because I have never seen any of it made. And if you are astounded, imagine that those who saw them and ate their fruit were no less so, considering the terrain of the spot which is high mountains. These vines grow a lot with poplars and elms, which having climbed over they are so abundant in foliage and branches that they can only be separated from them without breaking with great difficulty. I am sure that if these vines were cultivated they would produce good wine. In which we have to recognize a great marvel, which is that this good bush grows in all four parts of the world and is everywhere prized, as I have observed: however these natives, oddly, not knowing their virtues, it is the birds who feed on them.

It comes back to me that when I was in Arabia between the two gulfs, the Persian and the Red Sea, after having come out of the sandy deserts where neither herb nor greenery rejoices the sight, I arrived near a mountain in which I saw a plant which they name *Malazal*, which has leaves like a mulberry and is a foot high, which the Arabs feed to their horses and camels that have vives[53] or other malady, even if they have pursy.[54] As I was walking with some natives, who are not so objectionable as the Arabs near Judea, I saw on this mountain more than a hundred grapevines trained up some big trees, which already had some very small verjuice.[55] I asked what was this plant but they were unable to answer me. And not only there but under the Equator, or four degrees this side in an isle we named "of the Rats,"[56] which was never inhabited

52 This term appears, as *ozoba*, in Thevet's Second Dictionary, *Grand Insulaire*, chap. "Isle of Demons."

53 Inflammatory swellings of the submaxillary gland.

54 The heaves, or shortwindedness.

55 A juice made from unripe grapes; also the vines from which the juice is made.

56 This island has not been identified.

save by birds and small animals (about which I have spoken elsewhere), I found grapevines very thick in foliage and which clambered over the neighboring small trees, nevertheless not [1015r] appearing to have fruit. I think the birds had eaten it.

I shall not forget here an isle which is set at eight degrees ten minutes on the other side of the Equator to the south-southeast, which had never been discovered by anyone nor marked on any map. On this I landed in a skiff with some others to find fresh water after we had anchored because of contrary wind, with an agreement among us that the first to set foot on the isle would name it, which fell to me: wherefore it was named the Isle of Thevet [map 4]. The inhabitants and governors of it were only birds of divers plumages and sizes in great numbers, but also beautiful fruit trees of several kinds and colors. And when we thought to go into the isle, because of its thick woods, I perceived some hills and on these I discovered that there were some grape leaves. As for the trees I never saw any like them, and you would have judged this place to be a second earthly paradise: nevertheless I never saw any of these in the Antarctic country, and even less on the Guinea coast going straight towards upper Ethiopia. To be sure I have seen several trees and plants having leaves similar to that of the grape: and although these grapevines are wild and like brambles, if they were cultivated they would become more tractable like the rest of [the cultivated] trees and plants.

As for me, I believe that all the fine and good grapes which produce our good wine have their origin in wild plants, such as you can see, even from the history of the first to cultivate the grape. Further there is a tree there which the Canadians call *Guiabar*, similar to a Service-tree[57] in its twigs, but its leaves are very wide, like a half-foot wide and the same in length. You can write on it with a bodkin or knife or something having a fine point, and the letters are easy to read because the surface of the leaf does not rub off and the letters appear all white there, with the leaf very green with a reddish tinge. This *Guiabara* bears a fruit very similar to grapes, very clear and dainty [in color], of a reddish-rose verging on reddish-violet. They are good to eat, although there is not too much flesh because the seed takes up too much room. If I wanted to take the time to tell you about everything that grows there and in the neighboring provinces (which are Baccaleos, Newfoundland, and Labrador), more

57 Thevet has transferred the Guiabar from Brazil to Canada. It appears in the South American section of the *Grand Insulaire*. See Lussagnet, *Le Brésil et les Brésiliens*, pp. 318–19 and 318n3. A "service tree" is the Mountain Ash (a species of the genus *Sorbus* of the rose family).

in some, less in others—although they are all pretty much the same—I should never be done: wherefore I must continue with the rest I have to describe about this country.

Canada (although there are plains) still is a very mountainous country. In the mountains you find stones which in weight and color smack of gold ore: but when they tried to assay them to see whether they were good they could not endure the fire, but were immediately reduced to ashes. Not that I want to imply from this that anyone who would dig deep into the mountain might not find some vein of gold whose ore might equal that of the Isles of Peru [South America]. As for veins of iron and copper, many are found there. Further, stones are found there in the flat land as well as the mountains which are so beautiful and well-cut by nature alone that the first to find them thought, as they told me, themselves very rich believing them to be real diamonds, of which they have the color and shape. But on their return they found their mistake, whence the proverb: That is a Canada Diamond. And indeed they greatly resemble those brought from Calcutta and the East Indies, not that the lapidaries do not know the difference. Of such diamonds as those of Canada, I have seen [some] in the mountains of Auvergne and the Alps which are so beautifully carved by nature under their rocks that the cleverest lapidary [1015v] would be put to it to imitate their naturalness. They are prized not for their value but only because men, who are curious about rare things, are also pleased to see how great nature is in her effects. Having tested both, I find that the Canadian one is much harder than the one we find in Europe. Some say it is a kind of crystal, of the hardest one can find: on which I can give no other solution than that it could be, because crystal, as I have said elsewhere,[58] being concreted from glass and ice could be formed in Canada, drying and hardening and then solidly converted into this body gleaming like crystal.

But if this opinion were correct it would only be in very cold lands that crystal were found: experience shows the contrary, since in the Isles of Cyprus and Rhodes and in the country of Egypt, which are hot regions, I have found crystal in abundance. So I say that it is not created only of snow or frozen water or by cold, [but] rather by water dried out by the heat. Whether crystal was greatly prized in the past, Thevet is not going to discuss it now for you: I will only say that I saw in the Holy Land and in several parts of Palestine and Egypt temples built about the time of the Apostles which are all decorated about with little rocks of gilded crystal; and I really believe there is a Church like that of Bethlehem which would

58 See above, *Singularitez*, chap. 81: "On the Earthquakes and Hail."

cost a mint [illegible word] whoever would like to re-do it in its present state. The Ancients, who searched for crystal everywhere, did not send to the cold regions for it but rather to the warm ones. At present crystal is not in such demand as in the past by emperors and monarchs, unless to make vases, goblets, or mirrors, since it is too fragile and easy to break. And when I told you that in Cyprus, which is a hot country, you find crystal do not think it is in the mountains, as I have observed on the spot (so that we will not return to cold as the cause of its formation), but rather it is found in the flat country and in the bowels of the earth. When farmers turn or spade and dig in the ground, if they go rather deep they do not fail to find the said crystal, both in small and rather large pieces.

Moreover in Canada and the neighboring countries are found jasper and chalcedony in great abundance. And there is a mountain there which the natives call *Quea*, which means woman[59] (because from this mountain one sees ordinarily and continually smoke come forth), and it is some eight and one-half leagues distance from the *Hochelaga* River. In this mountain are found stones which occur naturally in the rock, gleaming with the color of the sky, which the savages call *Quanhia*[60] and the natives of Newfoundland *Kyph* because of its brightness.

The interior of the province of Baccaleos is very subject to hail and marvelously afflicted with great earthquakes. This people—which ignores natural causes as well as that which depends on heaven, although they are familiar to them as things they see everyday—are thus constantly in fear and say that it is *Ysmay* and *Assomaha* who cause this because they have offended them. As for the hail, it is no marvel that it is so frequent due to the intemperance of the air and distance from the sun, which does not approach it closer except when it is in our tropic. Which is the reason that when water falls from the sky, due to the perpetual coldness of the air, it freezes and is converted into snow or hail and frost.

In several places in this country and especially into the interior the people are idolators and make certain idols which they worship, [but] not as rich as those of Peru [South America]. As soon as they feel the great colds they retire into their lodges with some [1016r] domestic animals which they feed, and there they cherish their idols whose form

59 Here is a clear case of a misreading of Thevet's manuscript by the typographer. *Quea*, according to the Cartier-Ramusio vocabulary, means smoke (*fumée*), which the typographer misread as *femme*, or woman. This was an easy mistake to make, since the acute accent mark was usually used only over a final "e" by Thevet and most French Renaissance writers. We have found no source for Thevet's smoking mountain in Canada.

60 *Quenhia* (sky) in the Cartier-Ramusio vocabulary.

scarcely differs from the fabulous Melusine, so often sung by the ignorant cosmographer or by the old lying Romances; that is half-woman and half-serpent, since the face with the hair (as they picture her) represents the face of a woman, with all the rest of the body in the form of a serpent. I saw one of these in the hands of an English pilot, which Roberval gave him to present to Henry the Eighth, King of England. She was of the size of a foot-and-a-half, and they named her in their language *Miroph-quemeth*,[61] which means teller of news: because when they want to know something about their enemies they consult these fine dolls several times and the ones which are best-made are the ones with the most power.

In that country sometimes the earthquakes are so violent that for five or six leagues around will be found more than two thousand trees, in the mountains or valleys, knocked down and uprooted, rocks piled on top of one another; all this proceeding from this violent concussion of nature. This people, feeling itself thus subject to such upheavals and fearing the fury of the lightning, have been taught by this same nature that there are trees and animals upon which this heavenly fire never falls. Therefore when they go fishing far from their dwellings they place in their little boats, which they call *Casnouy*, branches of a tree named Cahene[62] because of an isle where they get it having a similar name in which no other trees are found save this one. Having [pieces] of this tree with them, they say that never do the lightning or storms harm them. They also cover their *Casnouis* with the skins of seals, since they attribute the same properties against storms to this sea-monster.

While on the subject I remember that when I was on the Isle of Pathmos, on which in the past the Holy Apostle [St. John] was exiled in the Mediterranean Sea, the inhabitants of the flat country usually have their houses surrounded by laurels planted about, and they told me when I was there that it is the surest remedy against lightning, which never falls on this tree. And this isle is one of the most subject to it that I ever saw, more than all the Cyclades. And I assure you that as we were approaching its port, which lies to the northeast, we all thought we were going to perish, and shortly before a lightning-storm (according to the Greeks) had struck three men and several horses and other domestic animals, reducing them to ashes. This is why the Corsairs do not land there.

Also, in the places where the Canadians think there are serpents and

61 This word is not found in the Cartier-Ramusio vocabulary, nor have we found it elsewhere.

62 In Thevet's vocabulary the word appears both as *Caheya*, and *Quahoya*, meaning nuts or walnuts. See *Grand Insulaire*, chap. "Isle of Demons."

poisonous beasts, they just sprinkle around leaves or branches of this *Cahene* tree or its bark, and right away not one of these beasts remain alive. It is remarkable when these vipers flee the odor of the Cahene tree, and the savages are building fires in the places where there are not any of these leaves, the serpents prefer to cast themselves into the fire or let themselves be taken and killed than to approach this thing they detest so. They also have a tree which has leaves like the wild agrimony[63] that I saw in "happy Arabia," [*Arabia felix*] which they call *Hoguada*,[64] which has the same strength and virtue against poison and harmful beasts as the above-mentioned tree: thus has nature provided for the defense of what she has created.

To this land is joined, as mentioned, that of Baccaleos at forty-eight degrees from the line towards the Arctic, and the country is very cold. The people are quite brutish, except near the coast where our people have traded and have labored so well and in such a short time that some of them have been received into our holy religion. These Baccaleans are not cannibals, although they formerly were, for their king would punish it severely.

[1016v] On the Country Called New[found]land, and on the Isle of Demons

CHAPTER 5

Fifty-six degrees[65] on this side of the equinoctial line lies the country which is vulgarly known as New Land, which from the time of its discovery until today has borne and still bears this name. This country is at the same latitude and has a similar climate to Moscow, where the sea is frozen and very close to the North Pole, which is under the Northern Sky and therefore extremely cold. This region of Newfoundland constitutes one extremity of Canada and shares that of Baccaleos, being completely maritime. In it is the great river called that of the Three Brothers, quite

63 Tansy or silver-weed.

64 This word is not in the Cartier vocabulary. Thevet may have combined *Hoga* (leaves) and *Haueda* (tree).

65 Fifty-six degrees is too far north on most maps, including Thevet's own map, to intersect any part of Newfoundland. But Thevet, here at least, considers Newfoundland as part of the continent, along with Baccaleos. He might have received this impression, for example, from the "Pseudo-Agnese" map (1556-60), which has the legend "La Nova Terra de Bacaliaos." See Ganong, *Crucial Maps*, p. 350; see also *Grand Insulaire*, chap. "Isles of the New Lands," and map 11.

close to the Island of Orbellande[66] which is in the said sea. This river is one of the greatest of all this land, and anyhow like those I saw beneath the Equator and in our Antarctica. This country is inhabited by barbarous people, cruel and inhuman just like those of Canada, ungracious and unapproachable unless by force, as those who go there to fish for the cod we eat over here know well.

They dress in skins of wild animals, in imitation of all their neighbors, peoples of the north. They live on hardly anything but fish, which they catch in great quantities because the sea there abounds in it more than any other place in the universe, and especially in seals whose meat seems very good and delicate to them. They use this fish in several ways since from its fat they make a certain oil, which being melted is converted into a reddish liquid and they drink it with their meals, as we do with wine or other beverage, or as they themselves do with water, which they call *Hame*.[67] They also prepare the skin of this fish, which is large, strong, and thick, as if it were that of some large land animal. They make coats of it and other clothing in their fashion, such as I described to you in the preceding chapter. It is a thing which Pliny refused to believe (and others also), that in the sea, an element which is not only wet and cold but which is wetness and coldness itself, there lives an animal whose skin toughens and dries to be used for warmth in such a cold region. There are also many other fishes who like this one are covered with a hard skin, such as the porpoise and the dog-fish. Others [are] armed with very hard shells, as turtles, oysters, and mussels, and others have only simple scales.

It is in this place that is found a great quantity of whales, and not in the Mediterranean Sea and hot countries, as he said who dared commentate the Cosmography of Munster [Belleforest], in which he was sadly mistaken as I have told you elsewhere. This monster is named by the savages of Mexico *Altapatli*, by the Syrians *Tanim*, and by others *Leviathan*. The Hebrew text calls him *Dagh-gadol*, i.e. great fish, and the Persians *Nuna rabba*. And I understand that it is in the open ocean that this monster is taken, since he never approaches the coasts, and feeds on fish which are scarcely larger than salmon: an incredible thing for one who has not witnessed it. The reason for it is very simple—it is because, although the whale is of monstrous size and grandeur, yet its throat is quite narrow and the conduit through which his food passes even smaller than the pro-

66 This island, not mentioned in the *Singularitez*, appears on a number of maps including those of Desceliers (1546) and Ramusio (1556). See also *Grand Insulaire*, chap. "Isle of Demons," and map 14.

67 Both Cartier and Ramusio have *ame*.

portion of his body would seem to require, which results in his liking little fish, being unable to swallow larger ones. Which [thing] I wanted to test, seeing a dead whale, which these Newfoundlanders call *Ainne honne*[68] and the Ethiopians *Echueuet*, which means [1017r] big fish: which is certainly a great discovery and a curiosity worthy of imitation, since the Ancients, however great researchers they may have been, never took the pains to perform this as I did, nor have the moderns either,[69] although they have undertaken to write and describe for us the history of fishes. The female of this Behemoth has only one little one at a time, to which she gives birth as do the quadrupeds, without eggs, contrary to the nature of all other fishes. Furthermore, the whale gives milk to her little whalelet once he is on the outside: and for this reason she has breasts on her stomach under the navel, which no other fish does either in the sea or in fresh-water, unless it is the seal or the comiaco, a very large fish which is caught in the Red Sea and in the great lake of Alexandria in Egypt.[70] And I caught more than fifty of this species one day with a large group of Arabs who were our servants, on another occasion which I mentioned before.

Moreover the whale is a dangerous beast for sailors to meet up with because of its hugeness, as those of Bayonne and the Spaniards know well. They experience this often and take them professionally with certain instruments and machines with which they wound them; and when they are wounded pursue them in medium vessels until they approach land and are dead, then they hook on to them and tow them to land. Then God knows [how many] people are employed to cut them to pieces and fill their vessels with them. Then they sell the meat and blubber to foreigners [which] you can see by the present illustration which appears above [fig. 5].

And in this connection I remember that when I was in the Antarctic it happened that a merchant who was going by boat from one land to another with fourteen sailors to trade was sunk by meeting up with this sea animal which struck [1017v] the boat with his tail and upset it in the depths of the sea, so that all of the men who were in it were lost except one who survived on a plank, who told us his story. Thus, cold places are where this monstrous fish most often frequents because of the great quantity of fish. This is why beneath the equator and near the two tropics

68 Thevet copies Ramusio exactly here.

69 Although the syntax of this passage is confusing, it appears that Thevet claims to have done an autopsy on a dead whale and to have been the first to do so.

70 There is a fish called the *comico* or *catalufa*.

Figure 5 Thevet's illustration of the conclusion of a whale hunt
Thevet's *Cosmographie universelle*, fol. 1017r.
Courtesy John Carter Brown Library at Brown University

they seldom are seen, because fish are scarcer there also but [are] in great quantities near the two poles: which I have faithfully and diligently observed as elsewhere I have more amply discussed than in this passage. And what I say about fish you can imagine to be true about wild and fierce beasts, since they abound more in northern regions (except lions, tigers, elephants, rignoseros [sic]), which are found in other countries. This is proved by the beautiful pelts which come to us from the northern regions where the cold is perpetual and beasts [are] in great quantities and well-fed, as I hope to discuss for you in the [appropriate] time and place.

In these areas where the whale is found frequents also a fish, the perpetual enemy of this behemoth and pursues it wherever it goes. Approaching it, it slides under its belly, which is the tenderest part of this marine beast, where it thrusts with its tongue, five feet long or thereabouts and which is as sharp as a barber's lancet, and attacks so fiercely that only with great difficulty can the whale escape death. So the fishermen who frequent Newfoundland assured me, and also the natives who name it in their jargon *Kourt*, others *Strich*, and it has various names according to the region.[71] On this seacoast is caught also another kind of fish which the barbarians call *Hecquy*, which has a beak like a parrot and [is] moreover quite deformed. I have seen this species in the Red Sea. And [there are] others which would be long in telling, like the cod which our people seek for there, which are so numerous that the barbarians take no account of them, and very often those who go fishing are hindered from pulling them out one after the other, so many are there. You see there also porpoises, which incorrectly are called dolphins, which often show themselves in the waves and on the surface, leaping and cavorting above it. Some have thought this to be a presage and sure sign of a coming storm and violent and stormy winds, which would approach from the direction in which these porpoises had taken their course.

As for terrestrial animals, there is as I have said such an abundance as you never saw, especially of bears, almost all of which are white and the same is true of the birds, which tend to be whitish. These bears are a great nuisance around the cabins and lodges of the savages, eating the oils they make from the fat of the fish. As for our men, when they have got a catch of cod, they [the bears] stuff themselves so well with their piles [of fish] that they [the fishermen] are obliged to start over again.

71 In the *Grand Insulaire*, chap. "Isle of Demons," Thevet is more specific in his information. There he says that the inhabitants of Canada call the whale *Kourt*, while those from Baccaleos use the word *Strich*.

These barbarians, angry at such importunity, pursue [the bears] in this manner. They prepare certain deep trenches near trees or rocks close to their lodges, then cover these trenches with branches and foliage, especially near some tree where there is a swarm of honey-bees, since this is the food which bears seek more than any other, either to satiate themselves with it or to get rid of pain in their eyes, which is common to them—and also when they are stung by the bees they bleed which greatly relieves their brain. Then attracted by this honey and wanting to go after the fish, he crosses these trenches into which he falls, and there is clubbed by these barbarians. I had forgotten to tell you that [in] the area which extends from one tropic to the other there is not found a single one of these ursine beasts, no more than wolves, lions and elephants. There are besides, certain beasts large as [1018r] buffalo, having rather large horns and the hair all greyish, from whose hide they make clothing.

Moreover, the country is little cultivated, little inhabited, and disagreeable for long stays. This people wants only what it has, which is very little, to sustain its life without worrying about a provision of foods or things which are in neighboring or foreign countries. They are almost always healthy because their nourishment is simple and without variety. They do not make war to conquer territory nor to enrich themselves at the expense of their neighbors, since they are practically equal in goods, distributing to each person what is necessary. Thus they never go to law, and nobody instigates a quarrel against his neighbor, since they do not know what it is to wrong one another: and so they need no laws, any more than the other savages, unless it be that which nature has inscribed in the soul of each one. They have neither cities nor castles nor machines of war like us, any more than the others.

Their religion is like that of the Canadians, except that the Devil has so betwitched them that they imagine that those who die of their fine natural death disappear like smoke and that the soul perishes with the body and is changed into wind and nothing, like a bird or beast. But those who die by their own hand, when one of their relatives or lords goes from life to decease, these [the former?] go to heaven with their *Tuira*, who is their god. [They] bear with them in dying fruits and fish, hoping to eat them in the other world.[72]

I have said that they are very seldom ill: however, sometimes with the change of weather, and not often, they fall into an illness which

72 This material on the religion of the Newfoundland natives, including the word *Tuira*, does not appear in other sources. These data may derive from oral information given to Thevet by Donnacona, Cartier, and others.

besides being disagreeable is also as contagious as the plague. It begins with the legs, then rises higher and renders the mouth so stinking that it is impossible to endure the breath of a man attacked by this illness. The feet and legs swell, and they are so feeble that they could not move from one place to another. Our people being there were surprised by this sickness from having associated with the savages who came into their fort, although this was forbidden. Therefore despairing of recovering and not telling [the natives] in what straits they were, they found out how the savages cured themselves, using a decoction of the leaves and even the wood of a certain tree named *Quahoia*[73] because it resembles a walnut except its leaves are wider and thicker, which they put on the swelling and used [drank] the decoction. A single one of these trees was more efficacious in four days than the doctors with all the drugs they get from the Levant would be in a year. Further, to tell you about the effects of this malady, they opened one of those who had died of the infection and found out that the disease had seized his entrails had ruined his spleen and his liver, which were covered with little drops of blood all rotten. In sum, all the internal parts were as if someone had rubbed them against something red, and also the whole of it dotted with whitish spots like blisters. So that if God had not succored them with the information about the above-mentioned tree, never would they have returned to their longed-for country of France.

Now this Newfoundland is not so small that it does not extend from the forty-eighth to the sixtieth degree of latitude, the coast continuing to the north for at least 350 leagues.[74] It is dangerous because of the whirlpools and abysses which are there and also because this land is surrounded from the east to the west by a girdle of rocks which are under water, made in the shape like an eel.[75] You have to go more than three hundred leagues to avoid this peril and skirt all this girdle, either taking the northern turn in the direction of Labrador, or the western route as if going to Florida, and then doubling back to the [1018v] Cape of Arcadia as far as Cape Breton, and follow the coast of Canada and Newfoundland, which

73 Compare this account with the narrative of Cartier's second voyage, where three whole chapters are devoted to the scurvy that afflicted the French and its cure (Biggar, *Voyages*, pp. 204–15). It is unclear why Thevet says that the tree is called *Quahoia* since Cartier says that the natives called the tree *anneda*. Cartier's word-list has *Hanneda* and Ramusio gives *Ameda*. The native term for walnut, given by Cartier, is *quaheya*. Thevet says the tree resembles a walnut. See also *Grand Insulaire*, chap. "Isles of the New Lands."

74 See also *Grand Insulaire*, chap. "Isles of the New Lands."

75 This description appears to be based on the Gastaldi map found in Ramusio's *Terzo volume* (see map 5).

contains near the mainland an infinite number of isles and islet-banks, rocks, some higher than others: as for example, the Isles of the Birds, of Newfoundland, of the two Castles,[76] and that of *Aaia yascou* – which is equivalent of an arm in their patois, since it is made in the form and semblance of a man's arm, and that of *Aggonzi*,[77] a word also in their language meaning head – since in the middle of the said isle is seen a mountain at the summit of which there is a large round rock made like a man's head – and the one they call [Isle] of the Demons, which is the largest and most beautiful. [This island is] at present uninhabited because of the great illusions and fantoms which are seen there, through the trickery and deceit of the devils. This has also been experienced even by Christians and that is why they gave it this name of Isle of Demons, or devils, as is said – and it is a great pity considering the beauty of the place and that it is closer to us than any of the others. People go there fairly often in the daytime for fishing and hunting: but if you get too far inland you will not fail to meet up with these accursed spirits, which make a thousand assaults on you in the woods and lonely spots in broad daylight.

There are demons which are divided into good and evil, the ones we call angels and the others devils, and both are included under the appellation of spirit. Devils have passible bodies, which being struck suffer pain and are burned if they approach the fire. But I will leave all these matters for others to discuss, because it is not the subject for a cosmographer. I also do not want to discuss here by what charms they conjure these spirits who resist obeying and are rebellious to those who try to conjure them. All this may be learned in the books of the philosophers who have busied themselves writing on the nature of demons. But I will tell you a very true thing, without feeding you lies, like those who never saw except through a hole[78] what is to be seen on this isle and the neighboring areas of the sea (where also, they say, there are spirits which torment men day and night). Which is true, and I have been told so by not just one but by numberless pilots and mariners with whom I have long traveled; that when they passed by this coast, when they were plagued by a big storm, they heard in the air, as if on the crow's nest or masts of their vessels, these human voices making a great noise, without their being able to

76 Thevet's "two castles" is a misreading for Baye des Chasteaux.

77 *Aaia yascou* is mentioned by Thevet in his *Grand Insulaire*, chap. "Isle of St. Julien," and both terms appear in his Second Dictionary, ibid., chap. "Isle of Demons."

78 This expression, which does not appear in dictionaries, is evidently a metaphor for bad or restricted vision or understanding.

discern intelligible words, only such a murmur as you hear on market-day in the middle of the public market. These voices caused them a hundred times more astonishment than the tempest around them. They well knew that they were close to the island called the Isle of Demons, but they paid no heed to this fact until some good people offered up prayers and invoked the holy name of Jesus; and little by little the murmur died away, although the storm continued for a long time afterwards.[79]

Often the savages where I was staying were tormented by the evil spirit who is their familiar. When I used to travel through their country and talk with them (often thinking only of philosophizing and inquiring about the rarest things), they would come with great fright and throw themselves into my arms, shouting *Hipouchi Agnan*, *Omamo Atoupaue*: the evil spirit *Agnan* is beating and tormenting me excessively, help me I beg of you. Immediately upon such happenings I would seize their body and recite the Gospel of St. John, *In principio*, etc. which being only half said, these barbarians felt themselves delivered from the evil spirit, and I assure the reader I performed this most holy and Catholic act more than one hundred times at least.[80] But on this isle be assured that they are so common there that the inhabitants tormented by the little rest they had on it were forced to move back to the mainland.

[1019r] History of Three French Persons Being in New-land, and of a Nestorian Bishop
CHAPTER 6

After the first voyage made by Jacques Cartier, as the great king François was desirous, both of learning much, and of hearing about all that was rare and exquisite in foreign lands, he ordered Roberval, a French gentleman, to go to this country of New-land and from there to go into the land of Canada proper with a good company, and (if he could) to populate this country with native Frenchmen since such a good start had been made and the trail broken: hoping that even though this country did not bring him in much revenue it would at least bring him immortal

79 These voices in the air heard by mariners appear to have a relationship with those heard by Rabelais' voyagers in his *Quart Livre* (chap. 56); see Stabler, "Rabelais, Thevet, l'Ile des Démons et les paroles gelées," *Etudes Rabelaisiennes* 11 (1974): 57–62.

80 Thevet's Agnan is most likely the Agnen of Tupinamba mythology. *Agnen* was greatly feared and was considered to be one of the evil genii present at creation. The "where I was staying," etc., refers to Thevet's brief stay in Brazil with the Villegagnon expedition. In addition, there is this interesting reference to his exercise of the priestly function of exorcism.

honor and the grace of God to have rescued this barbarous people from the ignorance in which it was plunged and to render it the son and ally of the Christian Church.[81]

Roberval, my familiar, as well as the said Cartier, having equipped himself as required for entry into this country through the liberality of his prince, and also employing a good part of his own wealth,[82] took with him a good company of gentlemen and artisans of all kinds and several women: among others a Damoiselle who was a rather close relative of his, named Marguerite,[83] whom he greatly respected and to whom he confided all his affairs since she was of his blood. Among the gentlemen of good birth who accompanied him there was one who went along more for the love of the said Damoiselle than for the service of the king or respect for the captain, as became evident a short time afterwards. Once on the sea, this gentleman wasted no time in paying such private attentions to the said Damoiselle that despite the perils and dangers which are common to those who expose themselves to mercy of the winds, they played their roles together so well that they passed beyond promises and mere words. Now all this was prompted by an old servant-woman of the said Damoiselle named Damienne, a native of Normandy and a very clever bawd, who played the sentinel while the two lovers were about their business. Several persons reported this to Roberval who, clever and wise, disguised his wrath, which he conceived more against his relative than against the gentleman. And to punish her, without wronging the said young man, as they were near the Isle of Demons of which I spoke in the preceding chapter, he separated them and put them in separate ships. Then seeing that he could not conquer their affection and that they cherished each other more than before—having been landed on terra firma at the solicitation of the servant—[Roberval] being God-fearing, yet bursting with spite since he was chief of such a great expedition, decided to give them a surprise. Therefore having embarked all of their equipment, and having let Cartier leave before him, he [Roberval] set

81 This passage reflects the wording of Roberval's commission from the king (H.P. Biggar, *A Collection of Documents Relating to Jacques Cartier and the Sieur de Roberval* [Ottawa, 1930], pp. 178–85).

82 Thevet may have inferred that Roberval used some of his own wealth for his expedition from the statement in the account of Roberval's voyage (Biggar, *Voyages*, p. 263) that Roberval "furnished 3 tall Ships, chiefly at the kings [sic] cost." As noted in our Introduction, it is clear that Thevet knew this account. In any case, historians of succeeding centuries have generally repeated this statement of Thevet's.

83 For a detailed study of the tale of the exiled damsel see Arthur P. Stabler, *The Legend of Marguerite de Roberval* (Pullman, Washington, 1972).

sail after him.[84] But when he reached this Isle of Demons, he made his relative land there and the old woman her servant, telling her this was the place he had ordained for the penitence of her crime and of the scandal she had done him. He had four arquebuses given her and ammunition for her defense against the animals.

The poor woman, having returned to France after living two years five months in that place, and having come to the city of Nautron in the country of Perigord when I was there, gave me an account of her past adventures and told me among other things that the gentleman, seeing this cruelty and fearing lest they do the same to him in some other isle, was so beside himself that forgetting the peril of death into which he was hurling himself and fearful tales he had been told about this land, took his arquebus and clothing, with a fire-steel and a few other commodities, some measures of biscuit, cider, linen, iron tools, and a few other things necessary for their use, and precipitated himself[85] onto the isle to accompany his mistress. [1019v] There Roberval left them, angry at the wrong his relative had done them and joyous at having punished them without soiling his hands with their blood.

Being there, they prepare their little household, build a dwelling of foliage and make beds of the same [fig. 6]. They killed a lot of animals, whose meat they ate, and lived off fruits, for of bread they had no way to have any. But it was a pity to hear the ravages which those evil spirits made around them and how they tried to destroy their little dwelling, appearing as divers kinds and shapes of frightful animals. But [they were] finally vanquished by the constancy and perseverance of these Christians, contrite over their sins, and did not afflict or trouble them any more except that at night they often heard such loud cries that it seemed as if there were more than 100,000 men together.

During this time this woman became pregnant (whose portrait together with the isle, with the manner and fashion that this female warrior fought against those "varmints" [Fr. *vermin*] who continually sought to surprise her and devour her and her child, I also represent for you above) [fig. 7], and when she was near her time the poor gentleman died of sadness

84 Compare this flashback with the account of Cartier's third voyage (Biggar, *Voyages*, pp. 250–1). As noted in our Introduction, Thevet was apparently familiar with this account also. For more information see Arthur P. Stabler, "En Marge des récits de voyage: André Thevet, Hakluyt, Roberval, Jean Alfonse, et Jacques Cartier," *Etudes Canadiennes/Canadian Studies* 17 (1984): 69–72.

85 The expression "precipitated himself" was taken literally by some subsequent tellers of this tale, including some who inferred that Marguerite's lover swam ashore, carrying all these provisions and equipment. See Stabler, *Legend*, p. 65.

Figure 6 The exiled damoiselle Marguerite on her island
Thevet's *Cosmographie universelle*, fol. 1019v.
Courtesy John Carter Brown Library at Brown University

Figure 7 The exiled lovers on their island
Marguerite d'Angoulême, Queen of Navarre,
The Heptaméron (1558), in an English translation
published by Gibbings & Co (London, 1894)

disappointment: [and] in the eight months he had been there no vessel had passed which might afford them help, succor, and liberty. This death was distressing to the woman, but anyhow making of necessity virtue, the mistress as well as the servant, they defended themselves very valiantly against the fierce beasts with their arquebuses and the sword of the dead man. She was so adroit at firing the arquebus that on one day she assured me she killed three bears, of which one was white as an egg. Having given birth to her child and baptized it in her own way in the name of God, without ceremonies, fortune is about to give her another shock. It was her servant who followed the path of the gentle lover, the sixteenth or seventeenth month that they were on the island, and shortly afterwards the child [1020r] went following the road of the two others.

It was now that the poor indiscreet woman was disheartened, no longer having anyone to talk to, unless it were the beasts whom she warred against day and night: and if the grace of God had not sustained her she would have despaired since, as she told me, for two months she continually saw the strangest visions that one could imagine—but just as soon as she prayed [to] God these fantoms vanished. Finally, having, as I said, for the space of two years five months remained in that place, as some ships from lower Brittany passed by there fishing for cod, she was on the edge of the water shouting for help and signalling with smoke and fire. And although to begin with they thought they were seeing illusions of the demons which deceive passersby, and since the island was never inhabited by a living soul, only predatory animals and birds, and "varmints," still finally they drew near and realizing what she was, took her into the vessel and brought her back to France. [Where] from her mouth I learned and heard of this pitiful story of her penance.

And although I had heard tell of these evil spirits as being an established fact, yet she further assured me about them and told me however that after the first two nights they had never approached their little lodge nor shown themselves visibly until the time when she was left alone: and that even then they did not persist, except during the times of the greatest realization of her misfortunes. And she told me moreover that when they embarked on these Breton ships to return to France, that a certain desire seized her not to leave, and to die in that solitary place like her husband, her child, and her servant; and that she wished she were still there, moved by sorrow as she was [fig. 8]. I know that some hare-brained wags, after hearing me tell this story (as happened), have added to it follies and lies which they have inserted into their fables and tragical stories, plagiarized

Figure 8 "At the moment of departure . . . a painful regret seized her, a pious memory arrested her . . . "
Ferdinand Denis and Victor Chauvin, *Les Vrais Robinsons* (Paris, 1863)

from here and there.[86]

When this woman was recalling for me her hardships, it reminded me of two Portuguese, who being shipwrecked on the Isle of Rats, lived there two whole years as you have heard, when I was speaking of this same island. . . . [87]

86 The "hare-brained wag" is a reference to Rabelais, while the (teller of) the tragical stories is Belleforest. See two studies by Stabler, *Legend*, pp. 17–24, and "Rabelais, Thevet, l'Ile des Démons et les paroles gelées," pp. 58–9.

87 Thevet ends his discussion of the New Lands here and begins to tell us about the adventures of a Nestorian bishop travelling in the Middle East.

Grand Insulaire

[143r] Isles of the New Lands

Before entering upon the description of this new country I have two points to make, one on its discovery and the other on the great extent of this coast. On the one hand I see the Spaniards and the Portuguese, who wish to have the discovery attributed exclusively to them; [and] on the other, I understand the objections put forth by the French, who granting that the Portuguese went somewhat farther than their predecessors, maintain that they penetrated no farther than the suburbs of Paris. If it were up to me to decide and render judgment in the quarrel I should have little difficulty. However, since I am an interested party, I prefer to put forth the simple facts and the naked truth, leaving it up to the gentle reader to award such free judgment as it may please him.

In the year 1500 Gaspar de Port-real [Corte-Real] a Portuguese, sailed this coast, and pushed by the tempest navigated as far as fifty-six degrees of latitude where he discovered a river which he named Rio Nevado which means river loaded with snow.[1] Afterwards a Venetian undertook this voyage under the authority of King Henry VII of England, passing as far as sixty-seven degrees, but both of these were obliged to return without accomplishing anything either because of the extreme cold or because they had insufficient equipment to maintain themselves and remain among these people.[2] Thus the honor of the discovery of these New Lands must be principally attributed to Jean Verrazzan, Florentine, and to Jacques Cartier, Breton pilot (my great and particular friend,

1 A Rio Nevado is given on the Sebastian Cabot map of 1544 and is also mentioned in Francisco López de Gómara, *Historia general de las Indias* (Saragossa, 1552; reprinted 2 vols. Barcelona, 1954), 1: 22. On Corte-Real see Eduardo Brazão, *Os Corte Reals e o novo mundo* (Lisbon, 1965). See *Grand Insulaire*, chap. "Isle of the Assumption," for Thevet's denial that Corte-Real had been in Canada before the French.

2 The "Venetian," of course, was Sebastian Cabot. There is, however, disagreement among accounts of Cabot's voyage concerning how far north he sailed. On Cabot see James A. Williamson, *The Cabot Voyages and Bristol Discovery under Henry VII* (Cambridge, 1962), esp. 145–72.

who voyaged there with the company which Messire Charles de Moüy, chevalier Lord of Milleray and Vice-admiral of France gave him in the year 1534). [Verrazzano and Cartier] did not content themselves with a simple passade but rather made profitable and advantageous conquest, as you shall hear hereafter.[3]

All this New Land extends from the forty-eighth degree of latitude as far as the sixtieth, the coast running always north for at least three hundred leagues. The new Munster[4] extends the boundaries of this country much more, stretching it from the twenty-fifth degree on this side of the equinoctial line up to the sixty-fifth and clear to the Arctic Pole, which would make it about six hundred leagues or thereabouts. It is all very easy to make such a calculation on paper, but it would be very hard to verify it in the presence of those who formerly sailed into these very regions of [143v] the New World. These [regions] lie at fifty-six degrees above the equinoctial line, at the same latitude and in a similar climate as Moscow, where the sea is icy and quite close to the Arctic Pole.

This region of New Land constitutes one extremity of Canada and is part of Baccaleos which is indeed quite northerly and maritime. I give it only forty-eight degrees thirty minutes of latitude and 327 degrees of longitude, although the new Monsterian Cosmographer [Belleforest] finds this very strange. If he had had very good glasses, he would have seen that Hierosme Girave[5] places its latitude no higher than forty degrees, and that reference to the globe and the situation of this country

3 For more on these voyages see Lawrence C. Wroth, *The Voyages of Giovanni da Verrazzano* (New Haven, 1970), and H.P. Biggar, *The Voyages of Jacques Cartier* (Ottawa, 1924), esp. 3n2 for Charles de Moüy. Gustave Lanctot has argued that Cartier sailed with Verrazzano in 1524 in his "Cartier's First Voyage to Canada in 1524," *Canadian Historical Review* 25 (1944): 233–45, and *Jacques Cartier devant l'histoire* (Montreal, 1947), pp. 108–36. Also see the refutation of this thesis by Marcel Trudel, *Histoire de la Nouvelle France: les vaines tentatives, 1524–1603* (Montreal, 1963), pp. 58–60. For a discussion of the relevant evidence see Bernard G. Hoffman, *Cabot to Cartier: Sources for a Historical Ethnography of Northeastern North America 1497-1550* (Toronto, 1961), pp. 112–14.

4 This is a reference to the *Cosmographia universalis* of Sebastian Münster, reworked by François de Belleforest in 1575. Thevet's quarrel with Belleforest here rests upon variant definitions of the "New Lands."

5 Hieronymus Girava was the author of *Dos Libros de Cosmographia* (Milan, 1556), and a sea-atlas (1567). His world map may be consulted in Adolf Erik Nordenskiöld, *Facsimile Atlas to the Early History of Cartography, with Reproductions of the Most Important Maps Printed in the XV and XVI Centuries . . .* (Stockholm, 1889; reprinted Dover, 1973), plate 45. From this source it would appear that Belleforest's information was more accurate than Thevet's, as Girava's 40th parallel apparently intersects what now would be the Carolinas.

necessarily shows this isle at precisely the latitude I have quoted, and not at sixty degrees above the line.

Now this isle, which you see here set on the flank of the Isles des Moulües [Isles of Cod] to the west [map 6], bears the name of the region of Baccaleos, so called because of a fish of the same name which is found there. As for the name of these Isles des Moulües, disregarding what others have chosen to say about it more lightly than seriously, the great abundance which there is there of cod has caused them to be qualified with this name. It witnesses to the fact that there was the fish-tank and storehouse where they kept them to sell them to the foreigners who went there to fish, so as to make use of their superfluity of cod, of which they have such an abundance[6] that the barbarians take no account of them but heap them up in great piles and sell and trade them *en masse* to the foreigners. Not that I wish to subscribe here to the error of the Monsterian reformer [Belleforest] who, speaking of the country of Norway, writes that from this region the entire rest of Europe is supplied with these fine hake which he claims are hardened by cold and strung out on great poles. As if everyone did not know that immediately [when] this fish is taken, after removing its entrails and tripes, it is salted down in the ships just as one does with the cod in this country of the New Lands; this I have seen. For otherwise it would stink, and there is no cold, however extreme it might be, which could prevent after passage of time the corruption of this seafood. That is the trouble with a lie, from it must emerge and jet forth a billion. For if it is not assumed that the Norwegian coast were swarming with hake, there would have been no problem in marketing them, but since [144r] he had so suddenly filled the country with them, he necessarily had to describe the means by which these goods might be preserved until the time that they might be marketed. Not that I wish to deny the existence of hake in that sea, but then to set up such great shiploads of them that they might be spread over the whole of Europe there is no probability. Furthermore, in the light of the frigidity of the country, it would be unlikely that the supply more than meets the demands of the islanders.

I am further constrained to pause in this Norwegian country in view of the fact that since this Munsterian commentator has given himself leave to place there his monstrous whales of a hundred cubits length, [and] further ascribing characteristics so far removed from the properties

6 This statement about the abundance of cod and the natives having piles of them is similar to a description given by Cartier in his first voyage (Biggar, *Voyages*, p. 62). The fish that Cartier saw, however, were mackerel, not cod.

of these great fish, the absurdity of his reveries is palpable. *Inter alia*, he has them utter such frightful cries that there is no reader, however gentle and polite he may be, that is not annoyed at hearing the buzzing of this prevaricator about his ears. For although Munster has stooped to the writing of such nonsense, he [Belleforest] should have struck it out. He could not have been unaware that if the whale is a fish, the native taciturnity of the scions of damp Thetis[7] necessarily makes the sound dead, dull, and muffled in the throat of such a great and fearful monster.

Further, he made many other big errors, for example confusing this country of the New Lands with the Southern Land [Southern Hemisphere], willingly joining heaven with earth. And since I have elsewhere disabused him of these errors, I am happy to take position against the funereal funeral doctor who is not content to add to the tomb of his beautiful funerals the things he has fished out of my Cosmographie, but would like for me to confess that along with the dupes I am confusing the Southern Land with the New Lands. I shall not bother to show him the conclusive reasons upon which I have founded the distinction between these countries, since in my Cosmographie I have sufficiently cleared up this point. I only wish to refute him on the authority which he [claims to] derive from the first chapter of the twenty-first book of my Cosmographie. If it is found that my discussion there has to do with the New Lands, Thevet will yield the match to funeral-director Guichard.[8] If it will please the reader to read what I wrote about it in the above-cited spot, immediately without liti-contestation he will condemn this young scribbler as abusing my writings; which he either does not understand, or perhaps if he dimly comprehends is trying to pervert and picture me as espousing the false conclusions of his Belleforest, which I fervently deny having published, [144v] [about] the enormous and frightful size of the whales which swim in the sea of cod. The field [of the Atlantic] was much more open to disport oneself in than the Mediterranean Sea and warm countries. But possibly from ambush he was trying to probe and persuade of a thing not only difficult to believe but completely false, so that he should be considered all the more clever a man since he was making it appear that he was arriving at conclusions which the boldest

7 In Greek mythology Thetis was a Nereid and mother of Achilles. Thevet is, of course, wrong in identifying the whale as a fish. Recent studies on the "cries" of whales lend interest to the assertion of the Münster-Belleforest account.

8 Claude Guichard (d. 1607) was a French scholar whose principal work is *Funérailles et diverses manières d'ensevelir des Romaines, Grecs et autres nations, tant anciennes que modernes* (Lyon, 1581).

and best informed would not have dared to assert. In a word, thinking to show himself off to advantage, he himself has dimmed the lustre of the good reputation which had been conceived of him.

But I feel that this digression has transported me and caused me to divagate outside my subject, which again taking up I shall return to our New Lands which abound in cod and whales, porpoises and sea-wolves, from which they derive particular profit as I have described in the fifth chapter of the twenty-third book of my Cosmographie. As for wild beasts, there are very few countries where there is such an abundance of them, and particularly of bears which do great damage to the inhabitants. The country is healthy enough so that the islanders are rarely sick, except for a disease closely resembling plague, tak, or sheep-pox, a sovereign remedy for which is a decoction of the tree called Quahoia, which resembles a walnut except with wider and fleshier leaves. Furthermore the coast of these New Lands is very dangerous because of the gulfs and abysses which are there, and also because all this land is surrounded from east to west by a girdle of rocks which are under the water [map 5]. [It is shaped like] an eel, so that one must go more than three hundred leagues to avoid this peril and skirt this girdle, either taking the northern route by the coast of Labrador, or the western route (as if heading for Florida), and then passing the Cape of Arcadia as far as Cape Breton and following the coast of Canada and Newfoundland, which presents near its terra firma an almost infinite number of isles and islets, shoals, and progressively more high-jutting rocks.

So among others is the Isle of Birds,[9] so called because of the great multitude of three species of birds, named tinkers, gannets (difficult to take because they peck those who think to take them) and the aporrahs

9 This passage is based on Cartier's first voyage, and Biggar has identified this island as Funk Island. See *Voyages*, pp. 6–8. It is clear from mistranslations and misprints that Thevet is using the translation of Ramusio. For example, here in writing of Cartier's *Apponatz* Thevet has *Aporrah*, which is evidently based on Ramusio's *Apporrath*. Furthermore, Ramusio says that these birds are as large as *graculi neri* (black grackles or jackdaws), hence Thevet's "the size of a jay"; but Cartier more accurately described them as "large as geese" and marvelously fat. Cartier also states correctly that these birds could not fly in the air, but "fly as easily in the sea as other birds do in the air." [Our translation; Biggar's is incorrect here]. Thevet, however, follows Ramusio who has them flying *a pelo d'acqua* (at water level) rather than submerged in the water as Cartier does. See Giovanni Battista Ramusio, *Terzo volume delle navigationi et viaggi nel quale si contengono le navigationi al mondo nuovo . . .* (Venice, 1556), fol. 371v. Ganong says that the name *Apponatz* is first used by Cartier. See his "The Identity of the Animals and Plants Mentioned by the Early Voyagers to Eastern Canada and Newfoundland," *Transactions of the Royal Society of Canada*, 3rd ser., 3, sec. 2 (1909): 203.

[Great Auks] (which are the size of a jay), which Jacques Cartier (my good friend) found there; and he [145r] made a great heap in a very short time to salt down for a long voyage. They are very fat, very good and appetizing, white and black with very short wings, and thus flying scarcely higher than the surface of the water. As for the isle that you see in my maps surnamed with my name, Thevet, this came to pass in that I was the first who set foot on it among my companions who landed there with me in a skiff in order to find some fresh water. This happened on my first voyage, as I have described in the fourth chapter of the twenty-third book of my Cosmographie.

Our isle [Newfoundland], about which I am telling you, is very wide and long, covered, as I said, with woods and on which it is very cold. Some mountain fishermen occupied themselves building there little huts[10] of very strong wood both for sleeping at night while awaiting proper winds for fishing, maintaining fire in them day and night, and for securing their fish inside fearing lest the beasts might eat it, among others the bears which are smart, tricky, and fond of this fish. The sea is troublesome in several places and principally at high tide. Of roadsteads and ports there are fine and good ones, capable some of them of anchoring a hundred large ships. The ground is high in the north-east part, [and] there are many currents there dangerous to medium vessels.

A thing certainly most admirable about this seacoast is that it so teems with fish, among others these cod, that in one year there is sold in Spain, France, and also England, Flanders, and Denmark (and other places) the cargo of more than three hundred ships.[11] Of such species of fish there is not found a single one in the Mediterranean Sea, nor in that of Bacchus or Caspian, nor are hake, whales, mackerel, calamaries, albacores, herring, [and] dorados, such as are in the Atlantic, and swarms of other species all different the ones from the others. There is no point of my describing here the details of the routes of this coast of the Isle of Newfoundland from Cape Race, which lies to the west, to the Pates River, and from

10 Thevet has *Longilles*, which is probably some variant of *loge* (dwelling, cabin).

11 Another contemporary observer, Anthony Parkhurst, estimated that 350 ships fished for cod off the coast of Newfoundland in 1578. See Richard Hakluyt, *The Principal Navigations Voyages Traffiques & Discoveries of the English Nation*, second ed. (1598–1600; reprinted in 12 vols., Glasgow, 1903–5; New York, 1965), 8: 10–11. For more on the cod trade see H.P. Biggar, *The Early Trading Companies of New France: A Contribution to the History of Commerce and Discovery in North America* (Toronto, 1901; reprinted St. Clair Shores, Michigan, 1972), chap. 2: "The Birth and Growth of Trade and Commerce, 1497-1597," pp. 18–37; and Charles de la Morandière, *Histoire de la pêche française de la morue dans l'Amérique septentrionale*, 3 vols. (Paris, 1962–6).

there bearing north to Cape Loux and then to Cape Bonavista and the Isle of St. Julien which lies northward, since various pilots and mariners are well-versed in the route and cognizant of these, among others those of Bayonne and St. Jean de Luz.[12]

[145v] Isle of Roberval

When I was discussing Iceland[13] I remember remarking that there phantoms are found who show themselves visibly and perform services for men. For the most part they appear in the remembered forms of those who have been killed or drowned in some violent misadventure; and they appear to those who know them, and show themselves so openly that those who are unaware of their death fancy them to be alive and offer them their hand. I have no need here to go into the question of whether it is possible that the spirits of the deceased return and show themselves, preferring to leave this research to the theologians and others who have more leisure to occupy themselves in such disputes. Moreover, at present I would have other and much more difficult matters to untangle if I should take the time to discuss some points which indeed would delight the reader, but which could not be cleared up without straying too far from my subject.

Here then, I shall set foot on an isle named by me the Isle of Roberval because he was the first person to set foot on its soil. It is given the name Isle of Demons because the Demons raise a terrible uproar there. I find that they have also left their traces there to such an extent that it is today renowned under no other name, title, or quality than "of Demons." These have achieved such mastery over it that although the isle is beautiful and of great size, nevertheless it is for the most part uninhabited. Although people go there in the daytime for fishing and hunting, still they dare not penetrate too far inland because of the attacks which those people receive constantly who, being too adventurous, insist on advancing too far into the thick woods and staying too long in them.

I remember having formerly read that a house, because it had been cursed (others say plagued or haunted by evil spirits) was abandoned, and the renter absolved by the order of the Roman Senate from the contract which he had made for the price of the rent. Which if true, there is little wonder if this Isle of Demons is so little frequented by inhabitants

12 These names are on various maps of the period. For Thevet's more lengthy description of the Isle of St. Julien see the relevant chapter of *Grand Insulaire*.

13 *Grand Insulaire*, fol. 19r. We do not publish this part.

since it serves as the haunt of these evil and tormenting spirits, who carry on there in horrible fashion.

I learned this from the poor miserable damsel named Marguerite, who was marooned there by Captain Roberval, her uncle, to expiate the crime and scandal she had done to the company which had voyaged to the country [146r] of Newfoundland and the country of Canada by command of King François, first of the name. And because I have rather lengthily and in detail set down the story (printed at Paris [in] 1575) of this damsel, in the sixth chapter of the twenty-third book of my Cosmographie, I will forbear recounting it again here for fear of boring the reader with a too tedious prolixity.

I shall content myself with recalling what I learned from her, that if this isle were frequented perhaps the malignity of these depraved spirits would vanish in smoke. The reason on which I base myself is that she had not been plagued and persecuted by these hideous phantoms which appeared to her in this isle until after she had lost the gentleman her lover, her servant Damienne, native of Normandy (an old bawd aged sixty years, [who] served as sentinel to prevent the discovery which might have been made of their wanton and lascivious amours), and finally the infant which had been procreated from this illegitimate and lubricious conjunction, in which they had both mutually accoupled themselves. The illation is (in my opinion) conclusive, since she was not afflicted with these fearful visions when she was in the company of her stallion, her old Norman woman, and her child, and was only assailed by them being all alone on this great isle. It is not improbable that if she had had considerable company the demons would rather have selected some retreat other than this ill-fortuned isle. And to tell the truth, solitude greatly reenforced the effect of these apparitions, as truly there is nothing in the world more inimical to the assurance which one could wish to maintain than to be alone in a place, deserted and abandoned by everybody in the world. Accordingly the wise Solomon, in his proverbs, detests such fearful solitude because it makes us tremble on the brink of keen and vehement temptations, [and] that no matter how steadfast one might be, it is very hard to remain firm, high, and mighty without being if not floored and cast down, at least mightily shaken. The experience of this is so manifest that he who would attempt to deny it would merit rather a firm and rough reprimand than a simple remonstrance.

And not to digress from my subject in this Isle of Demons, I related that this poor sinner, during the lifetime of her companions, while marooned, [146v] amused herself by hunting bears and venison, of which with her lover and her maid she made a terrible butchery. But after she was deprived of their company it was no longer a question of aiming at these earthly animals—the fire of the harquebus could not touch these invulnerable phantoms. Her arms, her hands, her legs, and all her body became numb, the powder had no strength, being bewitched, to explode out of the muzzle. Frozen, the ball, the bullet, the shot, or the charge, what else? This poor disconsolate woman was assailed from within and from without, since she must daily sustain the alarms which the beasts roaming this isle gave her, and who persecuted her with raging fury because they sensed that she was alone and unable to resist them and fit to be their prey. Nevertheless, whenever they showed their noses ever so little to her advantage, she gave them such a dose of bullets that they hastily retired. Half overcome and weakened from overwork, she was awakened by very much stronger, more powerful, cunning, and hardy enemies, against whom neither lead nor her weapons aught availed. Only the grace of the Almighty, which supported her in so long and wearying a state, served her as shield, buckler and arms, defensive as well as offensive, as this woman related to me upon her arrival in France after having spent two years in that place. [She then came] to the city of Nautron, country of Perigort, when I was there, where she gave me a full account of all her past adventures.

The isle is as cold as possible, populated only with woods, full of various wild animals which come from the continent, island to island as they well know how to do. Among other [animals], [the island] is populated with bears. The damsel told me that they are the animals which tormented her the most (and sought to devour her and her child), [more] than all the other beasts and that on one day she killed four of them. [She] then gradually withdrew into her dwelling which her lover had built before his death [fig. 6]. Roberval had left them some food and other commodities to help them and provide for their necessities, as he himself told me three months before he was killed at night near Saint Innocent at Paris.[14] Since that time I have marked and given the name Roberval to this present isle, and so marked it in my [147r] maps for the great friendship I bore him in his lifetime.

From a similar account which I published some time ago, there are certain ignorant garblers, never stirring from their homes, tellers of tragical

14 Roberval was killed during a riot in Paris in 1561. The site was the twelfth-century church and Charnel House of the Holy Innocents. For a discussion of the validity of Thevet's datum here see Arthur P. Stabler, *The Legend of Marguerite de Roberval* (Pullman, Washington, 1972), p. 12; see also Samuel Eliot Morison, *The European Discovery of America: The Northern Voyages A.D. 500–1600* (New York, 1971), p. 454.

tales,[15] who have profited [from it], blathering about certain fantastic apparitions which they claim I have imagined to exist on this isle. Others, using whatever might come to hand, greatly exaggerating the matter, have taken such advantage of [my account], that they confound the hubbub of Iceland with the pandemonium of this desolate isle, distilling in the alambic of their ill-assorted brains certain frozen voices which they make so much of, that to read the fabrications which they have advanced, one would say (in light of the cleverness which they are credited with having) that they themselves have spun through the atmosphere, apprehending these preposterous voices with which they presume to regale the ears of the reader.[16] As for the first [category], I will class them with Aristotle (who, according to John Wier, denied the appearance and existence of evil spirits) and such people who wish to question the existence of cacodemons.[17] Or if they tell me that although demons exist it does not necessarily follow that they ravage this isle, I will request them (since they refuse to believe it without seeing) to kindly take the trouble to go there in person, or to commission worthy persons seasoned by experience, ones who are of course capable and up to the task and in whom above all they place their trust to inspect the place, to test the shocks, attacks, and violence which customarily shock those who dwell alone on these isles. However, to avoid the expense (and since I realize that the cost makes people lose the desire to undertake such distant travels), I am happy to furnish them a way which, without exposing oneself to the perils of the sea, will make them clearly understand that there is nothing novel in the bedevilment of this isle by demons.

They will discover that all those who work with metals testify that in the recesses of mountains and mines there are demons.[18] Indeed, furthermore, they are happy when delving in the bowels of the mountains [if] they find that the little devils are swarming about, because this is a virtually sure sign that they have found a good and productive mine. So

15 This is a reference to François de Belleforest, *Le Premier [-septiesme] tome des histoires tragiques* . . . 7 vols. (Paris, 1564–1616).

16 Thevet has here considerably expanded the brief accusation of plagiarism made in his *Cosmographie* so as to leave no doubt about his targets. See Arthur P. Stabler, "Rabelais, Thevet, l'Ile des Démons et les paroles gelées," *Etudes Rabelaisiennes* 11 (1974): 57–62.

17 On Jean Wier (Johann Weyer) see Jean Céard, *La Nature et les prodiges: L'insolite au XVIe siècle, en France* (Geneva, 1977), pp. 353–6 and passim. Wier, a skeptic with reference to various supernatural manifestations, wrote *De Praestigiis Daemonum et incantationibus ac veneficiis* (1563).

18 For another contemporary account of demons in mines see Sebastian Münster, *Cosmographia oder Beschreibung aller länder* (Basel, 1564), pp. ccclxxix–ccclxxxij.

if it were permissible to make a generalization, I would say that since this isle [147v] is so populated with demons it would be fit for profitable exploitation if it were well populated with inhabitants.

But that therefore I should permit these Panurgical garblers to Pantagruelize in their gibberish about these frozen voices, which without foundation of proof they say are warbled in icy tubes by these phantastic demons, I shall certainly not do; rather, holding steadfastly and firmly to the pillar of the truth which I learned not from just one but several pilots and navigators with whom I have long traveled, I will say on their authority that when they passed by this coast, as they were being beset by [a] great tempest, they heard in the air, as if up in the crow's nest and masts of their vessels, confused sounds of human voices resembling the murmur one hears at a fair, market, or great assembly of people conversing. From this these quintessentialists have forged these pretty little scraps of frozen voices and half-frozen voices which melted in their hands when they handled them. But this is such thick and arrant twaddle that I myself am ashamed of their too impudent effrontery and of the time which they have miserably squandered plotting and weaving such yarns. This would be small loss if they had not also wasted several of the readers' hours devoted to reading such nonsense, which could satisfy them as much as if they had dined on wind.

Anyhow this isle lies at 340 degrees of longitude and fifty-eight degrees latitude. The most conspicuous and remarkable features such as isles, promontories, and regions of all this New Land and their elevation including that of Baccaleos and Labrador, are as follows, to wit: the elevation of the aforesaid isle is as I have just said; Cape Las or Raz at forty-six degrees twelve minutes of latitude; Cape Spear at forty-seven [degrees] eighteen minutes; Baccaleos at forty-nine degrees; Cape Bonavista at forty-nine degrees twelve minutes; the Espere Islands at fifty degrees; the Degrat of Quir Pont at fifty-one degrees zero minutes; Belle Isle at fifty-two degrees; La Grand Baye [the Strait of Belle Isle] at fifty-four degrees; Blanc Sablon at fifty-two degrees; the Isle of Frere Louis fifty-four degrees thirty-four minutes; La Croix Blanche fifty-three degrees; La havre du Barbu fifty-four degrees; L'Isle de Nostre Dame fifty-one degrees; The Isle of Souls fifty-one degrees twelve minutes. And as for the elevation of the land of Labrador, I shall begin at the Bay of Eudecqo which lies at fifty-seven degrees thirty-four minutes; Baye d'Escureul [Squirrel Bay] at fifty-eight degrees; Doprasse River at fifty-eight degrees thirteen minutes; Bonne Veue River at fifty-eight degrees twenty minutes; Le Cap du Grand Feu fifty-nine degrees; Riviere Doree [Golden River] sixty degrees; Maguin Bay sixty degrees; Baye de Place sixty-one degrees. These are the places that pilots should favor or prefer to anchor [when] sailing along the coast of Canada or Newfoundland.[19]

[148r] Belle Isle of Canada

Some people wonder why this Isle (located between the Isle of St. Julien which is to the south and Cape de Gade which extends north into the River of Canada [the St. Lawrence]) was characterized with the name Belle since it is uninhabited [and] without buildings except a few shacks for fishermen and finally uncultivated for the most part—thus giving no obvious motive for Jacques Cartier to so baptize it. He explained it in a conversation between him and myself in his house (and assured me that he was nine or ten days there ill with gravel [kidney stones] and that some savages cured him forthwith with the juice of a tree called Oppeth). To dwell on the the beauty, delicacy, or luxury of the buildings on [such] an isle would be to stand (as they say) on trifles and to take the suburbs for the city. The reason is that mariners take the name of an isle entirely otherwise than do the legal experts, who would claim that in certain respects our isle, being desert and uninhabited, was ill and improperly named Belle by its godfather. That is to say, if one takes the name of the isle from the houses which are separate from the others of the city and are not joined with the others, but rather have their entrances, exits, courts, grounds, and wings so arranged as not to touch any other building.[20] It is about this kind of houses that you must understand that Spartian[21] is speaking [when he says] that fire once destroyed in Rome three hundred and thirty-five isles.[22] But (as I said) it is not the mariners who argue over the fine distinctions made by Bartole[23] and other logicians, over whose science I have not greatly wearied my head nor they over mine, I think—but they [argue] rather according to the data which they [the mariners] gather from experience, as well as [from] the observations of the quadrant, compass, and other instruments

19 For these place names Thevet appears to be following Cartier, Alfonse, and the Mercator 1569 map—some names, however, cannot be identified.

20 Thevet does not complete this sentence.

21 Aelius Spartianus (fl. 117-28) was one of the authors of the *Augustan History*, a series of biographies of Roman emperors.

22 Thevet is here using the word isles in the sense of a building or block of buildings surrounded by streets.

23 Bartolus de Sassoferrato (d. 1357) is commonly regarded as the greatest Italian civil lawyer of the fourteenth century. He taught law at the University of Perugia.

of pilotage. And accordingly they consider the isles only for their land, which on all sides is surrounded by water and principally in the sea. So that they do not inquire whether the walls, palaces, and houses there are superb and magnificent, rather only whether this land which is supposed to be an island is anywhere joined to the continent.

This was the reason that my great and intimate friend Jacques Cartier accorded to this isle the name of Belle Isle, for the love of one which is in our Gaul on the coast of Little Britain [Brittany], lying at forty-seven degrees of latitude and nineteen degrees of longitude. The occasion which moved him to attach to it [148v] this name of Belle Isle was that he wanted to have a namesake for this isle of his province in this foreign land discovered by him. Added to which is the fact that there is a great similarity in the appearance of these two isles, as the reader may see if it pleases him to compare them together, for while the interior of the Brittanic Isle is furnished with a number of places, towns, and houses, exteriorly and [in] its superficial circumference one will find that there is very little argument. There are still other isles of the same name, and I remember having seen one above in the Orcades [Orkneys], so that the reader, hearing so many Belle Isles spoken of, will not mistake and confuse the one with the other and will not ascribe to the one that which is peculiar to the other.

As for our isle, it lies at 332 degrees longitude and fifty-two degrees thirty minutes latitude. The stags and hinds fawn there prolifically.[24] On the east coast is the Promontory of the Birds, so called because of the multitude of birds that nest in the trees which are near there. The most frequent are the gannets, which give much trouble to the sailors who want to waste their time catching them, since they defend themselves so fiercely with their beaks that without great danger one cannot catch them. It is true, however, that although they can peck finally they are obliged to surrender. It is not that their flesh is so good and delicate but that they are so abundant, which is very convenient for people who are planning a long voyage. One has only to sprinkle it with salt to prevent rotting. Today, although it is not ordinarily inhabited it is often visited by the Bretons going after cod, who stop on the south coast there and not on the north, for as you see noted on this map[25] the coast there is very dangerous because of the numerous reefs scattered around at surface

24 Thevet adds "and their fawns are slender and agile" in the *Description de plusieurs isles* (hereafter DPI).

25 It is not clear what map Thevet is referring to here, as his data seem to be inconsistent with those of his map of the I. of St. Julien (map 7).

level which break up and destroy a vessel into so many crumbs if it comes and scrapes upon them.

I do not want to forget to tell you that it was on this isle that the soldiers and sailors of the captain [Cartier] took two great bears, of which one was so old that he was as white as new snow and, having skinned him and dressed his hide, it was carried to St. Malo-on-the-Isle. Jacques Cartier, after having made his report to King François, the first of the name, made him a present of it along with the skins of other wild animals and some slips of trees and seeds of the rarest [plants] of the country of Canada. His Majesty commanded that they be planted in the garden at Fontainebleau. Furthermore, this isle is surrounded with a number of reefs and shoals. The tides there are high, in two places there are heavy currents, wherefore it is necessary that the pilot be heedful in circumnavigating it from coast to coast.

[149r] Isle of St. Julien

This isle[26] is not wrongfully called large by our mariners and [it is] marked on my maps since it contains a very large compass of land which distinguishes it from another bearing the same name about which, if occasion arises, I intend to discourse.[27] It lies in the latitudes of fifty degrees to fifty-three degrees, in longitude from 327 degrees to 336 degrees. [It is] in as beautiful and pleasant a site as any other that is on this coast, and it promises a great abundance of products if it were frequented and cultivated by the inhabitants, or if some foreigners should seize it by force or by friendship to make a new colony of it, as the Spaniards and Portuguese have done with the isles which they hold at present. But there is one thing: if the French and English tried to settle there or fortify [it] as they tried to do in Florida, the Spaniards would not fail to make war on them immediately to expel them. Alas, is not that a marvelous abyss of avarice and ambition in those people, to want to occupy if they could ten thousand times more land than they need and can settle? They would not be content and would like to be monarchs and command in heaven, on the earth, on the seas, and over the fish if it were possible for them, with no thought as to what end things might come.

26 According to Ganong, the name St. Julien arose from a misreading of *S. Juhan*. See his *Crucial Maps in the Early Cartography and Place-Nomenclature of the Atlantic Coast of Canada* (Toronto, 1964), p. 182. See also map 7.

27 Thevet does not discuss a second Isle of St. Julien. His geographical data indicate that he is using the Mercator map of 1569 or a similar map.

As for the two horns of the isle that you see in the division, which is pictured for you to the north on this map,[28] the isle must be very large since they [the horns] extend toward Belle Isle, [which is] the northernmost [isle] (which bears the name of another, which is in Brittany), and the isle called Assumption[29] and others which are inserted into this notch. Its entry is rather dangerous because of the shoals, banks, and reefs which are very dangerous and cause ships to be wrecked if they do not detour from the north to north-east and east. It is very full of large trees and thick forests, which are the principal product of this isle (at least so far as we know), since the wild beasts have seized and [are] in possession of it [and] prevent men from remaining there. This is a loss of no little consequence, since so great and ample extent of country would suffice [149v] to give occupation to many people. Not that I can guarantee the fertility or the fecundity of the terrain, which appears to be rather unsuitable; however, it would be a small matter to put in into shape, and even though it might not produce *pro rata* [sic] as well as here, it is certain that doubling, tripling or quadrupling the [cleared] area, it would produce richly. On which I am sure I will be opposed due to the difficulty of plowing it, which may be equal [to] (if it does not surpass) the seeding and price or estimate of the land. But [if it were not] for him who would wish to be aggressive and speculative, many regions which we see today flourishing with a fertile abundance and benediction of goods would have remained wild and abandoned.

Among a number of isles which surround this one, I admire especially that of Saint Catherine[30] since it is for the most part, and as well as you can imagine, cleared of these bushes which smother the fertility of the others. The only problems I see there is that it is low and in a plain, so that it is subject to wetness which be-swamps the principal products

28 It is not clear what map Thevet is referring to here.

29 Cartier named Anticosti Island Assumption because he discovered it on 15 August 1534, the feast day of the Assumption of the Virgin. The name is on the Desceliers map of 1546 but does not reappear until Mercator's 1569 map. Jean Alfonse uses Ascension, almost certainly an error for Assumption. The modern name Anticosti apparently derives from the native Natistco(s)ti. Thevet's Naticousti is the earliest recorded use of the name, and as Thevet claims to have obtained his information verbally from Cartier, along with the plan of this island which Thevet says Cartier gave him in 1550, it appears that the name goes back to Cartier himself. See Ganong, *Crucial Maps*, pp. 300–1.

30 According to Biggar (*Voyages*, p. 14n5), this island—now Schooner Island—was confused by Mercator with Belle Isle North. Although Cartier does not claim to have named this island, it is possibly named for Cartier's wife Catherine des Granches or her patron saint.

which one might hope from it. But for that, nevertheless, one should not give up on the hope of its fertility since Holland, Zeeland, and other regions, even though bogged down in the marshes, do not fail to excel in their reputation of fecundity. Furthermore, towards the north coast the land is somewhat higher and so escapes this marshy wetness; however, that produces inconveniences for mariners who are constrained to make a rather tiresome detour, because the ground there is dry and unsuitable for landing.

This isle and the Port of Chateau Bay lie north-northeast and south-southwest, whence some young pilots have taken occasion to say that the Isle of Saint Catherine is the Port of Chateau Bay—very incorrectly, since Jacques Cartier, from whom they say they drew and extracted their information, would have been most unwilling to agree with them. On the contrary, the reader will find that because of the circuit which must be made, they are fifteen leagues distant.[31] But it was not hard for a certain [150r] commentator [Belleforest] in his study to cut off and remove this detour and lump together the Isle of St. Catherine and the Port of Chateau Bay. On trying it, perhaps he might have had difficulties.

The coast of the isle teems with fish of all sorts, [and] the savages most of the time live on nothing but this fish which they prepare very handily after their custom, without sauce, bread, wine, or vinegar. Nevertheless, these people are hale and vigorous and are long-lived even though they lack the comforts which some of our lovers of delicacies here [have]. Others make flour in the [same] manner as do our savages of America [Brazil], as I related in detail in my book of my Singularitez.

The isle whose maps I represent for you [map 7] is set in the River of Canada [the St. Lawrence].[32] It is indeed one of the most pleasant and largest of all this country, provided with full-grown timber, full of harbors, and not too mountainous in the southern part. Its principal port faces east, of three and a quarter leagues in its greatest length. At times you find here two hundred ships for fishing cod, [for] it is here that the best fishing is and where merchants traffic with the savages of the country.

31 After leaving St. Catherine Island, Cartier sailed fifteen leagues across the Strait of Belle Isle and entered the Bay des Chasteaux. See Biggar, *Voyages*, pp. 14–15.

32 P.E.H. Hair has pointed out that on Thevet's map of Isles de Terres Neuves (map 6), the strait between Terres Neuves and the Isle of St. Julien lies between fifty-one and fifty-two degrees latitude, with Newfoundland stretching up to nearly fifty-two degrees. But on the separate map of the Isle of St. Julien [map 7] Newfoundland is not shown, although the strait now lies south of fifty-one degrees. See his "A Note on Thevet's Unpublished Maps of Overseas Islands," *Terrae Incognitae* 14 (1982): 105–16, esp. 113–14n33.

Moreover, I want to disabuse from error before passing on a number of new pilots and mariners who believe themselves to be important, among others three from the Bayonne country, who discoursing of pilotage in this present year 1586 tried to make me believe that the country of Canada and those of Norombegue and Bacchaleos are all one. But this is so far from the truth as I told them in view of the fact that [the country] of Norombegue is at forty-three degrees and that of Canada and the great river Dochelagua are at fifty-one degrees, fifty-two degrees and fifty-three degrees. That is what it is to lack experience the mistress of all things.

Before coming to the country and continental land of Norumbegue, and before getting to the Canadian land, there appears before you an isle encircled by eight very small islets which are near the country of the green mountains and the Cape of the Turtles. From there you come to the mouth of the said river [of Hochelaga], the entrance to which is dangerous because of a great number of large and high rocks and many reefs even though its entrance is almost half a league wide. [150v] About three leagues up the river, in the very middle, a little square isle presents itself before you: it is true that it has a promontory extending to the northeast which might be about four small leagues around, and [is] inhabited only by a few fishermen and by birds of various species. It is called by the local people Aiayascon, because the isle is shaped (seeing it from a distance from the east) in the form of a man's arm which is so named. It, as well as several other little islets which are quite some distance from it, could be easily settled and a fine fortress could be placed there to control the entire coast.

It is of this [island] that I have spoken so much to a number who have undertaken voyages to no good purpose and which failed, protesting to them that if they had taken possession of this isle and fortified it, that they would exercise control over all the savages of the countries of Bacchaleos, Norombegue, the Canadians and others, and that no one would in any wise dare to cast anchor there. The commodities which would be found in this country would be as great or greater for those who would command this land and the neighboring countries, as [for those who] go looking for gold mines in the Isles of Peru [South America]. For to begin with, mines of the metals copper, iron, lead, steel [*assier*] and others can be found in Norumbegue.[33] Secondly, an abundance of salt could be produced there since the country is flat and very clean. Thirdly, [there could be] a great

33 Thevet's mention of mining may have its roots in Cartier's 1535 voyage. The natives had told Cartier of a rich land to the west beyond a freshwater sea which they described as the home of copper-mining natives. See Biggar, *Voyages*, pp. 169–72.

commerce of furs. Fourthly, since the country is provided with full-grown timber of all kinds, with the aid of artisans one could build there many large and medium vessels, rowing or otherwise. Fifthly, it could be filled with warehouses of salted fish since this is the true fishing country where the sea teems with cod and more so than the other regions of Canada. Many hundreds of boats return [from there] every year loaded, and in truth I do not know any place more fit for some prince or great lord who would wish to found a new colony than to take possession of and fortify himself in these regions, so advantageous [and] having such a benign, gracious, and favorable appearance. Also the winds are such that in one year from our France or from England two round-trip voyages can be accomplished.

The people there are benign and gracious who seek only the friendship of the foreigner and I remember that when we had set foot on land, which was on my first voyage returning from the Southern Lands, we were reluctant to accost these barbarians. A kinglet of the country all clad in skins of wild beasts accompanied by some others, believing that we were angry and that we feared them, said to us in a quite friendly way in his language, Cazigno, Cazigno, Casnouy danga addagrin: which means, Let us go, let us go, on shore [disembark] my brothers and friends; Caoaquoca Ame Couascon, Kazacomy: Come drink and eat of what we have; Arca Somioppah, Quenchia dangua ysmay assomaha: We swear to you by the sky, the earth, the moon and the stars that you will have no more harm than our very selves. Seeing the good will and intentions of this old man we were with him an entire day. [On] the following day we took the route for the gulf of Canada.

[151r] Isle of the Assumption

This isle was discovered by Jacques Cartier on the day of mid-August in the year 1535, as he said in his second relation of the voyage that he made to Canada, Hochelaga, Saguenai, and other countries by the command of King Francois, the first of the name, which is why he baptized this isle with the name of the Assumption: because on the fifteenth day of the month of August is celebrated the feast and solemnity of the decease of the Virgin Mary, mother of the Saviour and Redeemer of the whole world.[34]

To touch here on the singularities of the isle is not my intention, since I could for the present do no more than recall its hideous and frightful

34 Cf. Biggar, *Voyages*, p. 104.

lairs of wild beasts which seem to command in the fortified waves of thick forests which for the most part thickly cover this country. However, it would not be a great affair to uproot and clear away and to populate these woods, [and] after having cleared them, chase away the bears which more than all the others hold sway there [and] give a thousand torments to those who fish for cod. If they do not take good care, a troop of these animals does not fail to enter at night the cabins and shacks and often into the boats to devour what they find there of fish; they are more fond of it than anything in the world, and when they are famished you see them going fishing in the lakes and rivers.

A number of other animals are also found on this isle as well as on the continent, among which is seen a kind like large bulls which have horns only a foot and a half long. I brought back two, which I still have in my den at Paris [from] when I came back from my first voyage. This animal has on its back a growth and hump just like that of a camel, [and] long hair whose color is close to fawn all over its body and especially under the chin. Its tail is like that of a lion, and this species is to be found in Lithuania and Poland which they call Zubex, and the Tartars Roffert [fig. 11].[35] The savages of the country arm themselves with their skins against the cold, and their horns are highly esteemed for their efficacy against venom; so the barbarians keep them as protection against the poisons and vermin which they often encounter going through the country to do their fishing.

But the thing which renders this isle so little frequented by inhabitants is that its approach is very dangerous, and even more difficult because of its sand-bars, shoals, and reefs which border it both on the side of the great River of Canada and of the gulf, basin, or Sinus of Saint Laurens

35 Álvar Núñez Cabeza de Vaca described the bison in the following terms: "They have small horns like the cows of Morocco; the hair is very long and woolly like a rug. Some are tawny, others black. . . . They come as far as the sea coast of Florida from a northerly direction ranging through a tract of more than four hundred leagues and throughout the whole region over which they run, the people who inhabit nearby, descend and live upon them." See Morris Bishop, *The Odyssey of Cabeza de Vaca* (New York, 1933), p. 98, cited by Wilma George, "Sources and Background to Discoveries of New Animals in the Sixteenth and Seventeenth Centuries," *History of Science* 18 (1980): 79–104, esp. 89. Cabeza de Vaca's *Relación* was published in Gonzalo Fernández de Oviedo, *Historia general y natural de las Indias* (Seville, 1535), and in Ramusio's *Terzo volume*. Also see Thevet's section on Florida in the *Singularitez* and *Cosmographie*. Thevet claimed to speak twenty-eight languages, and his Polish here is essentially corect: *zubr* means a (European) bison. For Thevet's claims as a linguist see J.B. Mencken, *The Charlatanry of the Learned*, trans. F.E. Litz, ed. H.L. Mencken (New York, 1937), p. 118, cited by Manoel da Silveira, "Some Remarks Concerning André Thevet," *The Americas* 1 (1944): 15–36, esp. 26 and n53.

which lies at some fifty-two degrees of latitude. It is however true that on the side of [151v] the Strait of St. Peter the way is a bit more sure and for this reason Jacques Cartier, who gave me the map of this isle and others also (which was in the year 1550), told me that he took this route in making his discovery.[36] The flat country that he speaks about is that of Nurembeg, otherwise called New France, which has to the north this Isle of Assumption. Others call it Jaisple, which I particularly wanted to warn the reader about, for fear lest he be over-troubled if in some sciographic[37] maps he might notice that mention is made of this Isle of Assomption or rather that of Jaisple, which I have no intention of separating from that of Assomption. Four degrees from the equinoctial line on my first voyage, which was around the year 1551, we found another isle inhabited only by birds [and] named Assomption, distant from the other by at least twelve hundred leagues, which I marked in my maps and mappemonde as well as the Canadian one. The variety of names of our isle that I am telling you about has come about because of divers voyagers who have come upon this isle, [and] who finding it inhabited and populated only by birds and wild beasts have concluded that they were the first who had discovered it, and so they baptized it with whatever name it pleased them. The elevation of this isle is such that for latitude it lies from the fifty-first degree up to the fifty-third, [and] for the longitude from the 312th to the 319th.

In this isle there are several mountains on the summits of which are the most beautiful and fragrant wild pastures that one can imagine. But since it is deserted and uninhabited they remain fallow, barren, and of no productivity. I know that certain herborists, who sought relaxation by going some way into the interior of the isle to ferret out its singularities, came back loaded with a number of exquisite plants which

36 The terms Sinus Saint Laurens and Strait of St. Peter were used by Cartier on his first voyage. The former appears on Mercator's map of 1569, which erred in placing the Estroict de S. Pierre south of Anticosti instead of north as Cartier had it. In place of the real Strait is Sinus S. Laurentii, evidently extended from Cartier's S. Laurens nearby. This is the crucial step which led to the extension of Cartier's local name St. Lawrence to the entire gulf and later to the river. See Ganong, *Crucial Maps*, p. 421; and map 3.

37 Thevet's use of this term appears to be the first in French. The *Oxford English Dictionary* cites Richard Haydocke in a translation from Giovanni Paolo Lomazzo, *Tratto dell'arte, della pintura* . . . (Milan, 1584), which could well have been Thevet's source for the word. There are various shades of meaning for the term, which was used primarily in architecture (a schematic representation of a section of a building) and drawing (delineation of an object in perspective with its gradations of light and shade). This latter definition would seem to be close to the sense in which Thevet uses the word, since in maps shading was used to indicate topographical features.

they made much over, regretting that conditions did not permit their making immediately a second foray. But they feared that if they tarried longer they might be rewarded with perpetual exile, and that as a reward for the trouble they had taken to wander among these mountains and to set up a colony of poor derelicts exposed to the mercy of the fierce beasts.

There are also some plains which appear to be good land, not so much for grain but for pasture, as well as [152r] very beautiful meadows useless to men who could not introduce a single beast there: for even if [animals] were to be shipped there, the cost of guarding against the incursions of the bears and other wild beasts would outweigh the value of all the income that could be got out of either the principal or the increase in several years.

When our people had landed [there] to seek out the rarest things, some here some there, with no fear of the barbarity of the people, they lived there well enough because the inhabitants of distant regions brought them more fish and game than they wanted; for they are very skillful with the bow and arrow and take the beasts with many fine tricks. Among others they use a kind of rackets, woven and made with ropes of animal tendons, square, and whose holes were very small like those of a screen, in the proportion of two and a half feet and almost as wide. They use these, tying them on to their feet (as much for the cold as for not sinking into the snow), when they are hunting the wild beasts and also because they do not slide on the icy places.

They dress in skins curried and accoutered in their fashion, in winter with the fur inside towards their skin and in summer the leather touching their flesh and the fur towards the outside. To take these beasts then, you will see them in groups of ten or twelve, armed and provided with long staves like spears or halberds, lances or pikestaffs, some being of twelve, others of fifteen feet [in] length, armed at the end not with iron or other metal but with some fine bone of stag or other beast, a good foot long and well pointed [and] carrying bows and arrows made in the same way. Thus armed they go through the snow all year long which they are very accustomed to; and pursuing stags, wild boars, wild asses, and reindeer through the deep snows they mark their trails just as our hunters do so as not to get lost. These savages make lodges of cedars in which the region is very abundant and hide under these verdant lodges and wait until the stags come there. As soon as the beast approaches they leave their ambushes and attack him with their spears and bows and with their halooing make him lose the beaten path. When the beast is dead they drag it to their houses – which the people call Canocas. [These houses] are arranged in the fashion and figure of a semi-circle [and are] of twenty-five or thirty paces large and long and ten wide, some covered with tree bark and others with skins and sea-rushes.

[It was] the Bretons who were the first [152v] to set foot in this country, penetrating as far as fifty and sixty leagues in the lands before Cortereal, who never saw more than small parts of it, in spite of the fact that some have wished to give him credit and praise of having been the first—a thing which Thevet will never grant them since we learned from the oldest savages that the French were the first who have given fame to their country.

One must not be surprised if our Isle of Assumption has few inhabitants for the reasons I have given you. It has many good harbors. In my day one could still see wooden forts which the French had built there, the same as on the river of Hochelaga and on that of Norembeg.[38] This country is very northerly and approaches that which is under the Arctic Circle which we call one of the poles or pivots sustaining the sphere, and consequently you can imagine how cold the land must be (but not for this reason uninhabitable). Now Canada means the same thing as land and this name came from the first who landed there, for as someone asked them what it was that they were looking for in this place they answered that they were Segnada Canada, that is men seeking land, and since then this name has remained as a name given at random, as are most of the names of the isles and provinces newly discovered.

To the north it extends to the icy and hyperborean sea, which is why all this country, Baccaleos as well as Labrador, is contained under the name of Canada. In this land there is a province named Campestre de Berge which extends to the southeast. In this province to the east lies the Cape or Promontory of Lorraine, so named by us. Others have given it the name of Cape of the Bretons because it was there that the Bretons, Biscayans, and Normands go and sail along the coast to fish for cod. Near this Cape is located another isle named Huree which extends from the north, having some five leagues circumference and rather close to the mainland. Another is seen which is two leagues away from it which is triangular, called by the natives Carbassa and by us was named the Isle of the Virgins. This land [*Campestre de Berge*] begins near this cape extending to the south and lies east-northeast and west-southwest. This coast of Canada from Cape Lorraine southwards projects into the sea

38 See Biggar, *Voyages*, p. 174n7. A great wooden stockade is also mentioned by Parmentier at the Baye des Chasteaux. See Bernard G. Hoffman, "Account of a Voyage Conducted in 1529 to the New World, Africa, Madagascar, and Sumatra, Translated from the Italian, with Notes and Comments," *Ethnohistory* 10 (1963): 14. Ganong believes that this is the origin of the tradition of a "Fort of Norembega" (*Crucial Maps*, p. 429).

as does Italy between the Adriatic and Ligurian seas in the manner of a peninsula.

I will leave off here about our Isle of the Assumption, deploring the weakness of many Christian princes for being so negligent and abandoning this flourishing province, and that they do not send [people] to populate it and evangelize since it is so close to us, as formerly did the Spaniards and Portuguese in so many lands which they hold at present. From the great riches which they receive from these they aggrandize themselves daily, and in truth if this Canadian land were inhabited they [the Christian princes] could receive as much or more profit as the kings of Scotland and Denmark receive from their Hebrides and Orkneys or the Grand Turk from his Cyclades isles.[39]

[153r] Isle of the Demons

It is impossible (it seems to me) to take away this stupid fancy from men, among others pilots and mariners who undertake the voyage to the New Land, that in this isle (the map of which I represent for you)[40] there are demons and devilry which torment those who cast anchor there, as I told you about another isle which I named Roberval rather close to this one.[41] It is not my intention here to remind the reader why this present isle has borne the same name of Demons nor to declare to you likewise how formerly these demons were classed by the philosophers among the good Genii, among which they listed six species, for example the sylvan demons and adjutant – that is to to say assisting-demons.

And as for our isle which is near the land of Baccaleos and New France, as I have described to you elsewhere, it certainly is uninhabited [and] you would say [it is] due to the tempestuousness of the great winds which are daily there and sometimes storms. The four elements fire, water, earth, and air, although each of these differs from the other by virtue of the fact that they are corruptible, and by exchanges are transmutable from one to the other: all these elements at a given moment are inimical to the men who set foot on the aforesaid isle. For whoever would simply consider

39 Thevet continues his discussion of the Isle of Assumption after his section on the Isle of Demons, adding information obtained from the work of Jean Alfonse.

40 There is no longer any map here given by Thevet.

41 Having already described, as he says, the Isle de Roberval (as the place of exile of the *demoiselle*) and having situated it at 58 degrees latitude and 340 degrees longitude, Thevet now describes the Isle des Demons as well. Below, he describes another Isle de la Damoiselle, based on Jean Alfonse. See also Biggar, *Voyages*, pp. 284–6.

the location of it according to the map and description very particularly done by myself, would say that it is a different world and uninhabitable place even though it is situated in a rather temperate and cold climate. [It] lies at fifty-nine degrees latitude on this side of the equinoctial line and at 343 degrees longitude. [This is] almost at the same elevation and the same climate as the most distant isles of the [Atlantic] Ocean where the sea is frozen and very close to the Arctic Pole in the direction of the northern sky. [It is] consequently the coldest isle of New Land, which constitutes one extremity of Canada and particularly of Baccaleos, [and is] completely maritime. In this isle [of Baccaleos] are found great rivers which are called of the Three Brothers, rather close to the Isle of Orbelande which is in the said sea. This river is one of the great[est] ones of all this country and in any case like those I have seen under the equator and in the Antarctic.

The mainland is inhabited by barbarous people, cruel and inhuman just like those of Canada. [They are] unapproachable and ungracious unless by force, and this is well known by those who go there to fish for cod that we eat here. They dress in skins of wild animals as do all their neighbors and people of the north. They often go to our Isle of [153v] Demons, sometimes twenty or thirty light boats [full], by which these people navigate going from isle to isle and place to place in them. [They] never return to their huts without bringing [back] a great number of wild animals which are nourished and engendered by this demonic isle, which is divided and separated into several others—principally on the eastern side where the good fishing is. [It is] a remarkable thing to see in this great ocean isles and islets distant from the mainland, some a hundred, three hundred, four hundred, twenty, and others ten leagues, nevertheless inhabited by various species of terrestrial animals and birds of various plumages.

But before entering into this discussion and speaking of the beasts which are nourished in this isle, I should like to consult some excellent personage who would explain to me the pros and cons of how it is possible that in this place and on a thousand other isles, which as I said never were inhabited any more than this one, you see teeming such a diversity of beasts and birds, and in what way they were procreated and engendered. I of course know that warmth and moisture causes the generation of lower forms of life, but also you have to realize that in any generation you have to pay attention to the matrix; for they [the lower forms] must live off that from which they are engendered. Now sentient beings must necessarily come from the commingling of semen, and for this reason I am in doubt (speaking according to natural reason) how these beasts were engendered in this isle.[42] To say that the putrefaction of a moist warmth produces such a generation of vermin I cannot understand nor grant, inasmuch as this place is extremely cold and also because this is contrary to the nature of matter. It must be that these bodies which are composed of all sorts of entrails receive nourishment from the blood circulating through the conduits of the veins [and] must likewise be formed and take their growth from this blood which vivifies and animates them. Just as man can only be engendered by the effusion of seed and nourishment which he takes from the matrix of his mother, likewise animals cannot be procreated from the mere humor of putrid earth, this being prevented by the lack of the radical warmth which through the blood causes this nourishment and life. However, one must not be surprised if there is an abundance of beasts there since these savages, in order to support and maintain themselves and to wear their skins after eating their flesh, load up their small boats with them. As for the birds, since their bodies are more tenuous and participate of the nature of the air, even if [154r] they may not have been there since the beginning of the said isle, still they may have come and still be coming there from elsewhere, since it is well known that cranes and swallows are migratory birds. I have made for you this little digression for the contentment of intelligent people and those who have never traveled.

Moreover in these seas there are found not only cod but seal whose flesh seems to them very good and delicate. They use the grease and make an oil of it which being melted is converted into a reddish liquor like we make wine and other beverages, or like the Moors of upper and lower Ethiopia [make] from olive oil, which is common and habitual with them when they are thirsty. They likewise have other fish enough, such as porpoises and dog-fish, which are covered with tough leather, and others having very hard shells such as turtles, oysters, mussels, and others which have only simple scales. It is in this place that is found a great quantity of whales and not in the Mediterranean Sea, as has been given us in writing by the commentator of Munster [Belleforest] in which he is very greatly deceived as I have mentioned to you elsewhere.

From this isle to the extremity of Florida the coast has been visited and discovered, the mainland as well as the fresh and salt water rivers which separate the kingdoms and provinces of this barbarous people.

42 Here Thevet shows a scientific curiosity which is one of the earmarks of the "Renaissance Man." Note, however, his parenthesis cautiously referring his thought to "natural reason" — he is, after all, a friar.

These rivers from the Gulf of Merore are frozen almost half the year.[43] The entrance to the said gulf is between fifty-nine degrees and fifty-eight degrees extending to the Isle of Gonse and to the large Isle of Fiche so that vessels which go cast anchor there often place themselves in danger of the ice if they do not take care.[44] Between the said Isle of Fiche and that of Gonse toward the reefs of St. Lawrence northerly this coast is extremely dangerous because of the current. In this Isle of Fiche was banished the damsel about whom I have told you (which since was named the Isle of Roberval by me), distant from the mainland, from Blanc Sablon, from the Isle of Baccaleos, and from that of Foulques,[45] and from Cape Bona Vista three leagues and no more. Having traversed these dangerous passages the pilot is in surety as far as the river and country of Saguenay, which the savages call Thadoyzeau; and the pilot may make full sail as far as the the Isle of Assumption which the same savages [154v] name Naticousti, [which is] rather dangerous of approach because of an infinity of banks and reefs, of which dangers the sea is full as far as Chaleur Bay, which the barbarians call Mechsameht.[46] Those who voyage in this sea or

43 Thevet may have derived the Gulf of Merore from Mercator's map of 1569 which includes a Golfam de Merosro. There is a letter of 1580 to Richard Hakluyt from Gerardus Mercator, who states: "Concerning the gulfe of Merosro and Canada, and new France which are in my mappes, they were taken out of a certaine sea card drawn by a certaine priest out of the description of a Frenchman, a Pilot very skilfull in those partes, and presented to the worthy prince George of Austria, bishop of Liege: for the trending of the coast, and the elevation of the pole, I doubt not but they are very neere the trueth: For the Charte had, beside a scale of degrees of latitude passing through the middest of it, another particularly annexed to the coast of New France, wherewith the errour of the latitude committed by the reason of the variation of the compasse might be corrected." See Hakluyt, *Principal Navigations*, 3: 280–1. Thevet, a friar who knew Mercator, is almost certainly the priest who gave him the map drawn by a French pilot, most likely Jean Alfonse or perhaps Jacques Cartier himself. See map 2.

44 Gonse may be Thevet's misreading of Ye. de Conques, which is on the east coast of Newfoundland on the Desceliers map of 1550. The Isle of Fiche appears on the same map. See also map 1.

45 The origin of this name is unclear.

46 Ganong identifies the names Thadoyzeau, Naticousti, and Mechsameht as a first record of three surviving major native place names: Tadoussac, Anticosti, and Miramichi, "none of which appear in Cartier's narratives or any known earlier source, though the last-mentioned occurs on 'Portuguese-Cartier' maps as *mecheomay* . . . Thevet could have had no imaginable source for them except Cartier's conversation, perhaps in part reflecting the third voyage: but the fact of their survival amply attests their genuineness and the existence of a continuous local tradition from Cartier's day to the end of the century." Ganong identifies Thadoyzeau and Naticousti as Huron-Iroquois and Mechsameht as Montaignais (*Crucial Maps*, p. 430). Hoffman adds that these terms "give undeniable proof of the

gulf, which borders the land extending straight to the north, find another land shaped like a peninsula named Athanicq which is on the right hand. Large ships are not suitable for this coast, rather small and medium ones of forty, fifty, and sixty tons, which can go clear to the extremity of the great river [where there is] a rather sandy region which they call in their patois Hananyer.[47]

I had forgotten to tell you that an isle named by the French Orleans, and by the savages Minigo, is the place where the river is the narrowest and from the entrance of the said river begins the Isle of the Virgins, which is near another river named Islee about sixty leagues distant, and from that [Isle] of Orleans to the Lake of Angouleme [there are] thirty-four leagues.[48]

If it is a question of going farther north and northeast you will find in one direction as well as another several large rivers, among others the one named Estendue which comes from and has its source in the high mountains of Chilague[49] and those of Tortimage.[50] To the left you have likewise the rivers of Monmorency which water the country of Chambriant,[51] and that of Gotin which borders rather closely the Promontory of Raguine[52] and that of Passer. Between these countries and that of the Magots[53] is located a large lake which might have twenty-

---

authenticity of Thevet's sources for Canada" (*Cabot to Cartier*, p. 173).

47 Ganong thinks that *Athanicq* is the peninsular land of the Magdalens. *Hananyer*, according to Ganong, sounds like a Huron-Iroquois term. See *Crucial Maps*, p. 430.

48 Ganong believes it probable that Cartier gave Thevet the name *Minigo*—the Micmac word for "the island"—when telling him of the I. du Massacre (*Crucial Maps*, p. 431). Also see Silas T. Rand, *Dictionary of the Language of the Micmac Indians* (Halifax, 1888), p. 148; and Hoffman, *Cabot to Cartier*, p. 176. The Lake of Angoulême, mentioned in Verrazzano's letter but not named in Cartier's narrative, is identified by Biggar as Lake St. Peter (*Voyages*, pp. 145–6 and 145n15). For Verrazzano's letter see Wroth, *Verrazzano*, p. 137n11.

49 Hochelaga (which appears as Chilaga on some maps).

50 According to Ganong (*Crucial Maps*, p. 431), all of these names, except *Gotin*, appear in various forms on the "Portuguese-Cartier" maps, "but are here given in a way more suggestive of dictation than copying from these maps."

51 Hoffman suggests that the Monmorency is the Richelieu River and the plain of Chambriant is lower Quebec (*Cabot to Cartier*, pp. 175–6).

52 In a similar account above, *Cosmographie*, chap. 3: "On the Land of Canada and Baccaleos" (fol. 1011v.), Thevet does not mention this place name, which may derive from the port raquina or pora quina of the Le Testu and Velho maps. See Ganong, *Crucial Maps*, p. 332.

53 Ganong states that Thevet's country of the Magots is that of the Iroquois, and that

seven leagues circumference, called by the natives Pathnos,[54] which has a beautiful isle in the middle populated by barbarians which might be three leagues in circumference. It is named Minigo, about which I told you above. This Isle of Minigo serves as a refuge for the people of these regions whither they retreat when they are pursued by their enemies and [it is] there that they place them when they have taken them alive to keep them several moons and days in order to massacre them afterwards in the fashion and manner that their enemies had formerly done to them when they had taken them on sea or on land.

Around the said isle there is the most beautiful fishing that there is in all of the [Atlantic], and [it is] where the whales repair at all times. Those of Bayonne, the Spaniards, and others go there fishing to take these great monsters called by the Mexicans Altapatli, by the Syrians Janim, by the Hebrews Dagh-gadol, which is to say great fish, by the Persians Nunarabba, by the vulgar Greeks Phalena, by the Moscovites Bellouga, and by this Canadian people Kourt and by the Turks Hyounos, [155r] and by those of Baccaleos Strich. A great number of them are taken each year and principally at the Saguenay River which may have a half league entrance.

Near this place our French made a wooden fort for security against the barbarians (who are rather good people and gracious if you do not irritate them). They do not believe in God at all. They live without faith and without law, worshipping nothing in the world. They are very lazy. You have to give them many presents either to gain their friendship or to get them to work and help in the fishing. The Christians who go there ask them to do this since this is the most important traffic which merchants can carry on there with these whales whose grease they have melted. They also traffic in divers beautiful and fine pelts with these barbarians who trade these and other merchandise to the foreigners.[55] As for gold and silver money they have no knowledge of it any more than do the savages of the austral lands.

I had forgotten to tell you, speaking of whales, that they are found in these rivers of Ochelaga, Saguenay, and others, [and] as I said they come

---

Magots is presumably identifiable with the later Maguas or Mohawks, "here mentioned for the first time" *(Crucial Maps*, p. 431). Ganong's opinion is supported by David H. Pentland, "A Historical Overview of Cree Dialects," *Papers of the Ninth Algonquian Conference*, ed. William Cowan (Ottawa, 1978), pp. 104–15.

54 Thevet has already referred to the I. of Path*m*os in the Mediterranean, see *Cosmographie*, chap. 4: "On the Utility of the Said Country of Canada."

55 On trading in pelts during the Cartier voyages see Biggar, *Voyages*, pp. 52–3.

there in various seasons and months and come from the open sea. From which it must be thought that these great aquatic beasts are migratory as well as the other small and medium-sized fish. There are also found in these regions a great number of marine horses[56] which are amphibious fish as are crocodiles[57] and seals. When the savages can catch them they do not leave one behind but kill them with arrows and large wooden clubs and then eat them avidly, [for] their flesh is very good and delicate. I will tell you furthermore what I have observed about whales, that the female has but one little one at a time, which she produces without eggs as do quadrupeds, contrary to the nature of all other fish. Moreover the whale gives milk to her little whale-calf once he is born, and for this function she has breasts on her belly below the navel, which no other fish in the sea or in fresh water does, unless it be the seal or the comiaco, a very large fish which is caught in the Red Sea and in the great Lake of Alexandria in Egypt as I have seen.

The whale is a beast dangerous to meet for sailors because of her monstrousness, as those of Bayonne and the Spaniards (whose trade is to take them with certain instruments and machines [155v] with which they strike them) well know and often experience. Having wounded her they pursue her with medium-sized vessels until she approaches land and dies, or until she is harpooned and pulled near land, and then God knows how many people are employed hacking her to pieces and filling several vessels with her. The natives traffic in the meat and oil with foreigners, hence the good fishing which these animals furnish. It is in cold places where most of these monstrous fish repair because of the great quantities of fish there, which is why below the equinoctial line and near the two tropics she seldom frequents since fish are not too plentiful there, but [are] very much so near the two poles as I have seen [and] faithfully and diligently observed. Although the whales are the greatest monsters of the sea they all have such a small throat that it is only with difficulty that they can swallow a fish of the size of the average salmon.

There remains only for me to remind the pilots and sailors that the country which adjoins our Isle of Demons and the Bay of Canada, on the coast of the New Land, extends far into the mainland possibly three

56 In 1535 Cartier applied the term *chevaulx de mer* to the walrus, which he had described in the previous year without giving it a name. See Biggar, *Voyages*, pp. 34, 110, 193, 199.

57 It is unclear whether Thevet's reference here, and elsewhere, is to the crocodile, which he may have seen in Egypt, or to the American alligator, *Alligator mississippiensis*. In his section on Florida, Thevet simply copies Laudonnière's *crocodil*.

hundred leagues to the southwest and west. The latitude of Canada is about forty-six degrees north of the equinoctial. Through the middle of this bay [the Gulf of St. Lawrence] descends a river of fresh water which flows from a city which is called Ouyslayna[58] around forty-three degrees north of the said equinoctial. The Canadian land is quite temperate and fertile like that of Gascony, fit for producing all sorts of grains.

In several regions of this coast fine grapevines have been found growing wild and without cultivation by a living soul, which bear large grapes which the savages call Oroba, and they are good to eat; but I do not know if their wine is good because I saw none made from them. These wild grapes like to climb up in poplars and young elms, to which being joined there are so many branches and leaves that it is hard to pick them without breaking them. I have seen similar species flourishing in Arabia in places among the high mountains. I also remember seeing some not only in this place but also in others in the region of Mt. Sinai. As you take the direct route to Gazera (which the Arabs call Gazer) (in the place where the mighty Samson was) [there are] some hills, and on these I discovered that there were grapevines. This constitutes a great marvel, namely that this good shrub [156r] being found in all the four corners of the globe is universally favored.

Moreover, hemp is found in the said region of Canada and of New Land, although the barbarians do not know how to process it and use it. [There are] great quantities of large filberts, walnuts, apples, wild pears, [and] chestnuts in great quantities, many species of wild animals who live for the most part off these fruits and more so than do the natives of the country. Stags, wolves, bears, martens, lynxes, buffalo and wild cows are also found there. There are no lions, tigers, elephants, camels, horses, mules nor asses, as are found in Africa; but great numbers of honeybees are found there even though the country is very cold, in sum many other species of terrestrial and aquatic animals. The earth produces such and similar plants as ours: oaks, pines, firs, hawthorns, and blackthorns which produce certain little fruits, and a number of other sorts unknown to us which posses great virtues in them; you would think you were in Gascony or Languedoc. They have prunes which they dry for winter which they call honesta; and have rather large figs which do not come to maturity; and large white broad-beans which they call Sahu; and the walnuts, Cahenya. They do not eat anything that tastes salty. When we showed them preserved grapes they gave a shake of the head saying

58 We have located no source for this name.

Nohda, which is to say we do not know these.[59]

And the Christians built a high wooden cross to which was affixed a large fleur-de-lis, around which was written, Long live the King of France.[60] When this cross was planted the savages who were present were greatly astonished as to why we were doing such a thing. And these brutes, noticing that certain Christians of the company were prostrating themselves to the ground before the said cross with joined hands, thought that these signs were intended to deceive them and that we would charge upon them and trick them into coming near so as to kill them. Eight days following this there arrived a king from sixty leagues distance from the place where the Frenchmen were staying. This kinglet, all clothed in skins, accompanied by six score of savages (each of whom had bows and arrows, others armed with pieces of wood and clubs), was likewise irritated and interrogated our men and wanted to know by sign language [why] this cross had been set up, whether it was to trick them and put [156v] them to death, or whether they wanted to take hereditary possession of that region and make themselves masters of it.[61]

At this juncture there arrived another king, the most feared of all these regions, named Donnacona (accompanied by another king whom they called Agouhanna, no less prestigious and feared by his people as much as anyone), who came to see the Christians who had already fortified themselves in several places. This king then, accompanied by fourteen boats and some hundred savages to reconnoiter our vessels, at first attempted to frighten those who were inside, but his anger passed when he was informed by an interpreter that we wished only to be their friends and to establish a new colony in their country to support them and protect them from their enemies. This king then began to approach our men and to make an oration using certain ceremonies according to the barbarian custom. This lord was accosted by and followed by another character extremely dangerous who was named Taignoagny. Following a general reconciliation the barbarians as well as the Christians wound up as good friends. They brought to them [the French] straightaway provisions from all sides, venison, as much or more cooked fish, so that there were more than sixty persons all loaded with meat, fish, and fruits.

59 See Biggar, *Voyages*, p. 63 and nn16–18.

60 Thevet has embellished Cartier's account of this incident; cf. Biggar, *Voyages*, pp. 64–7.

61 Brian Slattery suggests that France did not officially assert territorial rights in North America before 1560. See his "French Claims in North America, 1500-59," *Canadian Historical Review* 59 (1978): 139–69.

[These] coming up to our people began to cry out loudly, uttering these very words Aguyase, Aguyase, which means in their jargon nothing other than Joy, Joy my friends, you are very welcome, feast well.

Their royal houses are built of wood and covered with tree bark and foliage. As for the poorer houses they are also made of wood, and oftentimes when it is cold they are covered with snow and ice. The person who pictured the lodge of King Agouhanna is greatly mistaken and is using his imagination, since he shows it as circular and like the great houses and fortresses of the kings of Barbary.[62] [It is] a thing of his invention, and just as badly conceived as his having the people going around stark naked in the fashion of the Americans [Brazilians].[63] I leave it up to the reader whether people could be going around naked like that in countries so cold that the rivers are frozen all year round.[64] Indeed our people at first were so stunned by such cold that they could not get around from place to place. The barbarians, big, tall, strong, and powerful, taking pity on them, carried them on their shoulders to the places where they desired or wished [157r] to go.

It happened one day that a young Angevin gentleman who was in the company asked a certain savage to carry him and give him a joy-ride, which the savage did. The third day this fine Angevin, after he had dined and had a few drinks, ordered the said savage to do his pleasure as he had previously. The Angevin being on the shoulders of the Canadian savage and holding a stick in his hand, as the savage was going down a certain hill [the native] happened to stumble because of the snow on the rough and rocky road. Whereupon the gentleman began to beat unreasonably with blows of his stick on the aforesaid savage, who feeling himself offended came up to the edge of the sea and took my Angevin by the scruff of the neck and having strangled him threw him into the depths of the sea. Immediately after he had done this deed a certain French captain, a rather modest person, wishing to prevent this savage from throwing his companion into the sea, drew his sword thinking to frighten the barbarian but was not quick enough to strike with it before the said savage did the

62 This is a notable example of Thevet's hypocrisy. The "person" in question is Ramusio (or his illustrator). If Thevet had named him, he would have risked revealing his great debt to the author of the *Delle navigationi et viaggi*.

63 Cf. the illustration [fig. 9] of Hochelaga and its inhabitants in Ramusio, *Terzo volume*.

64 Elsewhere Thevet refers to the Canadian land as quite temperate, e.g. *Grand Insulaire*, chap. "Isle of Demons." Cartier said that even in the bitter cold the natives went about nearly stark naked (Biggar, *Voyages*, pp. 158, 185–6).

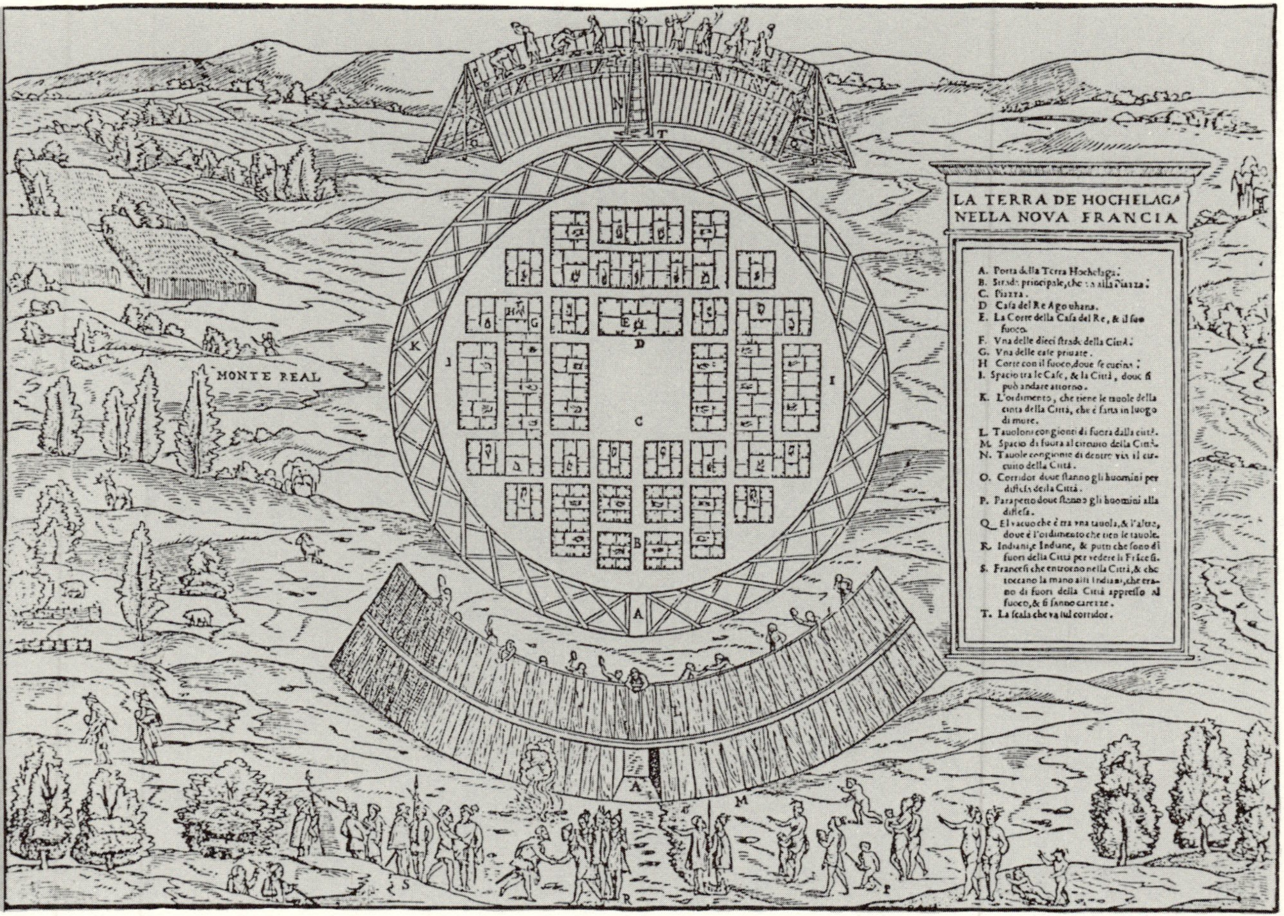

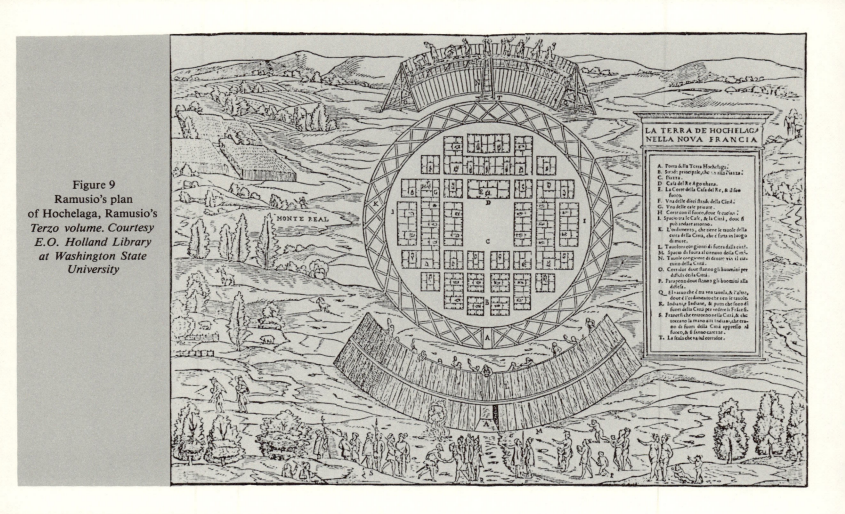

Figure 9
Ramusio's plan
of Hochelaga, Ramusio's
*Terzo volume. Courtesy
E.O. Holland Library
at Washington State
University*

same as he had with the first, and publicly strangled and felled in this way these two personages which greatly terrified the company. Thus I was informed by Captain Jacques Cartier when I was staying in his house at St. Malo-en-l'Isle.[65]

Now having left the Canadian land, Isle of Demons, Baccaleos and the rest of New Land, [for] those who wish to sail north [if they have] favorable winds there will immediately appear before them the Cortereal peninsula which is made a peninsula by the Gulf of St. Lawrence and that of Merore, as is "fortunate Arabia" by the Gulf of Arabia and that of Persia. After the Isle of Gonse which is easterly and that of Caravelle which neighbors another Isle called [Isle] of Fortune which are westerly, there appears to the left a port capable of giving anchorage to one hundred large vessels.[66] Its entry is from east to west and may be a half league wide and three in its greatest length. On entering there you must watch for two low-lying rocks which are near the entry, and also two islets which are in the middle of the port where one could fortify oneself. [For] those who would wish to settle in these regions or establish a new colony there the said isles are well-suited. Those who wish to go farther and sail towards our [157v] pole must not hug the land because of the great dangers that are there, rather they must keep to the large in the open sea five or six leagues for the danger of reefs and rocks which lie near the mainland.

And I can say the same for those who want to undertake from Canada the route to Florida and the Peruvian [South American] regions, who having left the Promontory of the Bretons and the Isle of Thevet so marked on my maps the pilot must avoid approaching too closely to the land unless in small vessels and skiffs, and take the straight route as far as the river of Arnodie, and that of Juvide which you leave to the right. It is a long and dangerous coast as far as the great river called Norambegue which is one of the most beautiful rivers after that of Ochelaga which is in all these regions. I have spoken to you (so it seems to me) someplace about the said river of Norambeg and of the beautiful isle which is at its mouth which may be two leagues around, which could be populated and fortified even though the said river is full of numerous shoals and rocks.[67] It is there that the good cod fishing is.

65 There are two references in Cartier to natives carrying Frenchmen. In the latter case, the Frenchman is carried "as on horseback" (Biggar, *Voyages*, pp. 147, 172). This is also pictured in the illustration (fig. 9) of Hochelaga in Ramusio, *Terzo volume*.

66 Caravelle and Fortuna appear on the Mercator map of 1569.

67 This predilection of Thevet's for "fortifying oneself" on an island in a harbor perhaps

Anyhow, continuing your route straight south you come to the river of Buemadre distant from Norambegue some eight score leagues. Having passed it you discover Grand Bay and then the river of St. Christopher, and you pass straight to the southeast as far as Cape St. Jacques, which having passed you find another Cape called "of Traverse," then the river of Mallebregue, which is the entry to the lands of Florida which is ninety leagues distance from it.[68] Those who wish to go beyond must govern themselves according to the latitude and the points of the compass, and avoid the continent because of the sudden squalls which could cause them to lose their lives and their goods. That is what I have wanted to discuss so that pilots and sailors might have occasion to be grateful to me and avoid the perils which threaten them from all sides.

The country about which I have written in the foregoing is very large. Its people all live in more or less the same disposition and fashion without religion nor faith nor laws any more than the southern Brazilians. They differ in language the ones from the others, especially those of the New Lands – formerly called the Land of the Bretons – from those of the great river of Ochelaga and the country of Saguenay, and since these regions are presently frequented by the French and the English I have wished for the contentment of the reader to append here a little dictionary of some of their own words and the main ones of their patois.

[158r] Language of the Inhabitants of the New Lands

God – cudrani
the sun – Isnez
star – suroe
Heaven (or sky) – camet

---

reflects his experience with Villegagnon in Brazil.

68 Most of these names appear, in various forms, on several early maps. *Malabrigo* appears on Mercator's 1569 map in the Gulf of Mexico; Thevet may have Gallicized it into *Mallebregue*. There is a R. di Travesa on the Homem map of circa 1534. Thevet also mentions Traverse in the Florida section of the *Cosmographie*. For more information see Ganong, *Crucial Maps*, pp. 150–1, 245.

69 Cartier used the word *conquedo* for throat. Ramusio has this word defining *gola*, which is throat rather than mouth.

70 Ramusio has *hehonguesto*.

71 In Ramusio, in the second column across from *Pelle* (skin, pelt), he has an entry "Vna pelle da coprire le parti Vergognose" (a skin to cover the private parts), for which he gives the native words *ouscozon uondico*. Thevet has confused the two columns, putting this definition in his first column, then not knowing what to do when he got to "Vna pelle

day – (no definition)
night – Aiagla
water – Ame
sand – estogas
sail – Aganie
head – Agonaze
mouth – conguedo[69]
nose – gehonguesto[70]
teeth – Hesangue
fingernails – agetascu
feet – ochedasco
legs – Anoudasco
death – Amocdaza
skin (pelt) – Aionasca[71]
a man's nature – ouscozon uondico[72]
that (demonstrative) – yca
a hatchet – Asogne
codfish – gadogoursere
good to eat – (no definition)[73]
almonds – Anougasa[74]
figs – Asconda
gold – Henyosco
the natural member (penis) – Assegnega
a bow (for arrows) – (no definition)
latten (sheet metal) – Aignetase[75]
the forehead – Ansce
a feather – yco
the moon – casmogan
earth (land) – conda
wind – canut
rain – onnoscon
bread – cacacomy
sea – Amet
ship – casaomy
man – Undo
hat – Hochosco[76]
eyes – ygara[77]
mouth – heche
ear – hontasco
arm – Agescu
woman – enrasesco
invalid – Alouedeche
shoe – Atta
red cloth – Cahoneta
knife – agoheda
conger eel – Agedoneda[78]
nuts (walnuts) – Caheya
apple – Honesta
beans (fava) – Sahe
sword – achesco[79]
green tree – haueda
an earthenware pot – (no definition)[80]

. . . " in the second column. He thus has two definitions for penis in the first column.

72 See preceding note.

73 Ramusio has written *Quesande*.

74 Ramusio has *anougaza*.

75 Ramusio has *aignetaze*.

76 Thevet mistranslates Ramusio's *Capelli* meaning hair.

77 Ramusio has *ygata*.

78 Ramusio defines this as *sgombro* (mackerel) and writes *agedoneta*.

79 Thevet omits Ramusio's *Vna frezza – cacta* [arrow].

80 Ramusio has *undaco*.

[158v] Second Dictionary of the Kingdom of Hochelaga and Canada and Other Countries

One – segada
two – tignemi
three – Hasche
four – Hannaion
five – Ouiscon
six – Indahir
seven – Aiaga
eight – Addigue
nine – Madellon
ten – Assem

There follow the words for the parts of a man

The head – Agononzi[81]
The Forehead – Hergueniascon
The Eyes – Higata
The ear – Abontascon
The mouth – esahe
The teeth – escongai[82]
The tongue – osnache
The beard – hebelim[83]
The throat – Agonhon[84]
The face – Hegouascon
The hair – Aganiscon
The arms – Aiayascon
The groins – Hetnanda[85]
The flanks – Aissone[86]
The stomach (breast) – Agruascon[87]
The belly – eschehenda

81 Ramusio has *aggonzi*.

82 Ramusio has *esgongai*.

83 Cartier used the term *Le Menton* (chin); Ramusio translates this as *La Barba* (beard). Thevet follows Ramusio and translates *La Barbe*.

84 In Ramusio "beard" follows "throat."

85 Thevet has here mistranslated Ramusio's *le alette, scagli* (the armpits); Cartier has *les esselles*, so Ramusio's translation is correct.

86 Thevet and Ramusio both have "flanks." Ramusio translated Cartier's *Les coustez* (ribs) as *li fianchi*. Thevet has *Les flans*.

87 Ramusio has *aggruascon*.

88 Cartier has *Les cuysses* and Ramusio *Le coscie*, both of which mean "the thighs." Thevet mistranslates this as *Le gousier*, "throat."

89 Cartier has *Le vyt*, or "penis." Ramusio has bowdlerized this term to "the member of a man," and Thevet follows this emendation.

90 Cartier has *Le con*, meaning "the cunt." Ramusio and Thevet have again expurgated Cartier's vulgar language.

91 Thevet at first wrote the word *paillard* (lecher) here, having misread Ramusio's *putto* which he probably associated with the French *pute*.

92 Again, Thevet first wrote the word for "whore" here for Ramusio's *putta*, which recalls the French *putain*.

The throat – hetnegradascon[88]
The knees – Agochinegodascon
The legs – Agouguenehonde
The feet – onchidascon
The hands – aignodascon
The finger – Agenoga
The fingernail – Agedascon
A man's member (penis) – Ainoascon[89]
The nature of the woman (vagina) – Castaigne[90]
A man – Aguehum
A woman – Agruaste
A child – Addegesta[91]
A girl – Agnia questa[92]
Small child – Exiasta

There follow other words

A dress – Cabata
A cassock (shirt, skirt) – Caioza
Stocking – hemondoha
Shoe – Atha
Shirt – Amgoua
Wheat – Osizi[93]
Bread – Carraconny
Water – Ame
Meat (flesh) – quahouascon
Currants – queion[94]
Plums (prunes) – Honnesta
Figs – absconda
A bunch of grapes – ozoba[95]
Nuts (walnuts) – quahoya
A hen – Sahomgahoa
Lamprey – Zisto
A salmon – ondacon
A whale – Ainne honne

93 Cartier has written *"Ilz appellent leur bled,"* meaning "they call their wheat." Ramusio simply uses the word *Formento*, and Thevet, *Fourment* denoting wheat or corn. Initially, Thevet wrote the word *castrua*, but then crossed it out in favor of *Osizi*. In Ramusio, the word *castrua* was the definition for the preceding word on the his list, *Vna berreta* or cap, but Thevet gives up on this word.

94 This is either a mistaken translation of *poisson* [fish] from Cartier by Ramusio, or a typographical error. Ramusio wrote *passi*, [raisins] which was probably an error for *pesci*. Thevet has *coryntes* meaning raisins or currants. This word reveals a fascinating history of dried grapes, and later currants, which are associated with the Greek port of Corinth, from which the Levantine specialty was often shipped.

95 Cartier defines *ozoba* as raisins. Thevet often writes *orobá*.

96 At this point in the Cartier and Ramusio vocabulary lists there is the entry "a squirrel – caiognem." Thevet omitted this word in his list.

97 Ramusio has *cudragny*.

98 Ramusio has *quazahaquea*.

99 Cartier has *Donnez moy a desieuner*, and Ramusio, *Datemi di far colation*, which means "give me breakfast." Thevet wrote *Donne moy a faire collation*, or "give me an evening snack" [Cotgrave].

100 Ramusio has *aignag*.

101 Biggar interprets this phrase as "to gamble."

102 This is Thevet's amusing mistranslation of Ramusio's *andiamo con la barca*, which accurately translates Cartier's *allons au bateau*, or, let's go to the boat. Thevet has written

An eel—esgneny[96]
[159r] a snake—undegnezi
Tortoise—Heu lexime
Wood—Conda
Tree leaves—Hoga
God— Cudrany[97]
Give me something to drink—
quaza hoaquea[98]
Give me something to snack—
quazahoa quascaboa[99]
Give me supper—quazahoa
quatfriam
Let's go to sleep—casigno
agnydahoa
Good day—Aignah[100]
Let's go play (or gamble)—Casigno
caudy[101]
Come talk to me—Assigni
quaddadia
Look at me—Quagathoma
Shut up—Aista
Let's go wash our beards—Casigno
casnouy[102]
Give me a knife—quazahca
agoheda[103]
A small axe—Adogne
A bow—Ahenca
An arrow—quahetan
Let's go hunting—Casigno
donnascat[104]
A stag (deer)—Aionnesta
Sheep—Asquenondo[105]
A hare—Sourhanda
A dog—Agayo
A goose—Sadeguenda[106]
The road—Adde
Seed of cucumbers or melons—
Casconda
Tomorrow—Achide
The Sky—Quenhia
The Earth—Damga
The Sun—Ysmay
The Moon—Assomaha
Stars—Signehoham
The Wind—Cahoha
[159v] The Sea—Agogasi[107]
The waves of the sea—Coda
An Isle—Cahena
A mountain—ogacha
The Ice—Honnescha
The snow—Camsa
The cold—Athau[108]
The warmth—odazani[109]
The Fire—Azista

Allons laver la barbe.

103 Ramusio has *buzahca agoheda.*

104 Ramusio has *Quasigno donnascat.*

105 This translation is evidently a mistake by Ramusio's typographer—for it is intended to summarize the statement in Cartier (See Biggar, *Voyages*, p. 244), *de dains ilz dient que se sont moutons & les appellent Asquenondo,* which means "of deer they say they are sheep and call them *Asquenondo*." Ramusio may have then written, *Per daini, Montoni,* for deer, sheep, which appears in his list as *pedaini Montoni*.

106 Cartier and Ramusio have given the word for "geese."

107 Ramusio has *agogasy*.

108 Ramusio has *atahu*.

109 Ramusio gives the adjective "warm."

The smoke – quea
A house – Canoca
(Fava) beans – sahe
A land – Canada[110]
My father – Adatthy[111]
My mother – Aadanahoe[112]
My brother – Addagrim
My sister – Adhoasseue
Cinnamon – Adhotathny

[403r] Isle of the Assumption [Continuation]

Furthermore, on the subject of this Isle of Assumption:[113] [it] lies to the northeast and west-southwest of Cape Trenot[114] and is at fifty degrees latitude, and the end of this [isle] is to the southwest at forty-eight degrees and a half, being five leagues long. Its [other] end is toward the mainland to the north. Cape Trenot and this Isle of Assumption lie southwest, northeast, and southwest a little to the northwest and are thirty-four leagues distant from each other.[115] It is a beautiful land without any mountain lying over white rocks like alabaster, all covered with trees up to the edge of the sea with many wild beasts like bears, lynxes, [and] porcupines. In the direction of Cape Breton there could be fifty leagues distance between them.[116] Taking the northwest route from there to Cape of Mount Nostredame, which is in the land of the southern part,

110 Cartier has *ils appellent une ville* [city] (*Canada*). Ramusio simply wrote *una terra* to mean city or land. Thevet followed Ramusio and wrote *une terre* meaning land or country.

111 Ramusio has *addathy*.

112 Ramusio has *adanahoe*.

113 In the interim between the writing of the first section of the Isle of the Assumption and this addition, Thevet has come across the *Routier* of Jean Alfonse (see Introduction). Most of the remaining Canadian section is from this source. We have used the text of Alfonse's *Routier* contained in Biggar, *Voyages*, pp. 278–303.

114 This name appears in several variations on early maps. Alfonse's spelling (*Thiennot*) agrees with that of Cartier. See Biggar, *Voyages*, pp. 77, 99, 286; and Ganong, *Crucial Maps*, p. 332.

115 Alfonse says twenty-four leagues; Hakluyt's text gives twenty-two. See Biggar, *Voyages*, pp. 286 and n10.

116 This sentence, about the fifty leagues distance between the Isle of Assumption and Cape Breton appears in Thevet and Hakluyt, but not in Jean Alfonse, as read by Biggar and Musset. Biggar, *Voyages*, p. 288n3, says that Hakluyt inserted this sentence, but the chances of both Hakluyt and Thevet doing so independently, and in the same place, are very small. Our inference is that Hakluyt copied this from a version of Alfonse's *Routier* furnished by Thevet (see Introduction).

you have only fifteen leagues. This Cape lies at fifty-nine degrees,[117] [and] it is very high land. The point of the Isle of Assumption and the Cape of Ognedor,[118] which projects two leagues into the sea, are northeast and southwest and are twenty-five leagues distant. Cape Ognedor has a point at the very end which is white. This cape on the northeast is all white rocks.[119] Between this cape and our Isle of Assumption, on the side of the southwest and the east west [sic], the route is only twenty leagues and the Bay of Cods is [at] forty-eight degrees. The coast lies north and south and at a quarter of northeast and southwest as far as Chaleur Bay which is distant from the Mountains of Notre Dame some fourteen leagues.[120] All this land is high and covered with trees. As for Ognedor it is another bay which lies to the north-northwest and the south-southwest, having a very good port whose entrance is on the north side. At the end of this entrance there is a very long point extending into the sea. If thou wouldst drop anchor there thou wilt find there fifteen or twenty fathoms of water.[121] People often take on fresh water there because there are two fine rivers the source of which comes from the northwest and which discharge their water to the southeast.

On this coast there is much cod fishing and the fish there [are] much better than in Newfoundland. There are several species of flying animals such as ducks, wild geese, [and] herons, and there are all sorts of trees like we have, even rose-bushes, raspberries, filberts, pears, and wild walnuts. Also I can inform the reader that in this Isle of Assumption it is warmer in some months of the year than in many parts of France. And as for the seven islands which are on the north side they lie southeast, west, or northwest. There are twenty-four leagues distance from Cape Ognedor to the Seven Isles and thirty-five from Cape Nostre Dame [and] for him who wishes to go from it to the other one has to go north. The Seven Isles are at fifty and one-half degrees of latitude. From the aforesaid Seven Isles to Point d'Ongea which lie northwest to southwest there might be fifteen leagues. And there are between the two several uninhabited isles which are in rather distant vicinity to Point d'Ongea and the Nostre Dame

117 Alfonse and Hakluyt give forty-nine degrees. See Biggar, *Voyages*, p. 288 and n4.

118 Hakluyt gives *Ognedoc*, Biggar has *Onguedo*, and Musset *Ouguedo*. See Biggar, *Voyages*, pp. 103n68 and 288n6, for a discussion of the various spellings of this name.

119 In the DPI Thevet here adds the sentence: "They say there is a silver mine there."

120 Here Thevet is closely copying from Alfonse, but has added the distance of fourteen leagues, given by neither Alfonse nor Hakluyt. See Biggar, *Voyages*, p. 290.

121 Sporadically from here on, Thevet (uncharacteristically) uses the *tu* forms of the verb.

Mountains. On the south side Point d'Ongea and the Caen River lie east and west. The route is but twelve leagues from the one to the other. In sum, all these lands between the Isle of Assumption and the Caen River are good and there are found all kinds of trees.

Point d'Ongea is at forty-nine degrees one-quarter and the Caen River and the Isle of Raquelle lie northeast and southwest and are twelve leagues distant.[122] The Isle of Raquelle is at forty-eight degrees and two-thirds. Eight leagues from there you will find another low isle which is rather close to the land. If you go on further to go around, [403v] Cape Marble[123] presents itself before you, which you discover from three good leagues distance in the sea. Between this cape and Raquelle there is very little distance, and they come close to the mainland to the north about two leagues. The Isle of Raquelle and the entrance to the Saguenay River are east-northeast [and] west-southwest: the distance is fourteen leagues.

The entrance of the Saguenay is a white rock which lies at forty-eight degrees forty-two minutes of latitude. The entrance is no wider than a quarter league. It is as dangerous as possible for large vessels because it can have no more than eight to ten fathoms of water. It bears to the southwest. Having gone two or three leagues up the said river it begins to widen and seems like a large arm of the sea. The savages told us that, having learned from their forefathers, they believed that this arm of the sea continued on to the Pacific Ocean which they call Quastroy.[124] About this these poor barbarians might be mistaken, just as Gemma Frisius and some ancients and moderns are judged to be mistaken and deceived, marking on their maps a northern detour. In which was mistaken Martin Fourbicher, Englishman, who for five years has been beating his brains out to pass from the [Atlantic] Sea to that of the South [Sea] through this northern detour, as Magellan and Pigafete did through the Southern Strait.[125] Moreover, this Saguenay is marvelously full [of water] and four or five leagues wide as I have mentioned in several places, having many

122 The names in this sentence and preceeding paragraph are clearly based on Alfonse's account (see Biggar, *Voyages*, pp. 289–91, 290n8, 291n7). See also Ganong, *Crucial Maps*, p. 347, fig. 92, for the *sep[t] isles* on the 1554 map of Lopo Homem.

123 Biggar identifies Cape Marble as Cape Arignole (*Voyages*, p. 292n3).

124 Ganong accepts *Quastroy* as one of Thevet's "interpolations presumably supplied by Cartier" (*Crucial Maps*, pp. 431–2).

125 "Fourbicher," of course, is Sir Martin Frobisher. On Frobisher's voyages see George Best, *The Three Voyages of Martin Frobisher in Search of a Passage to Cathay and India by the North-west A.D. 1576–8*, ed. Vilhjalmur Stefansson and E. McCaskill, 2 vols. (London, 1938). Thevet's *Singularitez* was in his ship's library. See George B. Parks, *Richard Hakluyt and the English Voyages* (New York, 1928), p. 46.

banks and rocks. In which gulf [the St. Lawrence] you will find the Isle of Raquellay and the Isle of Hares, which lie northeast and southwest and a little east-northwest.[126] The crossing from there to Saguenay might be eighteen leagues. The entrance of the Saguenay and the Isle of Hares lie north-northwest. The crossing is of five leagues. So there you have the route of the [main]land as well as of the Isle of Assumption which lies next to it, begging the reader if I have been too prolix to excuse the zeal that I have to show new mariners the route they must observe in these regions, which they should greatly esteem.

[404r] Isle of the Damoiselle

It seems to me that I have rather fully discoursed to you on the mores and fashions of the Canadians and other peoples who are their neighbors. There only remains, methinks, to speak to you of an isle named La Damoiselle and of the route one has to take to make land there. I know well that the way I shall take will be a bit dangerous for the reader, [but] nevertheless useful and profitable for pilots and mariners. And because hitherto I have found no one whatever who has wanted to take the time to explain to us the route to those regions,[127] it seemed good to me not to practice ingratitude with respect to those who are experts in pilotage by proposing to them this route, [and] the dangers and inconveniences into which they might get if they are not sure about the passages and the localities, capes, rivers, gulfs, harbors, promontories, and roads, and the latitudes in which these dangers are to be found. For which you should note that I have spoken to you in several places before of Cape Race and the way to the Great Bay, not very well known to the moderns and to the ancients because of not having researched it.

Cape Race then and Cape Spear both lie northeast and southwest, counting from one to the other one degree which makes seventeen and one-half leagues. Cape Race is at forty-seven degrees of latitude and [Cape] Spear at forty-nine and two-thirds of a degree. Between the two is found the bay of Rongneuse.[128] There might be a distance of two good leagues one from the other by sea. In the middle of the route there is a bad rock very much feared and very dangerous of approach, shaped in the likeness of a ship. Cape Spear and the land of Baccaleos lie north and

126 The Isle of Hares is also mentioned by Cartier and Alfonse. See Biggar, *Voyages*, pp. 234 and n80, and 293.

127 This is another example of Thevet's hypocrisy, since most of this is being closely copied from Alfonse.

128 This is present-day Renewse harbor. See Biggar, *Voyages*, pp. 240, 279.

south a quarter of northeast counting fourteen leagues from the one to the other. Baccaleos lies at forty-eight degrees and a half in latitude, and Baccaleos, Grand Bay and the Isle of the Apponas [Great Auks] lie north and south, taking a quarter of northeast and southwest and there is in the route thirty-five leagues at fifty degrees and a half [latitude]. The sea in these localities is somewhat weedy and dangerous to large and medium vessels because of the rocks [which are] low and at water-level [and] are often covered with water when the sea is agitated by winds. Especially are to be seen two rocks between the Isle of the Apponas and the Belles Isles, which lie northwest and southeast taking a quarter of north and south, counting from one to the other some three leagues. These Belles Isles are at fifty-one degrees thirty-two minutes of latitude.

If you want to sail from the Belles Isles and take the route northeast-southwest, beware when you are about twelve leagues from them of a little uninhabited isle named le Carpon [Carpunt], which is at fifty-two degrees latitude. Carpon and Belle Isle, which is in Grand Bay, lie north-east and southwest. To go anchor at Belle Isle about which I have spoken to you before and presented a map, and it lies at fifty-two and one-half degrees.[129] If you want to take on water there you have to beware of the east wind [404v] (which is very much against you and [blows] almost daily), for fear that you may shipwreck by lying over against the west coast. From its coast a half league or thereabouts you will approach a rock which is between the said Belle Isle and the Carpon. And on the east there is another flat uninhabited islet populated by birds. If you go northwest again you will find a flat rock, which might be a quarter league long surrounded by reefs and sands.

And as to Carpon, if thou wouldst go anchor there on the port or starboard side, thou shouldst approach as directly as possible. And thou mayest anchor between this Carpon and three little uninhabited isles. Having weighed anchor thou wilt leave the port on the northeast following the coast to the west as far as a shoal which thou shalt leave on the port side. And [thou] wilt take the north because of the dangers which might ensue, until thou gettest as far as the buttes which are three little points of land sticking up, which thou wilt sail by rather distant from the north shore a league and a half from the mainland.

Having passed beyond and avoided the dangers, the coast is followed to Belle Isle of Grand Bay and the Isles de Sablon which are rather close to it, continuing to pursue the route in order to learn the dangers of

129 Thevet has obviously omitted a thought in the middle of this sentence. There is no map here.

this Canadian [coast]. Thou wilt take the northeast-west and a little of the southwest. One counts thirty leagues from Grand Bay, which has an entrance of seven leagues, as far as Blanc Sablon some thirty-three leagues, and thou wilt continue the route as far as the Three Castles,[130] which are three high mountains which can be seen in the open sea from four to five leagues [distance]; between which[131] was found a gold mine at least as good as that of Peru [South America]. This was long kept secret for fear that the Spaniards and others might take possession of it and fortify themselves there. Blanc Sablon has eight leagues open sea to the mainland. All this coast of Blanc Sablon is low and healthy and lies north and east; and Blanc Sablon is at fifty-two and two-thirds degrees. This place is so named because the sea is very sandy there with a certain fine sand white as new fallen snow.

From Blanc Sablon to go to France Roy[132] which is the country of Canada proper is found on the way this very beautiful island called the Isle of the Damoiselle, so called because it was on it that was exiled the niece of Captain Roberval. Afterwards she was transported with her lover to another isle which might be about seventeen leagues distant from this one as I have rather fully described in my book of the Singularities.[133] This isle, which is surrounded by several islets and little islands, and [the Isle of] [405r] Blanc Sablon lie east-northeast, east, southwest and a little east and west. It lies at fifty-three and three-quarters degrees latitude and has a good port which opens up from the northeast, and [the] said port has in its width no more than about the length of three pikes. At its entrance a little to the left is found a rock which you leave on your port side and you will cast anchor after having heaved the lead [taken soundings] at twenty fathoms across from rather near to a little cove.[134] If thou wouldst leave it having weighed anchor it must be by the

130 This is again probably a misreading of Cartier's baye des Chasteaux (The Strait of Belle Isle).

131 Written above, then continued in the margin. No known source of Thevet mentions any gold mine in this location.

132 Alfonse's text does not name the fort, but the term France-Roy appears in Hakluyt. See Biggar, *Voyages*, p. 295. The map of Nicolas Vallard of 1547 gives us what may be the best contemporary illustration of France-Roy (see map 15).

133 Thevet does not tell this story in the *Singularitez*. Other versions of the story do not have her changing location from one island to another. This location and ensuing description of the island point definitively to Alfonse as Thevet's principal source for this information.

134 This "little cove," originating in the account of Alfonse, and transmitted by Thevet, has appeared in most of the derivative accounts of the exiled *Damoiselle*.

southwest side, leaving the said isle to the starboard, and when thou art outside (with the square foresail or mizzen, for fear of being surprised by a squall) thou wilt approach several other uninhabited islets covered with trees, which thou wilt keep on thy starboard. Then thou wilt take the southwest until thou seest five rocks about a half league from land. Leaving the Isle of the Damoiselle, thou wilt sail for Newfoundland which is not more than thirty-four leagues distant. From there thou wilt sail for Cape Breton running north-northeast and south-southwest.

I had forgotten to tell you that between the Isle of the Damoiselle and that of Blanc Sablon there are a greater number of little isles and islets, for the most part uninhabited, in which there are good ports and harbors where vessels can be in surety, some populated with men and the others with birds of prey such as falcons, lanners, tiercels, and others, [and] of eagles, as many or more.[135] Having passed the said isles you raise Cape Trenot which lies northeast and west-southwest. There are en route eighteen leagues. Cape Trenot lies at fifty-one and one-quarter degrees.[136] It extends well into the New Land seventy leagues from Cape Breton. And there are between the Isles of the Damoiselle and Cape Trenot six or seven other isles. Furthermore, the said Cape is very close on both sides to an isle named The Lost Isle which is dangerous for vessels.[137]

I believe that it was in this [Isle of the Damoiselle] that Lord Roberval intended to construct a fortress when one day he made his Saguenay River voyage accompanied by the Gentlemen de Lespinay, Labrosse, Longeval and others, and by a number of soldiers embarked in another little ship; there came up a wind which overturned the ship in which were the said soldiers who were all drowned.[138] This Cape is near to another Isle named Assumption lying west-northwest which I told you about above.

[405v] Isle of Orleans

It is a question of knowing that when this Canadian land was first discovered by the French in order to found a new colony there, they penetrated

135 Neither Alfonse nor Hakluyt mention eagles.

136 Thevet here again agrees with Hakluyt, and both differ from Alfonse, who has fifty degrees (cf. Biggar, *Voyages*, p. 286).

137 Thevet here appears to be confusing Alfonse's statement that five or six leagues from Cape Thiennot is "a lost isle." See Biggar, *Voyages*, p. 286.

138 This information appears to have been available only from the account of Roberval, now known only from the English translation in Hakluyt. Thevet, however, may have possessed this narrative (see Introduction). For more on the names of Roberval's men see Biggar, *Voyages*, p. 263.

the coast of this country as well as the environs and rivers of the same, being desirous of immortalizing the name and memory of the kings and princes of France. Having set foot on land in some noteworthy spot or on some isles, they gave them the name of a prince or princess of France as they did with this Isle of Orleans in honor of a French royal prince who was alive then and was named Louis [error for Charles] of Valois, Duke of Orleans, son of this great King François of Valois, the first of the name, of which isle I represent the map for you.[139]

One must also know that having passed by in this great River of Hochelaga several promontories, such as that of Saint Peter in the Gulf of St. Lawrence, Cape of St. Lois, Cape of Mount Morency, Isle Serree,[140] the Isle Jayple, the Seven Isles which adjoin the mainland to the right, the Saguenay River, and the River of Canada, which bears the name of the whole country, there presents itself nearby another isle which is called the Isle of the Hares, which lies northeast and south-southwest at five leagues from the Saguenay River [and] eight from [the] Raquelle River which lies northwest and south-southwest. Having traversed all these islands and islets, leaving behind New France which was the country of Canada and Hochelaga proper, all the country tends to the southwest [it is] a beautiful country luxuriant and fertile. The flat country, which one could cultivate and make flower if there were not so much barbarity among this people which inhabits it, [is] all covered with trees down to the water's edge.

The north coast is higher is some places because of the mountains which lie southward starting from the Isle of the Hares, so named by a friend of mine who being the first to set foot on land, perceived before him a number of hares similar to ours except that they have longer and thicker fur.[141] At the location of this isle and that of Orleans this great River of Hochelaga at this point is no wider than four leagues at the most. The isle is at the very middle of the Hochelaga River on the route to the Lake of Angoulême, which is more or less where the said river widens out to more than fifteen leagues around. The length of our isle is almost east-west and might be about five leagues and one and one-half in [406r] width. This spot is navigable for vessels of forty or fifty tons. It is neighbored by a great number of little isles and rocks. The air there is rather temperate. [These isles there are][142] often inhabited by savages

139 If the map were ever part of the manuscript of *Grand Insulaire* it is no longer there.

140 This name may be a deformation of the baie de Sois or Sorroies on the Le Testu map (1555). See Ganong, *Crucial Maps*, p. 265.

141 The account of the naming of the island by Cartier is in Biggar, *Voyages*, p. 234.

142 The words in brackets here are from the DPI.

who erect huts to take the fish with which the river is populated. From the Isle of Orleans to the Isles of Couldres [Hazelnut-trees] the route lies east-northeast and west-southwest distant one from the other some twelve leagues.[143] And you always have to hug the high land on the north. It [Isle d'Orleans] is surrounded by reefs and shoals as is the Isle of Couldres which is neither as wide nor as short. And because the sea [tide] runs into it there is greater danger. The Isle of Couldres is about one league long by half a league wide [and] all covered with trees in the area facing south, but this is all banks and sands. Isle of Couldres lies at forty-seven degrees three-quarters of longitude [error for latitude].

Having left this isle to go to the Isle of Orleans one must take the northeast and the southwest and the route is ten and one-half leagues. To avoid the banks and shoals you have to hug the high ground to the north about a quarter of a league because in the middle of this river as I have said there is nothing but banks and rocks. And when thou shalt pass by Round Cape[144] thou shalt traverse the south coast toward the southwest in which place thou shalt find seven to eight fathoms of water, and thereabouts begins the fresh water, and in this place the bitterness of the salt water ends. And when thou shalt pass by the Isle of Orleans where the fresh water begins, if thou wilt pass beyond thou shalt hold thy course to the middle of the river leaving the isle to the starboard side which is on the right hand. Although at this point the river is only a quarter of a league wide it is very very deep, fifteen to twenty fathoms. You will have the coast towards the south where you will find an abundance of isles for the most part uninhabited, all green with trees and bushes. This island route on the port side and point of the Isle of Orleans are [sic] pleasant [and] the air there is very fine and good. From the said Isle of Orleans to the great river there might be five leagues. It has about five leagues length and a league and a half width.[145]

On the north coast there is another river which is called Lestendue ["extended"] which is [on the] right hand and faces a promontory named Raguine, which is divided from another promontory named Passel by

143 In Alfonse's account and in Hakluyt, the distance to the Isle des Couldres from the Isle d'Orleans is ten leagues. The Isle aux Couldres was discovered by Cartier on his second voyage, and so named because his men found there a grove of trees bearing hazelnuts. See Biggar, *Voyages*, pp. 119, 294.

144 This name may derive from Alfonse's phrase *d'un hault cap, lequel est rond* "Of a high cape which is round." See Biggar, *Voyages*, p. 294.

145 This sentence has been crossed out by Thevet but like much of this description, is from Alfonse. See Biggar, *Voyages*, p. 295.

another river named in the language of the savages Pabecherib, which has its source in the Green Mountains inhabited by a certain people which wars on our Canadians. Once you have passsed the great Lake of Angoulême and also this little archipelago, which is right at the end of the river, you find the country of Chilague and that of Tortimage where those who inhabit these regions are worse than devils. They do not pardon their enemies and eat them like the Americans [Brazilians] do. Ships, as I have [406v] said, provided that they are not too large or too heavily loaded, can go cast anchor as far as our Isle of Orleans from which to the land of Canada proper are to be found several large and medium rivers. Some have their sources to the west, others in the northeast, and having made a thousand turns and meanders go render their tribute to the great river [of Hochelaga].

From the end of the above-mentioned isle to the west of Canada there are only three leagues to France Roy and when thou shalt be at the end of the isle thou shalt see a great river named Ochelaga which is rather distant from our Isle of Orleans. Franceroy [sic], where Roberval had a fine fortress constructed, is at forty-seven and one-sixth degrees. All these lands in my day were called New France (since it is just as good and as temperate as our France and at the same latitude). And the reason why it is colder in winter is that the fresh-water river is naturally colder than the sea; it is just as wide and deep in some spots. That happens also because the land is not cultivated nor inhabited by people plus the fact that it is all covered by trees which cause coldness. The sun has a meridian as high as the meridian of Angoulême the place of my birth, and has its noon when the sun is in the south-southwest. Also the North Star by the compass is in the north-northeast. And when in Angoulême [it] is noon, at France Roy and on our Isle of Orleans it is only nine-thirty A.M.[146]

The coast of New France as far as the Isle of Orleans has no point higher than fifty-six leagues [error for degrees]. From the entrance to Norambegue there must be 150 leagues by land, and from Norambegue to the Nodder River[147] [there are] three hundred leagues, and from

146 This passage is practically word for word from Alfonse, but the latter's comparison of times is between "Canada" (the town or province) and La Rochelle, and he says that when it is noon in the latter it is but six o'clock in the morning in the former. Hakluyt compares "Rochel" and France-Roy and says that at noon in the former it is "but halfe an houre past nine" in the latter. Thevet does the same, but substitutes the name of his birthplace, Angoulême, for La Rochelle and adds the Isle d'Orléans to France-Roy for good measure. Cf. Biggar, *Voyages*, p. 297n4.

147 It appears that Thevet's River *Nodder* is based on a misreading of Alfonse's sentence

Ochelaga about eighty leagues. From there, in this same gulf or river you have Saguenay, having left the great bay or extremity of the river which lies northeast west-southwest in the direction of Ochelaga. The lands are better and more fertile and furnished with soil than the other regions. This country is abundance [sic] in all goods, principally in wild game, fruit trees in abundance, very many figs, pears, and others.

I reckon if one dug in the summits and slopes of the mountains, gold and silver would be found there according to the accounts of these peoples. They assert that in the southwest there is a great city named Sebolla which is at thirty-five degrees. The houses of this city and temples of their idols are covered with gold and others with silver. According to them these lands abut against oriental Tartarie which [407r] is Asiatic according to the roundness of the world.[148]

[For] he who would like to travel this coast and see [it] from one end to the other, the pilot would have to observe from place to place and from one point to another the route as explained by me with two or three little ships of sixty-five tons to navigate the coasts in New France as far as Florida. Large ships are not suitable both on account of the entrance to the gulfs and for the dangerous rocks and reefs of which the adjoining and abutting areas are full; plus the fact that the soundings are reliable only for medium vessels if one does not wish to run the risk of shipwreck. From Norambegue to Florida[149] is the most pleasant passage there is in the whole universe and you would say, sailing along the land, that you were in the best [part] of France. You find there most of the same trees that we have here like oaks, ash, elms, maples, pines, firs, cedars, quaking aspen, wild walnuts, and several [kinds of] fruit trees.

The old men of the country say there is a beast bearing a single horn on the forehead, similar to those that Pliny and other authors tell of being

---

Et de Norombègue à la Fleuride . . . with *Fleuride* somehow transformed into *fleuve Nodder* (cf. Biggar, *Voyages*, p. 297). The same error appears in the text of the DPI.

148 These last two sentences are practically verbatim from Alfonse (see Biggar, *Voyages*, p. 298). For more on the seven cities of Cibola see Carl O. Sauer, *The Road to Cibola* (Berkeley, 1932); George Hammond and Agapito Rey, eds., *Narratives of the Coronado Expedition, 1540-1542* (Albuquerque, 1940); and Herbert E. Bolton, *Coronado: Knight of Pueblos and Plains* (New York, 1949). See also Thevet's section on Mexico in the *Cosmographie*, chap. 15: "On the Province of Mexico" (fol. 990r), where he says that Cibola is very rich in pelts.

149 The geographical limits of "Florida" during the early sixteenth century were indefinite, but by mid-century it was chiefly confined to the southeast region of North America. See William P. Cummings, *The Southeast in Early Maps* (Chapel Hill, N.C., 1952), p. 2. Whether by accident or not, Thevet is accurate in his description of this part of North America.

in Africa and Asia, which the simple people say must be unicorns. As for me I never believed it and I am a heretic on the existence of unicorns as I declared my reasons [for] in my Cosmographie, no more [than I believe] in euphones, dryads or hamadryads.[150] Also, in my day they sowed a little wheat which came to maturity and they found that there were twenty-eight grains to the head [ear], the same as we have here. It must not be sown before March and harvest can be made in mid-August. The waters are the best in the world. If the land there were cultivated and full of people, the country [would be] as warm and temperate as over here. The reason that it snows more there than in France is because it hardly rains [there], the rain being converted into snow. There are beautiful forests in which one can ride horseback and indeed charge with the lance if need be.[151]

Roberval, viceroy in Canada, arrived there accompanied by two hundred soldiers and mariners for his escort.[152] One month after he had visited the land he had a very beautiful house built, around which there were two rather strong towers situated on a small mountain in order to prevail against the barbarity of the inhabitants. He went to great expense in this since in the said house he had several bedrooms constructed, two living-rooms, and several cellars and granaries; but without having anything to fill them. Afterwards he had two water-mills constructed there and not being satisfied with the grandeur and beauty of the said dwelling, he had another begun at the end of a little river, named in the language of the barbarians Sinagua. Roberval, seeing that [407v] provisions were failing from day to day, sent several ships to France in the charge of the Seigneur de Sauveterre to inform the King François I that they could not keep this country, being deprived of all commodities as in truth they were, because of wheat, pork-fat, flour, cider, and wine there was none. Among other things what was left of wine had frozen in the ships and if he had not been succored by the savages he and his men would have been at an ill pass.

This poor people, even though it is barbarous and living without faith

---

150 These are various forms of forest nymphs.

151 The conclusion of this paragraph corresponds to the end of the account of Jean Alfonse as reported by Hakluyt. It is significant that Thevet's close use of Alfonse also stops at this point, and that Thevet here goes to the Roberval account, also known only from Hakluyt.

152 This figure, as well as most of the remainder of the text of the *Grand Insulaire*, is from Roberval's account. See Biggar, *Voyages*, p. 263. Morison guesses the number to be 150. See his *European Discovery*, p. 448.

and without law, are [sic] nevertheless charitable. Considering the poverty of [these] afflicted foreigners, deprived thus of all resources, they strove day and night to hunt wild game and to fish, so that having taken a quantity of fish like Alloses[153] and salmon, for a little knife or a brush hook they would give our men about thirty of these fish. This famine lasted six whole months, during which time there came among them a great illness of pestilential fevers from which most of the savages died.[154] Then our men were forced to go fishing or die of hunger, and had to gather hither and yon certain plants and roots to eat, having boiled them in seal oil or whale grease. And it was told to me by several of the company that some of them ate mushrooms, cooking them on the fire without salt or butter, of which several died from not having seasoned and prepared them as we do here. The vessels having returned, God knows how famished the poor soldiers and sailors were.

Captain Roberval was very cruel to his men, forcing them to work at their trades otherwise they were deprived of food and drink. He insisted on their living in peace according to his decrees, which he caused to be strictly kept. For if someone transgressed he had him punished. And one day he had six of them hanged even though they were his favorites, [and] among others one named Michel Gaillon, Jehan de Nantes and others. He had several exiled on an island with irons on their legs for having been caught in a theft not exceeding five Tours cents.[155] Others were whipped for the same offense, men as well as women and for having fought and harmed one another. Even though the savages were barbarous some of them wept and lamented the misfortunes of our men.

These people are handsome and almost all naked, clothed [only] in the skins of animals cured in the open air; these skins being sown the ones against the others covering their entire body the men as well as the women. Their breeches, upper and lower, and their shoes are of leather. They have neither shirts nor bonnets but have their heads covered with their hair tucked up and tied with kinds of bands of bark detached from trees.[156] As for their food, they eat all their meat without salting it. They dry meat and fish which they carry with them in war. Cold is continual

153 These are similar to sardines, and are possibly smelt.

154 In Roberval's account it is "our people" who fell ill and died, not the natives. See Biggar, *Voyages*, p. 267.

155 This money, according to Littré's *Dictionnaire*, was weaker by a fifth than that struck at Paris.

156 These details are similar to those from the Roberval account. Thevet, however, has added the "bands of bark detached from trees." See Biggar, *Voyages*, p. 268.

in that country from St. Martin's Day [11 November] in the winter until mid-April and the ices are big and thick.[157]

157 Up to this point, Thevet's *Grand Insulaire* and *Description de plusieurs isles* contain virtually the same material on Canada. The latter work, however, contains additional material which is given in the next chapter.

Description de plusieurs isles

Isle of Orleans

[126r] . . . Before entering upon the description of this new country I do not want to forget to tell you that the sea in this place and in many others of this coast is very grassy [seaweed] and there is good fishing there, among others of whales and other fish which the savages dry as soon as they have caught them. These they sell and barter to foreigners, along with the furs which they use for their clothing. And as for the whale, when they have taken some they eat their flesh, of which they are marvelously fond. As for the grease [blubber], they melt it, and it becomes as clear as oil, and they use it as a beverage as do the Ethiopians with olive oil, which I have seen [them] drink. If anything is left over they rub themselves with it and anoint their entire bodies. The weeds that grow in this sea do not come so close up to the surface of the water as does that which you see in the Gulf of Cuba. It is in this sea [Gulf of St. Lawrence] that these whales come because of the seaweed which they eat, together with large quantities of fish which abound there, including mackerel, smelt, herring and divers other sorts of little fish which they [whales] swallow rather than big ones, because they have very narrow throats. [The whales] cause the little fish to come to the surface because they disturb the weeds which cover them.

Furthermore [illegible character] this present year 1588, from this Isle of Orleans certain savages conducted a merchant pilot of the Basque country, of the City of St. Jean de Luc [Luz] to [a place] one hundred leagues from there, to a certain mountain where they led him to believe that there was a good gold deposit. Having arrived at a port named by the barbarians Gaspay[1] which is rather near the South Sea, instead of

1 This name has an interesting history. It is given in the English translations of Alfonse by Hakluyt, Stephens, and Baxter, but not in the French versions of Alfonse given by Musset and Biggar. See, respectively, Richard Hakluyt, *The Principal Navigations*

finding gold they found only red metal, pure and net [rich], of which he brought back a quantity to France, and gave me some. From there they boated to a little islet named Nenan by the savages, on which no Christian had ever been, which afterwards was called the Isle of Metal.[2]

Voyages Traffiques & Discoveries of the English Nation, second ed. (1598–1600; reprinted Glasgow, 1903–5; New York, 1965), 8: 277; Hiram B. Stephens, *Jacques Cartier and his Four Voyages to Canada* (Montreal, 1890), p. 119; James P. Baxter, *Memoir of Jacques Cartier* (New York, 1906), p. 251; Jean Alfonse de Saintonge, *La Cosmographie avec l'espère et régime du soleil et du nord par Jean Fonteneau dit Alfonse de Saintonge, Capitaine-pilote de Français Ier, publiée et annotée par Georges Musset* (Paris, 1904), p. 487n1; and H.P. Biggar, *The Voyages of Jacques Cartier* (Ottawa, 1924), p. 289n3. Thevet, however, uses the word in a context entirely different from that of Alfonse. This would appear to be the first recorded use of this place name. It may derive from the Micmac word meaning "the end." Many versions of this word, including *gachepé*, have been given by various authorities.

2 Thevet's source of information about this island is unknown to us.

PART 2

Florida

Singularitez de la France antarctique

[146r] On the Peninsula of Florida

CHAPTER 74

Since in writing this account we have made some mention of this land called Florida (even though on our return, our route not being in that direction, we would not have come close to it; yet nevertheless we sailed that way to pick up the east wind), it does not seem inappropriate to say something about it, together with the country of Canada which neighbors it to the north, [there] being only a few mountains between them. So pursuing our route at the same latitude as Spain, [bearing] right to get to our Europe, not so quickly nor so directly as we desired, we found rather favorable seas. But, as by pure chance I happened to stick my head out to look at it, as far as my eye could reach I saw it all covered with plants and flowers in some places, the plants almost like our junipers. This immediately made me think that we were close to land, since I had not seen so many in any other part of the sea, but I learned that my opinion was incorrect, [146v] and that they came out of the sea; and so we saw it strewn with these plants for the space of fifteen to twenty days.[1] The sea in this area has hardly any fish, for these places resemble swamps more than anything. Immediately afterwards [there] appeared to us another sign and presage, a comet [going] from east to north: which presages I leave to the astrologers and to the experience anyone may have had. Afterwards (what is even worse) we were driven for the space of nine days by a very contrary wind up to the latitude of our Florida.

This place is a point of land extending a good one hundred leagues into the open sea, twenty-five leagues square, twenty-five and one-half degrees on this side of the line, and one hundred leagues from Cape Baxa

1 Thevet is here referring to the Sargasso Sea, a meadow of floating gulfweed in the mid-Atlantic. See also *Cosmographie*, chap. 1: "On the Peninsula of Florida."

Figure 10 Portrait of Paraousti Satouriona, King of Florida
Thevet's *Vrais Pourtraicts*, fol. 663r.
Courtesy The Newberry Library, Chicago

which is near there.[2] So this great land of Florida is very dangerous to those who sail in the direction of Cathay, Cambalu [Beijing], Panuco, and Themistitan, for in seeing it from afar you would guess that it was an island in the middle of the sea.[3] Further this place is dangerous because of the great, impetuous sea currents which are usual there. As for the mainland of Florida, on its east are the province of Chicoma [Chicora?][4] and the isles named Bahama and Lucaia. On the West there is New Spain, which is divided into the land they call Anahuac,[5] of which we have spoken before. The best and most fertile province of Florida is Paunac,[6] which borders New Spain. The natives of this country [are] strong and very cruel, all idolatrous, who when they need water or sunlight for their gardens and root crops go prosternate themselves before their [147r] idols carved in the form of men or beasts.[7]

Moreover this race is more ingenious and tricky in warfare than are those of Peru [South America]. When they go to war they carry their king in a large animal skin. Those who carry him, four in number, are clothed and adorned with rich plumages. And if it comes to fighting their enemies, they will place their king in the middle of them, all clothed in

2 There are many maps on which the words *baxa*, *baixo*, *baxos*, *basse*, or *bassa* appear. The terms mean low coast or coast of shoals, from the Portuguese.

3 See map 8. For a discussion of representations of Florida as an island, and on maps in general, see Lawrence C. Wroth, *The Voyages of Giovanni da Verrazzano* (New Haven, 1970), "Florida in Pre-Verrazzano maps – The Lusitano-Germanic Group: Cantino, Caveri, Waldseemüller, and their Derivatives," pp. 46–53. Also see David O. True, "Some Early Maps Relating to Florida," *Imago Mundi* 11 (1954): 73–84; and Giuseppe Caraci, "The Reputed Inclusion of Florida in the Oldest Nautical Maps of the New World," ibid. 15 (1960): 32–9.

4 Carl O. Sauer suggests that the term Chicora might come from *Shakori*, the name of a tribe displaced from its coastal home in South Carolina and Georgia and subsequently absorbed by the related Catawbas further inland. See Sauer's *Sixteenth Century North America* (Berkeley, 1971), p. 72. See also Paul Quattlebaum, *The Land Called Chicora: The Carolinas under Spanish Rule with French Intrusions, 1520-1670* (Gainesville, Fla, 1956).

5 For more on Anahuac see Thevet's section on Mexico, *Singularitez*, chap. 73: "Description of New Spain," and *Cosmographie*, chap. 14: "On the Rest of the Mainland."

6 Frederick W. Hodge defined Pánuco as "the region drained by the streams that empty into the Gulf about Tampico." See *The Narrative of Alvar Nuñez Cabeça de Vaca*, in *Spanish Explorers in the Southern United States 1523–1543*, ed. F.W. Hodge and T.H. Lewis (New York, 1907), pp. 1–126, esp. 14n3.

7 Compare Jacques Le Moyne's illustration, "Offering the Skin of a Stag to the Sun," in Stefan Lorant, *The New World: The First Pictures of America* (New York, 1946), plate 35, p. 105.

fine pelts, and he will never leave there until the battle is finished. If they feel themselves the weaker and the king appears to flee, they will not fail to kill him, which is the custom today of the Persians and other barbaric nations of the Levant. The weapons of this people are bows, provided with arrows made of wood bearing poison and pikes, which instead of iron are armed at the end with wild animal bones, well-sharpened however. Some of them eat their enemies when they capture them, as do those of America [Brazil], about whom we have spoken. And although they are idolatrous, as we have already said, still they believe that the soul is immortal; that there is a place set aside for the wicked, which is a very cold region; and that the gods provide punishment for the sins of the wicked. They also believe that there are an infinite number of men in heaven, and as many beneath the earth, and a thousand other follies which are better compared with the transformations [*Metamorphoses*] of Ovid than to anything more worthy than material for laughter.[8] Further they believe in all these things as do the Turks and the Arabs in what is written in their Koran.[9] The part of this country near the sea is infertile. This people is quite uncouth, more than that of Peru [South America], or America [Brazil], [147v] from having little contact with civilized people.

This point of land was named Florida in the year 1512 by its first discoverers, because it was all verdant and adorned with flowers of infinite species and colors.[10] Between this Florida and the Palm river are found divers kinds of monstrous beasts, among others you can see a kind of large bull, having horns only a foot long, and on its back a tumor or hump like a camel's [fig. 11]. The hair is long all over the body, whose color is close to that of a tawny mule, and the hair under his chin is even more so. They once brought two live ones to Spain; I saw the skin only of one of them, and they cannot [148r] live long there. They say that this

8 Ovid's *Metamorphoses* is an epic poem in fifteen books, telling stories ranging in time from creation to the death of Julius Caesar.

9 See also *Cosmographie*, chap. 1: "On the Peninsula of Florida," fol. 1004r.

10 Florida was named because it was discovered on Easter, *Pascua florida*. Although here in the *Singularitez* Thevet says that it was Ponce de Leon, a Spaniard, who discovered Florida, in the *Cosmographie* he asserts that the French and English had been in Florida first. Ponce de Leon's discovery of Florida occurred in 1513 rather than 1512. The question of the proper date is discussed in Henry Harrisse, *The Discovery of North America: A Critical, Documentary, and Historic Investigation* (London and Paris, 1892; reprinted Amsterdam, 1961), pp. 149–50 and esp. 800–1, and in Justin Winsor, ed., *Narrative and Critical History of America*, 8 vols. (Boston, 1884; reprinted New York, 1967) 2: 284n1. See also *Cosmographie*, chap. 1: "On the Peninsula of Florida."

Figure 11 Thevet's illustration of a buffalo
Thevet's *Cosmographie universelle*, fol. 1007v.
Courtesy John Carter Brown Library at Brown University

animal is the perpetual enemy of the horse and cannot bear to have one near him.[11]

From Florida going toward the Promontory of Baxe is found some small river where the slaves fish for oysters, which bear pearls. Now that we have touched on the subject of oyster-gathering, I do not want to omit the method by which the pearls are extracted, in both the East and the West Indies. It is to be noted that each head of a family having a large troop of slaves and not knowing what else to do with them, sends them to the sea to fish (as the saying goes) for oysters. Bringing back to their masters whole scuttle-fulls of them, they put them into certain large vessels, which being full of water cause the oysters, kept there several days, to open: and the water having cleaned them, they let go these stones or pearls into the vessels. The way they get them out is this: first they take the oysters out of the vessel, then draw off the water through a hole, under which is placed a sheet or cloth, so that the pearls do not wash away with the water. As to the shape of these oysters, it is much different from ours both in color and in shell, having each one of them certain little holes that you might think were made artificially in the place where the little pearls on the inside are tied together. That is what I wanted to tell you *en passant*. These [pearls] are also found in Peru [South America], and other [precious] stones in good number: but the finest are found in the Palm river and the Panuco river, which are thirty-two leagues distance from one another.[12] But they [the Spaniards] are not free to fish for them because of the savages [148v] who are not yet all converted, worshipping the heavenly bodies and attributing divinity to the breath,[13] as did those who dwelt among some peoples of the Scythians and Medes.[14]

Sailing along then with the Florida coast to the left due to the wind which was contrary to us, we came very close to Canada, and to another country they call Baccaleos, to our great regret in any case and especially

11 Thevet's information on the bison also appears in the *Cosmographie*, chap. 2: "On the Beverages Used by the Floridians," and in the *Grand Insulaire*, chap. "Isle of Assumption." In the *Grand Insulaire*, Thevet claims that he brought two of the beasts' horns back to Paris after his first voyage. Here, however, he claims only to have seen the skin of one that was brought to Spain.

12 Hodge identified the River of Palms as the Rio de Santander. The Pánuco River was named by Alonso Alvarez de Pineda. See Hodge, *Cabeça de Vaca*, p. 14n3, and Winsor, *Critical History*, 2: 237.

13 The traditional association of breath with the soul or spirit is attested to etymologically by the Latin *anima*, which means both breath and spirit, and by its French and German cognates *âme* and *Atem*, which still preserve this dual meaning.

14 In the remainder of this section of the *Singularitez* Thevet discusses Canada.

on account of the excessive cold which tormented us for the space of eighteen days. This land of Baccaleos extends very far into the open sea from the north coast in the form of a point a good two hundred leagues, at only forty-eight degrees distance from the line. This point is called "of the Baccales," from a kind of fish which is found in the surrounding seas, which they call *Baccales*: between this and Cape del Gado there are divers inhabited isles difficult to approach however because of the numerous rocks with which they are surrounded: and they are called the Isles of Cortez. Others think they are not islands, but mainland, attached to this point of Baccaleos.[15]

[Baccaleos] was first discovered by Sebastian Babate [sic] an Englishman, who persuaded the King of England Henry the Seventh that he could easily get from there to the country of Cathay by the north, and thus would find spices and other things, as had done the King of Portugal in the Indies: he also proposed going to Peru [South America] and America [Brazil] to colonize the country with new inhabitants and set up a New England there, which he did not carry out. To be sure he set three hundred men ashore on the North Ireland coast, where the cold killed almost the entire company, even though it was in the month of July.[16] Afterwards Jacques Quartier (as he [149r] himself told me) made two voyages to the same country, that is in the year 1534 and 1535.[17]

15 The general outlines of the area here described by Thevet are well illustrated on Mercator's map of 1538, which shows a protruding Baccalaos region with an *Insulae Corterealis* off the coast. Thevet's "Isle of Cortez" might be a misreading of *Corte*, as some maps abbreviated the *Terra Corterealis*.

16 This information appears to be based on the description given by Peter Martyr in his *De Orbe Novo: The Eight Decades of Peter Martyr d'Anghera*, Trans. from the Latin with Notes and Introduction by Francis A. MacNutt, 2 vols. (New York, 1912), decade 3, book 6, I: 347. It must be remembered, however, that Thevet claimed to have met with Sebastian Cabot for nine days at Cartier's home at St. Malo. James A. Williamson believes that Thevet here is confusing accounts of Peter Martyr, the proposed 1552 expedition of the Duke of Northumberland, and the ill-fated voyage of Sir Hugh Willoughby in 1553–4. See Williamson, *The Cabot Voyages and Bristol Discovery under Henry VII* (Cambridge, 1962), p. 155. See also *Grand Insulaire*, chap. "Isle of Cedars in Florida."

17 Thevet mentions neither Cartier's 1524 voyage (if it ever took place), nor that of 1541. However, there is some evidence that he was familiar with the account of the latter voyage (see Introduction).

Cosmographie universelle (Book 23)

[1000v] On the Peninsula of Florida and the Surrounding Country
CHAPTER 1

Before proceeding with the description of the country of Florida and the customs of the natives, I want to describe somewhat the distances of the places between Iucatan and it, in order to furnish information to mariners.[1] The entire Mexican or Iucatanic gulf (as it is named) extends from one peninsula to the other in the form of an arc or crescent which seems to complete a circle, since the two points extend into the sea towards each other and they could not be more than three hundred leagues from each other; while if you went from one to the other following the coastline it would be a good 1100 leagues according to my calculations. From the Promontory of Iucatan, which is facing north, to Round Promontory is ninety leagues. From this Cape to Grinialue River [there are] one hundred leagues, from Grinialue to that of Coacacoalco [Coazacualco] fifty, and from this to the Alvarado River another fifty.

From this river (which the savages call *Papaloapan*) to that which has been named the True Cross [there are] forty leagues; from that to the Panuque River, eighty leagues; from Panuque to the River of Palms, which is directly below the Tropic of Cancer, forty [leagues]. From this [River of Palms] to the Beautiful River, which is in the Province of Topiratoue, is one hundred leagues, and from it to the one called Magdelaine [River], seventy. Forty leagues from this lies the one called Golden, which falls from the mountains of Caspachy[2] in the direction

1 Thevet's geography here and in the following paragraph is similar to that given by Francisco López de Gómara in his *Historia general de las Indias* (Saragossa, 1552; reprinted 2 vols. Barcelona, 1954), 1: 23.

2 Thevet's reference here may be based on the *Capaschi* appearing on Mercator's map of 1569 [map 2].

of the unknown land which extends near to the Arctic Pole. From the Golden River to that of the Holy Spirit, which in the language of the country is called *Culata*,[3] you count forty leagues; from Culata to the one called the River of the Flowers, seventy-one; from the River of the Flowers to the River of Snows there are thirty; and from there to the Basses River more than one hundred leagues. From that to the Ponce River [are] fifty leagues, from it to Pearl River fifty-six, and from it to the point of Florida, some six score or more. Therefore experienced pilots must be diligent in recognizing these promontories, rivers, and dangerous places if they want to sail along this long stretch of land, as I did with great dangers to my person, otherwise they will fail in their entire navigation in that sea.

Now the point of Florida resembles a tongue-shaped band [of land] extending into the sea more than [1001r] one hundred leagues in length and thirty in width in its narrowest places. It faces directly south (which is meridional) [to] the Isle of Cuba, and in the direction of Iucatan to the east it faces the Isles of Bahama and Lucaya. To the north [is] the land of Canada and to the west New Spain,[4] which otherwise is called Anauac. This sea is shaped like a gulf. Some call it and mark it in their false maps the *Catayan* Sea (but this is incorrect, since Cathay is very far away), others the Mexican Sea, since this province is bounded on one side by the Mexican [country]. Some call it the Yucatanic [Sea], because of the Peninsula of Yucatan, and others the gulf of Florida, in reference to that province.

But before continuing we must know the origin of this name [Florida], since previously it was called *Iaquaza*[5] by the inhabitants and savages of the country. Some, e.g. the Spaniards, say that it bears this name because a certain Jean Ponce discovered this land on the day of Palm Sunday [*Pascua florida*] in the year 1512; but this reason is of no value,

3 This place name is given on the maps of Alonso de Santa Cruz (1542) and Sebastian Cabot (1544). The term means a depression. See Henry Harrisse, *The Discovery of North America: A Critical, Documentary, and Historic Investigation* (London and Paris, 1892; reprinted Amsterdam, 1961), p. 374.

4 Richard Hakluyt's version of this sentence is ". . . and toward the West the Bay of Mexico." See his *The Principal Navigations Voyages Traffiques & Discoveries of the English Nation*, second ed. (1598–1600; reprinted Glasgow, 1903–5; New York, 1965), 8: 451.

5 This name, for example, appears on the map given by Le Moyne: *Ab Indigenis dicta Iaquaza* [map 9]. For more on this map see *The Work of Jacques Le Moyne de Morgues: A Huguenot Artist in France, Florida, and England*, Foreword by Paul Hulton, 2 vols. (London, 1977), chap. 4: "The Le Moyne-De Bry Map," by R.A. Skelton, 1: 45–54.

and seems only to show that the Spaniards want to credit themselves with the first discovery of all of this. The truth is that before they ever visited the north and countries extending to the Arctic, Florida was already known and named both by the French and by the subjects of the King of England.[6] [The latter] seeking a route to Cathay, [and] having heard of the riches to be found in the East Indies, made three voyages to Florida all in vain, since it was not the way to the Indies, nor to Cathay either.[7]

All the land around in these regions is so rich in plants and flowers, and the sea also, that however deep it may be you would say it is a meadow, the prettiest and most verdant that you would see here in the springtime. Having seen it thus, our people and other Europeans called it Florida, coming closer to the Latin name than that given it by the various nations. And to tell you the truth, I have been upon it, and have navigated it, where I saw the marine plain so covered with flowers and plants, resembling our Juniper, that I thought I was on land. But I was immediately forced to change [my] opinion, since having taken a sounding we found it very deep and knew then that these plants proceeded from the nature of the sea, which is strewn with them like this for more than nine or ten days travel by water.

As you come to and sail around this sea in this area, it is sterile in fish in comparison with others where it is remarkably abundant. But to tell you the reason for this, I do not know if Aristotle himself, if he were living, could disentangle himself if you were to ask him about it. For if he were to answer that the place was marshy, and that these plants were produced from such muddy matter, it is impossible to prove it since (as I have said) the water there is very deep, and the currents such as are unknown in neighboring places (and the cause of that is raging torrents which run along this coast, since cheek by jowl you have great rivers, the least of which is a half-league or thereabouts: and also besides that the neighboring mountains, in which the winds are bottled up, cause the waves to swell so, and enter the sea with such vehemence and fury that you keep hearing a noise like the murmur of thunder. I reckon also that in this sea there are mountains and valleys just as on the mainland).[8]

6 Thevet does not mention this issue in the *Singularitez* and elaborates on it in the *Grand Insulaire*, chap. "Isle of Cedars in Florida."

7 Thevet's reference here is vague, but he may be thinking of the 1497 and 1498 voyages of John Cabot, and the alleged 1508 voyage of Sebastian Cabot. In the *Grand Insulaire*, however, he admits that Ponce de Leon was the first to "penetrate" Florida. See chap. "Isle of Cedars in Florida."

8 A very canny guess of Thevet's.

That is how we came to the elevation of Florida, having taken a long time, and wandered around and sailed in every direction over this sea thinking we were on our way back here [to France]. So several [1001v] factors cause the main coast of Florida [to be] dangerous for those who go there from the coast of Mexico: for its latitude,[9] for its currents, winds, and tempests which are frequent there. The point of this land is at latitude twenty-five degrees, having several provinces. Some parts [have been] discovered by Christians, and some have not come to our knowledge, except through some relation of the savages of the country who will tell you all sorts of tales: for they do not travel as do the Orientals, and the Indians [of India].

The first province then, and the most famous, is *Panuque*, which is bounded on one side by New Spain and on the other by the Gulf of Yucatan, which lies to the east. To the north it faces the mountains of Capachy. The natives of that country [Panuque] are brave and cruel in war and are cannibals, wearing no hair on their bodies except on their heads, which [hair] comes down to their shoulders. They pull out [the hair] of the eyebrows, the beard, the eyelashes, and that of the private parts, front and rear, which they cover with well-curried deer hide. The ones who live on the coast have other ways and have no religion, only doing some honor and reverence to the sun in the morning. However, those who live farther in the flat country have idols before which they prostrate themselves when they need rain or sunshine. They are more clever and tricky than the savages of Peru [South America], but are not nearly so civilized as the Mexicans nor so hard-working, except that they are good fishermen.

The other province of Florida is that of the Avanares,[10] who are in the northern part in the mountains which separate Florida from Canada, and they live far inland. This race is simple, and very slow-witted, and very poor, having neither maize nor dates, [but] only a certain fruit which they call *Tuna*.[11] This is round and big as an egg, part black and part reddish, and very tasty to eat. They store it up during the space of three

9 The term *hauteur* may mean either height, depth, or latitude; Thevet apparently means latitude in this case.

10 The Avanares (or Chavavares) are mentioned by Cabeza de Vaca. See Hodge, ed., *Cabeça de Vaca*, pp. 73, 78–9, 87 and n1. Hodge states that this tribe has not been conclusively identified with later tribes. Cabeza de Vaca's work was included in Giovanni Battista Ramusio, *Terzo volume delle navigationi et viaggi nel quale si contengono le navigationi al mondo nuovo . . .* (Venice, 1556).

11 The fruit of an *Opuntia* cactus, of which there are approximately two hundred species.

months that it is on the tree: and I can assure you that if it were not for that it would be very bad to land there, as that is all they have to eat.

These people are neighbors of those who are called *Albardaos*:[12] The country of whom is even less agreeable than that of the Avanares, because they are poorer in fruits [and] roots, and in some places very little water is found for the requirements of the inhabitants. But with this poverty they are clever, alert, and tricky, more than all the rest of the natives both of Florida and of Mexico, as well as all of Peru [South America]. Also they use different war tactics than all the others, since they make surprise attacks during the night, and tiptoe around and almost crawl along the ground on all fours to deceive their enemies. If they see that the said enemy is weak they assail him bravely, but they do not have skill enough to pursue their victory. On the contrary if they see great resistance they run away, assured that there is nobody who can catch them, so quick on their feet are they. So those who have to fight them must always be on the alert, since they are the most speedy and sleep the least of all nations under heaven: for when you think they are far from you, they are on your tail.

In another area are the *Iaquazes*, a cruel people and just as good runners as the Albardaos: but they are superior to them in that they are in a more fertile country, whether in fruit or in roots, from which they make a very good beverage with which they get marvelously drunk. And what I find strangest about them is that in case of necessity they eat all the nasties which all other nations avoid as dangerous. For they eat their lice as do also [1002r] the Margageaz [in Brazil], even worms, lizards, serpents, spiders, and vermin of all kinds—even to swallowing coals, and putting sand in the porridge they make of millet roasted in the fire.[13] They are all clothed, like the rest of the people of Florida, in the skins of wild animals.

There are still other lands such as *Apalachen*, *Ante*, [and] *Xambo*,[14]

12 This tribe is also mentioned by Cabeza de Vaca. See Hodge, *Cabeça de Vaca*, p. 80 and n3.

13 Compare Cabeza de Vaca: ". . . and the famine [is] so great, that they eat spiders and the eggs of ants, worms, lizards, salamanders, snakes, and vipers that kill whom they strike. . . " and Hakluyt: "In necessitie they eat a thousand rifraffes, even to the swallowing downe of coales, and putting sand into the pottage that they make with this meale." See Hodge, ed., *Cabeça de Vaca*, p. 65 and Hakluyt's version of Laudonnière in *Principal Navigations*, 8: 454. For the *Iaquazes*, cf. map 9, Jacques Le Moyne's map of Florida.

14 Thevet here appears to be following Cabeza de Vaca, who traveled from Apalachen to Aute (see Hodge, ed., *Cabeça de Vaca*, pp. 21–37). According to Cabeza de Vaca local natives told Pánfilo de Narváez, when he landed in Florida in 1528, about a province called

which have the same inhabitants, that is whose customs and manners are similar, living without government, humanity or religion, like those who live on the point at the place where the French had built the fort which they named Caroline in honor of the late King Charles.[15] The country is flat, sliced up by several rivers, and therefore humid and sandy near the seacoast. A great quantity of pines grow there which have no seeds in the cones they produce, [and] oaks, walnuts, and chestnuts, which are not natural [native] like the ones in our country. [There are] many cedars, laurel-trees, cypresses, palms, holly, and some wild grapevines which climb up in the trees bearing grapes, but they [the natives] have neither the industry nor the intelligence to convert them into wine: also they are not abundant. There is a kind of medlar whose fruit is better than that of France, and larger: also plums which bear beautiful fruit, but not very good: raspberries, and a little grain very good to eat which we call over here Blues.[16] There grow here also roots named in their language *Hasses*,[17] from which in case of necessity they make bread.

The commonest animals of this land are stags, hinds, goats, fallow-deer, bears, leopards, lynxes, divers sorts of wolves, wild dogs, turkeys, partridges, hares, conies, parrots, wood-pigeons, turtledoves, blackbirds,

"Apalachen" (or "Palachen") which contained much gold. Apparently the present name of the mountain range derives from this mention. The name appears on many maps, including those of Mercator and Le Moyne. The latter carries the inscription: *Montes Apalacti, in quibus aurum argentum & aes invenitur* (The Apalacti mountains in which gold, silver, and copper are found). See map 9. On the other hand, the real location of the Apalachee tribe in West Florida was given in *The Narrative of the Expedition of Hernando de Soto into Florida. By a Gentleman of Elvas* (Evora, 1557), which made it clear that this tribe was not associated with mountains. The name given by early writers varies. For example, the 1586 edition of René de Laudonnière's *l'Histoire notable de la Floride* (Paris) gives *Appalesseil* (fol. 3v), *palassi* (fol. 76v), and *Palacy* (fol. 104v). The 1587 edition of Hakluyt gives *Appalatcy* (fol. 2v), *Apalassi* (fol. 40v), and *Apalassy* (fols. 40v, 54v). *Ante* is a misreading of *Aute*. The source of Thevet's *Xambo* is unknown.

15 There is a plan of Fort Caroline in *Coppie d'une lettre venant de la Floride, envoyée à Rouen, et depuis au seigneur D'Everon; ensemble le plan et portraict du fort que les François y ont faict* (Paris, 1565). A second, different plan of Fort Caroline appears in Le Moyne. See Stefan Lorant, *The New World: The First Pictures of America* (New York, 1946), plate 10, p. 55.

16 E.A. Huguet, *Dictionnaire de la langue française du seizième siècle*, 7 vols. (Paris, 1925–67), cites this mention of the word, but indicates no meaning for it. Laudonnière gives *bleues*, in his *Histoire notable*, p. 5. *Bleuets* or *bluets* (also mentioned by Huguet) are equivalent to our cornflowers. We have used the Paris, 1853, edition of Laudonnière's work, reprinted Nendeln, Liechstenstein, 1972.

17 Laudonnière gives *hassez* in his *Histoire notable* (p. 5).

crows, tercels, falcons, lanners, herons, cranes, storks,[18] wild geese, ducks, cormorants, egrets of divers colors, and an infinity of kinds of game. [There is] such a quantity of crocodiles [alligators], that men are sometimes attacked by them while swimming. There are also serpents of several sorts and a certain species of beast which differs very little from the lions of Africa. There is also found another kind of beast (which for its rarity as well as for its deformity I should much dislike to omit) named by this peoples *Succarath* and by the cannibals *Su*.[19] That animal mostly inhabits the banks of rivers and is rapacious, and is very strangely built, such as you see pictured above [fig. 12]. [1002v] If it is pursued it takes its young on its back and covers them with its tail which is rather long and wide, and flees. However, the savages in order to capture it make a moat into which it falls without suspecting such a trap. Moreover, one finds there a certain grain and plants of which very good dyes are made, and paints of all colors. Also they are fond of painting [their] skins.[20]

The best land and the most fertile and richest is the point [of Florida] and that which is on the river of *Panuque*, which is so wide that it makes a good port. And [it] is proof against tempests, ships being sheltered against the wind there. Six days' travel from Fort Caroline, sailing northwest, you see the mountains of Palassie, out of which comes a little stream of gold or copper, so think the inhabitants of the country, from which they extract the sand with a dry hollow reed.[21] That being filled they shake it and find that inside there are many little grains of

18 Here Thevet, or his typographer, has written *cigrigns*. Probably he meant *cigoignes*, modern *cigognes* or storks. Laudonnière gives *cigongnes* in his *Histoire notable*, p. 5.

19 Thevet's Succarath had already been mentioned and pictured by him in his chapter on the Straits of Magellan and Darien in the *Singularitez*, fols. 108v–9r. It is, perhaps, some kind of ground-sloth. See Bernard Heuvelmans, *On the Track of Unknown Animals*, trans. R. Garnett (London, 1958), p. 281. The animal has appeared in numerous books about unusual creatures including Edward Topsell, *The Historie of Foure-Footed Beastes* (London, 1607), p. 660.

20 For Le Moyne's illustration of and comment on tattooing see Lorant, *New World*, plate 39, p. 113.

21 See Le Moyne, plate 41: "How the Natives Collect Gold in the Streams," in Lorant, *New World*, p. 117. However, D.B. Quinn suggests that nowhere in the narrative does Le Moyne say that he or any of the French actually saw natives collecting gold by panning or any other method. He does say several times that natives obtained gold, silver, and copper in the Apalatic mountains, and refers once to the method used—gathering silt from a stream in the foothills of these mountains by means of hollow-reed pipes or canes as shown in this illustration. Quinn adds that apart from Le Moyne, there is no evidence that at this early period the natives north of Mexico extracted gold from water by panning. See his remarks in Hulton, ed., *Le Moyne*, 1: 215.

Figure 12 Thevet's illustration of a succarath (a ground sloth?)
Thevet's *Cosmographie universelle*, fol. 1002r.
Courtesy John Carter Brown Library at Brown University

copper and of silver: which makes them think that there is some ore in the aforesaid mountain. Now the true situation of this point is taken from another point, named *Canaveral*, which is thirty leagues from it extending east, and which extends as far as the Cape of Basses, at which there is a great river, making three very small islands.[22] From this Canaveral to the Basses you count 107 leagues, which is the amount that Florida (I mean its point) extends into the sea. In the direction of Cuba extends a great promontory named Traverse: and it is made a promontory by the two rivers of Prince and of Saint Espirit.[23] And returning to the salt river, which ends up at the peninsula of Florida, there is a beautiful land at the end of which there are six little islets. Then [there is] Cape St. John, at the point of which there is a great number of reefs. Some have claimed that this Cape Traverse was Florida itself—which I will never concede, since its point does not extend so far into the sea.

Now on this point there are several regions inhabited by divers peoples such as the *Baiegoseppes*, *Caragoles*, *Inopens*, and those of *Lapa* and of the river that the Barbarians call *Canoas*.[24] When you approach the said point of land you see thirteen little isles and an abundance of rocks and reefs very dangerous for those who navigate. If you continue up the coast of the River of Mines, called the river of Canaval as far as the great river of Hostie, which is an arm of the sea, the entrance is dangerous for the currents and the reefs and rocks which are found there.[25] And you must not be surprised if the currents are very strong, as I said, since there are more than twelve hundred rivers, large and small, which discharge themselves into the sea in this peninsula and along the entire Mexican coast to the point of Iucatan, called the Areines.[26] Between this point and that of Florida lies an archipelago of isles, called by the savages *Michachaz*,[27] which means sandy place.

And more northwards, leaving this archipelago and going towards the

22 Although the name Canaveral does not appear on the Spanish *padron* type maps of the 1520s, it is given by Alonso de Chaves in his *Quatri partitu en cosmographia . . .* (Seville, 1537), fol. 42v. From the mid-sixteenth century it appears on maps with increasing frequency.

23 These terms, Cape of Basses, River of Prince, and River of Holy Spirit are common on maps of the mid sixteenth-century. For Traverse, see Canada, *Grand Insulaire*, note 68.

24 The term Canoas is given on several maps of the period. Thevet's names for these peoples derive from no source known to us.

25 The source of Thevet's geography here is unknown to us.

26 The word, common on maps, means sands.

27 The origin of this name is unknown.

land of Canada you see another isle where the people are much involved in fishing. And although they are very inhuman and cruel, still they were discovered by the French, whatever the Spaniards may say, who rendered them less barbarous and made allies of them. They began to visit them in the time of King François I and a long time before. Indeed Jean Verazze [sic], Florentine, the 17th of March 1524 left Dieppe by command of the said King François, sailed along all of Florida as far as the thirty-fourth degree of latitude and three hundred degrees of longitude, and discovered this whole coast. He put a number of people there to cultivate it who finally were massacred by this barbarous people.[28] At that time neither the Spaniards nor the Portuguese had come there. But I will speak more about this in [the section on] the land of Canada.

So I must return to our point [1003r] of Florida, where the people are just like those of the flat country except that they are not so cruel and nonetheless very stupid and simple. They are of sallow complexion, of large stature and well-proportioned, and dressed in all weather in skins of animals, the men as well as the women. Most of them have their bodies painted, on the arms and the thighs, with very pretty divisions [areas] which can never be removed because they are pricked into the skin. They are great deceivers and traitors, personally valiant however and fight well.

They have no other arms than bows and arrows, the cord of which they make from the gut and leather of the stag, as well made and of as many different colors as anyone could make in France. They tip their arrows with the teeth of fish and with stone which they prepare most cleverly. They exercise their young men at running and the use of the bow, and they have a prize which they give to the one who can hold his breath the longest. They also take great pleasure in hunting and fishing. The kings of the country make war on each other, warring only by surprise, and they kill all the men they can capture, then remove their heads to have the hair, which they carry off to exhibit in triumph in their houses.[29] However, they spare the women and children, whom they support and keep permanently with them. On their return from war they assemble all their subjects and in their great joy they dance, sing, and feast for three days and nights. And they even make the old women of the country

28 Verrazzano's departure from the Madeira Islands was 17 January 1524. See Hakluyt, *Principal Navigations*, 8: 424. Thevet's mention of a massacre here may refer to the death of Verrazzano himself. See Lawrence C. Wroth, *The Voyages of Giovanni da Verrazzano* (New Haven, 1970), "The Dispute Concerning Verrazzano's Death," pp. 255–62.

29 See Le Moyne's illustration, "How Outina's Men Treated the Enemy Dead," in Lorant, *New World*, plate 15, p. 65.

dance, holding in their hands the scalps of their enemies: and while dancing they sing the praises of the sun, attributing to him the honor of the victory.[30]

They have no knowledge of God nor of any religion, other than that which they see like the sun and the moon. They have priests whom they call *Jarvars*[31] to whom they lend all faith because they are great magicians, soothsayers, and invokers of the Devil, and they serve them as physicians and surgeons since they always carry with them a sack of herbs and drugs to treat the ill. They are very subject to women and girls, whom they call daughters of the sun, and most of them [are] sodomites.[32] The kings are permitted to have two or three wives, however only the first is honored and recognized as queen and only her children inherit the property and authority of the father. The women do all the housework, and they [the men] do not cohabit with them when they are pregnant, nor eat any food they have touched while they are menstruating.

When they go to war, their king whom they name *Paracousti* (others *Paraousti*)[33] marches at the head with a club in one hand and his bow in the other, with his quiver full of arrows, and is followed by his people also armed with their bows and arrows. [The king] before departing sits in a bower surrounded by the kings who are going to accompany him on this expedition. This done, gazing at heaven [he] begins to discourse of various things, and to urge his subjects to fight well and valiantly, picturing to them the glory and honor he will acquire if they should win a victory over their enemy, and contrariwise the shame it will be to them if they are defeated and lose the battle. Threatening with a furious look which he casts in the direction of his enemies, he gives his subjects to understand the desire he has to vanquish them [the enemy], and in the course of his speech casts often his look on high, asking the sun to give him a victory over the aforesaid adversaries. This having gone on for half an hour, he pours with his hand some of the water which is brought

30 Again, see Le Moyne's illustration "Trophies and Ceremonies after a Victory," in Lorant, *New World*, plate 16, p. 67.

31 This word may derive from *yuru*: to tremble, to be shaken or contorted. See Albert S. Gatschet, "The Timucua Language," *Proceedings of the American Philosophical Society* 16 (1877): 626–42; 17 (1878): 490–504; 18 (1879): 465–502, esp. 500.

32 See Le Moyne, "Hermaphrodites as Laborers," in Lorant, *New World*, plate 17, p. 69. Le Moyne's hermaphrodites were the transvestites known to American ethnology as berdaches. See H. Angelino and Charles L. Shedd, "A Note on Berdache," *American Anthropologist* 57 (1955): 121–6.

33 The spelling *Paraousti* is given in the account of Laudonnière, *Histoire notable.*

to him in a vessel over the heads of the *Paracousis* who surround him, and the rest he hurls as if in fury and spite on a fire which has been prepared there for this purpose. In doing this he thrice cries out the name of his enemy, which all those [1003v] who follow him do after him. This ceremony from what I have been able to learn of it, signifies that he is begging the sun to grant him a victory so heroic that he will be able to shed the blood of his enemies at will just as he has showered all this water around: also that the *Paracousis* sprinkled with some of this water will be able to return with the heads[34] of their enemies, which is the sole and supreme symbol of their victories.[35]

For when it is a question of fighting they utter great shouts and exclamations, and the king would not dare to budge before the battle is finished. For if he were so mad as to flee, seeing that his men were getting the worst of it, it would be all up with him and they would not fail to massacre him. And that is the way the Persians still do, and it has not been very long since the Turks did the same, and several Levantine nations. And if mayhap they obtain the victory, they take the heads of their dead enemies and cut off all the hair with a part of the scalp. This done they go home giving thanks to the sun and singing his marvels. Also, they send a messenger ahead to announce the victory to those who stayed behind to guard the houses, who begin immediately to weep. But when night comes, they have a great dance and celebration in honor of the occasion. The *Paracousi*, having returned home, has all the scalps of his enemies set before his door surrounded with laurel branches, showing with this spectacle the triumph of the victory he has obtained. Then begin the weeping and lamentations, which at nightfall are converted into dancing and pleasures.

Their weapons are bows with arrows whose tips are poisoned and in some places the wood also is poisoned. On the tips instead of iron they place bones of wild beasts or teeth of fish so sharp that I doubt if iron penetrates better than these bones, hurled by the steely hands of these barbarians. The coast-dwellers content themselves with killing their enemies without eating them, while the inhabitants of the interior (being idolatrous), eat them after having sacrificed them to their idols. The coast people, but not all of them (as I said before), adore the sun without building any altar to it or making any sacrifice to it. They are of good stature and live a long time; there are some who are 150 years old at least.

34 *Bestes* has been misprinted for *testes* in the French text.

35 See Le Moyne's illustration "Saturiba goes to War," in Lorant, *New World*, plate 11, p. 57. French writers usually spelled this name Satouriona. See fig. 10.

And Captain Laudonnière will be my witness to this: who in 1564 by the command of the late King Charles [IX] made the Florida voyage for the second time. There he had the fort of the *Carolina* built, on the May river, in honor of the said King. Having then arrived in this country and exploring the lands adjacent to his fort, he arrived at a mountain of medium height, along which he set foot on ground.[36] Having rested himself a while, [he] walked with some of his troops in the woods arriving at a reedy marsh. Finding themselves tired from the march, they went into the shade of a great laurel-tree to rest a bit and discuss some problem of their enterprise. They then discovered five barbarians of that region half-hidden in the woods who seemed somewhat afraid of our Frenchmen, who greeted them in their own language saying *Antipola Bonnasou*,[37] so that hearing such words they would approach more confidently, which they soon did. But since they noticed that the four last ones were carrying the train of the pelts [with] which the first was clothed, they suspected that he was of higher rank than the others, plus the fact that they called him Paracousti. So some of the [French] company approached him and sweet-talking him pointed to their captain (for whom they had made a bower of laurels and palms in the fashion of the country) so that by such signs they would see and understand that the French had formerly had association with their fellows. [1004r] This *Paracousti* having approached the captain, began to address to him a rather long harangue, whose effect was that he begged the Frenchmen to come see his dwelling and his family. Which having been granted him by the said Frenchmen, he gave to the said Laudonnière in token of his great friendship the very pelt with which he was clothed.

This done, [he] took him by the hand and struck off through the swamps: across which the Paracousti and the said captain with several Frenchmen were carried on the shoulders of these savages. The others who could not pass because of the mud and [under]growth went through the woods and followed a little narrow path which guided them to the dwelling of the *Paracousti*. From this [there] issued forth fifty of these savages the more honorably to receive the Frenchmen, and entertained them in their fashion. Following which they immediately presented [to] them a large earthen jar of curious style, full of clear spring water and very excellent, which they presented to each, following a certain order and ceremony as they carried it to the various persons to drink. Thirst having

36 The exploration was presumably by ship.

37 Laudonnière gives a slightly different spelling, *Antipola Bonnasson*. See *Histoire notable*, pp. 67, 72.

been quenched in this way and the Frenchmen refreshed, the *Paracousti* conducted them to the lodge of his father, one of the oldest living people on earth. The Frenchmen, respecting his age, began to gratify him by the use of the term Friend, Friend, at which the old man appeared very happy. They then questioned him about his age, to which he answered claiming to be the living ancestor of five generations. [He then showed] them another old man seated across from him, who was much older than he. Indeed it was his father, who more resembled the bark of a tree than a living man. He had the tendons, veins, arteries, bones, and other parts of his body showing under his skin so that you easily could have counted them and told them apart from each other; and his age was so great that the good man had lost his sight and could not, without a very great effort, utter a single word.

The Sieur de Laudonnière seeing such a strange thing approached the younger old man, [and] asked him to explain what he had said about his great age.[38] Then the old man called up a troop of the savages, and then striking his thigh two times and placing his hand on two of them, signed that these two were his children. Then striking their thighs, [he] indicated some others less old than these two first ones – which he continued in the same way till he got up to the fifth generation. Now although this old man had a father even older than he, it seemed by their appearance that they were still good for thirty or forty years, indeed the younger perhaps for 250 years.[39] That is what the said Captain Laudonnière told me, who through his diligence has discovered many countries on this Florida coast and other singularities – which I omit to avoid prolixity.

They confess that the soul is immortal and that there is a place set aside for the wicked; which they say is a very cold country, because the greatest unease they suffer is the cold. [They] also say that the sins of men are punished in the other life. They believe that there is an infinite number of men in heaven, and as many under the ground, and they have a thousand little follies in their beliefs, just as stupid as the transformations of our savages, which I have recited to you:[40] and they believe in them just as firmly as the Turks and Persians do in Mahomet.

38 In the accounts of Hakluyt and Laudonnière it is Monsieur de Ottigni, not Laudonnière, who asked the native his age.

39 Le Moyne mentions a sorcerer more than 120 years old, and a 300-year-old man with a 350-year-old father. See plates 12 and 28, respectively, in Lorant, *New World*, pp. 59 and 91.

40 Thevet here refers to the natives of Brazil.

The country closest to the north[41] is the most fertile because its inhabitants, having derived from several nations, have learned to sow millet, which they call *Tapolla*, and a root resembling the *Mahiz* of Peru [South America]. They also have a plant which they call *Cassina* [Cassava], which is like a lettuce from which they make their beverage. They [1004v] drink [this] very hot after boiling the herb in water, saying that it is very good for the stomach. [It] has the virtue that, having drunk it, they are all in a sweat – which having passed they are immune to hunger and thirst for twenty-four hours. They also use a fish for which they use the generic name *Caioupi*.[42]

The land there is beautiful, [and] always green; their nearby gardens being in their fashion, where they grow their plants and gather their grain as they were taught to do previously so that they are better provided with food and drink than the rest of the nations of the said country of Florida. They sow their millet twice a year, i. e. in March and in June, which takes three months to harvest time, and the other six months they let the land rest, which they do not manure: rather when they want to sow they set fire to the plants and burn them. This done, they work the earth with a wooden instrument made like a wide hoe used by the vine-growers of France.[43] When the lands are to be sown, the king has all his subjects assembled to participate in the work, during which he provides them with much drink. The harvest being done and gathered in, their gross [unmilled] millet is all borne to the public warehouse where it is distributed to everyone according to his rank and as much as they will need for six months. In the winter they retire for a period of three or four months into the woods, where they construct little houses of *Palimites* [palmettos?][44] for shelter, and live during that time off acorns, fish which they catch, oysters, venison, turkeys, and other animals [which] they catch. Among others [they eat] the flesh of the crocodile [alligator], which is pretty and white and which I would have often eaten if it had not such a musky

41 A typographical error here has *mort* (death) instead of *nord* (north).

42 Hakluyt, *Principal Navigations*, 8: 462, gives *Sallicoques*, and Laudonnière *saillicoques (Histoire notable*, p. 22).

43 Le Moyne's illustration "How they Till the Soil and Plant," in Lorant, *New World*, plate 21, p. 77, shows French (or Belgian) hoes. For more information see William C. Sturtevant, "First Visual Images of Native America," in Fredi Chiappelli, ed., *First Images of America: The Impact of the New World on the Old*, 2 vols. (Berkeley, 1976), 1: 417–54, esp. 418, and also his "Lafitau's hoes," *American Antiquity* 33 (1968): 93–5.

44 Hakluyt gives Palme in *Principal Navigations*, 8: 456.

smell.[45] They eat all their meats roasted over coals and barbecued (almost smoke-cooked), not keeping the primitive ferocity and barbarity of their predecessors who ate raw flesh and sucked the blood of their enemies.

They have a custom among them that when they feel ill, in the place they feel the pain (unlike us when we have ourselves bled), their doctor-priests suck them till they make the blood come. They have feasts which they celebrate at certain times with very strange ceremonies. The place where the celebration is held is a large circle of very smooth ground, in the round, near the king's house. From [this house] those who are charged with the responsibility of the solemnities carry out paints and plumages of various colors and go to the said place. Arriving there they place themselves in formation, and are followed by three others very different from them in painting and in their way of doing. Each of these three carries a tabor in his hand, [and] when they begin to come to the middle of the circle, dancing and singing plaintively, they are followed by others who respond to them. But after they have sung, danced, and gone around the circle three times, they take off running through the thick forests just like unbridled horses. And then the women continue all the rest of the day in weeping so sadly and lamentably that it is indescribable.

And in this madness they seize the arms of the girls which they cruelly incise with very sharp mussel shells so that the blood flows, which they sprinkle in the air with the branch of a tree, crying *He Toya*, *Toya*, *Toya* three times. The three who begin the celebration are named *Jaonas*,[46] and are like priests or sacrificers to whom they lend faith and credence—partly because they belong to a hereditary order of sacrificers, and partly also because they are such clever magicians that they can immediately locate any lost object. At the end of two days, those who had taken off into the woods return to the arena. Having arrived they begin a light-hearted dance [1005r] to cheer up their fathers who, because of their too great antiquity or else their natural indisposition, are not invited to this celebration. The dances over, they begin to eat with such avidity that they seem rather to devour the food than to eat it, since neither on the day of the celebration nor the following two days when they are in the woods do they drink or eat anything at all.

45 Laudonnière expresses this same taste in *Histoire notable*, p. 12; see also *Grand Insulaire*, chap. "Isle of Cedars in Florida."

46 *Jarvars*. For more information on the feast of Toya see Hakluyt, *Principal Navigations*, 8: 476.

On the Beverages Used by the Floridians, and Other Foreign Nations: and on the Massacre of the French

CHAPTER 2

And because I have spoken of their beverage named *Cassina*, you will note here that there is no nation on earth however barbarous and rude which does not prefer working to prepare some liquor to drink than to content itself with pure water, which seems to be the proper beverage for animals. This I have sufficiently experienced in all the four corners of the earth, which I have visited. . . [47]

As for the savages of Florida, they make their beverage as stated above. And it is up to the women, whom they call *Nya*, to compose and make this beverage, and anybody can see this if you visit them in their lodges, which they call *Tapecona*, and the other savages *Mortugabes*. Showing you signs of friendship, they will all say in turn to you *Antipola Bonnassou Tymale Desa*, which means, I am your brother, drink with us, and help yourself to what we have. They invited the French rather than the Spaniards because they do not like them, since [the latter] formerly took their wives and children to make them slaves: and they call them *Rotizze*, just like those of the Antarctic [South America] call the Portuguese *Peroptz*, which makes me think that it must be some insulting term. This people which dwells near the river which we christened the Seine, are very benign and affable as are those who live on the coast and on the River May.[48]

[On this river] was built the fort that the French made and named Caroline, which was taken and sacked by the Spaniards in the year 1565, on St. Matthew's Day, the twenty-first of September.[49] The twenty-sixth of that month, when the French ships came either to attack or to reconnoiter the enemy, they [the French] saw themselves so cruelly invested that they were killed, masssacred, and thrown into the water. And as two [more ships] would have been defeated and sunk two days later, which was the

47 Thevet digresses from the natives of North America at this point and begins to discuss the beverages used by other nations. This information has nothing to do with his main point—a description of the life of the Floridian natives and of the French colony in Florida. We have omitted approximately one page of text here.

48 Neither Laudonnière nor Hakluyt gives the vocabulary which Thevet includes in this paragraph.

49 Hakluyt, *Principal Navigations*, 9: 94, gives September twentieth.

28th of the said month, Captain Jean Ribaud of Dieppe[50] arrived who, seeing his forces unequal, began to parley with the chief of the Spanish army and having trusted in his word was treacherously killed with his friend and all the rest of his company. Present at this time was he who gave me the story of it, who is a pilot, and two others who were in his company and escaped from danger.[51] So in three different defeats and in different places, even though they had been warned by the savages of the coming of the *Rotizze* in the campaign, our people were massacred to the number of more than a thousand men. [The latter] are not so much to be criticized as you might think, since knowing of the arrival of their enemies and not anticipating this tragedy, they decided to engage them: but not realizing their danger, and too bold, they lost what they might very well have kept if they had remained on the defensive in the fort they had built.

They say it was on account of religion that the Spaniards plotted this defeat, as a pretext or otherwise, intending the ruin of the French (as indeed they executed it).[52] I am not certain of the truth of this: I know what I told some of my friends who undertook this voyage and who to my sorrow did not return, and how I pointed out the peril into which they were hurling themselves considering the proximity of lands, continental or insular, of which the Spaniards boasted of being the lords and of having been the first to have reached and discovered those lands (as I have said elsewhere). [I told them that they] would not suffer anyone to come so close to them to visit the lands of Peru [South America] and

50 Jean Ribault established the French colony at Charlesfort (Port Royal, South Carolina) in 1562. He was killed by the Spaniards on a subsequent expedition to Florida in 1565. Thevet apparently did not rely a great deal on Ribault's *The Whole and True Discovery of Terra Florida* (London, 1563). Hakluyt incorporated this narrative in his *Divers Voyages Touching the Discoverie of America* (London, 1582), but did not include it in his *Principal Navigations*. A modern edition has been published by Jeanette T. Conner, ed., *The Whole and True Discoverye of Terra Florida* (Deland, Fla., 1927). This work contains a facsimile reprint of the 1563 London edition.

51 Among those who escaped from the Spaniards were Laudonnière, Jacques Le Moyne, and Nicolas Le Challeux, each of whom wrote an account of his experiences. See Introduction.

52 According to Hakluyt, Pedro Menéndez de Avilés, the leader of the Spanish expedition against Fort Caroline, declared: "I doe not this as unto French men, but as unto Lutherans. . . " *Principal Navigations*, 9: 109. For more information on the religious aspects of French activities in Florida see Frank Lestringant, "Millénarisme et Age d'Or: Réformation et expériences coloniales au Brésil et en Floride (1555–1565)." In *Les Réformes: Enracinement Socio-Culturel, 25e Colloque d'Etudes Humanistes, Tours 1-13 July 1982)*, ed. Bernard Chevalier and Robert Sauzet (n.p. 1985), pp. 25–42.

Mexico, reminding them of what the Portuguese had done to our people at the fort of the river of Janeiro (where [1006r] however they did not do such a great massacre and they got a pretty good fight, even though our people were in very small numbers and that food and ammunition gave out on them).[53] What is most to be deplored, after the loss of the good troop of soldiers, is [that of] the expert mariners: which is not something which can easily be recovered. But these things being disagreeable to relate and which cannot be told without some regret, it is better to pass over them in silence than to dwell on them at length, since I have already touched on the principal point of the story which is the defeat.[54]

Not that I want to forget the great and brutal cruelty exercised in the case of Jean Ribaud, valiant captain and pilot, with whom I took a long time ago a voyage. His face with his beard, which was very long, his eyes, nose, and ears they cut off when he was dead and sent them all to the Isles of Peru [South America] to exhibit them.[55] This Jean Ribaud had previously in the year 1560 [1562] made a quite successful voyage to these lands, where he had built a fort to which he gave the name of Charlesfort; in which he had left twenty-six soldiers under the charge of Captain Albert [de la Pierria].[56] For a while [these] behaved very well, but finally they got into divisions and dissensions, which arose over the death of a soldier named *Guernache* (who was known as a drummer for French companies) who was rather cruelly hanged by his own captain. This was the reason that the soldiers mutinied and so harrassed the captain that finally they killed him. What incited them even more to do this

53 The Portuguese, under Mem de Sá, took Rio de Janeiro after two years of fighting, 1565-7.

54 Professor Lestringant concludes that Thevet, having suppressed Laudonnière's *Histoire notable* (cf. Introduction), abstains from further discussion of the massacre here because he risked "revelations which could become compromising"—that his own account was largely copied from Laudonnière. See Frank Lestringant, "Les Séquelles Littéraires de la Floride française: Laudonnière, Hakluyt, Thevet, Chauveton," *Bibliothèque d'Humanisme et Renaissance* 44 (1982): 13 and n24.

55 A contemporary account of the mutilation of Ribault's body by the Spaniards is in La Popelinière, *Les Trois Mondes* (Paris, 1582), f. 33v. Woodbury Lowery, however, has concluded that these descriptions are mere fiction. See his *The Spanish Settlements within the Present Limits of the United States: Florida, 1562-1574* (New York, 1911), Appendix P, "The Death of Ribaut," pp. 425–9.

56 For an examination of the controversy over the location of Charlesfort, with bibliography, see William P. Cumming, "The Parreus Map (1562) of French Florida," *Imago Mundi* 17 (1963): 27–40, esp. 37-8n45. The number of persons left behind by Ribault varies in the sources: Hakluyt says twenty-six, Laudonnière twenty-eight, and Ribault himself gives thirty.

was the military punishment he had meted out to another soldier named *Lachere*, whom he had exiled. Their plot carried out, they went back to seek the said soldier who was on a little island three leagues distant from *Charlesfort*, where they found him half dead from hunger. So having returned they assembled to elect a chief over them. This they did and elected one named Captain Nicolas,[57] a man indeed worthy of such a charge: in fact he aquitted himself so well that all rancor and dissension amongst them ceased, and they lived peaceably with one another.

Meantime they began to build a small brigantine, even though there was not a man among them who knew the art. Nevertheless, necessity mistress of the arts showed them the means. They hoped to return to France if help did not arrive as had been promised them, and which they awaited daily. Finally frustrated in their wait, and their brigantine having been finished, their thought was to equip it with all that would be necessary to their navigation. But the principal things were lacking, like ropes and sails, without which the enterprise could not succeed. So not having any way of getting them they were more demoralized than ever, and on the point of giving way to despair. However this good God, who never abandons the afflicted, succored them in their need: for while they were in this perplexity, two kings of the country named *Audusta* and *Maccou*[58] arrived accompanied by about two hundred barbarians. Our people went and explained to them their need for ropes, [and they] promised them to return within two days with such a quantity as would suffice to equip the brigantine. Happy at this answer they gave them some brush-hooks, smocks, and other cheap merchandise, and after their departure tried hard to find some pitch [resin] in the woods, incising the pines and firs on all sides, from which they got quite a bit to prepare the vessel. [They] also got a store of a kind of moss to serve as caulking. All that remained was the sails, which they made from their shirts and bed linen. [1006v]

57 Nicolas Barré was a pilot who accompanied Villegagnon to Brazil in 1555 and later voyaged to Florida with Ribault and Laudonnière, where he succeeded Albert de la Pierria at Charlesfort after the latter was killed by his men. Barré was one of those massacred by the Spaniards at Fort Caroline. His *Copie de quelques lettres sur la navigation du Chevalier de Villegaignon es terres de l'Amérique* . . . (Paris, 1556) is given by Henri Ternaux-Compans, ed., *Archives des voyages, ou collection d'anciennes relations inédites ou tres-rares de lettres, mémoires, itinéraires et autres documents relatifs a la géographie* . . . 2 vols. (Paris, 1841, 1845), 1 (1841): 102–16. Hakluyt also referred to Nicolas Barré as Nicolas Masson. See *Principal Navigations*, 9: 53.

58 The French and Spaniards appear to have commonly mistaken names of localities or tribes for that of individuals. Woodbury Lowery believed that perhaps Audusta was a chief of the Edisto [Orixa] tribe, but did not speculate about Maccou. See his *Spanish Settlements*, p. 40.

Several days later the Kings *Audusta* and *Maccou* returned to their fort with so much rope that there was enough to rig the little ship: at which the French extremely happy distributed largesse to them, leaving them everything they had left in the way of merchandise. [The natives] were so satisfied with that that they went away the most content in the world.

So they continued working on the brigantine, and so diligently that in a very short time it was completely ready. Meantime such a favorable wind developed that it seemed to invite them to set out to sea. So after loading on their artillery and other war materiel which had been left them they did not further postpone. Thus, then drunk on the too great joy they had of returning to their country, or else lacking in all foresight and consideration, and without taking into account the inconstancy of the winds which change in a moment's time, they set out to sea. Their food was so scant however, that the outcome of their plan was disastrous: for when they had accomplished a third of their way they were so badly becalmed that they did not advance twenty-five leagues in three weeks. During this time the provisions diminished and became so depleted that they had to ration themselves to twelve grains of millet each per day, which might be equivalent to twelve of our peas. In sum, the provisions were soon gone and they had nothing to eat but their shoes and leather collars. As for drink, some drank seawater, others their own urine: and they were in a state of desperate necessity for a very long time, during which some died of starvation. Besides the extreme famine which accompanied them, they were hourly losing hope of ever seeing France again; also they continually had to bail out the water which was coming everywhere into their boat.

Things went from bad to worse: for after they had eaten their shoes and collars, such a strong and contrary wind came up that in no time the waves filled their vessel half-full of water and stove in one of its sides. More despairing than ever of ever getting out of such extreme peril, they left off bailing out the water which was sinking them: and as if resolved to die, everyone sank back abandoning themselves to the will of the waves. At this point one of them, having somewhat regained his spirits, reminded them that there was only a little more way to go and assured them that before three days (if the wind continued) they would see land. This personage encouraged them so much that after having bailed the water out of the brigantine they remained three more days without eating or drinking, except for the water on which they were. But the time of his promise having expired, they became more discouraged than ever, not seeing any land. Whereupon in this ultimate despair, some of them proposed that it was more expedient for one person to die than for all of them to perish. They decided then that he should die on whom the lot fell: which was carried out in the person of *Lachere* of whom I spoke before, and whose flesh was divided equally among this companions and eaten raw, after having drunk his blood all warm. A thing so pitiful to recount, that my very pen hesitates to write it.[59]

After such long and grievous travails, the good God with his usual favor changed their sorrow into a great joy, causing the land to appear to them. On this they were so overcome that the pleasure made them remain a long time like people overcome, thus letting the brigantine wander here and there without keeping to path or route. Then a little English dispatch-boat passing by came up to this vessel, in which there was a certain French sailor who had been with a [1007r] Norman captain in New France: and so he recognized them easily and spoke to them, then had food and drink given to them. Having recovered their natural spirits,[they] told him in detail about their voyage. The English consulted long about what they should do, but finally they resolved to put the weakest ones ashore, and take the rest before the Queen of England, who at that time was thinking about an expedition to New France. . . [60]

And since that is enough about this subject, I will pursue the rest of my task. [1007v] In Florida, besides a great diversity of birds which are found there and very deformed fish very different from ours, you also see there monstrous beasts; among which there is a kind like large bulls, which the savages call Buttol [*Buffol*] which have horns only a foot long and having on the back a swelling and hump just like that of a camel, with long hair all over the body and principally under the chin, whose color is nearly fauve. Its tail is like a lion's, and similar species are found in Lithuania and Poland which they call *Zuber* and the Tartars *Roffert*. This animal is one of the fiercest known because it is never tamed unless it is taken very young and separated from its mother: and I give you its portrait here [fig. 11].

These savages arm themselves with its pelts against the cold and its

59 Neither Hakluyt nor Laudonnière state that Lachère's body was eaten raw, or that his warm blood had been consumed. See *Principal Navigations*, 8: 486; Laudonnière, *Histoire notable*, p. 58. However, as noted by Lestringant, "Séquelles," p. 19 and n43, this oratorical phrase featuring the hesitant pen is borrowed from Laudonnière.

60 The accounts of Laudonnière and Hakluyt differ slightly here. Laudonnière gives, for the objective of the expedition, New France, while Hakluyt has Florida. See *Histoire notable*, p. 59, and *Principal Navigations*, 8: 486. The reference may be to the 1563 expedition of Thomas Stukely. See Woodbury Lowery, "Jean Ribaut and Queen Elizabeth," *American Historical Review* 9 (1904): 456–9. Thevet digresses briefly here to give accounts of other shipwrecks, but this passage has been omitted.

horns are much prized for the efficacy they have against poison; so the natives keep them to protect against poisons and vermin that they meet up with going about the country and in fishing. Two of [these bison] were once taken to Spain. I saw the pelt of one but they cannot survive there at all. This animal is such the enemy of the horse that it cannot be with one. In fact it flies into rage and agitation at the mere scent of one. Let the naturalists work on this and explain the cause of this antipathy, since before the Christians discovered this country thirty or forty years ago, this beast had never seen any kind of horse in this land.

And although at the beginning of the other chapter I spoke of the currents of these waters, and assigned some reason for them, still however it seems to me I did not say enough to satisfy the mind of the man curious about all things. I know very well that the true cause of the currents of the open sea has never been duly understod, any more than that of the tides, which make the sea greater [1008r] in one place than another. This is attributed to the movements of the moon, by some to the orbit of the sun; by others to the configuration of the land; while others say the sea is a sentient thing, which breathing like an animal causes by respiration this movement of the waves which we call the ebb and flow. This is too much of dragging philosophy about by the hair. Some people of this country say that the water coming to this side against the northern section, which is considered the highest part of the earth, and [then] going downhill, causes this effort and fury of the currents—the same where there is a gulf. But this explanation, although it has a certain plausibility, does not fill the bill since in the Gulf of Uraba the currents come more from the east than the north—unless they would say that the water ricochets there and comes swinging around like you see in whirlpools. Other very expert pilots discoursing with me, have told me that it is a result of the great rivers which flow into it, carrying along sand and gravel build up the bottom and causing the water to boil, cause the currents. But this although it seems true cannot always be defended, since the rule would have to be valid in every sea in which there are currents. It may be so in all seas which tend southwards. You see there an infinity of very great rivers which have no issue other than the Straits [of Gibraltar], and yet they do not flow out of these; rather it seems that the ocean runs into them, and makes its turn to the right hand towards the coast of Barbary, and past this to Alexandria in Egypt, which is from West to East. Here the currents are not caused by the rivers but rather by the Ocean, which runs downwards, according to the reason given above.[61]

61 Thevet's discourse on currents is examined in Harold L. Burstyn, "Theories of Winds

Coming back to [the explanation of] the abundance of the water of the rivers, some say that on this coast [of Florida] there is a great quantity of grottoes and caverns, windy and full of water, which entering impetuously into the sea cause the said currents. [It is] as if they wished to flow southwards, and then finding an obstacle take a westward turn, but [they say] that the cause of this turning and veering is the course of the sun, which attracts to itself the course of the ocean. And the opinion of some, with which I should gladly agree, is this: that these waters running to the west, finding themselves imprisoned by the contours of the places, due to the islands and mountains which are in the sea not far from the coast, when they are at one of the capes of the gulf, retreat backward as if pressed; and not being able to go where they please, therefore turn around and cause with their currents great difficulties for the vessels and ships that pass there. And certainly at that spot in the sea you find this reason to be valid, and you easily understand the effect. For as you leave this gulf and have passed the Isles of Cuba and Hispaniola and head east some five leagues into the open sea, you are out of difficulty.

But for myself, I stick to my first explanation, [that the currents are] caused by the mountains, isles, and reefs which are in the sea, as in this gulf; and because of the large rivers flowing out with impetuosity, as I showed at Romada, at the entrance of the Euphrates and the Tigris into the Persian sea, and at Diu, where the Indus pays its tribute to the Ocean, and at the Gulf of Bengal, where the Ganges causes the currents to roar well out into the sea. You might have observed the same with the great rivers of South America, such as the Maragnon, Orellane, Guiaquil, and that of Manicongre in Africa where the fresh water thrusts aside that of the sea and flows as a river more than forty leagues into the open sea without losing its freshness and without the sea being able to make it lose its strength and break its course through the effort of its flow and tides.

I also wish to warn new pilots [1008v] and beardless mariners to be careful not to approach closer than two leagues to Florida from the east, because of shoals which are forty-six leagues long, and several diamond-pointed rocks at surface level, which are very dangerous. As for the rivers, which are at least twelve leagues wide, and others less, you should know that some of them are very difficult if you are at anchor and you have a violent south wind. Nicholas Barré my companion, native of Tours, one of the foremost young men of our age in the marine art, was

---

and Ocean Currents from the Discoveries to the End of the Seventeenth Century," *Terrae Incognitae* 3 (1971): 7–31. This passage appears to be based on Peter Martyr as translated in Ramusio's *Terzo volume*, fol. 29.

the first Frenchman, having conducted three vessels, who penetrated well into those [rivers] and the flat country: he gave me the map of the mouths of several. On his second voyage, having conducted the ships there, he was killed like the rest. So leaving Florida [which is] lost to us, I will pass on farther to visit the land of Canada, and the rest of Baccaleos, sailing toward the Cape and Promontory of Arcadia.[62]

62 W.F. Ganong believes that this is the first mention of Arcadia in a printed book. See his *Crucial Maps in the Early Cartography and Place-Nomenclature of the Atlantic Coast of Canada* (Toronto, 1961), p. 434.

Grand Insulaire

[176r] Isle of Cedars in Florida

In my day there were diverse opinions as to who was first to set foot in the land of Florida. Some hold that it was Captain Jean Ponce, a Spaniard who was subsequently killed with all his men in those regions by the barbarians. I admit that it was he who first penetrated into this country, but he did not take possession of it; rather it was the pilot Sebastian Gabotte, who was a Venetian, soon after the decease of the Genevan [error for Genoese] Columbus. In fact this Venetian Captain, having volunteered for commerce under Henry, seventh of the name, King of England, was sent to explore this Floridian coast. While I was at St. Malo-on-the-Isle, staying at the home of Jacques Cartier, there came Captain Gabotte, son of the great [Giovanni] Gabotte, honorable old man with whom I conferred nine whole days.[1] In his quality of a personage well versed in marine matters he in no wise degenerated from the virtues of his father, and most familiarly spoke to me about the whole coast from Canada to Florida. He was employed by Henry, eighth of the name, King of England, to discover a strait of the sea closer than that of Magellan.[2] He gave me at that time several memoirs on the terra firma of Cortereal and on the rivers lying from the Arctic Circle to the Gulf of the Isles of the Demons[3] (where he lost two ships and many of his English sailors and soldiers) and from there to the rivers of Ochelagua and Saguenai.

1 D.B. Quinn suggests in his *England and the Discovery of America, 1481–1620* (New York, 1974), p. 152 that Cabot visited Cartier to discuss a joint Anglo-French enterprise to ascend the Amazon and take the Spaniards in Peru from the rear. See also Frank Lestringant, "La Conférence de Saint-Malo (1552-1553)," in *La Renaissance et le Nouveau Monde*, ed. Alain Parent et al. (Quebec, 1984), pp. 37–44.

2 It is uncertain whether Sebastian Cabot's alleged voyage to find a Northwest Passage was in 1508 (at the end of Henry VII's reign), or in 1509 (at the beginning of Henry VIII's reign).

3 In the vicinity of Labrador.

Since that time Florida has been explored and all that coast where the French had already penetrated: for it has been more than sixty-eight years since they discovered the cod [for] which they call the land of Bacchaleos, which is fairly close to Canada. It was the Normans and the Bretons who discovered it in the year 1504 under the leadership of a Florentine pilot named Jean de Verrazzane,[4] who was there several times by command of King Francois I and of the most illustrious dame the Regent Louise of Savoy, his mother. Therefore I hold that our French and even the English have much more right there than do the Spaniards, who however continually make war on those who cast anchor in Florida, where they have killed so many wrongfully and against their conscience, as also in the lands of Norumbeg and elsewhere. In short, they would if they could make themselves masters of everything lying between the two poles. [176v] They showed it only too openly two years ago when they tried to close the Southern Strait which we vulgarly term that of Magellan, fortifying themselves there to control those who sought to pass,[5] [and] seeking to rule in the Atlantic as well as the Pacific as they have done with several kingdoms, duchies, and great provinces such as Naples, Sicily, Portugal, Milan and other countries our neighbors.

All these explorers have never really described the style of life of these peoples of Florida, nor the things which are remarkable there, the rarities which grow there as well as the dangers of the sea and secrets of pilotage. I may boast of being one of the first who has described to you truly how things are there at present. I know well that there is a Benzoni[6] [who], although [he has] never traveled, has sung its marvels, but these are only lies; [he] thinks by these to build a reputation and pry a few pennies out of the printers. Among other things, he said the peoples of Florida eat their enemies after having sacrificed them to their idols. O the impudent liar! Never did these people have idols, any more than temples or any religion, knowing no more of sacrifice or idols than the savage peoples of Brazil or others of the Antarctic. This is on a par with what he says afterwards, that the barbarians of Florida have red skin. He certainly mistakes the red for the tanned. And as for Florida, which he calls

4 Lestringant claims that Thevet took this passage from Urbain Chauveton's translation of Benzoni, but skipped some six lines of Chauveton's text, resulting in the error of the date of Verrazzano's voyage ("Séquelles," p. 35n113). Chauveton translated Benzoni into Latin in 1578 and into French in 1579. See below note 6.

5 In 1583 Diego Flores Valdés tried to secure the Straits of Magellan for Philip II.

6 Girolamo Benzoni, a frequent object of Thevet's criticism, wrote *La Historia del Mondo Novo* (Venice, 1565).

Antarctic France, the good fellow well shows his complete ignorance, not realizing that what is on the other side of the equator or equinoctial line we call Antarctic or Southern Lands, and what is on this side of the said Equator is called Arctic—does he not know that this country is twenty-five, twenty-six, and twenty-seven degrees in the direction of our Arctic Pole. We have to forgive him, as well as his pal Léry, who says that the *croisant* which one begins to see very low down when one is below the equator, is under the Antarctic Pole.[7] On the contrary, it is more than twenty-three degrees distant from the Antarctic Circle. That is what it is like to speak offhand without knowledge and experience.

Moreover, our Isle of Cedars,[8] the map of which I represent for you here,[9] is about two and a half leagues long and one-half in width. Its [surrounding] depth is about ten fathoms. The tides [177r] are rather bothersome as in the other rivers of the region. It is inhabited by savages who are almost all fishermen because there is an abundance of large and medium fish [and] the best simples [medicinal herbs] anyone could find in all the Cyclades Isles of Greece or in the Hebrides and the Orkneys. The country near the seacoast is the most fertile because the inhabitants have learned to sow their millet which they call Tapola,[10] and a root resembling the maize of Peru [South America]. They also have a plant called Cassine, similar to a crispy round lettuce I saw in Happy Arabia from which they make a certain beverage. They have an abundance of wild animals, like stags, bears, pigs, and other animals that we do not have over here. They eat the meat of the crocodile [alligator] which is fine and white, as do the Arabs living on the banks of the Nile, and which I would often have eaten had it not had too musky an odor. They eat all their meat roasted over coals or barbecued in the manner of the Brazilians. As for their beverage it is pure water and sometimes as I said they make a mixture with Cassine but with cleanliness.

You will note here that there is no nation in the world however barbarous or rustic which does not prefer to go to the trouble of making some kind of liquor for its drink than to just get along with pure water,

7 Evidently the Southern Cross, but we have been unable to find any example of this use of the French word *croisant*. *Lune croissante* is the crescent moon. For more on Léry see the Introduction.

8 In the *Cosmographie*, chap. 15: "On the Province of Mexico," Thevet mentions that the Isle of Cedars is called *Oracantin* by the natives.

9 There is no map here.

10 René de Laudonnière gives *Tapaga Tapola* in his *Histoire notable de la floride* (Paris, 1586), pp. 69–70.

which seems to be the drink proper to animals; which I have observed in all the four corners of the earth which I have visited. I call them beverages when they are made of divers combinations and simples, and so they are of divers tastes and flavors. Take, for example, the people of Guinea as far as upper Ethiopia more than six hundred leagues from the seacoast – they use the sap of the palm for their drink. Going further along to the East Indies, there are different kinds of drinks according to the different regions and countries; just as I have seen the beverage made by our savages of the Southern Land [Brazil] that they call Caouin,[11] made of roots, [and] large millet that they call Anati, [and] the Turks, Arabs, and Persians do the same since they are forbidden to use wine. In place of it they make a certain mixture of water boiled with cloves, sugar, and other cordial things.

Well, I will leave these fine beverages to return to our Isle of Cedars, so named because those who were the first to land there found it heavily populated with large cedar trees, the most beautiful to be seen in those regions and in all the four quarters of the world. They are just the [177v] same as those you see in the mountains of Lebanon or on Mount Carmel, formerly so greatly recommended and prized by the kings of Egypt who used them to make their oared ships [and] to embellish the temples of their god-idols whom the people worshipped. In my day when I was in Egypt I saw a number of those idols which are kept in the caves near the Pyramids. I have one in my den in Paris as big as your arm [and] being about a foot and a half in length, wearing a long pointed beard, and another more middle-sized bearing Moslem [*lettres mousques*] or hieroglyphic characters. Cedar wood never rots either in water or underground, no matter how humid the conditions. It was on this Isle of Cedars that some Frenchmen took refuge to escape the fury and rage of the Spaniards after the death of Jean Ribaud and Nicholas Barré my companion, who had previously conducted three ships over there; and if he had not been so treacherously murdered he would have been today the foremost pilot of our age.

I have rather fully recounted the history of the Frenchmen killed in Florida, [a story] I cannot tell without some regret. It is better to pass over them silently than to discuss them at such length. There is a little history of them, printed last year, which I had in confidence and good faith

11 In other parts of his work Thevet gives *Cahouin*. He has taken this information from an earlier section of the *Cosmographie* (fol. 916v, which we do not publish). See Suzanne Lussagnet, *Les Français en Amérique pendant la deuxième moitié du XVIe siècle: Le Brésil et les Brésiliens par André Thevet* (Paris, 1953), pp. 55–7, 56n1, and her fig. 15.

loaned to a certain Englishman named Richard Hakluyt, in manuscript. He, having communicated this to a young Parisian named M. Basanier, held it out on me for four months or thereabouts, at the end of which time they had it printed at Paris.[12] I have here to seek condolence with my friends against these plagiarists and impostors, who unable to put anything over on me through their sinister enterprises that they had hatched up in their hearts, thought they could take away the credit and authority which my peregrinations had acquired via the reports I had made in my Cosmographie and my book of my Singularities. These two characters having committed such a villainy against me, the both of them brought me one of the books they had had printed thinking to please me with my well-written copy, which book they dedicated to a great English milord named Walter Ralegh. Moreover the latitude of our Isle of Cedars lies at twenty-five degrees thirty-two minutes, and at 302 degrees of longitude.

12 Hakluyt paid for the publication of Laudonnière's *History of Florida* in Paris in 1586 under the editorship of his friend Martin Basanier. He also translated and published it in England in 1587. For a correspondence between A.P. Stabler and Frank Lestringant on the ramifications of this passage of Thevet's, see Lestringant, "Séquelles," p. 12, and "Notes complémentaires sur les séquelles littéraires de la Floride française," *Bibliothèque d'Humanisme et Renaissance* 45 (1983): 337–8.

PART 3

Mexico

Singularitez de la France antarctique

[144r] Description of New Spain and the Great City of Themistitan, Situated in the West Indies

CHAPTER 73

Because it is not possible for any man to literally see everything in his lifetime because of the constant mutability of everything below heaven, or from the long distances between places and countries, God has given us a way to be able to represent them not only in writing, but also by true portraits through the industry and work of those who have seen them. I see that people have well depicted many ancient fables in pictures, like those of Jason, Adonis, Actaeon, Aeneas, and Hercules, simply to give pleasure, likewise many other things we can all see every day in their own being, without pictures, like the various species of animals. Therefore I have bethought me to describe for you simply and exactly as possible the great and ample city of Themistitan,[1] knowing that very few among you have seen it – much less being able to go see it, because of the long, extraordinary, and difficult navigation you would have to make.

Themistitan is a city situated in New Spain, which begins at the strait of Ariane [Anian],[2] bordering Peru [South America], and ends

1 The name of this city is spelled in various ways by the early chroniclers. Martyr says that the name Themistitan derives from three different words: *tem*, meaning "of divine origin," *nucil*, meaning "fruit," and *titan*, or "something standing in water." Thus, the name would mean a divine fruit standing in water. See *De Orbe Novo: The Eight Decades of Peter Martyr d'Anghera*, trans. from the Latin with Notes and Introduction by Francis A. MacNutt, 2 vols. (New York, 1912), decade 5, book 10, 2: 192. For more on the derivation of the name see *Hernán Cortés: Letters from Mexico*, trans. and ed. A.R. Pagden (New York, 1971), pp. 459–60n2.

2 The "Strait of Anian," dividing America from Asia, apparently derives from Marco Polo's *Ania*. See *The Book of Ser Marco Polo the Venetian*, ed. G.B. Parks (New York, 1927), chap. 57, "Concerning the Province of Anin," pp. 195–6. The Strait of Ania,

on the north side with the Panuque river. [This country] was formerly called *Anauach*;[3] afterwards, since it was discovered and settled by the Spaniards, it received the name of New Spain. [144v] The first of its regions and provinces to be settled was Yucatan,[4] which has a point of land extending into the sea similar to that of Florida: however, our mapmakers have neglected to remark [upon] this fact, which would have improved their description. Now this New Spain is surrounded by the great Ocean on the east, west, and south. On the north side is the New World which, being inhabited, faces even further to the north another land still unknown to the moderns, which is why I abstain from any longer discussion of it.

Now Themistitan, which is a fortified city, large and very rich in the above-named country, is situated in the middle of a large lake. The road by which one comes to it is not more than two lances wide. It was so called from the name of him who first founded it, surnamed Tenuth, elder son of King Iztacmircoatz. This city has only two gates, one for entry and the other for exit. Not far from it is a wooden bridge ten feet wide, built because of the tides, for this lake has tides like the sea. And for the defense of the city there are still others, since it is built like Venice on the sea.[5] This country is all surrounded by high mountains. The flat country has a circumference of about one hundred fifty leagues in which are found two lakes which occupy a large part of the countryside. The said lakes have fifty leagues circumference: one is fresh water in which there are many small delicate fish, and the other [is] salt, which aside from bitterness is poisonous and hence cannot support any fish, [145r]

---

for example, is on the 1566 map of B. Zaltieri [map 10]. Also see Sophus Ruge, *Fretum Anian: Die Geschichte der Beringsstrasse und Ihre Entdeckung* (Dresden, 1873). For more information see Samuel Eliot Morison, *The European Discovery of America: The Northern Voyages A.D. 500–1600* (New York, 1971), p. 515. Having this strait "bordering Peru" (South America) is a notable example of geographical confusion on the part of Thevet.

3 Anahuac was the ancient name for Mexico. At first it was applied to the region around the lakes in the present Basin of Mexico, but it later came to have a much broader application and was extended to include all of Mexico.

4 For Thevet's etymology of this name see *Cosmographie*, chap. 14: "On the Rest of the Mainland."

5 The comparison of Themistitan with Venice was made by a number of authors including Peter Martyr and Tommaso Porcacchi. For example, in the 1566 Italian edition of Gómara's *Conquista de Mexico*, the publisher, Giordano Ziletti, closed his dedication of the work with compliments to Cortés, "discoverer of New Spain and the great city of Mexico, now called New Venice because it greatly resembles Venice in location, buildings, and wealth." Cited by Benjamin Keen, *The Aztec Image in Western Thought* (New Brunswick, 1971), p. 139; see also *Cosmographie*, chap. 16: "On the City of Thenuthtitlan."

which is contrary to the opinion of those who think there is but one lake.[6]

The plain is separated from the said lakes by some mountains, and at their end [they] are joined by a narrow [strip of] land through which the men have themselves taken with boats to the city, which is situated in the salt lake. From there to the mainland, on the highway side is four leagues, and no better comparison of its size could be made than with Venice. To enter into the said city there are four roads made artificially of rock where there are conduits two paces wide and of the height of a man, by one of which fresh water is brought into the city. This is five feet high, and the water flows into the middle of the city, which they drink and use for all their necessities. They keep the other canal empty for this reason: that when they want to clean the fresh-water canal, they conduct all of the sewage of the city in the other one to [the main]land. And because the canals go over by the bridges, and by the places where the salt water enters and exits, they carry the said water by fresh [water] canals, one pace in height. In this lake which surrounds the city the Spaniards have built some little houses and parks, some on little *rochotes*,[7] others on wood pilings. Moreover, Themistitan is situated at twenty degrees above the equinoctial line and 272 degrees longitude.[8] It was taken by force by Fernand de Cortes, captain for the emperor in this country in the year of grace 1521, containing then 70,000 houses large and small.[9]

6 Compare the description of Mexico City given by Robert Thomson in 1555: "It is situated in the middest of a lake of standing water, and environed round about with the same, saving in many places, going out of the Citie, are many broad wayes through the said lake or water. This lake and Citie is environed also with great mountaines round about, which are in compasse above thirtie leagues, and the saide Citie, and the lake of standing water, doeth stand in a great plaine in the middest of it . . . " See "The Voyage of Robert Thomson, Marchant, into Nova Hispania in the yeere 1555 . . . " in Richard Hakluyt, *The Principal Navigations Voyages Traffiques & Discoveries of the English Nation*, second ed. (1598–1600; reprinted Glasgow, 1903-5; New York, 1965), 9: 338–58, esp. 355–6; see also map 12.

7 Rocks or pilings? The word is found in no references.

8 In his accounts of Themistitan in the *Cosmographie*, chap. 16: "On the City of Tenuthlitan," and *Grand Insulaire*, chap. "Themistitan," Thevet gives eighteen degrees latitude.

9 The official history of Cortés's exploits was written by López de Gómara (see Introduction, "Sources"). The literature on Cortés is very large: see R.H. Valle, *Bibliografia de Hernan Cortés* (Mexico City, 1953). Peter Martyr claimed that Mexico City had 60,000 houses. See *De Orbe Novo*, decade 5, book 3, 2: 108. A number of other sixteenth-century sources give the population of Mexico City as 70,000 houses. See *Cosmographie*, chap. 16: "On the City of Tenuthlitan."

The palace of the king, who was named Mutueezuma,[10] as well as those of the lords [145v] of the city were very beautiful, large, and spacious. The Indians who then were in the city were acustomed to holding a market every five days in a permanent marketplace. Their commerce was in bird plumage from which they made a variety of beautiful things, such as dresses fashioned in their style, tapestries, and other things.[11] And in this were occupied mainly the old, when they wanted to go worship their great idol, which was erected in the middle of the city as a kind of theatre. When they had captured some of their enemies in war, they sacrificed them to their idols, then ate them as part of their religion.[12] Other commerce was in animal skins, from which they made clothing, breeches, and a kind of hood to ward off cold and certain little very stinging flies.

The inhabitants of today, formerly so cruel and inhuman, through the passage of time have so greatly changed in their mores and character that instead of being barbaric and cruel they are now humane and gracious and have abandoned their former uncivilized, inhuman, and bad customs such as killing one another, eating human flesh, having intercourse with the first woman they came across without respect for blood and kinship, and other such vices and imperfections. Their houses are magnificently

10 *Motecuçoma* is probably the closest to a correct phonetic transcription of this name. Moctezuma is the common modern Spanish form, which in English has become Montezuma (see Pagden, ed., *Cortés*, p. 460n3). Thevet included a chapter on Montezuma in his *Vrais Pourtraicts et vies des hommes illustres . . .* (Paris, 1584), 2: fols. 644–5.

11 Descriptions of the market in Themistitan are in Francisco López de Gómara, *Historia general de las Indias* (Saragossa, 1552; reprinted 2 vols. Barcelona, 1954), 2: 145–8, "Mercados de Méjico," and Alonso de Santa Cruz, *Islario general de todas las islas del mundo*, 2 vols. (1541, reprinted Madrid, 1918, ed. Antonio Blásquez), 1: 534.

12 There is a lively debate on the issue of Aztec cannibalism. Most scholars would probably disagree with Thevet's testimony on this point, but see Michael Harner, "The Ecological Basis for Aztec Sacrifices," *American Ethnologist* 4 (1977): 117–35. Aztec religion is known through a large number of contemporary documents. The most important description of Aztec religion written by a missionary is undoubtedly that of Bernardino de Sahagún, *Historia general de las cosas de Nueva España*. Most of this work was a detailed account of the beliefs and rites of the natives, dictated to Sahagún in Nahuatl (which he learned) by native priests and nobles. For an English version see *Florentine Codex: General History of the Things of New Spain*, 12 vols., ed. A.J.O. Anderson and C.E. Dibble (Santa Fe, 1950–69). In addition, Aztec religion is described in the Aztec sacred books, or codices, which were kept in the temples. Many of these were destroyed after the conquest. Among modern works on Aztec religion see C.A. Burland, *The Bases of Religion in Aztec Mexico* (London, 1964), B.C. Brundage, *The Fifth Sun: Aztec Gods, Aztec World* (Austin, 1979), and Davíd Carrasco, *Quetzalcoatl and the Irony of Empire: Myths and Prophecies in the Aztec Tradition* (Chicago, 1982).

built: among others there is a very beautiful palace where the arms of the city are kept. The streets and squares of this city go so straight that from one gate you can see the other with no hindrance.[13] In short this city, at present fortified and surrounded by ramparts and thick walls like those of Europe, is one of the largest, [146r] richest, and most beautiful of all the West Indies – from the strait of Magellan which is fifty degrees below the line to the uttermost [part of] Labrador which is fifty-one degrees north of the line.

13 Again, compare Thevet's description with Thomson: "The said Citie of Mexico hath streetes made very broad, and right, that a man being in the high place, at the one ende of the street, may see at the least a good mile forward. . . " See Hakluyt, *Principal Navigations*, 9: 356–7.

Cosmographie universelle (Book 22)

[984v] On the Rest of the Mainland, As Far As the Kingdom of Mexico
CHAPTER 14

From Cuba then you go to the mainland, in the province of Nicaragua, which is still Peru [South America], under which is included the Peninsula which we now call Iucatan. This was not [formerly] so called, rather it bore the name of Ananac, but the first Christians who discovered it gave it this title from the answer which the natives gave them. For when the Christians asked the native inhabitants what was the name of this great people, they answered [985r] *Tectetan-Tectetan*, which is to say, I do not understand you: whereupon the Christians thought that the others were saying that such was their name, and for this reason the land was called *Iucatan*, which name I imagine it will be a long time in losing.[1] Our savages of the Antarctic [Brazil], when at first we would ask them something, they answered us proudly in their patois *Necoauit*, *Arouiouiou*, *mahyre mohan* (We do not understand you, wicked people).

This land, from the time it was first discovered was believed to be an island because from all sides one saw that the sea surrounded it.[2] But they had not gone to the south of it where they would have found that this land was bounded by and joined to the province of Nicaragua, which extends to the Southern Sea beside Panama in the direction of the Isle of Pearls.[3] Iucatan lies at twenty-one degrees latitude, being in the shape

1 This story of the origin of the name Yucatan is also found in Francisco López de Gómara, *Historia general de las Indias* (Saragossa, 1552; reprinted 2 vols. Barcelona, 1954), 1: 84.

2 The Spaniards believed Yucatan was an island, and named it Isla de Santa Maria de los Remedios. See Justin Winsor, ed., *Narrative and Critical History of America*, 8 vols. (Boston, 1884; reprinted New York, 1967), 2: 220.

3 The Isle of Pearls, in the Gulf of Panama, is mentioned by several early writers

of a peninsula just as is Florida except that it is larger and has greater length and width than does Florida.[4] Now the principal cape by which one approaches this land, coming from Cuba, is named *Catoche*, which means house.[5] What caused the discoverers of the country to land there was that seeing this people nicely accoutered in dresses of cotton and of feathers such as I have mentioned before, and that they were wearing much gold and silver jewelry, and that the women ornamented their hair and bosoms with the same; they thought that these savages were rich in these metals and that the land abounded in beautiful and rich mining. But in this they were deceived, since neither in Iucatan nor in Nicaragua were to be found silver and gold ores of any worth or which were not of poor and low grade. Therefore they were not so insistent on building large cities there and [to] colonize them with Christians as in the lands where gold is produced in abundance.

These Iucatayans were idolatrous and sacrificed human blood to their gods and idols, although they never ate human flesh as did most of their neighbors. [This idolatry] was to be seen in a tower of stone of square shape and with steps which went on the outside to the top of the said tower, where you saw an idol resembling a man which nevertheless exceded the just proportion of [other men], on the two sides of which were two proud and frightful animals sculpted equally [in size] to the idol. Right next to them one saw a stone serpent seven feet in length and big as a steer, which was battling with a lion, with all [the figures of this group] stained with the blood of the animals sacrificed to the idol.[6] This country is fertile in partridges, turtledoves, and ducks (somewhat different from ours), many hares, coneys, stags, and other edible game.

A Spanish captain [was] passing through a corner of this peninsula which faces the Isle of Cannibals, (which place in their language is called

---

including Gómara and Girolamo Benzoni, *History of the New World* (Venice, 1565, trans. and ed. W.H. Smyth, London, 1857).

4 Thevet's information here appears to be based on the account of Gómara. See *Historia general*, 1: 83.

5 The name Catoche is said to have originated with the Spanish landfall in Mexico in 1517. While sailing by Cape San Antonio, the expedition of Francisco Hernández de Córdoba met a group of natives and aked them what land they were going to. They replied *conex Catoche* or "come to our houses." The Spaniards accordingly named the area Punta de Catoche. When the Spaniards landed, however, they were ambushed and many were killed. See Gómara, *Historia general*, 1: 84.

6 Thevet appears to be following the account given by Diego de Landa, written about 1566. See *Landa's Relación de las Cosas de Yucatan. A Translation*, ed. with notes by Alfred M. Tozzer (Cambridge, Mass., 1941), p. 11 and n54.

Chaupoton) [Champoton]. At that time their chief, who was called *Choroboch*,[7] asking the Spaniard what he sought in his country, understood finally that he was asking for water and food. He told him through the interpreter that a little further on from there there was a spring of water very clear and sweet to refresh himself. The Christian seeing these idolators all armed with clubs and that their countenance was not peaceful, being braver than wise, sent his men ashore as well armed as possible, especially as these barbarians looked like valiant warriors and would not take fright for a trifle. The Christian soldiers seeing this people all assembled and in [war] paint, and making themselves frightful with the said paint, armed with large bows and ready to fight, did not want to go on the campaign. But finally, whether through shame or the express command of the captain, they set out not without first having fired several canon-shots to frighten them.

At first the barbarians were astonished to see the fire and smoke coming out of the piece [985v] and were afraid, hearing the tone and noise of the artillery, but nevertheless did not flee. Rather (which is worse) immediately upon the cessation of the noise they began a great hue and cry against our men assailing them with rocks, clubs, and arrows. The Christians advanced also and engaging the enemy killed several with sword-thrusts, finding no resistance against the steel. But the barbarians, although they had never experienced such blows, infuriated at the wounding and death of their comrades and urged on by their chief, who was enraged seeing that so few men were holding out against so large a company, spurred them on so greatly that despite all efforts of the Christians they were forced to retreat and regain the ships and six score of his best men were killed. Most of those that escaped were bristling with arrows and two were captured and sacrificed before their idol. The captain was wounded in thirty places with arrows: in spite of which they had to embark, and depart without trumpet [of victory], more grieved over his shame than happy at having made such a disadvantageous discovery.[8]

And to tell the truth, those of Yucatan are the most valiant to be found in Peru [South America] either in the north or the south and you can throw in the cannibals or the giants who are on the Plata River. For arms they use the sling-shot, staves in the shape of a heavy club, long lances without iron [tips], bows and arrows which are not poisoned, and

7 Landa gives Mochcovoh. Tozzer says that this is undoubtedly the Yucatan patronymic Couoh. See his *Relación*, p. 11 and n56.

8 Landa's account says that Hernández received thirty-three wounds. See *Relación*, pp. 11–12.

they make cotton cuirasses which are good enough [to turn away] sword blows; and although they sacrifice those whom they take in war they do not eat them.

The principal city of the country is now called *Meride* and formerly *Xicalance*. One of their priests, who was the most learned in the art of divination and in the secrets of the Devil, was converted to the Catholic faith being already of the age of six score years. This good man was called *Alquimpech*, and Christian though he was, still he never ceased to weep for the disaster which had come to his nation that a people so fierce and barbarous should hold them in slavery, saying that he had seen a plague which carried off more than 150,000 persons but that it had not harmed his country as much as those who were rendering it solitary and deserted.[9]

At the approaches to this peninsula on the Florida side, which is like a gulf in the shape of a crescent (there being about six to seven hundred leagues from the one to the other), there lies an isle which the savages call *Coxumel*.[10] Although at present [it is] not populated, since it was formerly inhabited I have not wished to pass over it in silence since I seek out matters rare and worthy of memory rather than riches. In Coxumel is found among several sorts of trees and plants which grow there entirely through the benefit of nature, the earth, and influence of heaven, a tree which the savages told me (when we stopped there to get food) that it was called *Iaruma*[11] which they hold in great esteem: and not without cause if it is true what they say and claim they know by experience. For if the buds, twigs, and leaves of this tree [are] all crushed together and then with the juice pressed out over a wound no matter how old, it will not fail to cure it better than the best balm one could apply to it. This tree is like a walnut in size and is thickly branched, and its leaves are like those of a fig and are always green for when some leaves fall others take their place.

9 This account, including the name Alquimpech, also appears in Gómara, *Historia general*, 1: 87.

10 Cozumel was discovered by the expedition of Juan de Grijalva on 4 May, 1518, the feast day of the Intervention of the Holy Cross, and given the name Santz Cruz.

11 Martyr describes the Jaruma as resembling "a fig tree at least as regards it leaves. It is taller than a poplar. . . Its fruit is half a cubit long, and soft like a fig, with strong flavour, and is excellent for healing wounds. Its leaves possess miraculous virtues . . . " (*De Orbe Novo: The Eight Decades of Peter Martyr d'Anghera*, trans. from the Latin with Notes and Introduction by Francis A. MacNutt, 2 vols. [New York, 1912], decade 7, book 1, 2: 248). Also see Francisco Tamara, *El Libro de las Costumbres de todas las gentes del Mundo y de las Indias* (Antwerp, 1556), fol. 315r.

Returning to the mainland, leaving Iucatan toward the south you enter the land of Nicaragua which is contiguous with the country of Castille d'Or, which the natives call Berague.[12] To the north it borders the country of Mexico. To the south is a very famous lake [Lake Nicaragua] because of its size and for the isles which are in it, its length extending to [986r] within four leagues of the Pacific Sea; and on it one can go by ship into the province of Berague: and from that you can judge how large this province is. It is more healthy and fertile than rich, although some pearls are fished from the Pacific coast, in the Isles they call the Pearl Islands in the gulf which is between Parise [Paria][13] and the city of Panama: but they are not very good or much in demand. As for gold, some is found there but it is very low [inferior] and light and so it is not much prized.

In the middle of this region there is a slope and hill completely round called *Masaye*, which continually throws out fire and flames:[14] and you must know that at the summit of this little mountain there is an abyss-mouth [crater] which is about a half-league wide and around it no tree or plant whatever grows. Yet the birds fly over it although usually the fire vomits forth its flames from it. At the distance of a bow-shot from this abyss you see a sort of well whose mouth is fifteen to twenty paces wide, from which one sees the fire arise like a mass, or like the tail of a great comet, and throws so much light that the flames divide[15] themselves into twenty-five or thirty very frightful splendors which make such strange sounds that there is none who is not astounded, more than at anything he saw in his life. Anyhow, whatever this fire may be, you never see sparks nor ashes come from it to harm anyone or any living thing. You only see smoke and fire, which light up the neighboring hill so well that you have no need of a candle.

Some people having heard this noise rather close up and saying it seemed inside like the boiling of a cauldron, thought it was gold or other

12 Veragua originally defined a stretch of about fifty leagues between ChiriquíLagoon (Panama) and Punta Rincón. The Spaniards later considered it part of Castilla del Oro, the region from the Gulf of Urabá (Colombia) to Cape Gracias a Dios (Nicaragua). See Carl O. Sauer, *The Early Spanish Main* (Berkeley, 1966), p. 131.

13 The name Paria was originally given by Columbus to an island in the West Indian archipelago. It was subsequently applied to various areas in Central and South America, and also to Florida.

14 This popular story about the Masaya volcano also appears, with slight variations, in Gómara, *Historia general*, 1: 343–4: "El volcán de Nicaragua que llaman Masaya." Benzoni also tells the tale of a friar who lowered a bucket and chain into the crater of Massaya, only to see it consumed by fire. See his *History*, ed. Smyth, pp. 152–3.

15 Gómara's verb, *divisar*, "to perceive indistinctly," obviously has been mistranslated.

metal which was melted there by the vehemence of the fire which was burning in the sulphurous mine. But this is advanced without regard to the substances in question. In my opinion I would say it is indeed sulphuric matter which is in the mountain but that the noise the fire makes comes from water, which naturally nourishes it and makes it swirl and fly thus in flashes and flames just as the small amount of water thrown on the blacksmith's fire, instead of extinguishing it, fires it up more. And since this furnace throws out neither ashes nor rocks as you read about other similar places, the explanation must be that there is no subject upon which the fire can act and which resists it, as heavy things would if there were any nearby. Some persons[16] curious to learn about it, and what was the material upon which this fire fed, let down to it an iron pail attached to a long iron chain of about two hundred fathoms: but as the pail approached the said fire it was burnt up as quick as thought.

The thing that is most abundant in this province is trees, of which some are so large that six men would have difficulty in putting their arms around one of the sort that grows there. Among these is a kind from which they make their beverage, better than that made from maize or from the palm, and the Nicaraguans get good and drunk from it. Gourds grow there in one month[17] and bear the fruit which they use when traveling to contain this beverage, since in this country there are few or no rivers and springs (since there are not many mountains and also that it does not rain too often or abundantly). This is why this region is the least populated of all of Peru [South America].

Although they take as many wives as they wish they marry only one with ceremony, and if she is unfaithful to her husband they banish her, the husband returning to her what she brought him as dowry: but the man who seduced the wife is cudgelled roundly and not condemned to death.[18] If anyone commits a cowardly act they take his arms from him and [he] is broken from his company: [986v] and all that a soldier pillages from his enemy they cannot take away from him, but he uses it as his own without accounting for it to his captain. He must, however, sacrifice those whom he takes as prisoner and would not dare release and pardon them for whatever ransom, for if he did that he would be subject to the law of sacrifice.

16 Gómara identifies these persons as Fray Blas de Iñesta and two other Spaniards. *Historia general*, 1: 344.

17 Gómara says that gourds grow in forty days rather than a month. *Historia general*, 1: 344.

18 Cf. the discussion in Gómara, *Historia general*, 1: 345–6.

This people boasts of being descended from the *Mexican*, saying that in the land of Auauac, which is New Spain, the inhabitants left their country and came across the Pacific to live in Nicaragua: which is quite probable since their language is quite close to that of Themistitan, and the characters which they use to signify what they mean are similar to the others.[19] These are written on very badly made parchment or on curried skins, with azure, gold, and other beautiful and rich colors, and usually recall to memory the great deeds of their captains and the wars which they have had against their neighbors.[20] In this land their barbarity is not so grossly felt as formerly it was in the rest of Peru [South America], since they observe better order and discipline in everything they do, either because of their republic or because of their superstitions and ceremonies.

They have not yet abandoned the cruel custom of sacrificing their prisoners of war and their slaves, unless in the last seven or eight years they have been weaned away from such impious and brutal customs. When, then, the priest conducts this cruel office he has to go three times around the poor man who is to be sacrificed, singing a plaintive lament. Then he cuts open his chest, spraying his face with blood; then cuts his heart out of his stomach,[21] and hacks the body to pieces. The principal sacrificer gets the heart, the king the feet and by the same token the hands, [and] the capturer the shoulders.[22] The trumpeters get the entrails, and all the rest [go] to the people for in several localities they are anthropophages. As for the heads they are hung on certain trees on which are engraved the names of the provinces with whom they have warred.

If it is a slave who is immolated they bury the feet and the hands and also the entrails and burn the heart, and the rest with the head is placed on these trees on parade. The priest anoints the mouth of the idol and its knees with the blood of the sacrificed one, and doing this the others sing and the people pray with great devotion and tears, and then they form a procession carrying the image of the Devil on the end of a lance which

19 Gómara here gives "those of Culua" rather than "the others." *Historia general*, 1: 347.

20 This is a reference, no doubt, to the *Codex Mendoza*, which was in Thevet's possession. See Introduction, "Sources," and *Codex Mendoza: Aztec Manuscript*, ed. Kurt Ross (Freibourg, Switzerland, 1978).

21 In sixteenth-century French the *estomach* was the chest, and consequently the heart was spoken of as being in the stomach. Here, however, Thevet uses *estomach* in the first part of the sentence and *ventre*, meaning belly, in the latter part. Thus Thevet appears to indicate that the heart is indeed in the stomach.

22 Gómara has thighs rather than shoulders here. *Historia general*, 1: 348.

the oldest and most honorable of the priests carries to the temple. On arrival there they place on the ground their robes and many flowers and branches so that the idol does not touch the ground. I saw when I was in Portugal two of these idols and three of these figures; however, they told me that the said idols had been brought from Calcutta.

Meantime they keep praying then each one sprinkles himself with blood wherever he can find some, saying that in this way they are delivered from their sins; and during this ceremony the young men dance, wrestle, or combat to honor the feast. If anyone is wounded in this, they apply a certain juice made from plants soaked in the sacrificial blood. Think whether we should find strange what the ancients wrote about the Scythians, the Romans, and even the Gauls, sacrificing men, some to Diana, others to Saturn; since even in our own times such butchery is taking place (which I can testify is true, having got it from several who were present).[23]

It is true that in Nicaragua, going toward Mexico, [and] in New Grenada and Leon, there are many Christian churches and bishoprics, where the Christians dutifully win as many souls as possible. But to say that all this region is Christian, as did a certain galant a year ago in his thefts and rhapsodies, would be a mockery since our people have not yet discovered a tenth of it.[24] And [987r] where they have passed through they have not stayed at all to live and sow the doctrine of the faithful there.

This province extends on the east side toward Berague, to the west to the Kingdom of Parise [Paria] which is in Mexico, and to the south is still a neighbor of Berague, except one point [which] extends into the Pacific. Belonging to Nicaragua there is an isle far out into the sea which some have named the Gorgon because of the fury of the seas there, which are never without storms. However, before continuing with our discourse it must be noted that there are several Isles called Gorgons: e.g. those of Cape Verde (which properly are the Hesperides), another which is near Corsica in the Sea of Genoa, and this one which is located at some three degrees and a half on this side of the line. [It is] near another islet which the Spaniards named *Isla del Gallo*, or the Isle of the Cock, because they saw there some birds which resembled cocks like the ones

23 Compare Gómara, "Religión en Nicaragua," *Historia general*, 1: 347–9.

24 Thevet's reference here is unclear. He may be referring to François de Belleforest, whose *Cosmographie universelle de tout le monde*, 2 vols. (Paris, 1575) appeared in the same year as Thevet's *Cosmographie*.

we have here.[25] Gorgon Isle might have two leagues circumference and is all mountainous, abundant in streams and springs whose water is very healthful and good. [There are] as many fruit trees as one could wish and so many birds that it is a marvel: but to live there is impossible, since no one ever saw it without rains, thunder, tempests, lightning, and thunderbolts of such vehemence and impetuosity that you could think it would be engulfed.

The cause of this is completely unknown to me, except that I think that the coast being very low and nevertheless mountainous, and the isle very high and vaporous because of the currents, it is impossible that this enclosure of mountains should not catch the winds in its concavities, which [winds] wishing to escape free to the country, cause this thunder and rain and impetuous winds, just as we see them rise like smoke attracted by the sun during the heat of the "dog days" over the Pyrenees mountains, causing thunder, tempests, storms, and hail. Besides, this isle is very close to the equator, where I have told you so often that you find the great attractions of vapors by the sun which is perpendicular to them twice a year. And the coast being low and the summits of the isle very high, one should not be surprised if the thin air and the hot land fight against this grosser substance of the attracted vapors, and if in this combat the winds, rains, storms, thunders, and lightning are commingled. And the louder the noise the more furious the effort, the narrower and more rugged the place where this turbulence is engendered.[26]

On the Province of Mexico and Its First Inhabitants, Where It Got Its Name: and How They Sacrifice Men

CHAPTER 15

Almost as soon as you have left Nicaragua you enter into this great and rich kingdom of Mexico, which goes from the Pacific, at the point of Parise [Paria], to the Panuco River which separates Mexico from the land of Florida. So in the northernmost part Florida serves as [its] frontier, to the south the province of Darien;[27] going east the Atlantic

25 These islands are off the coast of Colombia and are associated with the expedition of Francisco Pizarro to Peru. For the Isles of Gorgona and Gallo see Gómara, *Historia general*, 1: 190.

26 Giovanni Battista Ramusio, *Terzo volume delle navigationi et viaggi nel quale si contengono le navigationi al mondo nuovo . . .* (Venice, 1556), fol. 29v, contains similar material taken from Peter Martyr's *De Orbe Novo*.

27 Darien is the traditional name given to the eastern part of the Isthmus of Panama,

[is] its barrier; and to the west it is the Pacific Ocean which bounds it. And thus this entire province runs from the regions of Nicaragua and Iucatan to Florida, some twenty degrees of latitude.

But before proceeding it has seemed well to me to give you to understand whence came this name Mexico and who were the first to inhabit this province, according to what I have been able to gather and hear from them.[28] This name is not the one which the natives [987v] use, rather they say *Exic*, or *Echich*, and later being corrupted has been pronounced Mexico. They claim to have come from a place named *Echi* (which is near the mountain of *Tholman*, which those of Florida call *Quivir*,[29] and others *Teucan*, from which flow three rivers which empty into the gulf of the red sea)[30] where there is a great rock at the foot of which is seen a cave from which comes the wind, and that near it formerly lived two brothers who ruled this country each adoring a god.[31] Now that of the younger one, seeing the discord which had arisen between them, and that the elder was oppressing and trampling on the smaller, addressed the younger and said: do not get upset, I shall lead you to a place where you shall be a greater lord than your brother, and so assemble as many people as you can and follow me: which the younger brother did and traveled with those whom he had gathered to a province named *Culiacan* [Culhuacan] (situated two hundred leagues from Mexico to the west, not far from the Pacific, and one of the most fertile I ever saw); in which they remained a long time, and there built temples and houses.

A long time afterwards, by the wish of their god, they moved from there to seek places more suitable and to their pleasure, and having traveled a long time they arrived at a place named *Toich* seven leagues from *Chuquipila*,[32] where there is a well-artificed rock on the summit of

---

extending from the Gulf of San Miguel to that of Urabá (Colombia). The province was seen by Columbus in 1503, and in 1510 the first European settlement in South America—Santa Maria de la Antigua del Darien—was attempted on the western side of the Gulf of Urabá. The Spaniards considered Darien to be the eastern part of Castilla del Oro.

28 Thevet repeats this information in the *Grand Insulaire*, chap. "Themistitan."

29 Gómara, *Historia general*, 1: 358–61, has two chapters on Quivira. Also see the 1570 map of Abraham Ortelius [map 13].

30 This is probably a reference to the Mer Vermiglio which appears on several early maps, usually depicting the Gulf of California.

31 Thevet is here following the account given in the *Histoyre de Méchique*, pp. 14–15. Hereafter the identification of places and deities follows the annotations of Edouard de Jonghe, "Histoyre de Méchique, manuscrit français inédit du XVIe siècle," *Journal de la Société des Américanistes de Paris* n.s. 2 (1905): 1–41, unless otherwise stated.

32 De Jonghe tentatively identifies Toich as Teul. For a discussion of these place names

which is a very beautiful fountain of the best water in the world. They did not lodge in this place very long but went to *Chypila* [Xochipila] where they built beautiful edifices on two little hills between which passes a river which separates them one from the other. Here they did not stay long, but came to *Chalpe*, eight leagues from *Chypila*, where they also stayed but a short time. However, they built a temple so sumptuous that I think its equal was never built by the ancient Romans, and take note that the first thing they did on arriving at any place was to build temples and oratories to their gods. These they named *Tezcatlipuca*, *Yhim*, [and] *Cylopucheli*,[33] whom they carried always with them and urged those whose territory they passed to serve them, treating them well: by which means they attracted many people to their friendship. Finally they left Chalpe and came to a place named *Tenainque*,[34] two leagues from Mexico where was built thirty [years] ago a convent of minor brothers [Franciscans]. [They] populated it, as they did at another place named *Chapultequet* [Chapultepec], which is to say house of solace,[35] since it is rather high and very pleasant and where there is a very fine spring.

From there they came in the year of our lord 1324[36] into the province of Mexico, which they found full of trees which they called *Metl*. Here afterwards they had beautiful temples and edifices built, giving it this name of Mexico, composed of the two words *Metl* and *Echic*, which is the place (as I said) from which they originally came. Finally these Mexicans elected ten persons from among them to govern them, that is to say *Ocelopan*, *Quayan*, *Acacitli*, *Ahuechotl*, *Tenuch*, *Tecineuh*, *Chomimitl*, *Chocoyol*, *Chiuhcaqui*, and *Atotolt*. These people elected afterwards *Tenuch* to whom they gave the power and authority to command as superior, under whom they governed the republic and the people as his lieutenants. Now these barbarians, having multiplied, began to dominate over their neighbors and rendered [them] tributary; and [placed] under their obedience the inhabitants of *Colhuacan* and *Tenaincan* their neighbors, all of this under the government and reign of the said *Tenuch* who reigned fifty and three years, at the end of which he died. So much for

---

see *Histoyre*, p. 15n2.

33 Tezcatlipuca "Smoking Mirror" was one of the main Toltec deities; Cylopucheli may be a variant of Xochipilli-Cinteotl. For de Jonghe's speculation concerning Yhim see *Histoyre*, p. 16n4.

34 Thevet's Tenainque appears in the form Tenayucan in the *Codex Mendoza*. This city was the center for Xolotl, chief of the Chichimecas.

35 Thevet's information here is incorrect; *Chapultequet* means "grasshopper hill."

36 Thevet is here following the chronology of the *Codex Mendoza*.

the origin and foundation of this country.[37]

Well, the Spaniards of our times named it New Spain both because it is the place where they are most successfully settled and because the country is most similar in temperature to Europe [988r] of any over there. At eight leagues from Mexico is located the city of *Texcinq* [Tezcuco], whose inhabitants say they and their ancestors were the first founders and issued from *Loli* [Tlotli], that is, sparrow-hawk, and from *Compahli* [Tzompachtli] his wife, who are supposed to have been engendered from an arrow which had been hurled from heaven to a place named *Tezcalque*,[38] where at present there is a city. From the aperture of the said arrow came forth Loli and his wife, who only had a human body from the armpits on up, the rest being like the trunk of a tree, and they only walked in jumps like a magpie. The said Loli engendered [children] by putting his tongue in the mouth of his wife.[39] [They] had six male children and one daughter, with whom they came to the place where now stands the city of Texcinq which then was only a mountain full of trees and all sorts of beasts, with whose skins they clothed themselves. They never shaved their hair, and they offered the earth a plant named in their language *Tlacocatl* [Tlacococatl], that is precious plant, so that the earth would furnish them food. They lived in such great peace and friendship together that they would never have dared do or say anything to one another at which they could take offense; and even if one of them found a dead beast killed by another he did not take it, but rather reported the matter so that the one who had killed it could go and get it, so lacking in malice were they. Finally this people having multiplied and increased, they exercised such abstinence towards women that as soon as one of them was married he knew no other woman than his own.

Now Loli and his wife being lords of this place, their children traveled to new countries so that they populated many places, but they did not settle there because they did not yet know the art of building houses. But [they] lived in caverns which they found [already] made, or else made little shelters of tree branches covered with plants without concerning themselves with the weather or even less counting the months or the years

37 The *Codex Mendoza* says that he died at the age of fifty-one. Thevet now returns to the *Histoyre de Méchique*.

38 Thevet may be referring here to Texcalpan.

39 Joined tongues was an Aztec symbol for sexual intercourse. In some relgious paintings the tongue itself was symbolized by a red stone knife between the mouths of naked figures. See C.A. Burland and Werner Forman, *Feathered Serpent and Smoking Mirror* (New York, 1975), p. 93.

until the Mexicans brought them calendars figured in characters. The first who brought the adoration of idols was one of the sons of Loli who, having lived a long time away from *Texcinq*, came back to his father and brought an idol named *Tezcatlipuca* and raised an altar unto him. At this time they also began to sow maize and friosoles [frijoles], which is a seed crop used in *Chalio* [Chalco], six leagues from Texcinq, from where it is brought. Loli was still living, but he died in this season and one of his sons succeeded him who soon afterwards married a daughter of the lord of *Culhua* [Culhuacan], which is near Mexico.

And as this nation was multiplying they married each other and began to be called *Otomis*[40] from the name of the second lord and to build dwellings and houses. This said lord had a son who married the daughter of the lord of *Theomuthilan* [Tenochtitlan], but he was immediately killed by the brothers of his wife who were angry about this marriage; and not content with having killed him fell upon his brothers and relatives and killed many of them. The oldest brother of the latter, a man of much genius who wanted to know the cause for everything, placed governors on his lands [and] had magnificent temples built for his idols (having the ones his father had built demolished because they were too small). It was he who first began to war and have men sacrificed, eating human flesh. He invented several of the mechanical arts, as carpenter, goldsmith, couturier, shoemaker, and others. Also he much profitted the republic, for he had 140 male children. He began to make laws and instituted a parliament in his country. He bore great reverence for the gods and had a marvelous care for the [988v] temples and ceremonies. He also commanded that the young men and girls dance in the temples from evening till midnight to give pleasure to the false gods. He installed in his house such officials as steward, butler, and others, and commanded that there be a market in his city of Texcinq. He had two men executed who were [sexually] abusing one another and ordered that all those who should be found in the future committing such acts should be killed and likewise with adulterers. He also ordered during his lifetime several other good things: and from that one can judge how the Devil makes use of the good institutions of mankind when he has them in his bonds, for some great enormous vice.

He was succeeded by one of his sons named *Necahualt pilciutli* [Neza-

40 For more on this people see Pedro Carrasco Pizana, *Los Otomíes: Cultura e historia prehispánicas de los pueblos mesoamericanos de habla otomiana* (Mexico, 1950), and Charles Gibson, *The Aztecs under Spanish Rule* (Stanford, 1964), chap. 2: "The Tribes," pp. 9–31.

hualpiltzintli], or Little John, who imitated his father as much as he could and won by arms (with the help of the Mexicans) much territory; to whom succeeded one of his sons who was reigning when the Spaniards first came into that country. But he died soon afterwards, and after him one of his sons was lord of Texcinq. The latter was a Christian and lived according to the Church, and died having received all the sacraments and having made his will. This was the last of the Otomians who ruled at Texcinq. The inhabitants of Texcinq held also that there is a certain goddess named *Citlaline* who sent from Heaven to the city of *Theotihuacan*, located near Texcinq, sixteen hundred of her children, who perished as soon as they arrived.[41] Also that after the creation of the world, there was darkness for about twenty-eight years.[42] At the end of this two gods and a goddess got together, that is to say *Tezcatlipuca*, *Ehecatl*, and *Citlaleeue* [Citlalincue], who decided to make the sun so that it would illuminate the earth, as I shall relate hereafter.

At this time there lived another God named *Pilciutentli* [Piltzinteutli] and his wife *Chuquiquecal* [Xochiquetzal], who had a son named *Choquipile* [Xochipilli], with another *Nanauaton*,[43] who was not their own although he was brought up in their house, but rather was the son of a certain *Izpatl*[44] and of *Cuzcamianh* [Cozcamiauh] (who could transform themselves at will into men, beasts, and other hideous figures). [These two sons] did penance and offered to these three great lords precious pearls, incense, and other very rich things in order to merit being the sun. However this *Nanauaton* being poor had nothing of which to make an offering, so he stuck himself fiercely and repeatedly with a thorn and sacrificed his blood to these gods. [The latter] commanded him to make a great fire before them and to assemble his brothers: and this done, they said that he who should place himself in the fire would be the sun. Then *Nanauaton*, who was very expert in magic, jumped into it and went down to hell whence he brought back many riches, and for this reason he was chosen to be the sun.[45] That is the belief of these barbarians of Texcinq who have not yet received Scripture: which [Texcinq] the Spaniards seized and established governors there to control this fierce and unfriendly people.

41 For more on this deity see *Histoyre*, p. 29n2.

42 The *Histoyre* gives twenty-six years (p. 29 and n3).

43 The augmentative for Nanauatl.

44 De Jonghe guesses that this is Itzpatli (*Histoyre*, p. 30n6).

45 For more on this myth see B.C. Brundage, *The Fifth Sun: Aztec Gods, Aztec World* (Austin, 1979), pp. 41–4, 228n18.

The provinces of this great kingdom are diverse, since leaving Nicaragua you come into the region called by the natives *Tecoantepech*,[46] which is along the Pacific coast near the Kingdom of Parise [Paria] – a rather fertile country not yet subjugated by the Christians because there is a valiant king there, and places to hide when they are closely pursued. Beyond and past Tecoantepech, along the Pacific coast and some two leagues distant from Mexico, is found the Kingdom of *Culhua*, whose people are called *Chichimecas*,[47] who say they are descended from the rest of the Mexicans who stayed behind in the country of Culiacan (which I have discussed above), as follows: [989r] a company of the inhabitants of Culuacan had gone out to fight their enemies and on their return, their lord being dissatisfied with their service, refused to receive them. So being constrained to seek a new habitation they went to *Tula*,[48] a dozen leagues from Mexico, where they remained for some time. Their lord having died they chose in his place a certain *Vemac*,[49] during whose rule a vision appeared to the people of a man who seemed to touch the sky with his head. Whereupon this lord and all the people, frightened, left that place and came to the said Culhua, which they settled and introduced their sacrifices and made an alliance with their neighbors. They were the first (they claimed) who brought the use of maize, paper, cotton, and incense, for previously the Otomis, inhabitants of Texcinq, lived simply with no usage of the foregoing. Nevertheless, always since that time they have been believed to be more noble and virtuous than all the others. It was also this people who leaving their country migrated to the site of the present Themistitan, and conquering the country more than the others who had come from the isles of the [Atlantic] Ocean, began to build on the lake of Mexico.

These Chichimecans were formerly valiant men of war and taught the Mexicans their civic customs, and especially how to build temples and to conduct various ceremonies and the cult of human sacrifice, as I have

46 *Tehuantepec*. Thevet's spelling is identical to that given on Ramusio's map [map 14].

47 The Chichimeca were the peoples on the northern border of the Mexican empire. They were nomadic hunters who remained independent until the seventeenth century. Cortés referred to them as "a very barbarous people and not so intelligent as those of the other provinces" (*Hernán Cortés: Letters from Mexico*, trans. and ed. A.R. Pagden [New York, 1971], p. 446).

48 Tula was the capital of the Toltec empire.

49 Huemac was the god who had led the original Toltecs on the long wandering that had finally resulted in the founding of Tula. From that time on Toltec rulers occasionally bore the god's name as their own. Brundage, *Fifth Sun*, pp. 97–8, and 235n62.

already mentioned. And when the area was well-populated some of them returned to Culhua where their men are still fit, whiter than any of their neighbors: the cause of this I believe must be referred to heredity, it being thus passed on from father to son. For if you consider the climate or the fact that all the rest of the people are colored, you will recognize that the other peoples of Mexico are chestnut-colored, between white and swarthy,[50] but I have discussed this matter elsewhere. The women are beautiful and rather gracious. Their cities are scarcely as large, nor their buildings so magnificent as those of Themistitan; although built of stone, they cover their houses with straw or tree leaves so well joined that rain is unable to enter.

It is true that those who now call themselves Chichimecas at Culhua are priests and diviners who do not live in the cities, but rather in the mountains, with no other occupation than pasturing the stock which they have there in abundance. And [on] the days set aside for the sacrifices they come celebrate the feasts of their gods and deliver their orations in the temples set up for this purpose. These Chichimecas live in the woods and the mountains, living from what the good people give them. They go around all naked except for the private parts, the men and women both, for what superstition I was not able to find out. [They] dye their entire body with suet and the juice of fruits. Their temple is also covered with straw, and in their walls there are round windows in which they place the skulls of dead men—that is of those who have been sacrificed to the idol—since the entire country is steeped in this devilish ceremony of sacrificing men to Satan, who is adored in some visible form or other.[51]

Before the temple is a great moat at whose mouth there is the figure of a monstrous serpent, carved in the round so that the point of the tail comes back to the head and is being bitten in its mouth. It is made just like the god Janus was formerly done, and under this figure it is shown that the month dedicated to this hero is the end and the beginning of the year.[52] This figure of the Culhua Serpent is all in gold and silver and [989v] other mixtures of metal, to which they make sacrifice in this manner: the one among them who is to be sacrificed is chosen by lot, since they are not like the others who sacrifice foreigners (for they think such sacrifices unclean), and is lead in great pomp before this idol. There

50 Thevet uses the word *basané*, which ranges in meaning from tan to black. He considers it darker than chestnut.

51 See Brundage, *Fifth Sun*, pp. 129–30, "Chichimec Religion."

52 In Roman religion Janus was the animistic spirit of doorways and archways. Its symbol, in addition to the gate, was a double-faced head.

they have many banquets, drink, eat, and sing, all crowned with flowers and branches.

After the banquet is done, they take the one who is to serve as holocaust and showering him with signs of friendship and joy, cover him with flowers and scented herbs. [They] then lay him upon a bed of flowers which is prepared over the aforesaid moat, without his being bound in any way. Each one then throws a stick of very dry wood upon him, and chanting they set fire all around him – whereupon this wretch rejoices and takes it as happily as if they were doing him some great favor. And he does not budge from the fire any more than if he were still on the bed of fragrant flowers and does not feel, so they try to tell me, any heat. Then gathering up his bones and skull (which they set in the windows as I have said), they adore him as a god and believe this fine parrot[53] to be holy during an entire year, until at its end another succeeds him in this honor. They also sacrifice their prisoners, but in another manner, without the use of such ceremonies and letting everything be reduced to ashes.

After passing through the country of *Culhua*, you enter the Kingdom of *Guatimala*, still heading west and along the coast of the Pacific Sea. In this country they call the Christians who come here *Malinxe*,[54] that is to say the little god descended from heaven, because of the astonishment they had seeing ships so large and the men thus armed, and also because a small group had the bravery to enter into battle against the infinite multitude of the natives of the country and easily beat them. Now this word *Guatimala* (more properly according to the native term *Quanthemallan*), signifies rotten tree, because *Quanth* means tree and *temalli*, poor or rotten.[55] It also means "place abundant in trees," but this is contrary to the fact, since the country is devoid of trees because it is between the mountains which often vomit fire and cause great earthquakes. It is true that when you draw away from these burning mountains you see very pretty and pleasant country, good for pasture and so fertile that maize bears there three times as much as in the surrounding countries. Cotton is raised there and balm but not so natural that it is not surpassed by

53 Thevet probably means here that the person was gullible, not that he was a "parrot" who merely repeated things.

54 This name derives from the Nahuatl name of Malinal or Malintzin, the native woman who helped Cortés in the conquest of Mexico. The name was also given to Cortés by the natives. See Federico Gómez de Orozco, *Doña Marina la dama de la Conquista* (Mexico, 1942), and Mariano G. Somonte, *Doña Mariana "La Malinche"* (Mexico, 1969).

55 Thevet is here following Gómara's account of Guatemala in the *Historia general*, 1: 351–2.

the kind that is made artificially. Indeed I cannot affirm that it is balm, because its effect is so different from the properties of that which was formerly found in Egypt and which is still being harvested at the time that I was there, even though the plant is similar to it in shape. Alum is also found and sulfur, which is not surprising if you see those fires, since the earth is so full of sulphur. And I believe that the fires consume the gold which is in the mines of these mountains. The women there dextrously spin the cotton, and are very pleasant and of a good kind. The men [are] good warriors, and are champions in archery.

After the Kingdom of Guatimala, you come to that of *Xalisco*,[56] which in its occident is opposite the orient of the Kingdom of Quinsay [Hongzhou], being in the same climate and latitude. There is from *Tecoantepech* to the uttermost limits of *Xalisco* some 536 leagues which terminate at Cape Deception [Capo del Enganno]. Near this Province are those of *Centliguipac*, *Chiatmelan*, *Tonalla*, *Cuixco*, and *Chamollac*, from which the Spaniards have removed their prior names and call *Centliguipac*, Great Spain. *Xalisco* is called New Galicia because [990r] the country is rough and mountainous like in Galicia in Spain and the people irksome and difficult in their ways and manners of doing. *Tonalla* is now *Guadalajar*.[57]

In all these countries the men are very warlike and valiant and people who care nothing about exposing themselves to death; therefore it has been difficult to approach them. Indeed, so far as being made subject they are not at all, and the most one has been able to get out of them has been some alliance and confederation. At the time of *Monctezume*, King of Mexico, these people sided with the Christians in order to revolt against the Mexican tyrant. The women dress in long dresses, rather carelessly made, which trail on their feet; the men wear them short down to their knees. They have shoes made of the skins of animals with the hair. The men are larger of stature than all the other inhabitants of this land – but one must not draw the conclusion that they are giants, as Cardan has tried to make one believe when he says that along the coast of Mexico there is a country where the men are giant, and their king greater than all the others.[58] And yet (he says) that in the neighboring regions the people

56 Xalisco is covered in Gómara's *Historia general*, 1: 355–6.

57 Cf. Gómara, *Historia general*, 1: 356.

58 We have not located this reference. Girolamo Cardano (1501-1576) was an Italian physician and mathematician. For more on Cardano see Angelo Bellini, *Gerolamo Cardano e il suo tempo* (Milan, 1947), and Alfonso Ingegno, *Saggio sulla filosofia di Cardano* (Florence, 1980).

are very small. I do not know where he fished up this lie. The fact is that the stature of these people does not surpass that of the Germans, and those of the neighboring countries are not so small that you cannot see that not a single people of our Europe surpasses them [in stature]. So there is no need for Cardan or anybody else to torment themselves to find the cause of this great size and refer it to the midwives who receive the children, or else to the beverages given to the women before they go to bed with their husbands, since it is obvious that the climate, and the location of the region, and the food, cannot cause any monstrosity of body in these people.

Furthermore, this country being midway between warm and cold could not nourish these gigantic bodies which the region of the Plata River towards the Antarctic nourishes, or those in the coldest regions of the Arctic. I regret having to attack so often the savants, but they do not for that reason lose anything of their reputations. If they were present where I am, or were still living, they would not find it strange that I should point out their mistakes, as I did to the aforesaid Cardan, to Rondelet,[59] and to Gesner,[60] even by letters to Munster three years before his death (he took pleasure in the good information I gave him and thanked me in a missive, which was the year 1553, which I still have).[61]

Having left the Kingdom of Xalisco you find a gulf and arm of the sea which comes from the direction of north-northwest and extends to a place called Mountains of Snow [the Sierra Nevadas], which is the uttermost limit of all this country.[62] Between Cape Deception and these mountains there are 320 leagues, and from this cape you can go to the oriental kingdom of China [and] to the Indies subject to the great Cham of Tartary. There is counted between this cape to China, according to the calculations of pilots and good mariners, some thousand leagues: and if the mainland is continuous, as some hold, you could go from this cape to Asia and India. These mountains are distant from the land of labor [Labrador] some one thousand leagues, and before you could get there, leaving Xalisco, you must pass the lands of the Kingdom of Sybola

59 Guillaume Rondelet (1507-1566) was a naturalist and physician who made substantial contributions to the study of zoology through his detailed descriptions of marine animals from the Mediterranean Sea.

60 Conrad Gesner (1516-1565) was a Swiss scientist and bibliographer. See Willy Ley, *Konrad Gesner: Leben und Werk* (Munich, 1929).

61 Karl Burmeister suggests that Thevet did have correspondence with Münster but offers no specific evidence. See his *Briefe Sebastian Münsters* (Frankfurt, 1964), p. 9.

62 It appears that Thevet is looking at Ramusio's map at this point. See map 14.

[Cibola], a region very rich in pelts. The land there is cold and it freezes and snows there, for it is already quite northerly. Going further, you arrive in Quivira and from there to Cicuic,[63] all peoples to be mentioned more for the diversity of their names and customs than for any good, pleasure, or profit you could get out of them, the men being barbarous, cruel, and idolatrous, and the land infertile and cold in the extreme. In Quivira, which is at latitude forty degrees, the country is better than at Cicuic, for there are good [990v] waters there, plenty of herbage, walnuts, melons, and other fruitages and raisins, but of gold and silver there is none. The inhabitants there dress in cow leather and furs, products of the hunt.

When you come back from Quivira you pass an arm of the sea that they call the red sea, partly because it resembles in its configuration that sea which separates Egypt and Ethiopia from Arabia, and partly because the sands in some parts of it are red like [those of] the other, and for the same reason. Near one of the capes of this sea which faces the Pacific to the west, directly under the Tropic of Cancer, lies an isle named Isle of Cedars,[64] and by the barbarians *Oracantin* because of the great quantity there is of these trees, of which some are so large that two men could not embrace them. The people are so savage there that of all who have been discovered, east or west, north or south, never have such ferocious ones been seen; so that civilities profit nothing in taming them, and [they] are not frightened by any threat. They live so long that there was an old man who having been converted to Christianity admitted to being seven to eight score years old. If you wish to go further than to the places I have described, as far as the Sierra Nevadas, you need another guide than myself since this is all that has been discovered in my time and of which I have been able to get knowledge.

63 This name is also found in Gómara's *Historia general*, 1: 359–60. See also the 1570 map of Ortelius (map 13).

64 The Isle of Cedars appears on many early maps. Cf. Richard Hakluyt, *The Principal Navigations Voyages Traffiques & Discoveries of the English Nation*, second ed. (1598–1600; reprinted Glasgow, 1903–5; New York, 1965), 8: 464.

On the City of Thenuthlitan, or Themistitan, and the Number of Isles: and Notice to All Pilots

CHAPTER 16

This great city of Mexico, of which the entire country bears the name, is called Themistitan, even though the locals call it Thenuthlitan, from the name of him who first founded it called Tenuth, oldest son of *Istacmicoatz*, King of Mexico, which means spring or source of a brook. Those who built it gave it this name because when they were founding it they continually found springs and canals of fresh water, so that the lake became larger because of their digging there and is the reason that it is all on an island and that you cannot approach it save by bridges or boats or certain dikes. It lies at 272 degrees longitude and eighteen degrees latitude. And some people think that everything far from us is so barbarous that nothing good nor clever can come out of it, as in speaking of Cairo they thought that nobody except ourselves would think of building a city where there were fifty or sixty thousand houses. But those who have seen Themistitan, or Mexico of Thenuthlitan, will inform them that within its walls are sixty thousand houses and in the least of these ten to twelve persons live, like you would say in Paris, people living in furnished rooms. From that we can infer that this people is as barbarous as compared to us, as formerly we were in comparison with the Romans. And whoever would contradict me, seeing such a beautiful, large, rich, and superb city as Themistitan, which is no wise inferior in riches and commmerce to those two ornaments of the orient and royal capital of the Great Tartar, that is to say Catai [Cathay] in the Kingdom of Cambalu [Beijing], and Quinsay [Hongzhou] in that of China.

[Themistitan] is built in the water and on piles. You would think you were seeing the plan and situation of [991r] the rich city of Venice, except that this surpasses it for around the lake there are such large cities that those that are called large in France and Italy do not at all deserve to be compared to these: for example *Istacpalapan*, in which there is said to be ten thousand houses.[65] But the way they are all arranged with bridges they seem to constitute a single city. But if you consider the number of people certainly Themistitan is well-populated, not I admit as much as Paris, or so well governed, or the administration of all things so well conducted: and no offense to the constructors of histories, among

65 Cortés, in his second letter, says that Iztapalapa contained 12,000 or 15,000 inhabitants. Pagden, ed. *Cortés*, p. 82.

others to Munster who makes her first in the world, for it misses it by the hundredth part.

There was in the time that this city was captured from King Moctezuma an old Mexican named Cudragni (which means "high thing") who, having seen a number of signs which I will mention later, had prophesied to them more than five years before the Christians had come into all that country that a foreign nation would subjugate them and cast down their gods and plant there a religion unknown to them.[66] This Cudragni was a great physician, knew the nature of medicinal herbs, foretold the changes of weather, and had books full of characters on these subjects. After his death (which took place two years after the capture of this city), they accorded him such honors as they would have to the deceased king, whom they revered as a god, and they spoke of him constantly because of his predictions and his medicines. He lived very frugally. That is why he reached such an old age, so that when he died he had six score seventeen years, as was told me by those of the country. He ate only once a day, about one hour after noon, and used no fish except one which the others deemed poisonous. It is true that when he went for a walk in the morning he took a certain herb in his mouth named *Gruascon*, which comforted his stomach.[67] And so you see the intelligence of those who inhabit this region and how it is possible that their city be so excellent, since they had the industry to found it in the middle of a lake, [so] it is not impertinent to say that they had the intelligence to construct excellent edifices of their own type.

Moreover, another controversy must be settled: for some, having heard tell of a certain city under the rule of the great Cam and also of Themistitan and then of Quinsay [Hongzhou], have thought that they were all the same.[68] But they are mistaken, just like earlier [writers] (and notably

66 Cudragny, the local deity of Hochelaga in Canada, has evidently been transplanted by Thevet to Mexico. Gómara, in his chapter on "Señales y Pronósticos de la Destrucción de Méjico," does not mention him (cf. *Historia general*, 2: 268–9). For Thevet on signs and portents see *Cosmographie*, chap. 17: "On the Customs of the of the Country of the Mexicans."

67 Thevet lists the word *agruascon* in his vocabulary in the *Grand Insulaire* as being the native Canadian word for stomach.

68 The confusion concerning Themistitan and Quinsay [Hongzhou] was made by a number of sixteenth-century geographers including Franciscus Monachus and Johann Schoner. For more information see Henry Harrisse, *The Discovery of North America: A Critical, Documentary, and Historic Investigation* (London and Paris, 1892; reprinted Amsterdam, 1961), pp. 284, 524.

the learned Melanchthon),[69] since the latter [Quinsay] is not in the west, rather [it is] near the Northern Ocean, but not so near that from the lake to the Northern Sea there is more than fifty leagues, and from the Pacific west more than 150. Quinsay [Hongzhou] is built on a lake, engulfing itself in the Sea of Mangi, and is the most oriental country of all that have been discovered: and the two cities are so close to each other that the least their distance might be is 1800 leagues. Is that not a good one to try to make these two cities one? which would have been ill-advised on the part of Melanchthon, as I wrote him once. [He confessed] to me his mistake in response, since with the division made between the kings of Spain and Portugal,[70] if the Spaniard had taken away from him the commerce of the west, which he would have done if Themistitan and Quinsay [Hongzhou] were one and the same. But since there are so many men flitting about on the sea and seeking out rarities, as I have done, he would find out for sure that Themistitan is under the subjection of the Spaniard and that the inhabitants today are Christian. On the contrary, since hardly a Christian European has passed into East India farther than Quinsay [Hongzhou], [he would find] that [991v] the great Cam is the lord of it, and that the people are partly idolatrous and partly Mahometan, as I sufficiently informed you when I was [writing] on that place. So you have to believe those who have seen (as I have done) and who are informed about it by the foreigners who are close neighbors of it, rather than imagining ideas in the air and casting doubt on everything. It is impossible for any living man, never having left a place, however good a rhetorician he may be, to describe foreign countries unless he wishes impudently to lie.

This great city is situated in the middle of a lake more than thirty leagues long and on which there are more than thirty cities and towns built which embellish the whole country. Because everything is on water, the inhabitants have found a way to make a walkway thirty feet wide on each side of the two gates (since this is the only way there is to enter the said city), one to enter and the other to exit. Not far from the city is erected a ten-feet-wide bridge which accommodates the flow and ebb of the water, for this lake flows and ebbs just like the sea. And for the defense of the city there are several others, because it is built like Venice in the sea and like Quinsay [Hongzhou] in the Kingdom of Mangi, which is situated on a lake flowing into the sea. On the side of the temple to

69 We have found no such statement in the works of Melanchthon.

70 Thevet is here referring to the Treaty of Tordesillas (1494), which divided the lands newly discovered between Spain and Portugal.

the north you see dikes made like what they call in Languedoc fisheries, which are made with many faggots and earth to prevent the water of the lake from ruining buildings with its floods. And though there are only two principal streets, there are several others partly in water and canals like at Venice and partly on land which are well paved as are ours over here.

The surrounding country is mountainous and in these mountains there are volcanoes,[71] that is to say places where you ordinarily see fire, flames, and smoke. Coming from the springs which go from these mounts to the city and neighboring country there are various conduits. Also there are two lakes which occupy the country, one of which is fresh water abounding in good fish, and the other is salt water (which besides its bitterness is very poisonous and deadly, which is why nary a fish could live in it). And on this are mistaken those who say it is all one lake, since experience shows the contrary. For the inhabitants, since most of their city is built on the bitter lake, have industriously made conduits and aqueducts two feet wide and the height of a man, which end at the square in the middle of the town, out of which they drink and use for their other necessities. They have also built another aqueduct which they keep empty except when they clean their houses: for having thrown all the refuse into the canal, they open this aqueduct which carries it to the salt lake. The high tide then carries it to land where it is used for fertilizer in the fields and gardens. Some people draw water from wells or springs and put it in boats and carry it to sell in the city and canals serving the area of the salt lake. These fresh water conduits are cleaned every year to keep the city healthy. And since there are many birds and fish, they have holding-areas for both kinds of nourishment.

On this freshwater lake there are several beautiful buildings which the ancient kings and lords had built long ago like *Venizuele*, great and spacious place built well out into the lake and facing south, and *Mesquisque*[72] on the east, the garden of the lord and summer-house for the king, all this to the west and to the east, between a river which they conduct by canals and the square where formerly was the temple of their adoration and where at present the Christians have placed the seat of their bishop. All around the lakes the salt as well as fresh on the land, you see several beautiful [992r] cities, such as *Calmacan*, *Atacuba*,

71 There are two volcanoes in the vicinity of Mexico City, Popocatépetl and Iztaccíhatl.

72 The names Venezuola and Mezquique appear on the map of Mexico City given by Ramusio in his *Terzo volume* [map 12]. This map also gives the names Atacuba, Calmacam, and Iztapalapa, which Thevet also mentions in this same paragraph.

Istapalapan, [and] *Tesqua* [Texcoco], and an infinity of others, so that to see the beauty of this landscape and the cities built upon this lake you would think you were going along the river Loire in France or the Po in Italy. In the greatest width of the freshwater lake (which is long, whereas the saltwater lake has a round or oval form), is found much good fish where the people go fishing: for fishing in the conduits is forbidden unless for the lord and chiefs of the city.

In this same lake is found a fish large as a sea-cow, like those we catch five or six degrees on both sides of the equator. The savages of the Antarctic call it *Andura*, which means no more than some kind of bat, which often when they sleep bite them until they bleed.[73] It has a head and ears little different from a terrestrial pig, and five moustaches a half-foot long or thereabouts and similar to those of a large barbel. Its flesh is as tasty as that of the albacore of which I have already spoken. Formerly I had the skin of one in my cabinet, but because it was badly cured it was spoiled by vermin, which gave me the occasion to picture it for you here as I saw it in life [fig. 13]. I had forgotten to tell you that this *Hoga*[74] gives birth to its young alive as do whales and some others, which I have discussed previously. This fish is no less dangerous than the Velachif[75] and if you look at it when it is frolicking [and] swimming in the water you would say that it is sometimes green, sometimes yellow, and then red like the chameleon. The barbarians of this country call it Hoga, from the name of a tree so called which grows on the banks of the lake, having small, round, and very thickly growing leaves, and all densely surrounded by the branches. This fish, which tends to stick close to the banks, eats the leaves of this tree: which is why the natives have named it the Hoga. It has many teeth and is ferocious, killing [992v] and devouring the other fish, even those twice as large as it is. That is why it is pursued, hunted, and killed, and the one who kills the most of them is most favored, for if it entered into the conduits it would not leave one of them alive.[76] But nature has taken care of this, because the tree he likes and which is his principal food, does not grow in such places.

Also at the head of this lake is found a serpent which the natives call *Velachif*, and they eat it. This serpent is so large and hideous that when it is dead you would have trouble lifting two of them from the ground.

73 Thevet appears to be confusing a vampire bat with a manati.

74 This word appears in Thevet's Canadian vocabulary meaning "tree leaves."

75 In the next paragraph Thevet describes this animal in greater detail: it may be the *caltetepon*, or *Heloderma horridum*.

76 Presumably the "other fish."

Figure 13 Thevet's illustration of a hoga
Thevet's *Cosmographie universelle*, fol. 992r.
Courtesy John Carter Brown Library at Brown University

It is an amphibian like the crocodile [alligator], living on land and in the water, and so venomous that if either beast or man is bitten by it he is scarcely able to be cured. It has a round head except that its beak is like that of a parrot. Its body [is] enamelled in various colors, and especially reddish like a dull red jasper. Even so the Mexicans hunt it continually, catch it and eat it, cutting three fingers [length] off its head and its tail, and when it is cooked they say it is the most delicate meat you can eat.

Now the plain is separated from the said lakes by certain mountains. The place where was built the rich and superb [palace] where King *Moctezuma* lived can still be seen and is built on the east. It is so beautiful that it seems that all the riches of the orient could not make a more magnificent and sumptuous one than that, considering the great columns of marble of all sorts and divers colors. The masonry is made of certain green stones which are so beautiful and artfully cut that you would judge them to be true emeralds, and are of the same kind I think as are those which the barbarous savages of the Antarctic wear on their lips. . . [77]

[994v] On the Customs of the Country of the Mexicans and on Several Prophecies: and How Their Kings Were Formerly Consecrated

CHAPTER 17

Since I have often spoken of the King of Mexico, you must know that around the year of our Lord 1521 the Spaniards under the conduct of the valiant Captain Fernand Cortez (as I know from the stories of several old pilots who were of that period to whom I have always gone to get the truth about the things of the past and how they happened) went into that country, and were rather graciously received by the king of the land, named Motzume, a wise and intelligent man. Seeing the Christians apparently not intending to leave the country and wishing to become its rulers, whether it was true or that he falsely suspected it, he plotted to have them killed. In fact he began to speak of this with one of his vassals, who went about it too foolishly, for he [995r] started off by killing nine or ten Christians, the others being still in [their] troop. This was the reason that [the Spaniards], who were leaving him in possession of his city, stormed in furiously. However, they did not pillage or do any harm

77 Thevet here departs on an imaginary voyage through the Gulf of Mexico and the Carribean, giving bits of highly dubious information about places, people, flora, and fauna. After ff. 993r–994r Thevet returns to his discussion of Mexico on fol. 994v.

except for throwing down the idols of the temples and erecting in their place the figure of Jesus crucified and of the Virgin his mother. They then had *Qualpopaca*[78] burned (thus was named the lord of Nanthlan [Nautla], who had on the advice of Moctezuma killed the Christians), and the King of Mexico was put into prison and finally killed. Some say that it was in battle, but it is more likely that (like Atabalipa in Cuzco) this [king] was executed in Mexico.[79]

In spite of this it was three months before the Christians enjoyed this great city because the people defended themselves well and also because it was difficult to assault: so that if they [the natives] had had the usage of artillery it would have been hard for Cortez and his followers to set foot there. [The Mexicans] were great warriors who patiently suffered the travails of war and besides [they were] well-served by their soldiers because they treated them well. They were armed with certain links of mail which were of gold and silver in their style (that is, the great lords of the country) and had bows, arrows, and darts without any use of iron. But all that could not prevent their disaster predicted by Cudragny, of which I spoke to you previously. The city then being taken was subjugated and somewhat pillaged, but without expelling this great people (it being impossible); rather they had to win them more by courtesy than by threats of cruelty. Still *Quahutimocin*, king who was son of Moctezuma, by the same path where his father had walked there he went also.[80]

And since when speaking of Cudragny, who had prophesied their ruin, I told you I would tell you of the signs which appeared to him, I must keep my promise. This ruin was foretold by him like the taking of Constantinople by this good old Greek Theodore Tornichy, five years before it was beseiged by Mahomet II, he who was the first possessor of it.[81] Cudragni then and several others, knowing that the king had

78 Cuauhpopca was lord of Coyoacan. For details of his massacre of Spaniards see Pagden, ed. *Cortés*, pp. 87–91.

79 There are two versions of Motecucoma's death: that he died from a blow to the head, and that he was stabbed to death shortly before the Spaniards fled the city. For bibliography and sources concerning his death, see Ibid., pp. 477–8n89. For more by Thevet on Atabalipa see his *Vrais Pourtraicts et vies des hommes illustres* . . . (Paris, 1584), 2: fols. 641–3.

80 For the death of Cuauhtemoc see Cortés's fifth letter in Pagden, ed., *Cortés*, pp. 366–7 and 518n52. Also see Gómara, *Historia general*, 2: 323–5: "Muerte de Cuahutimoccín," where Cuauhtemoc is Moctezuma's nephew.

81 The major works dealing with the fall of Constantinople to the Turks do not mention a Theodore Tornichy. See, for example, Steven Runciman, *The Fall of Constantinople 1453* (Cambridge, 1965), esp. Appendix 1: "Principal Sources for a History of the Fall of

received a present from the foreigners (which was a sword and arms), reproaching him and threatening him with his ruin, he answered that these arms were from the treasury of his ancestors. Wishing to try him they asked him to unsheath his sword which, when he could not do it, they told him that it was a sign that he would not be able to defend himself from foreigners. They said also, and this story they also told the Christians, that a long time before they came to the country they had seen in the east, towards the Isle of *Haity*, the image of the Cross, just like the one they had planted in the temple, and flames of fire mounting to the heavens, and a man who seemed to touch the clouds with his head: [also] that several days before their landing they saw every morning two hours before dawn a great light coming from the direction of the Arctic Ocean, which being in the middle of the sky suddenly vanished and was lost to sight. It was a comet.[82] Also the said philosopher prophesied to the king that this light threatened him with death and ruin of his estates and high dignities and of all his house, [and] that the judgement of God should be executed and his word announced.

But what most impressed on the understanding and fancy of Cudragny the impending ruin of his country and of his prince and lord was an event which took place three years before the taking of Themistitan, when they were taking a man to sacrifice in the great temple. Seeing before him the picture of Satan, he began to cry and to invoke the name and help of the great God of Heaven. When he was at his contemplation and prayer (imagine that it was some Christian), here came a man who [995v] assisted him, telling him not to fear death and that God had compassion upon him, and that he should say to the priests of the idols that in a short time this pollution should be put to an end and that those who were to do it were not far away from their province. He said [this] to them and right away they sacrificed him. Several took good note of his words and saw the man who had spoken to the sufferer shortly before his death. [These persons] (after the Christians had conquered the country of Mexico and dedicated the temples of the idols to the honor of God) seeing the figures of the angels as we represent them, said that the man who had appeared to the said sufferer was of the same sort.[83]

Do not think that I want to draw up an Iliad of prodigies here for you. Nevertheless God at all times has given previous signs of his wrath or clemency to his people, as in the year 1566 when the late King Charles

---

Constantinople," pp. 192–8.

82 Thevet appears to be describing the Northern Lights.

83 The source of Thevet's story here is unknown to us.

IX was having a procession for Ste Genevieve at Paris for the famine which was assailing his people. A resplendent star was seen between ten and eleven o'clock in the morning: which I allege, because the memory of it is so fresh that there is not a man in Paris who does not remember it and saw it as well as I did. The chariots and horses which were seen in the sky in the time of St. Gregory predicted the coming of Attila the Hun, who did so much evil throughout all Christendom. And if one lends credence to several solid citizens of the city of Paris, in the year 1561 they saw in the air like an army drawn up, every morning at sunrise for the space of several days, which thing seemed to presage the cruel wars which have afflicted the country of France during the divisions and civil wars of my day. So nobody should find it strange to hear this story told by the Mexicans, who in their simplicity admired the celestial signs since so many examples have been proposed to us for our edification. There is no nation under heaven, however bestial and brutal it may be, which is not astonished to see these things which surpass the common course of nature and which contradict those who say that prodigies are all natural, which would be against Holy Scripture. If I wanted to cite here the prodigious signs which appeared in every capture of a great city or ruin of a great and remarkable people, like when the Christians took Antioch in the time of Godfrey of Bouillon, and in the times of our fathers when Mahometh the Turkish king conquered the Imperial city of Greece built by the great Constantine, we should never have finished.[84]

Therefore I leave that to the historians and continue with our insular city of Themistitan, at the taking of which died more than a hundred thousand of the natives, as I have been assured.[85] Whether it is true or not I leave open to question. The Christian camp had the alliance of an infinite number of those of the country, and they are such good soldiers that were it not for the gun-fire and artillery they would easily

84 If Thevet, as suggested by Jean Céard in his *La Nature et les prodiges* . . . (Geneva, 1977), was somewhat ahead of his time in his attitude toward the "monstrosities" of nature, the same could hardly be claimed with reference to his views on signs and portents—to which we may add his belief in the existence of demons (cf. Part 1 of our text, Canada: *Grand Insulaire*, chap. "Isle of Roberval"). Restrictions of time and space have not permitted us to determine Thevet's sources for this type of material—but among authors mentioned by him there are two who were very interested in monsters, prodigies, and the supernatural: Girolamo Cardano, *De Sapientia* (Nuremburg, 1543), and Jean Wier [Johann Weyer], *Histoires, disputes et discours des illusions et impostures des diables* . . . (French translation Paris, 1579); both works cited from Céard, p. 118.

85 Cf. the account given by Gómara in *Historia general*, 2: 267–8: "La Toma de Méjico." Of course it is impossible to compute with accuracy the number of those who died. Cf. Pagden, ed., *Cortés*, p. 491n77.

have withstood the European assault and as bravely as any nation alive. When they fight, they sing and dance and utter cries so hideous that those who are not used to such a cry are frightened. They do not spare their relatives but put everyone to the sword, and there is no woman exempt from it be she ever so sweet or beautiful: they only abstain from laying hands on the lords whom they capture from their enemies. Towards these they act in this wise: when they have captured some king or lord of their enemies, they keep him under heavy guard until certain celebrations they have; and then in some public square, in a high spot made like a theater where you have to climb up ten or twelve steps, they lead your lord and make him sit upon a round stone, having a sword in his hand and a round shield to defend himself with, if someone comes to fight him. [996r] Then the one who captured him stands forth who, if he can forthwith vanquish this lord, is honored and rewarded with some very rich present, as having given sufficient proof of his valor. So the victory consists in the death of the adversary. But if the king or lord prisoner is the stronger and beats his capturer that is not all, as he has to fight six others.[86] But if he is still the victor they free him, doing him great honor, and everyone restoring to him everything taken from him in battle. Mostly they go around naked, except in the city during hot weather they wear a very loose piece of fustian cloth which they tie in front, and it goes around their behind so as to cover their private parts.

In this city (as I told you) dwelt their kings who built their superb residences and palaces. If the king died it was not his son who inherited, but rather the brothers of the defunct or the eldest child of the said brother. And if there were no brother or nephew of the deceased king, the heritage and succession fell to the nearest relative. This was why before the capture of this beautiful city the kings gave positions and fiefs to their male children to sustain them and live according to their rank, and furniture to their daughters so that they might find a proper match worthy of their family and race. However, the one who was to succeed could give no orders or sovereign act, or bear the title, until the people accepted him publicly for their prince: and then the high priest annointed him with a certain precious liquor and said an infinity of orations over the future king. Then he had him swear to keep the ancient religion of the sacrifices to their gods, and that they would render justice to everyone

86 This section on "gladitorial sacrifice" is basically the same as that found in the Anonymous Conqueror, *Narrative of Some Things of New Spain and of the Great City of Temestitan Mexico: Written by the Anonymous Conqueror, A Companion of Hernan Cortes*, ed. Marshall H. Saville (New York, 1917), pp. 24–6. This work is included in Ramusio's *Terzo volume*.

equally observing the laws, usages, and customs of their predecessors, and a thousand other formulas which they observed at such solemnities. And after these ceremonies God knows what feasting and signs of joy these good people manifested wishing a good long life to their prince, whom they admired. And they knelt before him a whole moon when they served him at meal-time. In all these mysteries certain lords who were the first after the king had to be present, and these lords were called *Tecuitles*,[87] whom you might call the twelve peers or Chevaliers, of the order [of Charlemagne] in France.

As for the ceremonies used for a king's death, they were as follows: they washed his body and placed a beautiful and precious stone in his mouth, covering him with seventeen of his robes, the finest ones and best worked in their fashion and of divers colors; and placing rich plumages on his face. And having kept vigil over him for a night or so they bore him to the temple. It was there that they received the body and that the priests chanted over him some prayers in the native language. This done, they prepared a great fire where he was burnt with his jewels and a dog to keep him company in the other world as the Romans used to do, and as several nations of the East Indies still do, as I related to you in my History of Asia.[88] If there were some prisoner destined to be immolated it was then that his sacrifice was carried out. And while the defunct was lying in state in the house and in the temple they brought him flowers of all kinds and various meats, believing that the deceased partook of them. The day after the funeral they gathered up the ashes, the teeth, and the stones, putting them all in a chest painted with various hideous figures, which chest they carefully closed up, placing on top of it the effigy and portrait of the defunct.

The obsequies lasted four days after the gathering up of the ashes, during which time the women, wives, and daughters of the deceased bore great [996v] offerings to the temple and placed them before the chest of the ashes of their prince. Whither almost all of the inhabitants went with many tears and moans, showing they had much sorrow in their hearts. So much for the king and how they governed in times past in Themistitan before its capture sixty years ago or thereabouts. And they still do it in some of the regions of Mexico and this great area of the world. Also they hold that souls are immortal and that depending on their behavior in this life they have joy and sadness in the other, saying that there are

87 The native customs of succession and the like are taken from Gómara, *Historia general*, 2: 382–3. Thevet's *Tecuitles* are apparently based on Gómara's *Tecuitli*.

88 Thevet is here referring to his *Cosmographie de Levant* (1554).

nine places where the dead go to enjoy themselves on leaving this world. That is why they have such great ceremonies, so that if they are not in the happy places through these sacrifices they may finally be received there.[89]

It must be noted that all the writing used by this people is made in the form of various animals, just as formerly were the letters of the Egyptians, which were called *Hieroglyphics*, of which I saw the vestiges and marks in the obelisks and columns which are in Egypt. Of this writing I have some in my den engraved on two circlets of ivory, or of other fierce beasts,[90] which I recovered from the capture of a vessel which was coming from those regions.[91] In the middle of the said circlets you see certain letters made like toads or frogs and some other beasts, terrestrial as well as aquatic, around the said letters. There is also a place assigned for the girls where they are learning to spin cotton and to properly arrange feathers to make fancy-work of them.[92] These girls were supported by their parents, by the richest ones, until the time that they were spoken for by someone for wives.

In all of this country, except for the Chichimecas, Otomis, and Pignoles,[93] everybody married as many wives as he could keep in his house and made them work like slaves. [They did not marry] those closely related, as is falsely affirmed by the one who wrote, and the other who translated, this little history wrongly entitled The Indies of Peru.[94] There is no nation I have ever seen, however barbarous they may be, where the men take in marriage and have intercourse with their mothers, and

89 Cf. Tamara, *Libro de las Costumbres*, fol. 283r.

90 Perhaps the word "ivory" caused Thevet to think of "elephant" and hence "fierce beasts" here, as it is apparent that he is confusing the two. It may be merely coincidental that the word *ivoire* is derived from the same root as the Sanskrit word meaning *elephant* and that the medieval French word *oliphant* meant elephant, ivory, ivory horn (cf. *oliphant* in the *Song of Roland*). See the *Oxford Dictionary of English Etymology*, p. 489. As for "circlets" allegedly containing the "hieroglyphics" and other scenes, it seems likely that Thevet has invented them from the *Codex Mendoza*.

91 On Thevet's possession of the *Codex Mendoza* see Introduction, "Sources."

92 These details almost certainly derive from the *Codex Mendoza*. See, for example, the illustrations of a girl being instructed in weaving and of a youth learning feather-working from a master of the art, pp. 82, 114 (1978 edition). Subsequent references to the *Codex Mendoza* are to this modern edition.

93 In its modern sense "Pignole" (or Pinome) is a linguistic term, but in Aztec usage it was the equivalent of *Chocho*, *Popoloca*, or *Tenime*—a vague pejorative term for barbarian.

94 Whether Thevet is referring here to Oviedo's *Historia generale, & naturale dell'Indie occidentale* . . . included in Ramusio's *Terzo volume*, is uncertain.

much less their own sisters: that is what it is to speak and discourse without authority. When the rest of the people (and this is true today) get married, the woman goes to the home of the man and he comes to meet her at the door. They then perfume one another with incense, and the groom taking the bride by the hand conducts her to bed.[95] Wives who feel themselves to be pregnant do not allow their husbands to touch them – and that is why they take several wives.

When the child is born they say to it *Antamarayd*, *Aydey kad*, *matakader*, which is to say: O little creature, you are sick, be patient, you have come into the world to suffer.[96] Then they put a bit of earth on their knee to signify that which we all become when the soul is separated from the body. Similar observations and ceremonies are still used today by this poor people which is not yet converted (of which in truth there are fifty times more than the others). And from this you can show that the Spaniard holds only an inch of ground in those countries, compared with that which is not yet converted to Christianity. There you have the great philosophy of a people which was without knowledge of God.

The first day the mother did not give suck to the child and carried it around thus, having cotton coverings like you see these vagabond women that they call Egyptians [Gipsies] carrying theirs, wandering from country to country. They washed the child as soon as it was born in fresh running water, in springs if one were nearby: the reason for which is unknown to me. Which having done, if it were the son of some lord or rich man, they put an arrow into his hand as a sign of bravery.[97]

The Mexicans were rather good astronomers, for example those who measured [997r] the course of the sun, as I will tell you about later. Formerly these Mexicans believed (as do most of them today) that there were thirteen heavens:[98] in the first of which dwelt *Rintentli* [Xiuhtecutli], god of the years; in the second, *Rontli* [Tlaltecutli], goddess of the earth; in the third *Chalcintli* [Chalchiuhtlicue]; in the fourth *Tonatio* [Tonatiuh], the sun. In the fifth there were five gods of various colors, and because of

95 Cf. the illustration in the *Codex Mendoza*, where the bride and groom are seated on a mat (resembling a bed) before a hearth and a bowl of burning incense, pp. 79, 86.

96 Cf. Gómara: "It is the custom in this country to greet the new-born child saying: 'Oh little baby! Ah, little one! You have come into the world to suffer; suffer, endure and be silent'." *Historia general*, 2: 392. The origin of Thevet's "Mexican" vocabulary is unknown to us.

97 Cf. the illustration in the *Codex Mendoza* where the newborn, surrounded by symbols of the masculine and feminine occupations, is about to be washed by the midwife, pp. 69–70.

98 Here Thevet has returned to the *Histoyre de Méchique* (de Jonghe, pp. 22–5).

that named *Tonaleq*.[99] In the sixth was *Mitlantentli* [Mictlanteutli], god of Hades; in the seventh *Tonacatentli* [Tonacateutli] and *Tonacacilmatl* [Tonacaciuatl]; in the eighth *Tlalocatentli* [Tlalocoanteutli], god of the earth; in the ninth *Calconatlansi* [Quetzalcoatl], one of their principal idols; in the tenth *Tezcatlipuca*, another principal idol, of whom more anon. In the eleventh was *Yoaltentli* [Youalteutli], god of night or darkness; in the twelfth *Tlahuiz calpantehutli*,[100] god of the dawn; and in the thirteenth and last dwelt two gods named *Teotli* and two goddesses called *Omecinatl* [Ometecutli]. Besides these there were in each of the said heavens several other gods.

As for the creation of the world, they said they had it from their fathers that it had once been destroyed, and that in its first creation the gods were supposed to have created four suns under four figures.[101] The first of which was called *Chalchuich-tonaio* [Chalchiuh-tonatiuh], God of precious stones. Those who lived in those days (they said) were all drowned, and some of them were changed into fish and lived exclusively on a river plant called *Aciantli*.[102]

The second sun was called *Chalchiuh-tonaiuh*.[103] The people of those times lived on a plant called *Centencupi*,[104] and they were all burnt up by heavenly fire, by which some were changed into chickens, others into butterflies, and the others into dogs. Killed by the same fire were the giants who then inhabited the earth, which were very monstrous being twelve or thirteen feet tall, as can be judged by the proportion of the bones which are found in caves and ancient burials.[105] Myself, I believe that these giants were not of this country, since the proportions of the present-day inhabitants are nowhere near those but rather [these] were [the bones] of the inhabitants of the Subarctic, who because of the rigors of the cold had come into this more temperate region. They [The Mexicans] themselves tell that in the times of their earliest forefathers some cruel men had come into their country and that the gods had punished them because they were sodomites.

99 De Jonghe here gives Tonal-e-que. Ibid., p. 22n6.

100 De Jonghe states that Thevet gives the name of this deity correctly. Ibid., p. 23n2.

101 Cf. Brundage, *The Fifth Sun*, pp. 27–9.

102 De Jonghe, *Histoyre*, p. 23n6.

103 Ibid., p. 23n7.

104 Ibid., p. 23n8.

105 The legend of giants was a popular one throughout many parts of Mexico. Bones of large Pleistocene-Age animals were commonly mistaken for human remains.

The third sun was called *Yioanoatiuh* [Youaltonatiuh], dark or night sun. The inhabitants of that time lived on myrrh and on grapes coming from pines [piñon nuts] of which there is great abundance in this country, and they died from an earthquake and were eaten by wild beasts named *Quenamenti.*[106] The fourth was named *Ecatonatuich* [Eecatonatiuh], sun of the air, and those of that time lived on the fruit of a tree named *Misquitl,*[107] of which there are also many and from which nowadays they make a bread to carry on journeys which will keep for a year. Those of that day died in a windstorm and were changed into monkeys. As for the fifth [sun] which is the present one, they say that they find in their books that it will last longer than all the others, which were all lost with the people at the end of twenty-three years: and [the people] being lost, the gods created others.

This people also say they heard from their forebears that the world had been destroyed by the waters and all the people submerged for the faults and sins committed by them against the gods, and they descended to hell where their friends were burned. In consideration of which those who had been created since this flood burned the bodies of the dead and kept their ashes, because they expected that *Mitlantentli*, God of Hades, would let them leave and that they would again be resurrected. Look I beg you how the Devil made them believe a thousand lies under a truth.

As to the second creation,[108] they attribute it to [997v] their Gods Tezcatlipuca and Ehecatl (that is, the air), who after the water had drained away and the earth once more filled with everything necessary to man, they created heaven in the following manner: there was a goddess named *Tlaltentl* [Tlalteutli] (that is, the earth), who had the figure of a man (others say of a woman), through whose mouth entered Tezcatlipuca, and Ehecatl through the navel. And they got together in the heart of this venerable goddess (which is the middle of the earth) and formed a very heavy heaven, which is why some other gods came to help them raise it on high. [This heaven] being lifted up, some of them remained to hold it up for fear it would fall. This was done on the first day of the year, but they do not know how many [years] there are: they think there have been one hundred periods, which make 50200 years.

But since we are on this subject, it does not seem impertinent to me to explain their method of counting the years according to what I have

106 De Jonghe, *Histoyre*, p. 24n2.

107 Ibid., p. 24n4.

108 Ibid., pp. 25–9.

gathered from one of their books entitled *Xehutonali*,[109] that is to say book of the count of the years. They divide the years into four periods, as we do for summer, autumn, spring and winter, which they name *Tochtli*, *Acatl*, *Tecpatl*, and *Calli*, that is south, east, north, and west. Each of these periods has five months, one half of the year being of rain and warmth and the other of dry and cold. Each period is the equivalent of fifty-two years and has four hebdomads, which each contain thirteen years, each year eighteen months, and the month twenty days. They begin their first period with Tochtli, and that finished they go to Acatl: and thence from period to period until they return to Tochtli. And as long as the first hebdomad lasts, they count one, two, three up to the thirteenth that the said hebdomad lasts, and then begin over to count from one just as we do here up to one hundred. And this century complete we begin over again with one, so that according to their calculation the year amounts to 365 days.

But let us return to our subject.[110] These barbarians then say that the sky having been raised to where it is, the second year afterwards the stars were made by other gods named *Citlaltona* [Citlallatonac], and *Citlaluie* [Citlalincue] his wife, and the night by *Yoaltentli* [Youalteutli] and his [female] companion *Yacahuiztli* [Yacauizti]. This same year *Tlaloc* (who is the god of the waters) made water and rain. And because they say that the clouds come out of the mountains, they call these mountains *Tlaloqs*, that is lords.[111] The eighth year afterwards, Mitlantentli[112] created hell. All this having been done, the gods Tezcatlipuca and Ehecatl decided to create man so that he might possess the earth, and so Ehecatl descended to hell to ask Mitlantentli for some ashes of the dead to form other men. To which the infernal god agreed and gave him a bone four feet long and some ashes, which he regretted soon afterwards since the bone he had given was the most precious thing he had in his possession. So he followed Ehecatl to get back this bone from him, but Ehecatl fled, whereupon the

109 *Xiuhtonalli*. Ibid., pp. 20–1.

110 Ibid., pp. 25–9.

111 The Tlaloque were deformed beings and may have been thought of as parts of Tlaloc. They were said to live in a great palace of four halls in Tlalocan, the terrestrial paradise, and each hall represented one of the four directions. In the inner patio which these halls surrounded there were four tubs, each containing a different kind of rain or weather. On the order of Tlaloc, one of the Tlaloques would fill his great jug and pour water over the world. See Brundage, *Fifth Sun*, pp. 71–2; and E.T. Hamy, *Croyances et pratiques religieuses des premiers Mexicains: le culte des dieux tlaloques* (Paris, 1907).

112 Mictlantecutli. De Jonghe, *Histoyre*, p. 26n5.

bone fell to earth and broke into pieces, which is why man was created as small as he is, for before the time of the breaking of this bone men were tall as giants.

Anyhow Ehecatl brought back the rest of the bone with the ashes and went to the place where the *Paztli* [Apaztli] was, that is, a large book in which were written the names of the other gods and called on them to create man. Being assembled, they sacrificed [in] their tongues and began the creation of man, forming his body, which immediately stirred: and he was finished on the fourth day with his wife. They were not big right away, but grew little by little according to the course of nature and were fed by a god named *Cholutl* [Xolotl] (that is, turkey) with moistened bread, without ever having been breast-fed. Now they do not know the name of this [998r] first man, anyhow they say he was born in a grotto in *Tamoachan*,[113] in the province of *Quanhuahuac*, which the Spaniards now call *Cuernavaca*, which is in the possessions of the Marquisate of the Lord *del Valle*.[114]

All this done, being agreeable to the gods, they counseled among themselves: see, man will be all sad if we do not make something to delight him and take pleasure in the earth, so that he will praise us and sing of our marvels; which being heard by Ehecatl god of the air, he took thought where he might find some liquor to give man for his pleasure. Finally he remembered there was a virgin goddess named *Mayanetl*,[115] who was taking care of her grandmother[116] named *Cicimitl* [Tzitzimitl], also a goddess, whereupon he went to that place. Finding them asleep, he wakened the virgin and said to her: I am coming for you to take you to the earth. She immediately agreed, and they descended to earth, he carrying her on his shoulders. Having arrived they changed immediately into a tree which had two branches, one of which was called *Quecalhuexotl* [Quetzalcoatl], which was the one of Ehecatl, and the other *Choquicauitl* [Xochiquauitl], that of the virgin.

Now her grandmother having awakened and not finding her niece she called the other goddesses named *Cicimime* and they all descended to earth seeking Ehecatl and the said niece. And they separated the two branches from each other, and the virgin's was recognized by her aunt, who tore her to pieces and distributed her to each of the other goddesses

113 Tamoanchan is one of the common names for the Aztec paradise.

114 Cortés's title was Marqués del Valle de Oaxaca.

115 This important Aztec goddess was the personification of the Maguey, which produced Octli, the intoxicating drink of the Aztecs.

116 These goddesses become aunt and niece below.

to eat. As for Ehecatl's [branch] it was not broken, so as soon as the goddesses had ascended to heaven it took on its first form of Ehecatl, who gathered up the bones of the virgin and buried them. From these emerged a tree, called *Metl*, of which they make the wine which they use and get drunk on, although this is not due to itself, but because they [put] certain roots in it called *Tepactli*, which give it the strength and vigor which inebriates.

There are other of these barbarians who say that the earth was created by two gods named *Calcoatl* [Quetzalcoatl] and *Tezcatlipuca*, who brought from the heavens to earth the goddess of earth named *Atlaltentli* [Tlalteuctli], whose body joints were all full of eyes and mouths with which she bit like a wild beast, and she traveled on water which was created before they descended to earth – but they do not know by whom. Which seeing, the gods took counsel together and said that there was a need to create the earth; and to this end they transformed themselves into two great serpents, one of which seized the goddess from the right hand to the left foot, and the other from the left [hand] to the right foot, and pulled on her so that they broke her in half. From one of these [halves] (which was the one towards the shoulders) they created the earth, and the other was carried off to heaven – whereupon the other gods were very indignant with them. So to recompense the said goddess for the wrong she had received from these two gods, they descended to comfort her and decreed that from her should come all the fruit necessary for the life of men. And to do this they created from her hair trees, flowers, and plants [and] from her skin grass and little flowers. From her eyes they made wells, springs, and little caves; from the mouth rivers and large caves. From the nose and shoulders were made valleys and mountains. Now this nice goddess wept sometimes at night and refused to be appeased until they had offered her some hearts of men, saying she would not bear fruit until she had been watered with human blood. That is what these barbarians believe about the creation of the world.

It is true that there are other beliefs and those of the province of Chalco tell a different story,[117] and say that water was first created but they do not know by whom. Then afterwards some gods named *Cemecatl*, *Tezcatlipuca*, *Chiconaui*, and *Ehecatl*[118] descended from heaven, all

117 De Jonghe, *Histoyre*, pp. 31–4.

118 Cemecatl, Chiconaui, and Ehecatl are most likely Ce Acatl ("one reed" – the date name of the Toltec war god); and Chiucnahui Ehecatl ("nine wind"). These are two forms of Quetzalcoatl that originally were unconnected (Brundage, *Fifth Sun*, pp. 108–13, 237n22).

children of *Atlatime*,[119] goddess of the [998v] stars, who created the said stars, the sun, and the moon, and her children made man but they do not know in what year. Besides this they say that there are nine heavens, but they do not know in which are the sun, the moon, the stars, nor the gods. They also say that the root that they use (named maize) was created in this manner: The gods (they say), having descended into a cavern, found another god named *Pieciutentli* [Piltzinteutli] in bed with the goddess *Choquyceli* [Xochiquetzal], of whom was born a god named *Ciutentl* [Centeotl], who hid himself underground. From whose hair was produced cotton, and from one of his eyes a very good grain named *Sanctlhqez*[120] which they like very much. From the other eye was created another grain, from the nose another, named *Chia*,[121] which is good to drink in summer. From the fingers came a fruit called *Camotl*,[122] and it is like turnips; from the fingernails, wide maize, which today is their chief bread-grain; and from the rest of the body were produced many other fruits which they gather and sow today. For this reason this god was loved by the others, and they called him *Tlacopile* [Tlacopilli], that is beloved lord.

But since we have previously spoken so much of this god *Tezcatlipuca*, so greatly revered by this people, it has seemed to me appropriate to tell you where he got his name and what he was. This name then is composed of three words, that is of *Tezcatl*, or mirror; *Tlepuca*, or light; and *Puctli*, or smoke. This [was] because he always had with him a very shining mirror which smoked because of the incense and odiferous things he carried with him. This people also said that it was he who created the air in which he appeared as a black figure, holding a great bloody thorn as a symbol of sacrifice, and said to them: go beyond the sea to the house of the sun, with whom dwell many musicians and players of instruments (to give him pleasure) among whom thou shalt find three-footed ones, and others who have ears so large that they cover the rest of their body. And when thou shalt be on the shore, thou shalt call my nieces *Esacapachtli*,[123] which is the tortoise; *Acilmatl* [Aciuatl], half woman and half fish; and *Altcipatli* [Acipactli], the whale, and shalt tell them to convert themselves into a bridge so that more easily thou shalt pass and go to the sun's house

119 De Jonghe, *Histoyre*, p. 31n3.

120 Ibid., p. 32n1.

121 Ibid., p. 32n2.

122 Ibid., p. 32n3.

123 Ibid., p. 33n1.

to bring back to me the said musicians and players of instruments to do me honor. This said Tezcatlipuca vanished and was seen no more. Then the god of the air went and did what he had been commanded and passed over the water with the aid of the said nieces, who immediately obeyed the command of their uncle. Now the sun, seeing him approach his house, said to his musicians: there is a wicked one who is coming to ask for you, and so let none among you answer him, for the one who answers must go with him. Now these musicians were clothed in four colors, to wit white, red, yellow, and green. So the god of the air having arrived, he called the said musicians in singing: to which one of them answered, and so he went away with him and bore music, which is that still used in their dances honoring their gods, as we here do with organs or other instruments.

They also say that this god Tezcatlipuca appeared to them in the form of a monkey and spoke through his shoulders, at other times in the figure of a bird, which flapping and striking with its wings made a great noise and awakened those with whom he wished to speak. And since he saw that they were cruel and inhuman, he persuaded them to offer him human blood sacrifices,[124] which they did by opening the sides of slaves, and tearing out their hearts, made them eat it before they died. And they deemed that he who performed and accomplished this sacrifice with the greatest cunning and skill was most worthy of honor.

They relate also that in the time of this Tezcatlipuca there lived [999r] another god named *Quecalcoatl*, son of *Comachtli*[125] and of the Goddess *Chimalma* [Chimamatl], who died giving him birth at *Nichatlauco* [Tlachinol-tepec]. Since he was greatly beloved by his father, his brothers hated him, and so conspired his death. To do this they lured him with sweet words onto a rock named *Chalchoneltepetl* and set fire all around it to burn him, but he hid himself in a hole to escape this fire. And seeing that the brothers had gone away thinking him dead he came out, took his bow and arrows and killed a doe which he met on his path. [He] loaded it onto his shoulders and carried it to his father's dwelling and presented it to him before the arrival of the brothers, who on their arrival were astonished to see him.

[Once again] they immediately plotted to kill him: to do which some days afterwards they took him out into the fields and made him climb a tree, giving him to understand that from there he could more easily

124 Legend says that human sacrifice originated in Tula as the Toltec empire began disintegrating. Brundage, *Fifth Sun*, pp. 208, 249n26.

125 De Jonghe, *Histoyre*, p. 34n2.

shoot birds. He believed them, but he had no sooner climbed up there than they began to shoot many arrows at him: which seeing, (since he was wise and discreet) he let himself fall from the tree feigning death. So the brothers went away, but as soon as they were gone he got up and went and killed a coney which he gave to his father before the arrival of the brothers. Now the father, who suspected the conspiracy which the brothers had made against [the boy], asked him where the said brothers were, to which he answered that they were coming, and having said this he went away to another house near his father's.

Meantime the brothers arrived, of whom the father inquired where their brother *Quecalcpatl* was, and they answered that he was coming. Then the father scolded them angrily for having plotted to kill their brother. Irritated by this they took counsel to kill their father, which they did by taking him to a mountain. This done they came to seek their brother, giving him to understand that their father had changed himself into a rock, and so it was necessary to sacrifice unto him some animals such as lions, tigers, eagles, butterflies, and others impossible to take, so that they would have a pretext to kill him. Since he refused to do what they said, they sought to murder him but he escaped from their hands and fled to the same rock, whither he was pursued by them. He killed them by shots of arrows, and this done his subjects who loved him came to seek him and carried him off in honor along with the heads of his brothers, of which they made drinking bowls. *Quecalcoatl* departed from there and went away into the land of Mexico to a village named *Tulancinzo*,[126] where he lived some days, and from there to *Tula*, where they were still ignorant of what a sacrifice was. And since he was the first to bring them the custom he was reputed by them to be a god, to whom he taught to make temples to him and many other superstitions, and lived in this place like a little god for 160 years.

Now Quecalcoatl thus happily living at Tula, and since the truth cannot long be hid without coming to light, it happened that Tezcatlipuca came to that place disguised as an indigent. Being envious of the honor paid to Quecalcoatl, he changed himself into many different forms and frightened the inhabitants of Tula and Quecalcoatl too, although he too was a Devil. So there are greater and lesser Devils. Now one day it happened that Tezcatlipuca went into the temple wherein was the effigy of Quecalcoatl on an altar and guarded by many servitors, with a mirror much esteemed by these barbarians. Finding the said guards asleep, he stole the said mirror and hid it under one of the straw mats on which the said guards

126 Ibid., p. 35n2.

slept, who waking and not finding this mirror were very upset, since Quecalcoatl had informed them that by [999v] means of this mirror he would send them rain whenever and how much they need it.

Meantime, Tezcatlipuca, who had left, met in his path an old woman to whom he said: go to the temple and tell them that what they are seeking is under a straw mat, and they will be grateful to thee for this. And he transformed himself into various shapes of animals and monsters, trying thus to frighten the inhabitants of Tula. He also had his hair cut (a thing not yet customary among the barbarians). [He then] went to the Temple of Quecalcoatl, broke and demolished the statue,[127] knocked it to the ground, and changing himself into many shapes struck all the natives of Tula, who fled in fear and abandoned the city. So did Quecalcoatl, accompanied by several of his servitors, and went away to *Tenacuia*[128] where he stayed some time, and from there to *Cullinacan* [Culhuacan] where he also made his residence for some time.

From there he crossed the mountains and went to Quantiquchula,[129] where he had a temple built and himself adored by the inhabitants as a god. And he stayed in the place for 190 years. At the end of which he took the road to *Acholula* [Cholula] and left as his representative a certain *Maclalchochitl* [Matlac xochitl]. He stayed at *Acholula* 160 years, whose inhabitants built for him and edified a very magnificent temple whose ruins are still to be seen today. From there he went to *Cempoala*,[130] a city near the sea which is where the Marquis Don Cortez arrived when he first reached this country (but today it is all ruined like many others). In this city resided Quecalcoatl 260 years, to which place he was still pursued by Tezcatlipuca. Seeing that he was so greatly persecuted by him, Quecalcoatl fled to a desert and shot an arrow at a tree, in the hole of which he hid himself, and died there. Seeing which, his servitors burnt his body and that is the origin (they say) of the custom of their country of burning the dead. They also say that from the smoke of this fire was created the star *Hesperus*.

Now, as to the government and justice of the country:[131] if a judge who is appointed to try a certain case should take a present or give a favorable judgement, they cut off his hair, deposed him from office, and

127 Brundage says that the vandalism of this temple in Tula is a matter of archeological record. *Fifth Sun*, p. 237n27.

128 De Jonghe, *Histoyre*, p. 37n1.

129 Ibid., p. 37n3.

130 Ibid., p. 37n6.

131 Thevet has here returned to the account of Gómara, *Historia general*, 2: 403–17.

led him around for three different days on a horse without bridle or saddle throughout the entire city. And each father of a family was required to send some of their children or slaves after the delinquent judge, to do him greater affront and render him more odious and unworthy of his estate to the people, which is considered to be a great infamy and dishonor.

Now such were their laws, which seemed to be taken from some republic the best governed of the universe. For he who committed a murder, it was without any exception or conditions whatever that he had to die. The woman who killed her child was also executed. The thief who was sentenced for the first time was made a slave; if he were a repeater, he was inexorably hanged. The traitor was killed with various and sundry forms of torture. A woman who disguised herself as a man, or a man who wore women's clothing, was equally punished by death. A soldier who challenged another, unless in war, was also put to death.

Formerly, when they went to war it was with just cause and legitimate, the people had to be consulted and the very old and aged women entered into the council because they remembered other wars and what had transpired in them to their profit or disadvantage. They greatly honored him who had gained recognition in battle from some great or remarkable deed. The soldier who rebelled, or refused to obey his captains was severely punished as a traitor. When they had to fight, it was not permitted to soldier or captain to drink any beverage which could make him [1000r] drunk, as their Cacao, brewed as they did it, muddled one's head almost as quickly as our wine.

As for the priests and ministers of their crazy superstitions, they wore long white cotton robes and very narrow, in which they taught the mysteries of their sacrifices both orally and with figures to those who were apt enough to be received as a sacrificer. Laymen were not allowed to know anything of such secrets, and if anyone discovered any, the law decreed the death penalty. Some of these priests did not marry, to be considered more holy, although they were permitted to marry like the laity. And although there were several ministers in the temple in Themistitan, yet there were only a few chosen by the high priest who dared approach the sacrificial altars to immolate some offering. At present all this idolatry has ceased in the big city and in some parts of the province. They have learned our religion, the sciences we use, Latin and other languages, and observe the same customs and style of life that we do. In time some of the rest of them who believe in the superstition of the idols will be converted.

Grand Insulaire

[180v] Themistitan

I will refrain from repeating here what I set forth on this isle in my Cosmographie, from which I pray the reader to take that which, in order to avoid prolixity, I cannot discuss here. I shall only recall here what has not yet been touched on by others, and in which I have been helped by a certain personage, who lived seventeen years in that country.[1] And since I have nothing which I do not devote to the public, so I have been willing to share with you the history of it [Themistitan] which I have recovered. I will therefore silently pass over the proof that this is an island, since the thing is as clear as day, as its location amply shows[!]

The Mexicans are that people from which New Spain got its beginnings, and which inhabit the city which is the capital of the kingdom, and also it is situated in the most fertile area of the country. This word Mexico is a corruption, composed of Me which is a tree, and chic, and co, which is the possessive case. This is why the principal inhabitants of the country do not permit one to call them Mexicans, but rather Echicans, from the place whence they descended, which is a hollow rock which emits air from underneath it: so that going back to the origin of the Mexicans, from what I have been able to learn about it, is, that in that place were two brothers, between whom division and discord arose because each had his false god and they were jealous of the honor which was accorded more to the one than to the other. So that having come to blows, the younger got the worst of it and was forced to leave the country, and traveled to the province named Couliacan [Culhuacan], which is very fertile, two hundred leagues on the other side of Mexico to the west, not far from the South Sea where Nunnio de Gusman was when he conquered New Galicia.[2] In this province they remained a long time and had very

1 Thevet is most likely referring either to Andrés de Olmos or his superior, Juan de Zumárraga. On the latter see J. García Icazbalceta, *Don fray Juan de Zumárraga: Primer obispo y arzobispo de México*, 4 vols. (Mexico City, 1947).

2 Here Thevet is following *Histoyre de Méchique*, published by Edouard de Jonghe,

beautiful and magnificent edifices built.

After having lived there for some years, they left there to find another more agreeable place. Either the dissatisfaction of their gods incited them to do this, or [it was] the hostility of the original inhabitants, who did not like having these newcomers in their country who ruled over them. So they arrived at Trich [Toich], distant from Xuichipila about seven leagues. It is a place full of rocks and high mountains which seem to have the color of wax, and [there] is a peaked rock in the form and shape of a calabash. On the saddle of this rock there were a number of houses made of beautifully hewn rocks. At the top and crown of this rock there was a house like a fortress which overlooked all the other edifices and buildings of this mountain, on which was the dwelling of the demons, [and] in which place there was a fountain whose water was very tasty and beautiful.

Afterwards they decamped from these quarters and went to make their home at Cuchipilaa [Xochipila], where there is now a Franciscan monastery, and they populated two mountains which are separated from each other only by a river in the middle. On these mountains they had beautiful and magnificent edifices. From there they went [181r] to Xalpa [Chalpe] eight leagues from Cuchipila [Xochipila], where they built a temple so great and sumptuous that I doubt if the Romans ever built one like it. They also built other special edifices for their lord who led them, and for other chiefs, and particularly in this place as in the others where they had set foot. They took great pains to build temples to the gods which they carried with them, which were Tescachipouca [Tezcatlipuca], Yhiu [and] alopuchtli [Xochipilli-Cinteotl], and for this they invited their neighbors, whom they made their partisans by this means and also by the good treatment they gave them. Finally they left the city of Xalpa [Chalpe] and came to Mexico in the year 1324 after the arrival of our Saviour and Redeemer Jesus Christ, where they settled down after wandering around several other countries.

When they arrived the country was swimming in water or was all wooded: so that it seemed that they were being engulfed in a wilderness. They found a confluence of clean water which surrounded all these woods; it was in the form of a Saint Andrew's cross. And about the middle of this cross they found a large stone or rock with flowers, and above a great nest where a great eagle had his eyrie. They called this

---

in *Journal de la Société des Américanistes de Paris* n.s. 2 (1905): 15. Guzman's account appeared in Ramusio's *Terzo volume delle navigationi et viaggi nel quale si contengono le navigationi al mondo nuovo . . .* (Venice, 1556).

rock Quantytichinchan. In it [the nest] there were many bones of birds and feathers of various colors. And having explored around to discover and reconnoiter the country, they found that it promised great fertility and waters in great abundance. That is why they decided to construct a fortress here, settle in and hold out against their enemies.[3]

So they fortified themselves and called the place Thenuthlitan, from the name of the one who (as I remarked in my Cosmographie) founded it, who had the name Thenuth, [the] younger son of Istacmicotatz, King of Mexico, which means like a fountain and spring of fresh water. And they gave it this name, those who built it, because as they were building it they continually found springs and canals of running water: so that the lake became even larger from the fact of their digging, and [this] is the cause that it is all on an isle, and that one cannot approach it except by bridges or in boats, or [by] certain causeways. Others subtilize variously about this etymology and say that it is called Thenuthlitan, because of the tree Thenuth which grows on this rock.

Finally these Mexicans elected ten persons, to be better governed, namely Ocelopan, Quayan, Acacitli, Ahucchotl, Thenuch, Tecineuch, Chomimith, Chocoyol, Chiuhcaqui, and Atotolt, who then elected for their chief and lord Tenuth, for the wisdom, prudence, and ability that they recognized [181v] in him [as] capable enough to be able to exercise the seigniory, and that the others should be only subordinate and like the agents and captains of the rest of the people. Having grown in numbers and strength, as they were hardy and bellicose, they began to dominate over their neighbors and through force of arms to subjugate them and make them tributaries and vassals, and [place] under their obedience the inhabitants of Colguacan [Colhuacan] and Tenaincan their neighbors. This happened during the reign of Thenuth, who was lord fifty years, and at the end of these he died.

It is astounding the superstitions into which this poor people was plunged before the sun of the Gospel had shone forth over their country. I have in my possession two books about the idols writ by hand containing the genealogy and history of the kings and great lords of that country, and the pictures of the idols they adored, painted and pictured in two books, written by hand by a monk who lived there around thirty-four years, exercising the charge of a bishop in that country.[4] [These] books came into my hands after having been presented to the late Queen of

3 See B.C. Brundage, *The Fifth Sun: Aztec Gods, Aztec World* (Austin, 1979), "The Founding of Mexico-Tenochtitlan," pp. 144–5.

4 Thevet's reference here may be to either Olmos or Zumárraga.

Spain, daughter of King Henry II, King of France.[5]

Here are these beautiful gods and goddesses of the Mexicans. The first was named Vicilo-puchtli, which is the God of Virgins, for whom there was a great festival in his temple with many flowers. They have the goddesses whom they call Citalicue [Citlalincue], accoutered in beautiful plumages, whom they say is the lady of the heavens and of the stars, and her husband, whom they name Cistalcitonac, a name which has the meaning of star of heaven shining brightly. These are the most monstrous figures you can imagine, clothed very barbarously with hands and feet of griffins, as we over here have the custom of painting devils. Their festivals are solemn and celebrated on the tenth day of the month of May, in honor of chaste women who have not sinned with respect to their husbands. It would take a long time if I sought to go into the detail of all that I find about these idols. The reader who might be curious and want to go thoroughly into the matter will have patience, if it please him, to wait until I have published these books, which will be soon with God's help. Still, if he were too famished [to wait], I would advise him to come see me and I will show him something that will be able to satisfy him.

For [even] if these people were not so idolatrous, I would scruple to believe in what is revealed to be the deceptions of the Populacas, who are reputed to be very notorious sorcerers; and therefore some claim that they discovered fire in their country in this fashion.[6] It happened one day that one of these barbarians took a stick [182r] fashioned like a rod, scarcely larger than a spindle, and held it vertically above another little dry stick lying horizontally between his feet. The other end of the rod was placed on the aforesaid stick, then he kept on turning that rod like a drill, and turning it rapidly by the collision and contact of these sticks fire was produced in the dust coming out of these sticks, and from that they got their fire, which [process] they use today when they need it. The news of this invention having come to the chiefs and neighbors of the country, they were greatly pleased with it, and to make a great Alama-vool,[7] which means a miracle in their language, they cut on the highest mountains of

5 Thevet is here referring to his possession of the *Codex Mendoza* and possibly of the *Histoyre de Méchique*. This story of the acquisition of the books, however, is different from that given in the *Cosmographie*, chap. 17: "On the Customs of the Country of the Mexicans," and is almost certainly a fabrication, as the document never reached Spain. The Queen of Spain to whom Thevet refers is Elizabeth of Valois (d. 1568), third wife of Philip II.

6 De Jonghe, *Histoyre*, pp. 12–14.

7 This word is not in the account given in the *Histoyre*.

their province the greatest quantity of wood that they could, which they carried to the highest point of the said mountains, [and] then set fire to it. When the flames and smoke were at their hottest, the Otthonians perceived this new and sovereign miracle which engendered an emnity toward the Populacas, for when they had noticed this novelty they sent them messengers to inquire why they had dared do such a thing without their leave, because such inventions were their province. The Populacas answered that it was more fitting for them to invent that than for them [the Otthonians], and also that they could do it better. And so over this they went to war, and having drawn up on either side in battle-array they were ready to charge each other when the Otthonians demanded a truce to learn from their enemies if it were true, as they said, that their god was more powerful than their own.

Those Otthonians proposed three conditions to the Populacas. The first is that they obtain from their god, in the area where they were, that the dwellings which they saw there standing should be instantaneously razed. This the Populacas, since they were great sorcerers, immediately performed through their charms. The second is that in the countryside they should cause to die by their enchantments and magic, which they did and, according to their request, so impeded and dazzled their sight that nothing appeared of what had been done.[8] The third is because of its being late, that the sun should stop for the love of them to show if it were true that the sun, whom they made their god, loved them so much. The Populacas said that they would dispatch a Waldensian ambassador[9] to go stop the sun, which they did. And the one they were supposed to have sent found the demon in the guise of a bearded sun, who asked him where he was going; he answered, I come to tell you to cease your course [182v] otherwise our wicked enemies will think to have superiority over us. This sun answered: Look, I cannot stop because, as I am the great god and lord, I have several other children before me, who await me so that I cannot stop, and I have to go to them to help them; nevertheless, to satisfy you here are my beards which is the thing I prize most, which I give you for the love which I bear you above all others, and tell your malevolent enemies to give you the advantage, otherwise I will destroy them so that not one remains. And because among them they did not

8 Thevet does not tell us what was caused to die.

9 The Waldensians were, originally, followers of Peter Waldo, a twelfth-century reformer. In the sixteenth century Waldensians occasionally sent ambassadors to Protestant communities, particularly in Switzerland, in an attempt to establish alliances against mutual enemies.

have the custom of wearing beards and never had seen any, for they used a certain ointment which prevented it from growing.[10] And as soon as they [the Otthonians] saw this beard, they were afraid and were not slow to concede superiority to the Populacas.

When I am telling this it seems to me that I am wrong to insert it into this work, and indeed I have been of two minds several times about it, having no doubt that our renovators, calumniators, and critics will profit by this account, [and] make fun of it. But if they had in their possession, as I do, the information written in my books they would soon change, I am sure, their tune. The person who helped me with these accounts[11] tells of having touched these sun's beards with his own hands, which were longer than half an ell, reddish, [and] ample as the hair of a horse's tail. If this country had been provided with horses, I would say that he could have gotten these beards from their tails to deceive the poor ignoramuses; but they would have had to go a long way to find them.

For if their idolatry involved no more than an idiotic stupidity it would not be so bad, [but] along with their superstitious ignorance they mingle their bloody cruelty. For example their idol Maltheult, meaning god of paper, [is] bathed in the blood of men who are sacrificed to him. When the Spaniards arrived there, they counted eighty thousand principal slaves taken in war. Now here is how they went about sacrificing. When they won some battle, to thank their god for the victory obtained, they took the chief prisoner, removed his heart while he was still alive with a certain device, which their demon had taught them about, and with the blood of their [prisoner's] heart they soaked a piece of paper the size of a man's hand and they plastered it against their idol Maltheult. So many pieces of pasteboard [were] heaped one upon the other that upon the arrival of the Spaniards it was as tall as a man and [183r] so large that two men could not have put their arms around it.

As for the location of Themistitan, it is situated on the salt lake, and not at all in the middle. It lies at 272 degrees of longitude, and eighteen of latitude, containing within its enceinte sixty thousand houses, in the least of which there are ten or twelve who live there. To tarry longer over the details of this isle would be to indulge oneself in retelling that which I have sufficiently lengthily recounted in my Cosmographie. One point remains and which I cannot tolerate, about the dogs which the new Munster claims are castrated in Themistitan, to fatten them up for eating. I ask you to ruminate on the good taste he could get out of

10 Thevet does not complete his sentence.

11 This is probably a reference to Olmos.

using the flesh of these poor dogs. If he could furnish me a guaranty, since neither he nor his Pierre Martyr have ever known anything about Themistitan other than by hearsay, I would discuss it [and] philosophize on what he wants to allege, but these are monstrosities of the Kabbala[12] of those who, without proof, discourse of things which they do not know and understand even less.

I have no need to describe for you here the plan of this city of Themistitan with its aqueducts, gardens, [and] houses, nor the ways of the Spaniards who rule here for the moment peacefully. I only want to tell you that it is situated on a lake of salt water, though in truth not so [salty] as the open sea. To try to maintain that this lake has [the] flow and ebb of the tide, as the refurbisher of Munster [Belleforest] has done in writing, is to deliberately mock those who are gullible enough to believe it.[13] And when all is said and done there is no plausibility in such fables. You could say the same thing about the other lakes ten or twelve good leagues distant, that they too had the same flow and ebb as does the sea. I know that this comes from those who, for lack of experience, wish to fantasize their fleeting impressions. If you want to know why these movements of the water do not occur in this lake you must not just consider the diversity which is in the quality of the water, i.e. that one is salt, the other not.

It is marvelous how these toadstools of philosophers try to persuade us that they can delve into the most hidden secrets. Ignorant as they are, they seek to wish to argue with sophistry against what ordinary experience teaches us and uphold the position of those who have tried to make us believe that although our taste tells us that the sea is salty, by reason they wish to persuade us of the contrary, [and] maintain essentially as follows: the sea is the stream from which the waters arise, issue forth, and flow, which is so true that she is known as the mother of streams, lakes, [and] rivers. Now the waters which come from her [183v] are not salty, rather they are sweet, even those that flow in are sweet. It therefore follows that the sea is not salty.

I will refrain from going on here to demonstrate the contrary, since Aristotle, Albert,[14] and other Greek, Latin, and Arab philosophers have

12 This word derives from the Hebrew *qabbalah*, a Jewish tradition of mystical interpretation of Scripture. Thevet is perhaps using the term in its figurative meaning of a secret or mystical science.

13 Thevet himself appears to have believed it in his *Singularitez*, chap. 73: "Description of New Spain," and *Cosmographie*, chap. 16: "On the City of Tenuthlitan."

14 Albertus Magnus (d. 1280).

Figure 14 Portrait of Montezuma, last Aztec king
Thevet's *Vrais Pourtraicts*, fol. 644r.
Courtesy British Library, London

sufficiently developed this matter, also the various movements which are in the Atlantic Ocean causing this flow and ebb including why it is that the sea never overflows and gets neither larger or smaller; finally about the moon and how its waxing and waning help navigation. I have sufficiently treated this elsewhere to satisfy those who would wish to know something about it.

To return to our Themistitan, there is no person of good judgment who does not know that this city is very large in extent and built on an island, as I show you on the map which I had from him who provided me with these two books, which I told you about before. I have no more to tell you except that this great personage Ferdinand Cortez, by ruses and deceptions under the authority of his lord and prince, captured the king of Themistitan, named Montezuma, who always before his death had shown Cortez and his men the utmost good will, as you will see in what I have written about it in my Cosmographie and History of Famous Men, with the account of the main and most remarkable deeds of his life; from what race he was descended, [and] the brave and warlike conquests he made over his barbarous enemies [fig. 14].

When I see this all again before my eyes, and the end about which I have just thought—how it all came out and his great misfortunes—I cannot sufficiently deplore human misery, and that at the conclusion of such fine and glorious exploits the reward should be so slight: and that after so many trophies of victory won by Montezuma he had to serve as a plaything and subject for Cortez to mock the vanity of human deeds and to show an example of such treacherous and strange ingratitude. Do not think that Cortez got away with it, just as he had done to Montezuma so he was treated. After having exposed himself to reproach in this way and risking his life for his master, he was ousted from favor for a long time.[15]

15 Thevet's information here is perhaps based on the tradition that Cortés passed his last years in disgrace and poverty. In fact, Cortés was exonerated of charges made against him by enemies at court, and he was given the title of Marqués del Valle de Oaxaca. Significantly, he did not receive the post of Viceroy of New Spain, which he had requested. For Thevet's other remarks on Cortés, see *Vrais Pourtraicts et vies des hommes illustres* . . . (Paris, 1584), 2: fols. 385–8.

PART 4

Original French Text (Canadian Section)

Grand Insulaire Original French Text (Canadian Section)

[143r] Isles des Terres Neuves

Premier qu'entrer en la description de ce nouveau pays, i'ay deux poincts à devuyder, tant sur la descouverte, qui en a esté faite, que sur la longue estendüe de ceste coste. D'un costé je vois les Espaignols et Portugais, qui privativement s'en veulent attribüer la descouverte. D'autre part j'entends l'opposition formée par les François, qui, accordans, qu'à la verité les Portugais ont passé quelque peu outre que leurs devancjers, soustiennent que ce ne sont que les faulx bourgs de Paris, où ils ont donné. Si c'estoit à moy à decider, et donner arrest sur tel differend, je n'aurais pas beaucoup de peine. Toutesfois, comme j'ay interest à la partie, j'aime mieux proposer la simple fait et la verité nüement, laissant au debonnajre Lecteur à y asseoir tel et si libre jugement qu'il luy plairra.

En l'année mil cinq cens Gaspar de Port-real Portugais seillonna celle coste, et poussé par la tempeste fit course iusques a cinquante six degrés de latitude, où il descouvrit un fleuve, lequel il nomma Rio Nevado, qui signifie riviere chargée de nege. Du depuis un Venitien entreprint ce voiage souz l'authorité d'Henry septiesme de ce nom Roy d'Angleterre, lequel passa iusques à soixante sept degrés, mais et l'un et l'autre de ceux cy falut qu'ilz s'en retournassent sans rien faire, soit pour les grandes froidures, soit qu'ilz n'eussent ce qui estoit necessaire pour se tenir et arrester parmj ce peuple. Par ainsi l'honneur de la descouverte de ces Terres Neuves doit estre principalement attribüé a Jean Verazzan Florentin et à Jacques Cartier Pilote Breton (mon grand et singulier amy, qui s'y avoiagea avec la compaignie, que Messire Charles de Moüy, chevalier Seigneur de la Milleray, et Vice-admiral de France luy donna en l'an mil cinq cens trente quatre) lesquelz ne se contenterent pas d'y faire une simple passade, ains y firent proffit et conqueste fort avantageuse, ainsi qu'entendrez par cy apres.

Toute ceste Terre Neuve court des le quarente huitiesme degré de latitude iusques au soixantiesme, la coste, courant tousjours le Nord pour le moins trois cens cinquante lieües: Le nouveau Munster estend bien plus au large les fimbries de ceste contrée, laquelle il espand des le vingt-cinquiesme degré de latitude deça la ligne Equinoctiale, iusques au soixante cinquiesme et au Pole Arctique, qui viendroit a la concurrence de six cens lieües ou environ. Ce calcul n'est pas mal-aisé à tracer sur du papier, mais ce seroit bien plus difficile de la verifier en presence de ceux, qui ont autrefois cinglé iusques en ces parties neufves, du [143v] monde nouveau. Lesquelles gisent cinquante six degrés deça la ligne Equinoctiale, en mesme elevation, et souz pareil climat, que la Moscovie, où la mer est glacée et fort voisine du Pole Arctique.

Ceste region de Terre Neuve fait une extremité de Canada, et participe à celle de Baccaleos, qui ne laisse d'estre fort Septentrionale et maritime, encor que ie ne la marque qu'a quarente huit degrés trente minutes de latitude, et trois cens vingt sept degrés nulle minute de longitude, quoy que le nouveau Cosmographe Monsterien le trouve fort estrange: s'il eut eu de fort bonnes lunettes, il eut veu et que Hierosme Girave ne met son elevation plus haut qu'a quarente degrés et que le seul iugement du globe et assiette de ce pays rangent par necessité ceste Isle souz ceste seule elevation que i'ay cotté, et non souz les soixante degres de la ligne.

Or ceste Isle, que voyez icy posée au flanc des Isles des Moulües a l'ouest, porte le nom de la contrée de Baccaleos ainsi nommée, a cause d'un poisson de mesmes nom, que l'on y trouve. Quant est du nom de ces Isles des Moulües, laissant ce, qu'autres en ont voulu discourir plus legierement qu'á propos, la grande abondance, qu'il y a la de moulües, a fait qu'elles ont esté qualifiées de ce titre, pour tesmoigner que là estoit le vivier et magasin, où on les reservoit, pour les debiter aux Estrangiers qui alloient là à la pescherie, afin de servir de la superfluité des moulües, desquelles ils y ont tant a regorger, que les Barbares n'en tiennent compte, ains les entassent a grands monceaux, et en bloc les vendent et troquent aux estrangiers. Ce n'est pas que ie veuille souscrire à la bourde du reformateur Monsterien, qui, parlant du pays de Nordvvegue, escrit, que de ce quartier on porte par tout le reste de l'Europe ces beaux Merlus qu'il fait endurcir de froid et estend sur de grands bastons. Comme si on ne scavoit pas tres bien, qu'incontinent, que ce poisson est prins, apres luy avoir osté ses entrailles et triperies, on le sale dans des vaisseaux, tout ainsi qu'on fait les Moulües en ce païs des Terres Neuves, ce que i'ay veu faire.[1] Car autrement il s'y empuanteroit et n'y a froid, tant

1 In the *Description de plusieurs isles* Thevet has written here: "ce que j'ay veu faire

extreme soit il, qui sceust empescher, qu'avec le temps ceste marée ne se corrompit. Voila que c'est d'une menterie faut qu'en sortent et iaillissent[2] une milliasse. Que s'il n'eust[3] point supposé que la coste Nordwegienne fourmijoit en merlus, il n'eut esté en peine de les debiter, mais voyant [144r] qu'il en avoit si a coup remply le pays, faloit bien qu'il declairat les moyens, pour les conserver iusques au tems, que ces denrées pourront [sic] estre debitées. Je ne veux pas revoquer en doute qu'il ne puisse avoir des merlus en ceste mer là, mais aussi d'en dresser si grandes battelees, qu'on puisse les esparpiller par toute l'Europe n'y a point d'apparence: Attendu que veu la froidure du pays c'est tout s'il y en peut avoir pour la provision des Insulaires.

Encores suis ie contraint m'arrester en ce pays Nordwegien, d'autant que, comme ce gloseur Munsterien s'est licentié à y bastir ses balajnes monstrueuses de cent coudées de long, aussi bien a il baillé des qualités tellement esloignées des proprietés de ces grands poissons, que palpablement peut on toucher l'absurdité de ses resveries. Entre autres leur fait il jetter des cryes si espouvantables, qu'il n'y a Lecteur, tant doux et patient soit il, quj ne s'ennuye d'ouir bourdonner au pres de ses oreilles un tel bourdeur, quj, encores que Munster eut voulu escrire telle fadaise, devoit y donner un trait de plume, puis qu'il ne pouvoit ignorer, que, si la balajne est poisson, il faut que la taciturnite naturelle des enfancons de la moitte Thetis retienne aussi son son mort, sourd et estourdi dans le gosier d'une si grande et effroiable bellue.

Encores s'est il grandement mespris avec plusieurs autres, en ce que confondant ce pays des Terres Neuves avec le terre Australle, volontiers voudroit conjoindre le ciel avec le terre. Et pource qu'ailleurs je luy ay rabattu ce, quj l'entretenoit en telle verdure, je suis bien contant de me rengier contre le[4] funebre docteur funerailljer, quj ne se contente pas d'engrossir le tombeau de ses belles funerailles, de ce qu'il a pesché dans ma Cosmographie, ains prendroit bien a gré, que je luy accordasse qu'avec les abusés ie confonds la terre Australle, avec les Terres Neuves. Je ne daigneroje luy monstrer par raisons concluantes sur quoy i'ay fondé la distinction de ces pays, puis qu'en ma Cosmographie j'ay assez esclaircy

---

y estant." Hereafter this work will be abbreviated DPI, with Thevet's additions following. Only annotations concerning Thevet's language are presented here. For notes on content, see the English translation.

2 DPI: "Voilà que c'est, qu'il faille que d'une menterie il en sorte et iaillisse . . . "

3 DPI: "S'il n'eust . . . "

4 DPI: "Et pource qu'ailleurs ie l'ay combattu sur ce point, je le lairray pour m'attaquer à ce funebre . . . "

ce poinct. Seulement veux ie le battre de l'authorité, qu'il puise[5] au premier chapitre du vingt uniesme livre de ma[6] Cosmographie. S'il se treuve que mons discours doive estre prins[7] des Terres Neuves, Thevet quicte au funerailljer Guichard la partie. S'il plaist au Lecteur de lire ce que i'en ay escrit au lieu sus allegué, du premier coup sans litis-contestation condamnera ce jeune regratteur comme abusant de mes escrits, lesquels ou il n'entend pas, ou, peut estre, s'il y mord quelque peu, tasche de les pervertir, et me faire espouser les fausses impressions de son [144v] Belleforest, lequel ie m'esbahis fort n'avoir bien publié, l'enorme et effroiable grandeur des balejnes, qui noüent en la mer des moulues. Le champ estoit bien plus beau, pour s'esbattre qu'en la mer Mediterranée et pays chaleureux. Mais, possible, de guet à pend s'est il mis a prouver et persuader chose non seulement difficile à croire mais du tout fause, a fin que de tant plus il fut tenu pour habile homme puis qu'il se faisoit entendre pouvoir venir à chose de ce que les plus hardis et mieux advisés n'eussent osé entreprendre, en un mot se pensant faire paroistre il a luy mesme obscurcy le lustre de la bonne reputaion, que l'on avoit conceüe de luy.

Mais je sens, que telle digression m'a transporté et fait extravaguer bien loin hors de mon sujet, lequel reprenant je retourneray a nos Terresneufves, quj abondent en Moulues, balejnes, Kourts (ou Striches, quj sont ennemis mortels des balejnes) Hecquys, marsouyns et Loups marins, desquels ilz retirent un singulier proffit, ainsy que i'ay descrit au cinquiesme chapitre du vingt troisiesme livre de ma Cosmographie.[8] Quant aux bestes sauvages il y a bien peu de contrée, ou il y en ait si grande frequence,[9] et nommement d'Ours, qui en-dommagent fort les habitans. Le pays y est assez sain, de maniere que les Insulaires y sont bien peu souvent malades, si ce n'est d'une maladie, fort approchant à la contagion de la peste, du Tac ou de la clavelée, contre laquelle est fort souverajne la decoction de l'arbre, nomme Quahoia, qui ressemble à un noyer, sauf qu'il a les feuilles plus larges et plus charnües. Au reste la coste de ces Terres-neufves est fort dangereuse, à cause des goulfes et abysmes, qui y sont, et que aussi toute ceste terre est environée de l'est a l'oüest par une ceinture de rochers, qui sont souz l'eau, lesquels sont faits

5 Thevet first wrote "puisse," then crossed it out.

6 DPI: "ma dite Cosmographie . . . "

7 DPI: "pris . . . "

8 DPI: "ainsy que i'ay descrit ailleurs."

9 DPI: "multitude . . . "

en facon d'Anguille de sorte qu'il faut faire plus de trois cens lieües, pour eviter ce peril et contourner toute ceste ceinture, soit prenant la volte du Nord par la coste de Labrador ou la volte de l'Ouest, comme qui iroit à la Floride, et puis doubler au Cap d'Arcadie iusques au Cap Breton, et suivre la coste de Canada et Terre-neufve, laquelle contient pres de terre ferme un nombre presque infiny d'Isles et Islettes, bancs, rochers haut elevés les uns plus que les autres.

Si comme est entre autres L'Isle des Oiseaux, ainsi appellée à cause de la grande multitude des trois especes d'Oiseaux, nommée Godets, Margots, (difficiles a prendre a cause qu'ilz becquetent ceux, quj les pensoit prendre) et les Aporrah (quj sont de la grandeur d'un Geay) lesquelz Jacques Cartier (mon bon amy) y trouva, et dont il [145r] fit grand amas en bien peu de tems, a fin d'en saler pour un long voiage. Ilz sont tres gras, fort bons et de grand appetit, blancs et noirs ayans les aisles courtes, et par ainsi ne volant guere plus haut que du fil de l'eau. Quant a l'Isle que voyez dans mes cartes sur-nommée de mon nom, Thevet, cela survint, par ce que ie fus le premier, quj y mis le pied entre mes compaignons, quj y descendirent avec moy en un Esquif, pour trouver quelque eau douce, ce qui advint a mon premier voyage, ainsi que i'ay descrit au quatriesme chapitre du vingt troisiesme livre de ma Cosmographie.[10]

Nostre Isle de laquelle je vous parle est fort large et longue peuplée comme je vous ay dit de bois, et en laquelle il fait un tres grand froid. Quelques pescheurs des montaignes s'amusoient a y faire des Longilles[11] de bois tres fort tant pour coucher[12] la nuict en attendant les vents propres pour pescher y tenant feu jour et nuict, que pour serrer leur poisson dedans craignant que les bestes ne le mangeassent,[13] entre autres les Ours qui sont subtils, accorts et friands[14] de ce poisson. La mer est fascheuse en plusieurs lieux, et endroits,[15] et principalement lors qu'elle est en son croissant. De Raddes et de Ports il s'en trouve de beaux et de bons, capables tel qu'il y a[16] pour ancrer cent grands vaisseaux. La terre est haute de la part du Nord-est, il s'y trouve force courant [sic]

10 DPI: "ainsi que je vous ai dit ailleurs."

11 DPI: "des Logettes . . . "

12 DPI: "pour s'y retirer . . . "

13 DPI: "le mangent . . . "

14 DPI: "qui sont friands . . . "

15 DPI: "endroits de ces contrées . . . "

16 DPI: "capables pour la plus part . . . "

dangereux aux moiens vaisseaux.

Chose certes tres-admirable de ceste[17] coste de mer qui foisonne d'une telle sorte en poisson,[18] entre autres en ces[19] moulües que pour une année l'on y en vend la charge de plus de trois cens navires d'Espaigne, France, et aussi Angleterre, Flandre,[20] Dannemark et d'autres endroits. De telle espece de Poisson il ne s'en trouve un seul en Mer[21] Mediterranée, Mer Maior ne a celle de Bacchus ou Caspie, non plus que d'arencs [harengs], merlus, balejnes, maquereaux, casserons, Albacoures, dorades telles qu'avoit l'ocean, et une formilljere d'autres especes different tous les unes des autres. Je n'ay icy affaire de mettre par ordre les routes de la coste de ceste Isle de Terre-neufve depuis la Cap de Ra [sic] quj gist vers l'ouest, iusques à la riviere des Pates, et de la tirant vers le Nord au Cap de Lour, et puis au Cap de Bonne-veüe et l'Isle de Sainct Julien, qui tire vers Septentrion, veu que plusieurs pilotes et mariners sont versés à la Route et cognoissance d'icelles, entre autres-ceux de Bayonne et de Sainct Jean de Luct [Luz].

[145v] Isle de Roberval

Quant ie discouroje d'Islande, je me souviens avoir ramenteü[22] que la on trouve des fantosmes, quj se monstrent visibles, et font des services aux hommes, et principalement apparoissent les figures de la remembrance de ceux, quj ont esté tués ou noyés par quelque adventure violente, et apparoissent à ceux quj les cognoissent, et se monstrent si ouvertement, que ceux, quj ne sont point advertis de leur mort, ont ceste fantasie, qu'ilz sont vivans et leur donnent la main. Icy ie n'ay pas de besoin[23] d'entrer au fonds, pour sçavoir s'il est possible que les esprits de ceux, qui sont decedés, retournent et se representent, aymans mieux laisser ceste recerche aux Theologiens et autres, quj ont meilleur loisir de s'esbattre en telles disputes. Joint que presentement j'auroie bien à demesler autre chose, et beaucoup plus difficile, si ie me plaisoie a discourir des poincts, qui resioujroient vrayment le Lecteur, mais qui ne pourroient estre esclaircis,

17 DPI: "C'est une chose admirable en cette . . . "

18 DPI: "en plusieurs poissons . . . "

19 DPI: "de . . . "

20 DPI: "Flandres . . . "

21 DPI: "es Mers . . . "

22 DPI: "je me souviens vous avoir dit . . . "

23 DPI: "Je n'ay icy affaire . . . "

sans extravaguer trop hors mon sujet.

Icy donques je mettray pied en une Isle, nommée par moy L'Isle de Roberval, pour ce qu'il fut le premier quj mit pied en terre, on luy donne le nom d'Isle des Demons, pour ce que les Demons y font terrible tintamarre, je trouve qu'ils y ont aussi laissé leur trace de telle maniere, qu'elle n'est aujourdhuy renommée, que souz le nom, titre et qualité des Demons, quj s'en sont tellement rendus maistres, que, quoy que L'Isle soit belle et de grande estendüe, si est elle pour la plus part des-habitée, d'autant qu'encores que de jour on y alle [sic] assez pour le faict de la pescherie et pour la chasse, si est ce qu'on n'ose pas s'y fourrer trop avant à cause des atteintes, que fort continuellement recoivent ceux, quj, pour estre par trop adventureux, veulent s'avancer et demeurer par trop long tems dans les toffus boscages de ceste Isle.

Je me souviens avoir autresfois leu, qu'une maison, pour avoir esté malencontrée (autres dient mal genjée et tourmentée des malins esprits[)], fut delaissée, et le Louagier deschargé par arrest du Senat Romain de la promesse, qu'il avoit fait pour le prix du louage. Que si ainsy est n'est merveille si ceste Isle de Demons est si peu frequentée d'habitans, puis qu'elle sert de repaire a ces malins et bourrelans esprits, qui y rabatoit d'une horrible facon, ainsy que i'ay apprins de la pauvre des-confortee Damoiselle, nommée Marguerite, qui y fut releguée par le Capitaine Roberval, son oncle, pour l'expiation du forfait et scandale qu'elle avoit faict à la compaignie qui estoit avoyagée[24] au pays [146r] de Terre-neufve et pays de Canada par le commandement du Roy Francois premier de ce nom. Et par ce que i'ay assez au long et par le menu escrit toute l'histoire imprimée a Paris .1575. de ceste damoiselle au sixiesme chapitre du vingt-troisiesme livre de ma Cosmographie, ie me deporteray d'icy en faire de rechef nouveau escrit, crainte d'ennuyer le Lecteur d'une trop fascheuse prolixité.

Je me contanteray de ramentevoir ce que j'apprins d'elle, que si ceste Isle estoit frequentée, peut estre la malignité de ces depraves esprits s'esvanoüiroit en fumée. La raison, sur laquelle je me fonde, est, qu'elle n'avoit este tarabassée et persecutée de ces hideuses phantosmes, qui luy apparurent dans ceste Isle, sinon depuis qu'elle eut perdu le Gentil-homme son amoureux, sa servante Damienne, native de Normandie (quj estoit maquignonne vieille aagée de soixante ans [et qui] servoit d'eschauguette, pour prevenir la descouverte, qu'on eut peu faire de leurs folastres et impudiques affections) et finalement l'enfant, quj avoit esté procreé de ceste illegitime et lubrique conjonction, dont ilz s'estoient tous deux par

24 DPI: "qui avoit esté envoyée . . . "

ensemble accouplés. L'illation est (à mon advis) concluante, d'autant que si en la compaignie de son estalon, de sa vieille Normande et de son enfant elle n'avoit este affligée de ces efformidables visions, et qu'elle en fut seulement assaillie, estant seulette en ceste grande Isle, n'est pas hors de vray-semblance, que, si elle eut esté en bonne compaignie, les Demons n'eussent plus tot choisy autre retraite qu'en ceste Isle mal-encontrée. Et adire le vray la solitude donnoit grande force à l'esbloüissement de ces apparitions, comme à la verité, il n'y a chose au monde plus contraire à l'asseurance, qu'on desire avoir, que d'estre seul en un lieu, delaissé et abandonné de toute compaignie du monde. D'où est venu, que le sage Salomon, en ses prouverbes deteste telle et si farouche solitude, pour autant qu'elle nous fait chopper au precipice de si vifves et vehementes tentations, que quelque bien armé, que l'on puisse estre, on a bien faire a demeurer droict, haut et eslevé, sans estre sinon terrassé et du tout bouleversé, pour le moins bien esbranlé. L'experience en est si manifeste, que, quj voudroit la nier, meriteroit plustost griefve et rude reprimande qu'une simple remonstrance.

Et afin que ie ne m'esgare point hors de mon sujet en ceste Isle des Demons j'ay raconté, que ceste pauvre pecheresse pendant la vie de ses compaignons, pour la relegation [146v] s'amusoit à chasser aux Ours et sauvagine, dont avec son amoureux et chambriere elle fit une terrible boucherie, mais apres qu'elle eut perdu leur presence, ce ne fut plus question de viser aux animaux terrestres, la portée de l'arquebouze[25] ne pouvoit atteindre droit iusques a ces estoupés Fantosmes. Les bras, les mains, les jambes et tout le corps demouroit engourdy, la poudre n'avoit la force, estant charmée, de chasser hors du canon. Enfusté la balle, le boulet, la dragée ou la charge: quoy plus? Ceste pauvre desolée estoit assaillie et par dehors et par dedans, d'autant que iournellement falloit qu'elle soustint les alarmes, que luy donnoient les bestes rampantes parmy ceste Isle, quj d'une fureur enragée s'archarnoient sur elle, par ce qu'elles la sentoient seule suffisante[26] de leur resister et digne[27] d'estre leur proye.[28] Toutesfois dés [sic] qu'elles monstroient tant soit peu le nez à son advantaige, elle les servoit si à propos de prunes, que leur plus hastif estoit de se retirer. Demy atterrée et alangourje de travail estoit resveillée par bien plus durs, puissans, rusés et hardis ennemjs, sur lesquels le plomb

25 DPI: "harquebouze . . . "

26 DPI: "seule non suffisante . . . "

27 DPI: "et partant digne . . . "

28 In the DPI Thevet has made rather extensive revisions of the rest of the Marguerite story. Hereinafter, only revisions of significance to meaning will be indicated.

ny ses armes ne pouvoient rien. Seulement la grace du Tout-puissant, qui la maintint en un si long et ennuyeuse estre, luy servoit de targue, bouclier et armes tant deffensives que offensives, ainsy que m'a raconté ceste femme, estant arrivée en France, apres avoir demouré deux ans cinq mois en ce lieu là, et venue en la ville de Nautron, pays de Perigort lors que i'y estois, où elle me fit un ample discours de la mes-adventure de toutes ses fortunes passées.

L'Isle est froide au possible, peuplée seulement de bois, plaines [sic] de divers animaux sauvages quj viennent de terre continente d'Isle en Isle, comme ilz scavent tres-bien faire, entre autres, elle estoit peuplée d'Ours. La damoiselle me dit que c'estoient les animaux qui la tourmentoient le plus, et qui taschoient à la devorer elle et son enfant, que toutes autres bestes, et que pour un jour elle en tua quatre, puis se retiroit peu à peu a sa loge que son amy avoit fait devant mourir. Roberval leur avoit laissé plusieurs vivres et autres commodités pour leur aide et survenir a leurs necessités, comme luy-mesmes me dit trois moys devant qu'il fut tué de nuict pres Sainct Innocent a Paris, depuis lequel tems i'ay marqué et donné nom de Roberval a ceste presente Isle, et aussy marqué dans mes [147r] Cartes pour la grande amitié que ie luy portoye de son vivant.

De tel recit, que i'ay autrefois publié, il y a certains grabeleurs ignorans, acazanés a leurs maisons, conteurs d'histoires tragicques, quj ont fait leur profit, se lavans leurs gorges des phantastiques apparitions qu'ilz disent estre par moy supposées au dedans de ceste Isle. D'autres, mettans toutes pieces[29] en besoigne, ont bien enflé la matiere, tellement se sont avantages qu'il y en a aucuns deux [d'eux], quj, pesle-meslant les tintouins[30] d'Islande avec les tracas de ceste Isle desolée ont distillé dans l'alambic de leur cervelle mal disposée certaines voix gelées[31] dont ilz font si tresgrand cas, qu'à lire les bayes, qu'ilz ont avancé, diroit on, veu la dexterité d'esprit, dont on tient qu'ilz estoient habillés, qu'ilz ont eux mesmes vire-volté parmy l'air, pour digerer ces voix saugrenées, dont ilz presument repaistre les oreilles du Lecteur. Quant aux premiers je les renoyjeray avec Aristote (lequel, au rapport de Jean Wier, a njé les apparitions et existence des malins esprits) et telz autres, quj veulent revoquer en doute, qu'il y ait des Cacodemons. Que s'ilz me dient, qu'il n'y a aucune necessite de crojre, encores qu'il y ait des Demons, qu'ilz ravagent en ceste Isle, ie les prieray, puis que sans le veoir ilz ne le veulent crojre, qu'il leur plaist de prendre la pejne d'eux y acheminer en propre

29 DPI: "toutes pierres . . . "

30 We are indebted to Frank Lestringant for the correct reading of this word.

31 DPI: "certaines invectives mal à propos, et quelques discours . . . "

personne, ou commettre personnes dignes, routiniers en experience, à ce bien entendu, suffisantes, capables, et desquelles sur tout, ilz se reffient pour faire la visite des lieux, et se mettre à l'espreuve des chocs, attaques et efforts, quj resveillent ordinairement ceux, qui seuls s'habituent en ces Isles. Toutesfois, pour prevenir aux frais, et comme ie scay, que le coust leur faict perdre le goust d'entreprendre tel et si lointain voyage, je suis bien contant de leur ouvrir ce moyen, quj, sans s'adventurer aux perils de la mer, leur fera toucher au doigt que ce n'est nouveauté qu'il y ait des Demons, quj diablassent en ceste Isle.

Au creux des montaignes et mines ilz trouveront, que tous les metalliques raportent, qu'il y a des Demons: et s'il y a bien plus, que avec plus grande gaitté de coeur, ilz se mettent a fouiller les entrailles des montaignes, quant ilz appercoivent, que les petits diablotins y formillent, d'autant que cela est presque indubitable avoir trouvé bonne et feconde mine. Que s'il est loysible de faire rapport par ensemble, ie diray, que ceste Isle [147v] est tant peuplée de Demons, qu'il faut qu'elle soit bonne et propre a bien rapporter, si elle estoit frequentée des habitans.[32]

Mais que pour cela je veuille permettre aux Panurgiques grableurs de pantagrueliser en leur barragouin de ces voix gelées qu'ilz font à credit gringotter dans tuyaux glacées par ces phantastiques Demons, ie m'en garderay bien, ains me tenans ferme et arresté au pilier de la verité, que i'ay apprise, non point par un seul, mais par plusieurs Pilotes & Nochiers, avec lesquelz i'ay long tems voiagé, diray à leur rapport, que lors qu'ilz passoient par ceste coste, comme ilz fussent [sic] agités d'une grosse tempeste, ilz oyoient en l'air, comme sur la hune et mat de leurs vaisseaux des voix d'hommes confuses, ressemblantes a un bourdonnement qu'on entend en une fojre, marché ou grande assemblée de peuple devisant. De là ces quint-essentialists ont forgé ces beaux petits lopins de voix gelées, a demy gelées et quj se fondoient entre leurs mains lors qu'ilz le manioient: mais la faribourde est si grossier et espesse, que i'ay moy mesme honte de leur trop effrontée impudence, et du tems, qu'ilz ont miserablement perdu a tramer et tistre telles fadaises, quj seroit bien peu si aussy ilz ne desroboient aux Lecteurs plusieurs heures qu'ilz employent à lire telles niaiseries, quj les peuvent autant rassasier, comme s'ilz avoient humé le vent.

Au reste ceste Isle gist à trois cens quarente deux degrés de longitude,

32 The rest of this tirade on demons is missing from the DPI, and is replaced by a transitional sentence roughly equivalent to the one which ends: ". . . autant rassasier, comme s'ilz avoient humé le vent." Evidently Thevet had decided that it was best not to take on Rabelais.

et cinquante huit degrés de latitude. Les lieux les plus signalés et remarquables comme Isles, promontoires et contrées de tout ceste Terre neufve et hauteur d'icelle comprenant celle de Baccaleos et Labrador sont ceux icy, scavoir la hauteur de ceste dite Isle est telle elevation comme i'ay icy dict. Le Cap de Las ou Raze a quarente six degres douze minutes de latitude. Le Cap d'Espere a quarente sept dix huit minutes. Baccaleos sur les quarente neuf. Le Cap de Bonne Viste a quarente neuf douze minutes. Les Isles d'Espere sur les cinquante. Le degrat du quir pont sur les cinquante un degré nulle minute. Belle Isle sur les cinquante deux. La grand [sic] Baye sur la cinquante quatre. Blanc Sablon sur les cinquante deux. L'Isle de Frere Loüis cinquante quatre trente quatre minutes. La Croix blanche cinquante trois. La havre du Barbu cinquante quatre. L'Isle de nostre Dame cinquante un. L'Isle des Ames cinquante un douze minutes. Et quant a la hauteur de la terre de Labrador ie commenceray a la Baye de Eudecqo qui gist à cinquante sept degrés trente quatre minutes. La Baye d'Escureul a cinquante huit. Riviere Doprasse cinquante huit treze minutes. Riviere de Bonne Veüe à cinquante huit vingt minutes. Le Cap du Grand Feu cinquante neuf. Riviere Doree soixante. Baye de Maguin soixante. Baye de place soixante un. Ce sont les lieux que les pilotes doivent bien regarder ou volontiers vont mouiller l'ancre costoyante ceste terre de Canada ou Terre Neufve.

[148r] Belle Isle de Canada

Aucuns s'esbahissent pourquoy ceste Isle a esté embellie du nom de belle, attendu qu'elle est posée entre l'Isle de Sainct Julien quj est vers mydj et le Cap de Gade quj tire de la part du Nord dans la riviere de Canada, elle est deshabitée sans bastiments hors mis quelques logettes pour des pescheurs et finalement pour la plus part en frische, ne prenant pas esgard au motif, qui incita le Pilote Jaques Cartier d'ainsi le baptiser: suivant ce qu'il me dit discourant de l'Isle entre luy et moy en sa maison, et, m'asseura qu'il y fut neuf ou dix jours malade de la gravelle, et que quelques sauvages le guerirent incontinent apres avoir prins du ius d'un arbre nommé Oppeth, Car de s'arrester à la beauté, delicatesse ou somptuosité des bastiments, qui sont dans une Isle, seroit s'amuser (comme l'on dict) à la moustarde, et prendre les faulx-bourgs pour la ville. La raison est que les mariniers prennent bien d'autre facon le nom d'Isle que ne font les Jurisconsultes, lequelz confesseront bien, que pour certain regard nostre Isle estant deserte et desabitée a esté mal et improprement appellée Belle par son parrain, ascavoir si on prend le nom d'Isle pour les maisons, quj sont separées des autres de la ville, et ne sont enclavees avec icelles, ains ont leurs entrees, issues, cours, saillies et entours tellement ordonné qu'il ne touche aucun autre bastiment. De telle sorte de maisons se doit prendre ce, que dit, Spartian, que le feu devora jadis à Rome trois cens trente cinq Isles. Mais (comme i'ay dit) ce ne sont les mariniers, quj subtilisent selon les distinctions espluchées par Bartole et autres[33] Legistes, à la science desquelz ie ne me suis pas beaucoup rompu la teste, ne eux a la mienne, comme i'estime, ains selon les reglemens, qu'ilz tirent tant de l'experience et observations du quadran, boussole et autres instrumens du Pilotage. Et suivant cela ne prennent les Isles que pour la terre, quj de toutes parts est environnée d'eau, et principalement en la mer: Si bien qu'ilz ne s'enquierent si les murailles palais et maisons y sont superbes et magnifiques, ains seulement si la terre, quj doit estre jslée, joint d'aucune part au continent.

Cela a fait, que mon grand et intime amy Jaques Cartier a baillé a ceste Isle le nom de Belle Isle, pour l'amour d'une, quj est en nostre Gaule sur la coste de la petite Bretaigne, gisant à quarente sept degrés de latitude, et dix neuf degrés de longitude. L'occasion, qui le meut a luy communiquer [148v] ce nom de Belle Isle, fut, qu'il avoit envie de renouveller ceste Isle de sa Province en ce pays estrange par luy descouvert. Joinct qu'il y a grand rapport de ces deux Isles par ensemble pour le regard de la figure, ainsi que pourra veoir le Lecteur, s'il luy plaist de les conferer par ensemble, d'autant qu'encores qu'au dedans de l'Isle, la Bretannique soit garnje de quelques lieux, bourgs et maisons, par le dehors et a la superficiaire circonference trouvera on qu'il y a bien peu a redire. Il y en a encores d'autres Isles de mesme nom et me souviens en avoir remarqué une en dessus entre les Orcades, afin que le Lecteur, entendant parler de tant de Belles Isles, ne se mesprenne, et confondant l'une parmy l'autre, n'approprie, a l'une ce quj est de peculier a l'autre.

Quant a nostre Isle,[34] elle gist à trois cens trente trois degrés de longitude, et cinquante deux degrés trente minutes de latitude. Les Cerfs et biches y faonnent à outrance, beaux gresles et vistes. Au coste de l'Est est le promontoire des Oyseaux, ainsy appellé, a cause de la multitude des oyseaux quj se nichent aux arbres, quj sont là aupres. Les plus frequens sont les margaux, lesquels donnent bien de l'affaire aux nautoniers qui veulent s'amuser à les prendre, d'autant qu'avec leur bec ilz se deffendent si furieusement, que, sans grand dangier ne peut on les attraper. Bien est vray, que, quoy qu'ilz scachent becqueter, à la par fin faut qu'ilz se

33 DPI: "Bartole, Jason et autres . . . "

34 DPI: "Or, nostre Isle est posée entre l'Isle de Sainct Julien, qui est vers midy, et le cap de Gade, qui tire de la part du nord, dans la riviere de Canada. Elle gist . . . "

rendent. Leur chair n'est point si bonne et delicate, qu'elle foisonne beaucoup, et est de tant plus commode a gens, quj deliberent faire lointain voiage. C'est affaire seulement à la saupoudrer de sel, pour empescher la corruption. Aujourdhuy, quoy qu'elle ne soit d'ordinajre habitee, si est elle assez souvent visitée par les Bretons, allans aux moulües quj y font alte du coste du Sud, et non du Nord, par ce qu' ainsy que voyez remarqué en ce plan, la coste y est fort dangereuse à cause de plusieurs batteures entretaillés à fleur d'eau, quj desbrisent et[35] saccagent le vaisseau des que tant mje quant il vient là frayer.

Je ne veux oublier a vous dire que ce fut en ceste Isle que les soldats et mariniers du Capitaine prindrent deux grands Ours, dont l'un des deux estoit si vieux qu'il en estoit blanc comme recente neige, et l'ayant escorché et courroyé sa peau fut porté a S. Malo en l'Isle. Jaques Cartier apres avoir fait sa relation au Roy Francois premier du nom luy fit present avec d'autres peaux d'animaux sauvages et de quelques plantes d'arbres et graines des plus rares du pays de Canada. Sa Majesté commanda que on les planta au jardin de Fontaine bleau. Au reste ceste Isle est rongée de plusieurs batteures et escueils. La marée y est grosse, en deux endroits il y a force courantes, parquoy il faut que le pilote soit accort la tournoyant coste à coste.

[149r] Isle de S. Julien

Ceste Isle n'est point à tort dicte grande par nos mariniers et marquée du nom de grande dans mes cartes d'autant qu'elle contient un fort grand cerne de terre, joint que c'est pour la distinguer d'une autre, portant le mesme nom, de laquelle, si le sujet m'y appelle, je pretens discourir. Elle gist pour latitude des le cinquantiesme degré iusques au cinquante troisiesme, pour longitude des le trois cens vingt septiesme degré iusques au trois cens trente sixiesme degré: d'aussy belle et plaisante assiete, qu'aucune autre, quj soit en ceste coste, et quj promet une grande abondance de biens, si elle estoit frequentée, et cultivée par les habitans ou que quelques Estrangiers s'en emparassent par force ou par amitié, pour en faire nouvelle colonine [sic] comme ont fait les Espaignolz et Portugais aux Isles qu'ilz tiennent de present. Mais une chose y a, si les Francois et Anglois se vouloient habituer ou se fortifier comme ilz ont voulu faire à la Floride, les Espaignols incontinant ne faudroient à leur faire guerre pour les deschasser. Helas, ne voila pas un merveilleux goulfe[36] d'avarice et

35 DPI: "saccagent le vaisseau des ignorans mariniers."

36 DPI: "gouffre . . . "

ambition de ces gens là, de vouloir occuper s'ilz pouvoient dix mille fois plus de pays qu'il ne leur en faut et qu'ilz n'en peuvent peupler, ne seroient contens et se voudroient faire Monarques, et commander au Ciel, a la terre, à la mer et aux poissons s'il leur estoit possible, sans penser à quelle fin les choses doivent parvenir.

Quant aux deux cornes de l'Isle que voyez en l'entre-tailleure, quj vous est representée par ce plan au Nord, faut que l'Isle soit de bien grande estendüe, qu'elles prennent sur Belle Isle, la Septentrionale, quj porte le nom d'une autre qui est en Bretaigne, et l'Isle dicte de l'Assomption et autres, quj sont enserées au milieu de ceste eschancreure. L'entrée d'icelle est un peu dangereuse a cause des escueils, bancs, et batteures, qui sont tres-perilleuses pour faire naufrage le vaisseau, s'il ne se destourne du Nord au nord-est et Est. Elle est fort remplie de grands arbres et forests espesses, quj est tout le principal raport de ceste Isle, au moins, quj nous soit communiqué, d'autant que les bestes sauvages estant en saisine et possession d'icelle empeschent que les hommes n'y facent leur sejour. Quj n'est pas perte de petite consequence, puis qu'une si large et ample estendüe de pays suffiroit [149v] assez pour embesoigner beaucoup de peuple. Ce n'est pas que ie promette une fertilité, ou fecondité du terroir, quj y semble estre assez mal propre, ce seroit toutesfois a peu d'affaire de luy remettre au moins mal nouvelle face, et quj encores qu'il ne fut pro rata de tel raport, que celuy de par deca, ne pourroit que, doublant, triplant ou quadruplant les terres, il ne rendit grande foison de biens. Là dessus ie m'asseure, qu'on m'opposera la difficulté du labourage, quj a peu pres se rapporte (s'il ne surmonte) à la semence et prix ou estime du fonds: mais quj voudroit estre si fort, speculatif,[37] plusieurs contrées que voyons aujourdhuy fleuronnées d'une plantureuse abondance et benediction de biens demeureroient en friche et en herme.

Entre plusieurs Isles quj entourent ceste cy, i'admire sur toutes celle de Sainct Catherine, dautant qu'elle est pour la plus part et au moins mal que l'on peut penser desfrischée de ces buissons, quj estouffent la fertilité des autres. Tout le mal que i'y vois est qu'elle est basse et en une plaine, si bien qu'elle est sujette à des relentisseures quj en-marescagent le principal rapport qu'on doit esperer de là. Pour cela nean moins ne faut mettre souz le pied l'esperance de sa fertilité, attendu que l'Hollande, Zelande et autres regions, quoy qu'elles soyent embourbées dans les marestes, ne laissent pas à faire par tout esclater le los de leur fecondité et y a bien plus que du costé de Nord-est le pays est un peu plus eslevé et par ainsi exempt de ces moiteurs pallustres: mais d'autre costé cela apporte une

37 DPI: "Mais qui voudroit regarder de si pres, plusieurs . . . "

grande incommodité aux mariniers, quj sont contraints pour faire un assez ennuyeux destour, par ce que la terre y est seche et y a mauvais fond pour y prendre terre.

Ceste Isle avec le Port du goulfe des chasteaux regardent au Nord nord-est et Sud Sud-oüest, d'ou quelques uns jeunes pilotes ont print occasion de dire que l'Isle de Sainct Catherine est le port du goulfe des Chasteaux: fort mal a propos, attendu que Jaques Cartier, duquel ilz disent avoir tiré et extrait ce qu'ilz rapportent, eut esté bien marry de les joindre par ensemble, au contraire le Lecteur trouvera qu'à cause du circuit qu'il faut faire, il met de distance quinze lieües: mais il n'estoit pas dificile a un certain [150r] glosseur en son estude de couper et trancher tout ce destour pour emmonceler ensemblement tant l'Isle de Sainct Catherine, que le port du Goulfe des Chasteaux. A l'espreuve il se fut, peut estre, trouvé fort empesché.

La coste de l'Isle foisonne en poisson de toutes sortes, les sauvages ne vivent la plus-part du tems que de ce poisson qu'ilz accommodent tres-gaillardement à leur facon, sans saulce, ne sans pain, ne sans vin ne vinaigre, ne laissant pourtant ce peuple estre gaillard et dispos, ilz vivent longuement encor qu'ilz n'ayent leurs aises, comme aucuns friands de par deca, autres en font de la farine à la maniere que font nos sauvages de l'Amerique [du Sud], ainsi que je vous ay amplement discouru dans mon livre de mes Singularités.

L'Isle de laquelle je vous represente le plan est posée dans le fleuve de Canada, c'est bien l'une des plaisantes et grandes de tout ce pays là. Elle est peuplée de bois d'haute-fustee, fort portueuse et peu montaigneuse, si c'est de la part du Sud, son port principal vise vers l'Est, il tient en sa longueur trois lieües, et un quart, en sa plus grande largeur. Pour une fois, il s'y trouve deux cens basteaux pour y pescher des moulües, c'est là où est la bonne pescherie, et ou les marchans traffiquent avec les sauvages du pays.

Au reste Je veux oster icy d'erreur devant passer outre plusieurs nouveaux pilotes et mariniers quj estiment estre quelque chose d'eux, entre autres trois du pays Bayonnois, lesquelz discourant du pilotage me voulurent ceste presente année mil cinq cens quatre vingt six faire accroire que le pays de Canada, et ceulx de Norombegueien et Baccaleos n'estoient qu'un mesme paï̈s mais tant s'en faut comme ie leur dits attendu que cestuy cy de Norombegue est sur les quarente trois degrés et celuy de Canada et la grand riviere Dochelaga sont sur les cinquante un, cinquante deux et cinquante trois, Voila que c'est que d'avoir faute d'experience maistresse de toutes choses.

Devant que daborder le pays et terre & continuité de Norombegue et avant que parvenir à la terre Canadienne vous apparoist une Isle tournoyée de huit Isleaux fort petits, quj avoisinent la terre des montaignes vertes et le Cap des Tortues, de là vous venez tousjours à la bouche de ladite riviere, l'entrée de laquelle est dangereuse, à cause d'un grand nombre de gros et hauts rochiers et force basteures, encor que son entrée soit large presque de demie lieüe, [150v] Environ trois lieues dans la riviere a beau mitan se presente devant vous une petite Isle quarrée, vray est qu'elle a un promontoire qui vise de la part du Nord est, quj peut avoir quelques quatre petites lieues de tour, et habitée seulement de quelques pescheurs et d'oyseaux de diverses especes. Elle est nommée par ceux du pays Aiayascon, à cause que l'Isle est faite la voyant de loin de la part de l'est, elle vous apparoist en forme d'un bras d'homme qu'ilz appellent ainsy, L'on la pourroit peupler facilment aussi bien que plusieurs autres petites Islettes qui l'avoisinent d'assez loin, et en icelle faire une forteresse tres-belle pour tenir en bride toute la coste.

C'est d'icelle que i'ay tant discouru a plusieurs entrepreneurs de voyages qui font des levées de boucliers et puis ce n'est rien, leur remonstrant que s'ilz s'estoient saisis d'icelle Isle et la fortifier, qu'ilz tiendroient en bride tous les sauvages du pays de Bacchaleos, Norombegue, Canadiens et autres, et n'oseroient pour rien y mouiller l'ancre. Les commodités qui se trouveroient audict pays seroient aussi grandes, ou plus à ceux quj commanderoient a ceste terre et pays voysin, que d'aller cercher les mines d'or aux Isles du Peru, car premierement se peut trouver a Norombegue des mines de metaux de cuivre, de fer, de plomb, d'assier et d'autres. Secondement s'y pourroit faire abondance de sel attandu que le pays est plat et fort propre, Tiercement grand traffic pour la pelleterie, Quartement attandu que le pays est peuplé de boys d'haute fustaye et de toutes especes avec l'ayde des artisans il s'y pourroit bastir et faire plusieurs vaisseaux grands et moyens à rame ou autrement. Quintement se pourroit remplir de grands magasins de poisson salé, attandu que c'est le vray pais de la pescherie, où la mer formille en moulües et plus qu'aux autres contrées de Canada autant de centaines de navires en viennent tous les ans chargée, et ne scache à la verite lieu plus propre à quelque Prince ou grand Seigneur qui desireroit faire nouvelle colonine que de s'emparer et se fortifier en ces contrées là, si propres ayant l'air si benin, gracieux et favorable et les vents pareillement, que dans un an de nostre France ou d'Angleterre s'y peut faire deux voyages aller et venir.

Les peuples y sont benins et gracieux quj ne taschent qu'a tirer l'amitié de l'estranger et me souvient que quant nous eusmes mis pied en terre quj fut a mon premier voiage au retour des terres Australes nous faisions difficulté d'accoster ces Barbares. Un Roytelet du pays tout vestu de peau de beste sauvage accompaigné de quelques autres estimans que nous estions faschés et que nous les craignions nous dit assez amiablement en sa langue, Cazigno, Cazigno, Casnouy danga addagrin: c'est adire, Allons, allons, en terre mes freres et amys. Coaquoca Ame Couascon, Kazaconny, Venez boire et manger de ce que nous avons. Arca Somioppah, Quenchia dangua Ysmay assomaha: nous vous jurons par le Ciel, la terre, la lune et les estoiles: que n'aurez non plus de mal que nos propres personnes. Voyans la bonne affection & volonté de ce vieillard, fusmes avec luy un jour entier, le lendemain prismes la route du goulfe de Canada.

[151r] Isle de l'Assumption

Ceste Isle fut descouverte par Jaques Cartier, ainsy qu'il appert par la seconde relation du voiage, qu'il fit en Canada, Hochelaga, Saguenaj et autres pays, par le commandement du Roy Francois premier du nom, en l'année mil cinq cens trente cinq le jour de la my-aoust, [Thevet has added the following in the margin: "ainsy qu'il ma dit estant logé en sa maison de St. Malo en l'Isle"] et pour ce baptisa il ceste Isle du nom de l'Assumption, pour ce qu'au quinziesme jour du moys d'Aoust on celebre la feste et solemnité de la Vierge Marie mere du Sauveur et Redempteur de tout le monde.

De toucher icy aux Singularités de l'Isle n'est mon intention, d'autant que ie ne pourrois y ramentevoir pour le present que les repaires hydeux et effroyables de la sauvagine, qui seule semble commander dans les flots remparés des toffues forests, quj em-buissonnent pour la plus-part ce pays: Toutesfois n'y auroit pas beaucoup affaire à desfrischier et à desserter[38] ces bois, aprés les avoir esclaircys,[39] donner la chasse aux Ours, quj sur tous les autres animaux tiennent la leur canton, quj donnent mille tourments à ceux quj peschent les moulües, et s'ilz ne prennent garde de bien pres incontinent une troupe de ces animaux ne faillent d'entrer la nuit aux cabanes et logettes et souventesfois dans les barques pour devorer ce qu'ilz y trouveront de poisson, ilz en sont friands plus que de chose du monde, et estans affamés on les voit aller pescher dans les Lacs et rivieres.

Ilz se trouvent aussy plusieurs autres animaux tant en ceste Isle que en terre continente, entre lesquelz on en voit une espece comme de grands taureaux [margin: Buffol beste majestueuse] quj ont cornes longues seule-

38 DPI: "et de peupler . . . " Thevet first wrote "desfrichier et a desserter," then crossed them out and reversed the order.

39 Thevet has added here, and then crossed out the words "et fait claire voye."

ment d'un pied et demy, et en apportay deux que i'ay encore de present dans mon Cabinet a Paris au revenir de mon premier voyage, ayant cest animal sur le dos une tumeur et bosse, toute telle que celle d'un chameau, le poil long par tout le corps, la couleur duquel approche du fauve, et principalement sous le menton, sa queue comme celle d'un Lyon, et de telle espece s'en trouve en la Lituanie et Pologne qu'ilz nomment Zubex, et les Tartares Roffert. Les Sauvages du pays s'arment de leurs peaux contre le froid et sont leurs cornes fort estimés pour la proprieté qu'elles ont contre le venin, et partant en gardent les Barbares afin d'obvier aux poisons et vermine qu'ilz rencontrent souvant allant par pays et à la pescherie.

Mais ce, qui rend ceste Isle si peu frequentée d'habitans est, que l'abord d'icelle est fort dangereux, et encores plus difficile à cause des sablons, basteures et bancs quj la rengent tant du coste du grand fleuve de Canada, que de celluy du goulfe carré ou Sein de Sainct Laurens, quj gist à quelques cinquante deux degrés de latitude. Bien est vray, que du coste du [151v] destroict de Sainct Pierre la voye est un peu plus asseurée et pour ceste occasion Jaques Cartier, celuy qui me donna le plan de ceste Isle, et d'autres aussy, quj fut l'an mil cinq cens cinquante, me dit que pour faire sa descouverte, print ceste route. Le plain pays, dont il parle, est celuy de Nurembeg, autrement appellé la nouvelle France, quj a au Nord ceste Isle de L'Assumption. Laquelle d'autres nomment de Jaisple, dont i'ay bien voulu advertir le Lecteur, de peur qu'il ne se partrouble, si dans quelques cartes Sciographiques il n'appercoit que mention soit faite de ceste Isle de l'Assumption, ains de celle de Jaisple, laquelle ie n'entends aucunement separer de celle de l'Assomption. A quatre degrés de la ligne Equinoctiale à mon premier voyage quj fit environ l'an mil cinq cens cinquante un, trouvasmes une autre Isle habitée seulement d'oyseaux nommee de l'Assomption esloignée de l'autre de plus de douze cens lieües pour le moins, laquelle i'ay marquée dans mes cartes et Mappemonde aussi bien que celle du Canada. La varieté de noms de nostre Isle de laquelle ie parle, est survenue à cause des divers voiageurs, quj ont donné en ceste Isle, lesquelz la trouvans seulement habitée et peuplée d'oyseaux et bestes sauvages se sont fait entendre qu'ilz estoient les premiers, quj l'avoient descouverte, et pour ce l'ont baptisé de tel nom qu'il leur a pleu. L'elevation de la presente Isle est telle, que pour latitude elle gist du cinquante uniesme degré iusques au cinquante troisiesme, pour longitude du trois cens douziesme iusques au trois cens dix-neufiesme.

En ceste Isle il y a plusieurs montaignes, au coupeau desquelles sont les plus beaux et savoureux pasquiers, que l'on puisse estimer, mais d'autant qu'elle est deserte et deshabitée ilz demeurent en friche, infructueux et sans nul raport. Je scay que certains herboristes, quj se desbanderent pour aller un peu au dedans de l'Isle fureter les Singularitez d'icelle revindrent chargés de plusieurs plantes fort exquises, et dont ils faisoient grand cas, regrettans que la commodité ne leur permettoit d'y faire derechef un nouveau voiage. Mais ilz craignoient que s'ilz arrestoient davantage ilz ne fussent salariés d'une perpetuelle relegation, et pour guerdon des peines qu'ilz avoient prins à virevolter parmy ces montaignes, de dresser là une colonie de pauvres abandonnés et exposés à la mercy des bestes farouches.

Il y a pareillement quelques plaines quj ressentent assez leur bon terroir, non point tant pour le rapport du grain, comme pour le pasquier, d'autant qu'il y a de [152r] fort belles prayries inutiles aux hommes, quj n'y scauroient transmarcher une seule beste, et quant bien elle y seroit transmise, elle cousteroit plus à garder des incursions des Ours et autres bestes sauvages, que ne pourroit valoir tout le prix, qu'on scauroit retirer tant du principal que de l'accessoire en plusieurs annees.

Quant les nostres eurent mis pied en terre pour descouvrir les choses les plus rares, les uns espars d'un costé, les autres d'un autre sans aucune crainte de la barbarie de ce peuple [,] y vivoient asses bien a cause que les habitans des pays lointains leur amenoient plus de poisson et de sauvagine qu'ilz ne vouloient à quoy ilz sont fort duits à tirer de l'arc et prennent les bestes avec mille ruses gentilles: Et entre autres ilz usent d'une sorte de raquettes, tissues et faites de cordes de nerfs de bestes, carrées, et desquelles les trous sont fort petits, comme ceux d'un crible, et sont en proportion de deux pieds et demy, et presque autant de large. Et usent de cecy, les liant à leurs pieds, tant pour le froid, que pour ne s'enfoncer point dans la neige, lors qu'ilz chassent aux bestes sauvages, et que aussy ilz ne glissent point sur les glacons.

Ilz se vestent de peaux couroyées et accoustrées à leur mode, l'hyver le poil par le dedans vers leur chair, et l'esté le cuir touchant leur chair, et le poil estant par le dehors. Pour prendre donc ces bestes, vous les verrez assembler dix ou douze, garnis et embastonnes de longs bastons, comme espieux et pertuisanes, lances ou piques, ayans aucuns douze, autres quinze pieds de long, garnies par le bout, non de fer ou autre metail, mais de quelque bel oz de cerf, ou autre beste, long d'un bon pied, et pointu à l'advantage portans des arcs et et flesches garniz de mesme. Ainsi embastonnez ilz vont par les neiges le long de l'annee, quj leur y sont familieres, et poursuivant Cerfs, Sangliers, Alces et rangiferes par la profondeur de ces neiges ilz delaissent leurs brisées tout ainsy que font nos veneurs a fin de ne s'esgarer point. Ces sauvages font des loges de Cedres desquelz le pays en est fort peuplé et se cachant souz ces loges verdoyantes attendant que les Cerfs y viennent, des que la beste approche ilz sortent tous de leurs embusches et luy courent sus avec leurs piques et arcs, et avec leur huée luy font perdre le chemin frayé, et puis estans leur beste morte la trainent a leurs maisons faites en facon et figures d'un demy cercle, que le peuple appelle Canocas, grandes et longues de vingt-cinq ou trente pas et dix de largeur, et couvertes les unes d'escorces d'arbres, et autres de peaux et de iongs [joncs] marins.

Au reste les Bretons qui furent les premiers [152v] qui mirent pied en terre en ce pays là, et penetrerent iusques a cinquante et soixante lieües dans les terres devant Cortereal quj iamais ne vit que les chantillons d'icelle, encor que l'on luy ait voulu donner le los et iouange d'avoir esté le premier, chose que Thevet ne leur accordera jamais, d'autant que nous sceusmes des plus anciens sauvages que les Francois ont esté les premiers quj ont illustré leur pays.

Il ne se faut estonner si nostre Isle de l'Assumption n'est beaucoup peuplée pour les occasions que ie vous ay dites. Elle est fort portueuese, de mon tems il s'y voioit encor des forts de bois que les Francois y avoit dressé, mesme sur la riviere d'Hochelaga et sur celle de Noremberg [sic]. Ceste terre est fort Septentrionale et approche de celle quj est souz le cercle Arctique que nous disons l'un des Poles ou Pivot soustenans la Sphere, et par consequence que vous pouvez imaginer combien la terre doit estre froide et non pour autant inhabitable. Or Canada veut autant a dire comme terre et vint ce nom des premiers quj y firent descente, car comme quelcun leur demandast que c'est qu'ilz cerchoient en ce lieu ilz respondirent qu'ilz estoient Segnada Canada, scavoir hommes cerchant terre, et depuis ce nom est demeuré comme nom donne à plaisir, ainsi qu'à la pluspart des Isles et provinces nouvellement descouvertes.

Vers le Nort, elle tend à la mer glaciale et Hyperborée, parquoy tout ce pays est contenu tant Baccaleos que Labrador souz le nom de Canada, En ceste terre il y a une Province nommée Campestre de Berge, quj tire au Su est, en ceste Province gist à l'Est le Cap ou promontoire de Lorraine, ainsy par nous nommé et autres luy ont donné le nom du Cap des Bretons, à cause que c'est la que les Bretons Biscains et Normans, vont et costoyent allant en terre neufve pour pescher des Moulues. Pres de ce Cap est assise une autre Isle nommée Hurée quj tire de la part du Nort, ayant quelques cinq lieües de circuit et assez pres de terre firme. S'y voit un autre quj l'avoisine de deux lieues quj est en triangle quj se nomme par ceux du pays Carbassa et de nous fut nommée l'Isle des Vierges, et commence ceste terre vers le Cap devers le Mydj et se renge à l'Est Nord-est et ouest Sud-ouest, Ceste coste de Canada depuis le Cap de Lorraine tournant au Su, entre ainsi en mer comme fait l'Italie entre les mers Adriatique et Ligustique, y faisant comme une Peninsule.

Je feray fin icy de nostre Isle de l'Assumption deplorant les miseres de beaucoup de Princes Crestiens d'estre si negligents de laisser ceste florissante Province, et qu'ilz n'envoyent aussi bien pour la peupler et evangeliser ces pauvres Barbares attandu qu'elle est proche de nous, comme ont jadis fait les Espaignolz et Portugais en si grand nombre de terres qu'ilz tiennent de present, et par les grands richesses qu'ilz en recoivent ilz s'agrandissent de iour en iour, et à la verité si ceste terre Canadienne estoit habitée ilz pourroient autant ou plus recepvoir de profit, que les Roys d'Escosse et d'Annemark recoivent de leurs Isles Hebrides et Orchades ou le grand Turc de ses Isles Cyclades.

[153r] Isle des Demons

Il est impossible (ce me semble) d'oster ceste sotte fantaisie aux hommes, entre autres aux pilotes et mariniers quj entreprennent le voyage de terre neufve, qu'en ceste Isle de laquelle ie vous represente le plan, n'y aye des Demons et Diablerie qui tourmentent ceux, qui y vont mouiller l'ancre, comme ie vous ay dit d'une autre Isle que i'ay nommée Roberval assez voisine de ceste cy. Je n'ay icy affaire ramentevoir au Lecteur pourquoy ceste presente Isle a porté le mesme nom des Demons, ny vous declarer pareillement comme iadis iceux demons estoient estimés des Philosophes entre les bons Genyes, entre lesquels ils en avoient de six especes, scavoir Demons forestiers et Demons paredres, c'est a dire assistans.

Et quant a nostre Isle qui avoisine la terre de Baccaleos, et la Nouvelle France, comme ailleurs ie vous ay descrit, certes encor qu'elle ne soit habitée, diriez pour la tempestuosité des grands vents qui y sont iournaliers, et quelques fois les orages, les quatre elemens le feu, l'eau, la terre et l'air, encor qu'entre eux soient differens, toutesfois pour estre l'une et simple raison par lequelle sont corruptibles, et par eschanges transmuables de l'un a l'autre, que tous ces elemens en un moment sont contraires aux hommes qui mettent pied en terre en ceste dicte Isle. Car qui prendroit seulement esgard a l'assiette d'icelle, selon le plan et description par moy faite particulierement, diriez que c'est un autre monde et le lieu inhabitable, encor qu'elle soit posée a un climat assez temperé et froid, qui gist deça la ligne Equinoctiale a cinquante neuf degrés de latitude, et a trois cens quarente trois de longitude quasi en mesme elevation et pareil climat que sont le plus esloignées Isles de l'Ocean où la mer est glacee et fort voisine du Pole Arctique qui est de la part du ciel septentrional, et par consequent la plus froide Isle de terre neufve, laquelle fait une extremité de Canada et participante de celle de Baccaleos estant tout maritime, en laquelle Isle se trouve de grandes rivieres que l'on dit des trois freres assez proche de l'Isle d'Orbelande, laquelle est en ladicte mer. Ceste riviere est des grandes de toute ceste terre et toutesfois telles que celles que i'ay veues dessouz l'Equator et a l'Antarctique.

Le pays de terre continente est habité de gens barbares, cruels et inhumains, tout ainsy que ceux du Canada, peu accostables et mal gracieux si ce n'est par force, et le scavent bien ceux, quj y vont pescher les moulues que nous mangeons de par deca. Ilz se vestent de peau sauvagine a l'imitation de tous leurs voisins et peuple de Septentrion. Ilz vont souvent a nostre Isle des [153v] Demons, quelquefois vingt ou trente batteaux legiers desquels ce peuple naviguent allant d'Isle en Isle et de lieu en lieu dans iceux, et ne viennent iamais en leurs logettes qu'ils n'apportent grand nombre d'animaux sauvages que nourrit et engendre ceste Isle Demonienne, qui est divisée et separée en plusieurs autres, principalement de la part de l'Est où est la bonne pescherie. Chose tresadmirable de veoir en ce grand Ocean d'Isles[40] et Isleaux esloigniées de terre continente, les unes de cent, de trois cens, de quatre cens, de vingt et autres de dix lieues, peuplées toutesfois de diverses especes d'animaux terrestres, et oiseaux de plusieurs plumages.

Mais devant que d'entrer en ce propos et discours de telles especes de bestes qui se nourrissent en ceste dicte Isle, je voudrois bien ouïr quelque excellent personnage qui m'esplucha[41] cecy souz le merite et doute comment il est possible qu'en ce lieu et en deux mille autres Isles qui ne furent comme i'ay dit iamais habitées non plus que celle cy, on veoit formiller tant de diversité de bestes et oiseaux, et en quelle sorte ils ont esté procréées et engendrées. Je scay bien que la chaleur et humeur cause la generation des choses inferieures mais aussy faut il regarder que en toute generation il faut avoir egard a la matiere, et selon icelle il faut qu'ils vivent de ce dequoy ils sont engendrés. Or les choses qui ont sens faut necessairement qu'elles sortent de la commixtion des semences, et par ainsy ie dis que ie suis en doute (parlant selon la raison naturelle) comme ces bestes se sont engendrées en ceste Isle. De dire, que la putrefaction d'une chaleur humide engendre telle semence de vermine, ie ne puis le comprendre ny accorder, tant pour l'extreme froidure qui est en ce lieu là, d'autant aussy que la matiere y repugne et qu'il faut que ces corps qui sont composés de toutes sortes d'entrailles, recoivent nourriture par le sang s'espandant par les conduits des veines soient aussy formés, et prenant leur augmentation de ce sang qui les vivifie et anime, et tout

40 DPI: "tant d'Isles . . . "

41 DPI: "espluchast . . . "

ainsy que l'homme ne peut estre engendré sinon par l'effusion de semence et nourriture qu'il prend dans la matrice de sa mere, semblablement aussy les animaux ne peuvent estre procrées de la seule humeur de la terre putride, y obstant le defaut de la chaleur radicale qui cause par le sang ce nourrissement et vie. Il ne faut donc s'esbahir s'il y a abondance de bestes veu que ces Sauvages pour s'entretenir et maintenir et couvrir[42] de leurs peaux ayans mangé la chair, en chargent leurs barquettes.[43] Quant aux oiseaux pource qu'ilz ont le corps plus subtil et participant de la nature de l'air, quant bien [154r] ils ne [y] seoient des le commencement de ladite Isle si peuvent ils estre venus et y venir encor d'ailleurs veu que l'on scait bien que les Grues et Arondelles sont oiseaux passagiers. Je vous ay faict ceste petite digression pour le contentement des bons esprits, et de ceux qui n'ont iamais voiagé.

Au reste autour de ceste mer il s'y trouvent non seulement des molues, mais aussy des Loups marins desquels la chair leur semble tresbonne et delicate. Ils se servent de la graisse et font certain huille lequel estant fondu se convertit a une liqueur toute rousastre, et en boivent aux repas comme nous faisons du vin et autre breuvage, ou comme les Mores de la haute et basse Ethiopie de l'huile d'olif, qui leur est commun et propre lors qu'ils sont alterés. Ils ont semblablement d'autres poissons assez, comme marsoüins, chiens de mer, qui sont vestus de cuir dur, et les autres chargés de coquilles tresdures comme Tortues, huistres, moles,[44] et autres qui n'ont que la simple escaille. C'est en cest endroit que se trouve grand quantité de baleines, et non en la mer Mediterranée, comme nous a laissé par escrit le gloseur de Munster là où il s'est trop lourdement abusé suivant ce que ie vous en ay dit ailleurs.

Depuis ceste Isle iusques à la pointe de la Floride la coste a esté visitée et descouverte tant le continent que les rivieres d'eau douce et salée qui separe les Royaumes et provinces de ce peuple barbare. Ces rivieres depuis le Goulphe de Merore, sont quasi la moitié de l'année gelées. L'entrée dudit goulfe est sur les cinquante neuf et cinquante huit degres tirant iusques a l'Isle de Gonse et a la grand Isle de Fiche tellement que les vaisseaux qui y vont mouiller l'ancre se mettent souvent en danger de la glace si l'on n'y mect remedde bien tost. Entre ladite Isle de Fiche et celle de Gonse tirant aux batteures de S. Laurens de la part du Nord ceste coste est la plus dangereuse a cause de la courante. En ceste Isle de Fiche fut bannje la Damoiselle de laquelle ie vous ay parlé, Laquelle

42 DPI: "se couvrir . . . "

43 The DPI has "marquerottes" here, which is obviously incorrect.

44 DPI: "moules . . . "

a esté depuis nommée par moy l'Isle de Roberval, esloignée du continent du blanc sablon de l'Isle de Baccaleos et de celle de Foulques, et du Cap du Bonne Veue de quelques trois lieües et non plus. Ayant traversé ces dangereux passages, le pilote est en seurté iusques a la riviere et pays de Saguenay que les Sauvages appellent Thadoyzeau, et peut le pilote deployer toutes les voiles iusques a L'Isle de l'Assumption que les mesmes sauvages [154v] nomment Naticoustj assez dangereuse pour l'aborder à cause d'une infinité de bancs et de batteures desquels dangers la mer est pleine iusques a la Baye de Chaleur que les barbares appellent Mechsameht. Ceux qui voiagent dans ceste mer ou goulphe quj avoisine la terre tirant droit au Nord trouvent une autre terre faict en peninsule nommee Athanicq qui est à main droite. Les grands vaisseaux ne sont propres pour ceste coste ains les petits et moyens de quarente, cinquante et soixante tonneaux, lesquels peuvent aller iusques a l'extremité de la grand riviere pays asses sablonneux qu'ils appellent en leur patois Hananyer.

J'avois oublié a vous dire que une Isle nommée des Francois Orleans, et des sauvages Minigo est l'endroit ou la riviere est la plus estroite et depuis l'entrée de ladite riviere commence l'Isle des Vierges quj avoisine une autre riviere nommee Islee, esloignée pres de soixante lieues, et de celle d'Orleans iusques au Lac d'Angoulesme trente quatre lieues.

S'il est question de passer plus outre de la part du Nord et Nordest vous trouverez tant d'une part que d'autre plusieurs grands rivieres, entre autres celle nommée Estendue qui vient et prend sa source des hauts monts de Chilague et ceux de Tortimage: A gauche vous avez pareillement les rivieres de Monmorancy qui baignent les pays de Chambriant, et celle de Gotin qui avoisine d'assez pres le promontoire de Raguine et celuy de Passer. Entre lesquels pays et celuy des Magots se treuve un grand lac qui peut avoir vingt sept lieues de tour nommé de ceux du pays Pathnos, qui a une belle Isle au mitan peuplée de barbares, et peut avoir trois lieues de tour. Elle est nommée Minigo, de laquelle ie vous ay parle icy dessus. Ceste Isle de Minigo sert de retraite au peuple de ces pays pour se retirer lors qu'ils sont poursuivis de leurs enemis, et là où ils les mettent les ayans pris en vie pour les garder quelques Lunes et Jours pour apres les massacrer a la facon et maniere que leurs anciens ennemis faisoient d'eux quand ils les avoient prins ou sur mer ou sur terre.

Au tour de ladite Isle c'est la plus belle pescherie qui soit en tout le grand Ocean, et où les baleines y repairent en tous tems. Les Bayonnois, Espaignols et autres, y vont a la pescherie pour y prendre ces grands belues, nommées des Mexicains Altapatlj, des Syriens Tanim, des Hebreux Dogh-gadol qui est a dire grand poisson, des Persiens Nuna-rabbi, des Grecs vulgaires Phalena des moschovites Bellouga, et de ce peuple

Canadien Kourt, et des Turcs Hyounous, [155r] et de ceux de Baccaleos Strich. Il s'en prend tous les ans grand nombre et principalement a la riviere de Saguenay qui peut avoir demie lieue d'entrée, au pres de laquelle nos François y firent un fort de bois pour s'asseurer des barbares qui sont asses bonnes gens et gracieux si l'on ne les irrite. Ils ne croient point en Dieu. Ils vivent sans foy et sans loy ne n'adorent chose au monde.[45] Ils sont fort paresseux. Il leur faut faire beaucoup de presens tant pour attirer leur amitié que pour les faire travailler et ayder a la pescherie quand les Chrestiens qui vont de par dela les prient pource faire dautant que c'est le plus grand traffic que les marchands peuvent faire de par de la de ces baleines, la graisse desquelles ils font fondre. Ils traffiquent aussy avec iceux barbares de diverses peaux belles et fines qu'ils permutent avec d'autres marchandises aux estrangiers. Quant à l'or et argent monnoyé ils n'en ont cognoissance aulcune non plus que le reste des sauvages des terres Australles.

J'avois oublié a vous dire parlant des baleines qu'il s'en trouvent dans icelles rivieres d'Ochelaga, Saguenay et d'autres, comme i'ay dit qui viennent là en diverses saisons et moys et viennent de la grand mer. A quoy il faut penser que ces grandes bestes aquatiques sont passagieres aussy bien que les autres petits et moyens poissons. Il s'y touve en ces lieux mesmes grand nombre de chevaux marins qui sont poissons amphibiens comme sont les crocodilles et Loups marins. Quant les sauvages les peuvent attraper ils n'en laissent pas un en arriere mais les tuent à coups de flesches et grosses massues de bois et puis les mangent tres bien, la chair en est bonne et delicate. Je diray encor ce que i'ay observé pour le fait des baleines que la femelle ne fait iamais qu'un petit a la fois, lequel elle met hors tout ainsy que font les quadrupedes sans oeufs, au rebours du naturel de tout autre poisson. Au reste la baleine alaitte son petit baleinon apres qu'il est dehors, et pour cest effect elle porte des mammelles au ventre sous le nombril, ce que ne fait aucun poisson soit en mer ou en eau douce si ce n'est le loup marin ou le Comiaco, poisson fort grand qui se prend a la mer rouge et au grand Lac d'Alexandrie d'Egypte comme i'ay veu.[46]

La baleine c'est une beste d'une dangereuse rencontre pour les navigants a cause de sa monstruosité, ainsy que scavent bien les Bayonnois et Espaignols qui l'experimentent souvent et qui font mestier coustumier de les prendre avec certains instruments et machines [155v] desquels ils la ferissent. Estant blessée la poursuivent avec quelques moyens vaisseaux

45 This last phrase is repeated, then crossed out.

46 DPI: "y estant."

iusques a ce qu'elle approche de terre et soit morte où lors elle est cramponnée et tirée pres de terre, et alors Dieu scait le peuple qui est employé a la mettre en pieces et en remplit plusieurs vaisseaux, et de la chair et graisse ils traffiquent avec les estrangiers, parquoy la bonne pesche que l'on fait de ces animaux ce sont en lieux froids où se repairent le plus ces poissons monstrueux a cause de la grande quantité du poisson, qui est cause que sous la ligne Equinoctiale et pres des deux Tropiques elle ne frequente gueres dautant que le poisson n'y est trop frequente aussy, mais trop bien pres les deux poles comme i'ay veu, fidelement et diligemment observé. Encor que les baleines soient les plus grandes belues de toute la mer elles ont toutes le gosier si petit qu'a grand peyne peuvent elles avaler un poisson de la grosseur d'un moyen saumon.

Il ne me reste plus à ramentevoir aux Pilotes et Mariniers que le pays qui avoisine nostre Isle des Demons et la Baye de Canada qui est a la coste de terre neufve et s'estend loin dans la terre possible trois cens lieues au Sud-ouest et Ouest, et le lieu de Canada peut estre par les quarante six degres Nord de l'Equinoctial, par le milieu d'icelle baye descend une riviere d'eau douce qui provient d'une ville que l'on appelle Ouyslayna par les quarante trois degrés nord dudit Equinoctial. La terre Canadienne est bien temperée et fertile comme est celle de Gascoigne propre a produire toutes sortes de grains.

L'on a trouvé en plusieurs contrées de ceste coste de beaux seps de vigne y croissans sans labeur ou culture d'homme qui vive, qui portent de gros raisins que les Sauvages appellent Orobà, et sont bons a manger, toutesfois ie ne scay si le vin en est bon a cause que ie ne l'ay point veu en oeuvre. Ces vignes sauvages s'addonnent fort aux peupliers et hormeaux[47] ausquels estans iointes abondent en telle maniere en feuillage et branches qu'a grand peyne les peut on separer sans les rompre, et de telles especes i'en ay veu en l'Arabie heureuse en des lieux entre des hautes montaignes espesse d'arbres, et me souvient avoir veu non seulement en cest endroit mais en d'autres de la part du Mont Sinaj prenant la droite voye du chemin de Gazera que les Arabes appellent Gazer de la ou estoit le fort Sanson quelques colines, et sur icelles ie descouvray qu'il y avoit des feuilles de vigne. En quoy faut contempler une grand merveille, qui est, que ce bon arbrisseau [156r] se trouvant par toutes les quatre parties du monde est tousiours fort recommandé.

Au reste il se trouve en ladite region de Canada et terre neufve, du chanvre, encor que les barbares ne scachent comment il le faut appliquer

47 DPI: "Ormeaux . . . "

et s'en aider,[48] grande quantité de noisettes grosses, noix, pommes, poires sauvages, chastaignes en grande quantité, de toutes especes de bestes sauvages qui vivent la pluspart de ces fruits et plus que ne font les habitans du pays. Il s'y trouve aussy des Cerfs, Loups, Ours, Martes, Loups cerviers, bufles et vaches sauvages. Il n'y a ne Lyons, Tigres, Elephans, Chameaux, chevaux, mulets ne asnes, comme il s'en trouve en Afrique: bien s'y trouve grand quantité de mouches a miel, encor que le pays y soit fort froid, somme de[49] toutes autres especes d'animaux terrestres et aquatiques. La terre produit de telles et semblables plantes aux nostres, comme chaisnes, pins, sapins, espines noires et blanches, quj produisent certains petis fruits, et de plusieurs autres sortes a nous incogneues quj ont de grands vertus en elles, et diriez proprement que soyez en Gascoigne ou Languedoc. Ils ont des prunes qu'ils font secher pour l'hiver que nomment Honesta, et ont des figues asses grosses qui ne viennent point a maturité, et des febves grosses blanches qu'ils appellent Sahu et les noix Cahenya. Ils ne mangent chose aucune quj sente le sel. Lors que les nostres leur monstroient des raisins confits ils donnoient un estourdion de teste leur disant Nohda qui est a dire nous ne cognoissons point cela.

Et firent les Chrestiens une haute Croix de bois, contre laquelle estoit attachée une grande fleur de lis, autour de laquelle y avoit escrit, Vive Le Roy de France. Plantant ceste croix les Sauvages quj assistoient et estoient presens s'estonnoient grandement pourquoy l'on faisoit telle chose. Et contemplant ces brutaux que certains Chrestiens de la compaignie se prosternoient a terre devant Ladite croix les mains iointes, pensoient que par tels signes l'on les vouloit decevoir, et charger sur eux, et attirer a la pipée pour Les faire mourir. Huit jours suivans en apres arriva une Roy de soixante lieues de la ou estoient habitués les Francois, Lequel Roitelet tout vestu de peau accompaigné de six vingts hommes sauvages, chacuns desquels avoit l'arc et les flesches, autres garnis d'espées de bois et massues, fut mesmes irrité interrogeant les nostres, qui vouloit dire par tels signes d'avoir posé icelle croix, ou si c'estoit pour les decevoir et mettre [156v] a mort, ou bien s'ils vouloient prendre possession hereditaire de ce pays là et s'en faire maistres.

Sur ces entrefaites arrive un autre Roy le plus redouté de toutes les contrées nommé Donnacona accompaigné d'un autre Roy non moindre en authorité et craint de ce peuple que nul des autres qu'ils appeloient Agouhanna qui vint veoir les Chrestiens qui s'estoient desia fortifiés en

48 DPI: "il y a . . . "

49 DPI: "en somme il s'y trouve de . . . "

quelques endroits. Ce Roy donc accompaigné de quatorze barques et quelques cent sauvages pour recognoistre les vaisseaux des nostres, de prime face vouloit espouvanter ceux qui estoient dedans, mais sa cholere passée estant adverty par un Truchement que ne voulions que attirer leur amitié et faire nouvelle collonie en leur pays pour les maintenir et garder a lencontre de leurs ennemis, ce Roy commenca a s'approcher des nostres et faire une harangue usant de certains ceremonies selon la coustume barbaresque. Iceluy seigneur estoit accosté et suivy d'un autre mauvais garson dangereux au possible quj avoit nom Taignoagny. S'estans tous reconciliés tant les barbares que les Chrestiens furent a la parfin bons amis, leur faisant incontinent apporter vivres de toutes parts, comme chairs sauvagines, de poisson cuit tant et plus, et d'une telle sorte qu'ils estoient plus de soixante personnes tous chargés tant de chair, volaille[50] que fruicts. Lesquels s'approchans des nostres commencerent tous a crier a gueule desployée usans de ces propres motz, Aguyase, Aguyase, qui ne signifie autre chose en leur barragouin que Allegresse, Allegresse mes amis vous soyez les tresbien venuz faites bonne chere.

Leurs maisons Royales sont basties de bois et couvertes d'escorces d'arbres et feuillage. Quant aux autres maisons des plus pauvres elles sont aussy faites de bois, et souventesfois quand il fait froid elles sont couvertes de neige et de glace. Celuy qui a fait le plan du logis du Roy Agouhanna, se trompe grandement et la fait par fantaisie, d'autant qu'il la fait en rond et d'une facon comme sont les grandes maisons et forteresses des Roys de Barbarie. Chose inventée par luy, et aussy mal considerée que du peuple qu'il fait aller tous nuds a la facon des Bresiliens. Je fais juge le Lecteur si les hommes peuvent aller ainsy nuds aux pays froids ou en tous tems les rivieres sont glacées. Mesmes que les nostres au commencement sentans telles froidures estoient fort esbahis, ne pouvans aller d'une part a d'autre. Les Barbares gros, grands, forts et puissans ayans pitie d'eux les portoient sur leur col és lieux ou ils desiroient ou [157r] vouloient aller.

Advint un jour, qu'un ieune Gentil-homme Angevin qui estoit a la compaignie pria un certain Sauvage pour le porter et proumener a son plaisir, ce que le Sauvage feit. Le troisiesme iour que ce gentil Angevin apres qu'il eut disné et un peu haulcé le tems, voulut de rechef que ledit sauvage le menat s'esbatre comme au paravant. Estant l'Angevin sur les espaules du barbare Canadien tenant un baston a sa main, ainsy que le sauvage descendoit d'une certaine colline, luy advint faire un faux pas tant a cause des neges que du chemin qui estoit raboteux et pierreux.

50 DPI: "poisson . . ."

Lors le Gentilhomme comença a coups de bastonnades a frapper a tors et a travers sur ledit[51] sauvage, lequel se sentant offensé s'approche tout au pres du bord de la marine, et print mon Angevyn par le collet, et l'ayant estranglé le ietta au parfonds de la mer. Incontinant ayant fait le faict un certain Capitaine Francois, personnage asses modeste, voulant empescher iceluy sauvage de ietter son compaignon dans mer desguigna son espée estimant espouvanter le Barbare mais ne fut si prompt a ruer d'icelle, que ledict sauvage en fit autant qu'au premier et publiquement estrangla et culbuta en ceste sorte ces deux personnages qui espouvanta grandement la compaignie, et ainsy m'en fit le recit le Capitaine Jaques Cartier, estant logé en sa maison a S. Malo en l'Isle.

Or ayant quicté[52] la terre Canadienne, Isles des Demons, Baccaleos et le reste de Terre neufve, ceux quj veulent tirer de la part du Nord incontinant ayant vent propre vous apparoit la peninsule de Courte-real qui est faicte peninsule par le sein de S. Laurens et de celuy du Merore, comme est l'Arabie heureuse qui est pareillement faite peninsule par le sein Arabic et celuy de Perse. Suivant l'Isle de Gonse qui est Orientale et celle de Caravelle qui avoisine une autre Isle dicte de la fortune, qui sont Occidentales vous apparoit a gauche un port capable pour y mouiller l'ancre de cent grands vaisseaux. Son entrée tire de l'Est a l'Ouest qui peut avoir demie lieue de large et trois a sa plus grand longeur. Il faut se donner de garde devant y entrer de deux seches quj avoisinent l'entrée, pareillement de deux Isleaux qui sont au mitan du port, dans lesquels l'on se pourroit fortifier. Ceux qui voudroient habiter ces pays là ou y faire nouvelle collonie lesdites Isles sont fort propres. Ceux qui veulent passer outre et tirer vers nostre [157v] pole il ne faut pas qu'ils costoyent la terre pour les grands dangers de batteures et rochiers qui avoisinent la terre continente.

Autant i'en puis dire de ceux qui veulent entreprendre de Canada la route de la Floride et pays Perusiens [sic], lesquels ayans quicté le promontoire des Bretons et l'Isle de Thevet ainsy marquée dans nos cartes il faut que le pilote se donne garde de s'approcher trop pres de terre sinon dans petits vaisseaux et barquerottes, et tirer la droite route iusques a la riviere d'Arnodie, et celle de Juvide que laissez a droict. C'est une coste longue et dangereuse iusques a la riviere grande dicte Norambegue qui est l'une des belles rivieres apres celle d'Ochelaga qui soit en tous ces pays. Je vous ay (ce me semble) parlé en quelque endroit de ladite riviere de Norambeg

51 DPI: "ledit pauvre . . . "

52 DPI: "Or, cella fait, de peur d'encourir plus grande perte de nos gens, nous quittasmes . . . "

et de la belle Isle quj est a son emboucheure qui peut avoir deux lieues de tour; laquelle l'on pourroit peupler et fortifier encor que ladite riviere soit pleine de plusieurs escueils et rochers. C'est là ou est la bonne pescherie de molues.

Au surplus tenant tousiours vostre route droit au Sud vous venez a la riviere de Buemadre distant de Norambegue quelques huit vingts lieues. L'ayant passée vous descouvrez La baye grande, et puis la riviere de S. Christophe, et doubles droit au Sud-est iusques au Cap de S. Jaques, lequel l'ayant doublé vous trouves un autre Cap dict de Traverse, puis la riviere de Mallebregue, qui est l'entrée des terres de la Floride qui luy est distante de quatre vingts dix lieues. Ceux qui voudront passer outre il faut qu'ils se gouvernent selon la hauteur des lieux et rumbe des vents, et eviter le continent a cause des bourrasques soudaines qui leur porroient faire perdre la vie et les biens. Voila ce que i'ay bien voulu discourir a celle fin que les pilotes et mariniers ayent occasion de se contenter de moy, et eviter les perils tant d'une part que d'autre.

Le pais duquel Jay ci devant escript est de grande estendue duquel les hommes vivent quasi tous d'une mesme humeur et facon sans religion sans foy ni sans loy non plus que Bresiliens Austraux. Ilz different de langage les uns des autres principalement ceux de terres neufves, jadis nommee La terre aux bretons d'avec ceux de la grande riviere Ochelaga et pais de Saguenez. Et d'autant que ces contrees sont frequentees de present des Francois et Anglois Jay bien voulu pour le contentement du lecteur adjouster icy un petit dictionnaire de quelques motz propres et principaux de leur patois.[53]

[403r] Isle de l'Assomption
[Continuation]

Au reste aupres de ceste Isle de L'Assumption qui gist au nordest et oest susoest du Cap de Trenot et est acinquante degrez de hauteur et est le bout d'Icelle au Suest aquarante huit degrez et demi aiant cinq lieues de long Son bout tire a terre ferme vers le nort Le Cap de Trenot et ceste Isle de l'Assumption gisent au Suest nordest et Suroest un petit du nordest et sont distant l'une de l'autre trente quatre lieues[54] Cest une belle terre sans aucune montaigne assise sur roches blanches comme Albastre toute couverte d'arbres jusques au bord de la mer aiant force bestes sauvaiges

53 Fols. 158r–160v: the dictionary, from Ramusio, follows.

54 The DPI account omits the foregoing and begins here: "Au reste c'est une belle terre . . ."

comme Ours et Loups Serviers porcs espics [.] tirant au Cap Breton y peut avoir cinquante lieues distance lun de lautre prenant la route au noroest dela au Cap du Mont Nostre dame qui est laterre de la part du Sud Lon ne compte que quinze lieues [.] Ce dict Cap gist a cinquante neuf degrez cest une terre fort haute La pointe de l'Isle de L'Assumption et le Cap de Ognedor qui entre deux lieues dans mer sont nordest et suroest et y a de route vingtcinq lieues Le Cap de Ognedor y a un forillon tout a bout qui est blanc Ce Cap de la part du Nordest est toute roche blanche.[55] Entre celuy Cap et nostre Isle de Lassumption du costé du Suest et Lest oest la Route nest que vingt lieues et La Baye des molues est quarante huit degrez, La coste gist nort et sud et prend un quart du Nord est et Sur oest Jusques ala baye du Chaleur qui est eslonguee des monts de nostredame quelques quatorze lieues Toute cesté terre est haute et couverte d'arbres Quant a Ognedor cest une autre baye qui gist au nord nor oest et Su Suest aiant un tresbon port Lentree duquel est de la part du Nort Au bout duquel y a une pointe fort longue dans mer Si tu y veux mouiller lancre tu y trouveras quinze ou vingt brasses d'eau Lon y faict souventesfois aiguade a cause qu'il y a deux belles[56] Rivieres la source desquelles vient devers le noroest et se vont desgorger de la part du Suest

En ceste coste y a grande pescherie de molues et le poisson y [est] beaucoup la meilleure qu'en terre neufve Il y a plusieurs especes[57] d'animaux volatiles comme canards, oyes sauvages, airons [hérons], y a de toutes sortes d'arbres[58] mesmes des Roziers, framboises, noisettes poiriers et il y a aussy noyes sauvages et peux advertir le Lecteur quen ceste Isle de Lassumption il faict plus de chauld en quelques mois de l'ännee quen beaucoup dendroits de la France Et quant aux Sept Isles qui sont du coste du Nort elles gisent suest oest et noroest y a en la Route vingt quatre lieues au Cap Ognedor aux Sept Isles et trente cinq du cap du Mont Nostre Dame [.] qui veut aller de lun a lautre il faut tirer vers le nord Les Sept Isles sont acinquante degrez et demi de latitude Des dictes Sept Isles ala pointe Dongea qui sont nordoest et Suest y peut avoir quinze lieues Et y a entre les deux plusieurs petites Isles deshabitees qui avoisinent dassez loing la pointe Dongea et les montz de nostre dame De la part du Sud la pointe Dongea et la Riviere de Cay[59] gisent alest et loest. La Route

55 DPI: "roche blanche, là où lon tient qu'il y a mine d'argent."

56 The word "petites" is crossed out.

57 Crossings-out and illegible words follow; supplied from the DPI.

58 DPI: "comme avons . . . "

59 DPI: "Cau."

nest que douze lieues de lune a lautre Somme toutes ces terres comprises depuis LIsle de l'Assumption Jusques ala Riviere de Cau sont bonnes et la se trouvent toutes sortes d'arbres

La pointe Dongea est aquarante neuf degrez un quart Et la Riviere de Cay et lisle de Raquelle gisent nordest et suroest et y est en la Route douze lieues LIsle de Raquelle est a quarante huit degrez et deux tiers Ahuit lieues de là trouverez une autre Isle basse qui avoisine assez pres la terre Si vous passez plus outre pour tournoier [403v] se presente devant vous le Cap de Marbre que vous descouvrez de trois grandes lieues en mer Entre ce Cap et Raquelle y a fort peu de distance. Et avoisinent la terre continente de la part du Nort denviron deux lieues LIsle de Raquelle et l'entree de la Riviere Saguenay sont est nordest ouest suroest La Route en est de quatorze lieues

L'entree de Saguenay est une Roche blanche qui gist a quarante huit degrez quarante deux minutes de latitude Lentree n'a point plus de largeur que un quart de lieue Elle est dangereuse au possible pour les grands vaisseaux A cause quelle ne peult avoir que de huit a dix brasses d'eau Elle tire vers le Suroest Aians faict deux ou trois lieues dans lad[icte] Riviere Elle commence a s'eslargir et semble estre un grand bras de mer Les Sauvaiges nous disoient qu'ilz estimoient comme l'aians [ap]pris de leurs anciens peres que ce bras de mer passoit outre Jusques ala mer pacifique quilz appellent Quastroy A quoy se pouvoient tromper ces pauvres barbares [,] Aussy bien que Gemma Frizius et plusieurs antiens et modernes se sont imaginez trompez et deceuz marquans en leurs cartes un destour Septentrional A quoy sest trompe Martin Fourbicher Anglois lequel depuis cinq ans en ca sest rompu la teste pour passer outre de la mer Occeane a celle du Sud par ce destroit Septentrional comme ont faict Magellan et Pigafete par le destroit Austral Au reste ceste Riviere de Saguenay est merveilleusement desbordee et large comme J'ay dict en plusieurs endroitz de quelque quatre ou cinq lieues aians des bancs et Rochers tant et plus Dans lequel goulfre vous trouverez LIsle de Raquelluy et LIsle des Lievres qui gisent nordest et suroest prenant un peu de Lest et oest. La traverse de la Jusques a Saguenay peut avoir dix huit lieues L'entree de Saguenay a LIsle des lievres gisent nord nordest La traverse est de cinq lieues Voila la Route tant de la terre que de LIsle de LAssumption qui l'avoisine Priant le Lecteur si Jay este trop prolixe de supleer le Zele que Jay pour monstrer aux nouveaux mariniers la vraye voye quilz doibvent observer en ces pais lá, ce quilz doivent avoir en grande recommendation.[60]

60 The DPI has the following addition: "en grande et singuliere recommendation, de

[404r] Isle de la Damoiselle

Il me semble vous avoir assez amplement discouru, des meurs et facons des Canadiens, et autres peuples qui les avoisinent. Il ne me reste plus ce me semble qu'a vous discourir, dune Isle nommee La Damoiselle et de la Route quil faut tenir pour l'aller abborder. Je scay bien que la voye que je veux prendre sera un peu chatouilleuse au lecteur, toutefois utile et prouffitable aux pilotes et mariniers. Et parceque parcidevant je n'ay trouvé homme qui se soit voulu amuser a nous éclaircir la Route de ces pays la, il ma semblé bon de n'user d'ingratitude en l'endroit de ceux qui sont versez au pilotage en leur proposant icelle route, les dangers et inconveniens ou ilz se pourroient mettre s'ilz ne sont asseurez des passages et endroitz, Caps, Rivieres, Goulfes havres, promontoires, et Raddes, et les hauteurs ou sont exposez iceulx dangiers. Par quoy vous aurez ici a noter que Je vous ay parlé en quelques endroitz parcidevant du Cap de Ras et L'adresse de la grand' Baye asses peu cogneüe aux modernes et antiens pour n'en avoir faict la Recherche.

Le Cap de Ras donc et celuy Despere sont tous deux tendant au nordest et sur ouest, contant de l'un alautre un degré qui faict dix sept lieues et demie. Cap de Ras est a quarante sept degrez d'elevation, et celuy despere a quarante neuf et deux tiers d'un degré. Entre les deux se presente la baye de Rongneuse ou se peult avoir deux bonnes lieues distance l'un de l'autre en mer. Au mitan duchemin se presente un mauvais Rocher fort redoubté et tresdangereux pour aborder, faict en forme de navire, Le Cap despere et la terre de Baccaleos sont nort et Sud quart de nordest contans quatorze lieues delun alautre. Baccaleos gist aquarante huit degrez et demi en latitude, et gisent Baccaleos la grand Baye et LIsle des Apponas, nort et Sud prenans un quart du nordest et Sur ouest et y a en la Route trente cinq lieues a cinquante degrez et demi. La mer est en ces endroitz quelque peu herbeuse et dangereuse aux grans et moyens vaisseaux, et pour les Rochers bas àfleur deau, qui sont souventesfois couverts de la mer, quand elle est irritee et agitée des vens. Sur tout se voient deux Rochers entre les Isles des Apponas et les Belles Isles, qui gisent norouest et Suest prenans un quart du Nort et du Sud, contans de lung a lautre quelques trois lieues Ces Belles Isles sont acinquante un degré trente deux

---

peur que n'y prenans pas garde, et sans y penser ilx soient surpris des orages, et tempestes des vens, qui sont lá journaliers, et qui causent souvent naufrage à ceux, qui par leur ignorance s'exposent temerairement à la mercy de telx gouffres. Les marées y sont fort grandes, et tempestueuses, desquelles qui ne se prend garde, mesme le plus souvent les mieux advisez y sont trompez: On n'y sçauroit doncq trop apporter de consideration, de vigilance, et diligence, pour n'encourir point telx perilx, et dangers."

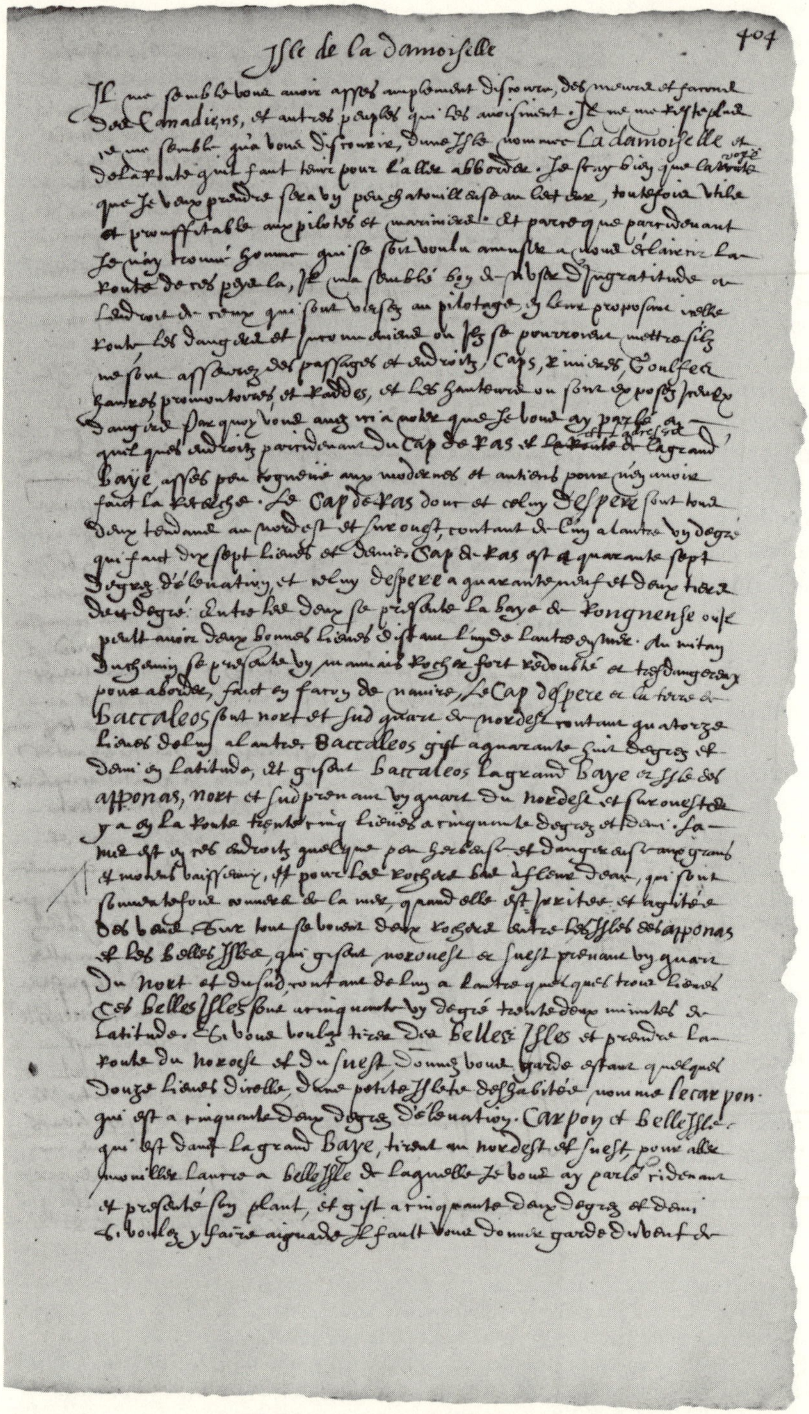

Figure 15 Folio of the *Grand Insulaire*
Thevet's *Grand Insulaire*, fol. 404r.
Courtesy Bibliothèque Nationale, Paris

minutes de latitude.

Si vous voulez tirer des Belles Isles et prendre la Route du noroest et du Suest, donnez vous garde estans quelques douze lieues d'icelles, d'une petite Islette deshabitée nomme Le Carpon[61] qui est a cinquante deux degrez d'elevation. Carpon et Belle Isle qui est dans la grand Baye, tirent au noroest et Suest, pour aller mouiller lancre a Belle Isle de laquelle Je vous ay parlé cidevant et presenté son plant, et gist a cinquante deux degrez et demi. Si vous voulez y faire aiguade Il fault vous donner garde du vent de [404v] lest qui vous est fort contraire et quasi journallier de peur que vous ne faciez nauffrage, et vous gisent ala coste de Loest. Du coste d'elle une demie lieue ou environ vous appercevez dun Rocher qui est entre ladicte Belle Isle et le Carpon. Et du coste de Lest y a un autre Islet plat deshabité et peuplé doyseaux. Si vous tirez du costé du noroest pareillement se presente un autre Rocher plat qui peut avoir demi quart de lieue de long tournoyé de battures et sablons.

Et quant a Carpon, si tu y veulx aller mouiller lancre du coste de Tierbot ou de Babort tu t'approcheras de Luy le plus doulcement que tu pourras. Et pourras ancrer entre celuy Carpon et trois petites Isles deshabitees. Aians levé les Ancres tu sortiras de la part du Nordest Rangians au long la Coste du Suest Jusques aune basse qui te demeurera du costé de Trierbot et prendras le Nort pour les dangiers qui s'en pourroient ensuivre Jusques quetuviennes[62] ala hauteur des buttes, qui sont trois petis forillons elevez en hault que tu rangeras assez loing de la bande du Nort distante de terre continente dune lieue et demie.

Aians passé outre et evité les dangiers la coste est saine Jusques a BelIsle de la grand baye et les Isles de Sablon qui l'avoisinent d'assez pres poursuivant tousiours la Route pour cognoistre les dangiers de ceste Canadienne Tu prendras le nordest oest et quelque peu du Suroest. Lon compte trente lieues de la grand Baye qui a sept lieües d'entree Jusques a Blanc Sablon quelque trente trois lieues. Et [. . .][63] tousiours laVoye Jusques aux trois Chasteaux, qui sont trois hautes montaignes qui se voyent en pleine mer de quatre acinq lieues[64] Blanc Sablon a huit lieues de large Jusques aterre ferme. Toute ceste coste de Blanc Sablon est

61 DPI: "l'Ecarpon . . . "

62 DPI: "jusques à ce que tu sois parvenu . . . "

63 Illegible word: DPI gives "iras."

64 In the margin, and appearing in the text of the DPI, is the following insertion: "entre lesquelles l'on touvera une mine d'or aussy bon pour le moins que celluy de Peru, laquelle a esté tenue secrete long tems de peur que les Espaignolx, et autres ne s'en emparassent, et s'y fortifiassent."

basse et saine qui tire du Nort et est [.] Blanc Sablon a cinquante et un degré deux tiers. Ce lieu est ainsy nommé a causeque la mer y est fort sablonneuse d'un certain menu sablon blanc comme recente neige.

De Blanc Sablon pour aller a FranceRoy qui est le propre pays de Canada se presente au chemin ceste tres belle Isle dicte LIsle de la Damoiselle ainsi nommée pour autant que ce fust en elle ou fust exillee la niece[65] de Capitaine Roberval Depuis fust transportee avec son amoureux en une autre Isle qui peut estre distante de celleci quelques dix sept lieües comme Je vous ay assez amplement discouru dans mon Livre des Singularitez,[66] Cest Isle[67] qui est avoisinee de plusieurs Isles et Isleaux et celle de [405r] Blanc Sablon sont les nordest, oest, suroest et prent un petit de l'est et oest. Elle gist a cinquante trois degrez trois quartz de latitude, laquelle aun bon port lequel tire de la part du nordest et n'a en sa largeur Iceluy port que environ la longueur de trois piques, A lentree duquel un peu a gauche se presente un Rocher qui vous demeurera ababort et Irez mouiller lancre apres avoir jette la sonde avingt brasses de travers assez pres dune petite Anse, Situen veux sortir aiant levé lancre il faut que ce soit par le costé du Suest laissans ladicte Isle a tierbot Et quant tu seras hors tu t'approcheras[68] de quelques autres Isles deshabitees couvertes darbres, qui te demeureront a tierbot puis tu prendras la Suest Jusques ace que tu verras cinq Rochers eloingnez de terre denviron Demy lieue. Laissans LIsle de la Damoiselle tu t'approcheras de la terre neufve nen estans elongné que de trente quatre lieues [.] dela tu tireras au Cap Breton courans le Nort nordest et Su Suroest

Javois oublié avous dire, qu'entre l'Isle dela Damoiselle et celle de Blanc Sablon ya grand nombre dIsles et Isleaux laplupart deshabitées, ausquelles y a de bons portz et Raddes, ou les vaisseaux peuvent estre en seurté, peuplees les unes dhommes les autres d'oiseaux de proye comme faul cons [sic] laniers tier celetz et autres. Des aigles tant et plus. Aians doublé lesdictes Isles vous tirez le cap de Trenot qui tire nordest et ouest Suroest. Il y a en la Route dix huit lieues. Le cap de Trenot est acinquante et un degré un quart. Il entre bien avant en la terre neufve soixante et dix lieues du Cap Breton. Et y a entre les Isles de la Damoiselle et le cap de Trenot six ou sept autres Isles Au reste ledit Cap[69] est avoisiné dune

65 The word "damoiselle" is crossed out.

66 The phrase "premier et second tome de ma Cosmographie universelle" is crossed out.

67 The phrase "de la Damoiselle" is crossed out.

68 Here there is a marginal insert, illegible but supplied from DPI: "avec le trinquet ou Papefix, de peur d'estre surpris d'une bourrache, et là tu rencontreras . . . "

69 The phrase "de Trenot" is crossed out.

part et dautre dune Isle nommee LIsle perdue qui est dangereuse pour les vaisseaux.

Jestime que cest en Icelle que se vouloit fortiffier le Seigneur Roberval lequel un jour aians faict le voyage de la Riviere de Saguenay accompaigné des Sieurs de Lespinay, Labrosse, Longeval et autres et de quelque nombre de soldatz embarquez dans un autre petit vaisseau vint un vent qui culbuta led[ict] vaisseau ou estoient lesdicts soldatz qui furent tous noyez Ce Cap[70] avoisine une autre Isle nommee de L'Assumption qui gist oest nordoest de laquelle Je vous ay cidessus parlé.

[405v] Isle d'Orleans

Il est question de scavoir que lorsque ceste terre Canadienne fust premierement descouverte par les Francois pour y faire nouvelle colonie et eussent penetré tant la coste de ceste terre que les environs et Rivieres dicelle estans curieux dimmortaliser le nom et la memoire des Rois et princes de France [,] Aians mis pied aterre en quelque lieu remarquable ou dans quelques Isles leur donnoient le nom de prince ou princesse de France comme ilz feirent de ceste Isle laquelle ilz nommerent Isle d'Orleans en lhonneur dun filz de France qui lors vivoit et se nommoit Lois de Vallois Duc Dorleans filz de ce grand Roy Francois de Vallois premier du nom. De laquelle Isle Je vous represente le plant[71]

Il est question de scavoir qu'aians doublé en ceste grand Riviere DOchelaga, plusieurs promontoires, comme celuy de Sainct Pierre au gouffre de St Laurens, Cap de St Lois, Cap de Mont moransi Isle Serree, LIsle Jay ple [Jaisple] Les Sept Isles qui avoisinent la terre continente adroit, la Riviere de Saguenay et celle de Canada qui porte le nom de toute la terre, se presente la aupres une autre Isle qui se dict Des Lievres qui tire nordest et Su suroest acinq lieues de la Riviere de Saguenay ahuit de celle de Raquelle qui tire de la part de noroest et Su suroest. Aians traversé toutes ces Isles et Isleaux, Laissant derriere La Nouvelle France qui estoit le propre pays de Canada et Ochelaga toute la terre tend au Sudoest beau pays plantureux et fertile, La terre plate laquelle on peut cultiver et fleurir sil ni avoit tant de barbarie entre ce peuple qui L'habite toute couverte d'arbres Jusques au bort de l'eau,

La coste du Nord est plus haute en d'aucuns endroitz a cause des montaignes qui tirent vers le Sud comprenans depuis L'Isle des Lievres ainsi nommee par un mien ami lequel aians le premier mis le pied en

70 The phrase "de Trenot" is crossed out.

71 The phrase "pour plus facilement vous donner son assiette" is crossed out.

terre sapperceut devant luy quelque nombre de Lievres semblables aceux de pardeca hormis quilz ont le poil plus[72] espois. Depuis ceste dicte Isle et celle DOrleans ceste grand Riviere dOchelaga en cest endroit na point plus de largeur que quatre lieues au plus L'Isle est au beau mitan de la Riviere dochelaga tirant La Route du Lac DAngoulesme qui est quasi ou ladicte Riviere seslargit de plus de quinze lieues en Rond. La longueur de nostre Isle [Orleans] est prise de Lest a oest et peut avoir en sa longueur quelques[73] cinq lieues et une et demie [406r] de largeur. Ce lieu est navigable pour les vaisseaux de quarante ou cinquante tonneaux Elle est avoisinee de grand nombre de petites Isles et Rochers Lair y est asses temperé souventefois[74] habitées de sauvages qui dressent des logettes pour prendre du poisson dont la Riviere est peuplee. De LIsle Dorleans aux Isles des Couldres gist la Route Lest nordest et Oest Suroest distante lun de lautre de quelques douze lieues. Et vous faut tousiours ranger la haute terre du Nord. Elle est tournoyee descueils et batteures aussi bien quest l'Isle des Couldres qui nest du tout ne si large ne si courte Et pour ce que la mer y court il y a plus grand danger LIsle des Couldres a environ une Lieue de long et demie de large toute couverte d'arbres devers le terroir qui vise au midi mais ce sont tous bancs et sables. LIsle de Couldres gist aquarante sept degrez trois quartz de longitude.[75]

Aians quité ceste Isle pour aller a celle d'Orleans faut prendre le nordest et suroest et ya en la Route dix lieues et demie. Il faut costoyer pour estre plus asseuré des bancs et battures le long de lahaute terre qui tire du Nort environ un quart de lieue pour raison que au mylieu de ceste Riviere comme J'ay dict ne sont que bancs et Rochers. Et quant tu feras la traverse du Cap Rond tu traver seras du costé du Sud tirans au Suroest auquel endroit trouveras sept ahuit brasses deau, et la aupres commence la Riviere doulce, et prend fin en cest endroit l'amertume de leau salee. Et quand tu feras la traverse de LIsle dorleans ou commence La Riviere doulce si tuveux passer outre tiendras ton chemin par le mylieu de lavitriere[76] et lairras LIsle du costé du tierbot qui est ala main droicte encores qu'en cest endroit la Riviere n'ait qu'un quart de lieüe elle est tres parfonde et de quinze avingt brasses d'eau. Et te demeurera la coste

72 The phrase "velu" is crossed out.

73 The word "trois" is crossed out.

74 DPI: "Ces Isles sont . . . "

75 Thevet means latitude. He makes the same mistake in the DPI.

76 DPI: "la Vitriere . . . " This word is apparently a metathetical flip of the pen for "la riviére." The copying of such absurdities in the DPI—as well as the different handwriting—argues for Thevet's use of a copyist for this manuscript.

vers le Sud outrouveras une fourmilliere dIsles la plus part deshabitees, toutes verdoyantes darbres et arbrisseaux Ceste Route dIsles dela part de babors et pointe de LIsle d'orleans sont plaisantes[77] Lair y est fort subtil et tresbon De ladicte Isle dorleans Jusques alagrande Riviere y peut avoir cinq lieues[78]

Du coste du Nort y a une autre Riviere que lon appelle Lestendue qui est main droite et vise un promontoire nommé Raguine qui est divisé par un autre promontoire nomme Passel [,] par une autre Riviere nommee en langue des sauvages Pabecherib qui prend sa source des montaignes vertes habitees dun certain peuple qui faict guerre a nos Canadiens. Passé que vous avez le grand Lac d'Angoulesme ensemble ce petit Archipelague qui est tout au Cul de LaRiviere vous trouvez le pays de Chilague et celuy de Tourtimage ou sont ceux qui habitent ces contrees pires que Diables Ilz ne pardonnent aleurs ennemis et les mangent ala facon des Bresiliens. Les navires comme Jay [406v] dict moiennant qu'elles ne soient trop grosses et chargees peuvent aller mouiller lancre Jusques a nostre Ile [sic] DOrleans depuis laquelle Jusques ala propre terre de Canada se trouvent plusieurs Rivieres grandes et moiennes. Les unes prennent leur source vers loest, les autres de la part du nordest et aians faict mille tours et virevoltes vont rendre leur tribut dans la grand Riviere.

Du bout de LIsle susdict aloest de Canada ni a que trois lieues Jusques a France Roy et quand tu seras au bout de LIsle tu verras une grosse Riviere nommee Ochelaga qui est assez distante de nostre Isle DOrleans. Franceroy ou Roberval avoit faict bastir une belle forteresse est a quarante sept degrez et un sixieme de degré [.] en toutes ces terres, lesquelles furent de mon temps apellees la Nouvelle France dautant quelle est aussi bonne et aussi temperee que nostre France et a la propre hauteur Et la raison pour quoy elle est plus froide en hyver est pourceque la Riviere douce y est naturellement plus froide que la mer, elle est aussi large et profonde en aucuns lieux. Cela advient aussi pour ce que la terre n'est labouree ni peuplee de gens; Joinct quelle est toute couverte d'arbres qui causent la froideur. Le soleil a son meridien aussi haut que le meridien DAngoulesme lieu de ma nativité et faict son midi quand le soleil est au Sud Suroest. Aussi Lestoille du nort par le compas demeure au Nort nordest Et quand a Angoulesme cest midi, A France Roy et a nostre Isle DOrleans n'ont que neuf heures et demie de Jour.

La coste de la France neufve Jusques en LIsle ni a point plus hault, de cinquante six lieues. De Lentree de Noranbegue y peult avoir cent

77 DPI: "est plaisante."

78 "Elle a en longueur environ cinq lieues et une lieue et demie de large" is crossed out.

cinquante lieües par terre, et de Noranbegue ala Fleur Nodder, trois cent lieües. Et DOchelaga environ quatre vingt lieues. De la en ce mesme goulphe et Riviere vous avez Saguenay estans sorti de la grand Baye ou extremite de la Riviere qui tire au Nordest oest Suroest tirant vers Ochelaga Les terres sont meilleures et plus grasses et peuplées de bois que les autres contrees Ce pays est abondant en tous biens principallement en sauvagine. D'arbres fruitiers tant et plus figuiers poiriers[79] et autres.

Jestime si lon fouilloit aux sommetz et costeaux des montaignes que sy trouveroit or et argent, suivant le recit de ce peuple, et tiennent pour chose asseuree que de la part de Sudoest y a une grande ville nommee Sebolla qui est par les trente et cinq degrez Les maisons de laquelle ville et temples de leurs Idoles sont couvertes d'or et les autres d'argent Ces terres aboutissent comme Ilz disent ala Tartarie orientale qui [407r] est Asiatique selon la Rondeur du monde

Qui voudroit ranger ceste coste et veoir dun bout alautre se faudroit que le pilote observast de lieu en lieu et de point en autre la Route par moy declaree avec deux ou trois petites navires de soixante cinq tonneaux pour destourner les Costes de la France Neufve Jusques ala Floride Les grands vaisseaux ni sont propres tant pour l'entree des goulfres et Rivieres que pour les dangereux Rochers et batteures dequoy les environs tenans et aboutissans sont pleines Joinct que la sonde n'est propre que pour les moiens vaisseaux si lon ne se veut mettre en dangier de nauffrage De Noranbegue a la Floride c'est le plus plaisant paisage qui soit en tout LUnivers et diriez costoyans la terre que vous estes au meilleur de la France Vous y trouverez la pluspart des mesmes arbres que nous avons pardeca comme, chesnes, fresnes, ormeaux, Erables, Pins, sapins, Cedres, trembles, noyers sauvages, noisettes, raisins sauvages, prunes rouges, et blanches y croissant les plus belles du monde, pois, febves, grozelles, frezes, et plusieurs autres fruitiers

Les bons vieillards du pays disent y avoir des bestes portans une seule corne au front, semblable acelles que Pline et autres auteurs antiens racomptent avoir en Aphrique et Asie que le simple peuple dict estre Lycornes Quant a moy Je ne le creus oncques Et suis heretique pour le faict du Lycorne comme Jay declaré mes raisons dans ma Cosmographie[80] non plus que des Euphones, Dryades ou Amadryadés. Au reste de mon temps lon semoncea quelque peu de Bled lequel vint a maturité et lon trouva a un espi y avoir huict vingtz graines de bled tel que nous l'avons pardeca. Il ne le fault semer qu'en mars et la cuillette se pourra faire

79 The DPI adds "pommiers."

80 DPI adds here "on les peult appeller Unicornes, mais non Lycornes."

Figure 16 "Figure of the *Maroli*, a very strange bird of prey."
Thevet's *Cosmographie universelle*, fol. 994r.
Courtesy John Carter Brown Library at Brown University

a la my oust Les eaux sont les meilleures du monde Si la terre y estoit labouree et pleine de gens le pays [seroit] aussi chauld et temperé que celuy de pardeca. La Raison pourquoy il neige plustost pardela quen France est pource qu'il ni pleut guerres la pluye se convertissans en neige. Il y a de belles forestz dans lesquelles on peut aller acheval voire y courire la lance sil en estoit besoing.

Roberval Lieutenans pour le Roy en Canada y arriva accompaigné de deux cens soldatz et mariniers pour son advenement Un mois apres quil eust visité la terre y feist bastir une tresbelle maison autour de laquelle y avoit deux touraces asses fortes, assises sur une montaignette pour se prevaloir de la barbarie des habitans et y feit une tres grande despence d'autant quen Icelle maison il feist faire plusieurs chambres deux salettes et autant de caves et de greniers, sans toutefois avoir dequoy les remplir. La aupres il feist faire deux molins à eau [et] ne se contentant de la grandeur et beaute dudict logis en feist commencer un autre au bout dune petit Riviere nommee en langue des barbares du pais Sinagua Roberval voians que [407v] les vivres luy defailloient de jour a autre envoia quelques navires en France conduitz par le Seigneur de Sauveterre pour faire entendre au Roy Francois premier quil n'avoit moien de garder ce pais la estant prive de toutes commoditez comme a la verité il estoit Car de bled & lard & farine & sydre ni vin navoit aucunement. Entre autres ce qui restoit de vin estoit gele dans les vaisseaux et sil neust este secouru des sauvages luy et les siens eussent esté mal acheval.

Ce pauvre peuple encor qu'il soit barbare vivans sans foy et sans loy sont neanmoins charitables [,] et considerans la pauvreté des estrangers affligez en ceste sorte despourveus de tous moiens s'efforcoient tant de Jour que de nuict de chasser aux sauvagines et ala pescherie, tellement qu'aians prins quantité de poisson comme Alloses et saulmons pour un petit cousteau ou une serpe Ilz donnoient aux nostres une trentaine de ces poissons. Ceste famine dura bien six mois entiers, sur lesquelles entrefaictes advint entre eux une grande maladie de fiebvres pestilentieuses de laquelle la plus part des sauvages morurent. Lors les nostres estoient contraintz d'aller ala pescherie ou mourir de faim Jusques a amasser dune part et dautre certaines herbes et racines pour les menger estans boullues avec de l'huille le loupmarins ou graisse de balesne Et me fust recité par quelquesuns de la compaignie que plusieurs d'eux mengeoient des champignons les faisans cuire aupres du feu sans sel ni sans beurre dont aucuns en moururent pour n'estre assaisonnez et accoustrez comme lon faict de pardeca. Estans les vaisseaux de retour Dieu scet comment les pauvres soldatz et mariniers estoient affamez.

Le capitaine Roberval estoit fort cruel alendroit des siens, les contraignans de travailler en leurs vacations autrement estoient privez du boire et du mengier. Il vouloit que chascun vescust en paix suivans les ordonnances par luy faictes. Lesquelles il faisoit garder fort soigneusement Car si quelqun defailloit[81] promptement il le faisoit punir. En ung jour il en feit pendre six, encores quilz fussent de ses favoritz, entre autres un nommé Michel Gaillon, Jehan de Nantes et autres et quelques uns qu'il fist exiller en une Isle aians les fers aux jambes pour avoir esté trouvez en larcin qui nexcedoit cinq souz tournois. D'autres furent fustigez pour le mesme faict tant hommes que femmes et pour sestre battus et Iniuriez. Encores que ces sauvages soient barbares plusieurs d'eux pleuroient et lamentoient la fortune des nostres

Ce peuple sont belles gens et presque tous nuds vestuz de peaux de bestes conroyees en leur facon ces peaux estans cousues les unes contre les autres leur couvrant tout le corps tant hommes que femmes Leurs chausses haut et bas et souliers sont de cuir et nont point de chemises ni de bonnetz mais ont la teste couverte de leurs cheveux troussez et liez avec certaines bandes descorces deliees darbres. Quant a leur vivre ilz mengent de toutes viandes sans saller Ilz font secher chair et poissons qu'ilz portent avec eux en guerre. La froidure est continuelle en ce pais la depuis la Sainct Martin dhyver Jusques a la mi Avril et les glaces grosses et espoisses.[82]

81 DPI: "à son debvoir . . . "

82 A Table of Contents follows, and at the end, "Thevet, 1586."

Description de plusieurs isles

Isle Dorleans

[126r] . . . Je ne veux oublier à vous dire que la mer en cest endroit là, et en beaucoup d'autres de cette coste est fort herbeuse et y a bonne pescherie, entre autres de Baleines, et autres poissons que les sauvages font seicher, incontinent qu'ilx l'ont pris, lequel ilx debitent, et permutent avec les peaulx des estrangers, [!] desquelles ilx font leurs accoustrementz. Et quant à la balaine, en ayans pris quelques unes, ilx mangent la chair, de laquelle ilz sont merveilleusement friandz. Quant est de la graisse, ils la fondent, et devient claire comme huile, et en usent pour leur boire comme font les Ethiopiens de l'huille d'olive, que j'ay veu boire: que s'il en reste quelque chose ilz s'en frottent et oignent tout le corps. L'herbe qui croist en cette mer n'est si haute et eslevée à fleur d'eau, que celle que lon voit au gouffre de Cuba, et c'est en cette mer ou ces Baleines repairent à cause de l'herbe qu'elles mangent, ensemble grande quantité de poisson, qui y fourmille,[1] et entre autres macquereaux, esperlans, harencs, et diverses autres sortes de petits poissons, lesquels elles engloutissent plus tost que de grands, a cause qu'elles ont le gosier fort estroit, et font venir ces petits poissons sur l'eau, ayans remué l'herbe, qui les couvroit.

Au reste [illegible character] ceste presente année 1588. De ceste Isle Dorleans certains sauvages conduisirent un marchant Pilote du païs de Basque, de la ville de Sainct Jan de Luc, à cens lieux de là, en une certaine montaigne ou ilx luy faisoient à croire qu'il y avoit bonne mine d'or. Estant arrivé à un port nomé des Barbares Gaspay, qui est assez voisin de la mer du sud, où estant arrivé, au lieu de trouver de l'or, n'y trouva que du metail rouge, pur, et net, duquel il en apporta en France quelque quantité et m'en a fait part. De là se embarqua en une petite Islette, nommée Nenan en sauvage, en laquelle jamais Chrestien n'avoit esté, qui despuis la nomma L'Isle de mettail.

1 The phrase "en cette mer là" is crossed out.

Bibliography

MAJOR WORKS WRITTEN BY ANDRE THEVET

Cosmographie de Levant

Cosmographie de Levant, par F. [Frère] André Thevet d'Angoulesme. Lyon, 1554; Lyon, Antwerp, 1556.

Cosmographia Orientis, das ist Beschreibung desz gantzen Morgenlandes, vor diesem frantzösisch beschrieben durch Andream Thevetum, jetzo aber in teusche sprache versetzt durch Gregor Horst. Giessen, 1617.

Cosmographie de Levant: Edition critique par Frank Lestringant. Geneva, 1985.

Singularitez de la France antarctique

Les Singvlaritez de la France Antarctiqve, avtrement nommée Amerique: & de plusieurs Terres & Isles decouuertes de nostre temps. Par F. André Theuet, natif d'Angoulesme. Paris, 1557; Paris, Antwerp, 1558.

Historia dell' India America detta altramente Francia antartica, di M. Andrea Thevet tradotta di francese in lingua italiana. Trans. Giuseppe Horloggi. Venice, 1561, 1583, 1584.

The New found vvorlde, or antarctike, wherein is contained wõderful and strange things, as well of humaine creatures, as beastes, fishes, foules, and serpents, trees, plants, mines of gold and silver: garnished with many learned aucthorities, travailed and written in the French tong, by that excellent learned man, Master Andrewe Thevet, and now newly translated into Englishe, wherein is reformed the errors of the auncient cosmographers. Trans. Thomas Hacket. London, 1568; Amsterdam and New York, 1971.

Les Singularitez de la France antarctique: Nouvelle édition, avec notes et commentaires par Paul Gaffarel. Paris, 1878.

Singularidades da França antarctica a que outros chamam de America. Prefacio, traducão e notas do Prof. Estevão Pinto. São Paulo, 1944.

As singularidades da França antarctica. Traducão de Eugenio Amado. São Paulo, 1978.

Les Singularités de la France antarctique. Ed. Jean Baudry. Paris, 1982; contains facsimile reprint of the edition of 1558.

Les Singularités de la France Antarctique: Le Brésil des Cannibales au XVIe siècle. Choix de textes, introduction et notes de Frank Lestringant. Paris, 1983.

Cosmographie universelle

La cosmographie universelle d'André Thevet, cosmographe du Roy. Illustrée de diverses figures des choses plus remarquables veües par l'auteur, & incogneües de noz anciens & modernes. 2 vols. Paris, 1575.

"The Cosmography of the Fraudulent Thevet," [extract] in *Magazine of American History* 8 (1882): 130–8.

"Grand Insulaire"

Le Grand Insulaire et pilotage d'André Thevet angoumoisin, cosmographe du Roy, dans lequel sont contenus plusieurs, plants d'isles habitees, et deshabitees et description d'icelles. 1588. 2 vols. BN MS fr. 15452 and 15453.

Vrais Pourtraicts

Les Vrais Pourtraicts et Vies des Hommes Illustres Grecz, Latins, et Payens, recueilliz de leurs tableaux, livres, medalles, antiques et modernes, par André Thevet Angoumoisin Premier Cosmographe du Roy. 2 vols. Paris, 1584.

Prosopographia or some select pourtraitures and lives of . . . illustrious personages . . . Trans. G. Gerbier, alias D'Ouvilly, etc. London, 1657.

Histoire des plus illustres et sçavans hommes de leurs siècles tant de l'Europe, que de l'Asie Afrique & Amérique avec leurs portraits en taille-douce tirez sur les véritables originaux. 8 vols. Paris, 1670–1; 1695.

The Lives of the Noble Grecians and Romans . . . To which are also added, the lives of twenty selected eminent persons of ancient and latter times translated out of the work of that famous historiographer . . . Andrew Thevet . . . and now in this edition are further added, the lives of several eminent persons, translated out of the aforesaid Andrew Thevet. Cambridge, 1676.

Les Vrais Pourtraits et Vies des Hommes Illustres. A Facsimile Reedition. Introduction by Rouben C. Cholakian. 2 vols. Delmar, New York, 1973.

Other Manuscripts

Description de plusieurs isles par M. André Thevet. 1588. BN MS fr. 17174.

Histoire d'André Thevet Angoumoisin, Cosmographe du Roy, de deux voyages par luy faits aux Indes Australes et Occidentales, contenant la façon de vivre des peuples Barbares, et observations des principaux points que doivent tenir en leur route les Pilotes, et mariniers, pour eviter le naufrage, et autres dangers de ce grand Ocean. Avec une response aux libelles d'injures, publiées contre le chevalier de Villegagnon. 1588. BN MS fr. 15454.

[Fragments] sur les Indes occidentales et le Mexique, comprenant, outre de l'Histoire naturelle et generale des Indes, l'Histoire du Mexique, et des fragments de divers livres. No date. BN MS fr. 19031.

De Jonghe, Edouard. "Histoyre du Méchique, manuscrit français inédit du XVIe siècle," *Journal de la Société des Américanistes de Paris* n.s. 2 (1905): 1–41.

Second Voyage d'André Thevet dans les Terres Australes et Occidentales. 1587-8. BN MS fr. 17175.

A SELECTED BIBLIOGRAPHY OF WORKS ABOUT ANDRE THEVET, AND REFERENCES FREQUENTLY CITED

Adhémar, Jean. "André Thevet Collectionneur de portraits." *Revue Archéologique* (1942-3): 41–54.

– *Frère André Thevet, grand voyageur et cosmographe des rois de France au XVIe siècle.* Paris, 1947.

Alfonse, Jean, see Saintonge.

Anonymous Conqueror, see Saville.

Atkinson, Geoffroy. *Les Nouveaux Horizons de la Renaissance française.* Paris, 1935.

Balmas, Enea. "Documenti inediti su André Thevet." *Studi di Letteratura storia e filosofia in onore di Bruno Revel.* Florence, 1965, pp. 33–66.

Baudry, Jean. *Documents inédits sur André Thevet, Cosmographe du roi.* Paris, 1983.

Belleforest, François de. *La Cosmographie vniverselle de tovt le monde. . . Auteur en partie Mvunster. . .* 2 vols. Paris, 1575.

– *Le Premier [-septiesme] tome des histoires tragiques . . .* 7 vols. Paris and other cities, 1564–1616.

Benzoni, Girolamo. *History of the New World.* Trans. and ed. W. H. Smyth. London, 1857.

Biggar, Henry P. *A Collection of Documents Relating to Jacques Cartier and the Sieur de Roberval.* Ottawa, 1930.

– *The Early Trading Companies of New France. A Contribution to the History of Commerce and Discovery in North America.* Toronto, 1901; reprinted St. Clair Shores, Michigan, 1972, pp. 231-42.

– *The Voyages of Jacques Cartier.* Ottawa, 1924.

Boyer, Abel. *Dictionnaire Royal François-Anglois . . .* London, 1759.

Brief Récit, see Cartier.

Brundage, Burr Cartwright. *The Fifth Sun: Aztec Gods, Aztec World.* Austin, Texas, 1979.

Cartier, Jacques. *Brief Récit, & succincte narration de la nauigation faicte es ysles de Canada, Hochelage & Saguenay & autres . . .* Paris, 1545. See also Biggar, *Voyages.*

Cabeza de Vaca, see Hodge.

Céard, Jean, ed. *Des Monstres et prodiges, by Ambrose Paré*, 4th ed., 1585. Geneva, 1971, pp. xvi, xxv, and passim.

– *La Nature et les prodiges: L'insolite au XVIe siècle, en France.* Geneva, 1977, pp. 282–9, 309–13, and passim.

Chiappelli, Fredi, ed. *First Images of America: The Impact of the New World on the Old.* 2 vols. Berkeley, 1976.

Chinard, Gilbert. *L'Exotisme américain dans la littérature française au XVIe siècle.* Paris, 1911.

Clark, James Cooper. *The Mexican Manuscript Known as the Collection of Mendoza and Preserved in the Bodleian Library Oxford.* 3 vols. London, 1938.

Codex Mendoza, see Clark; Ross.

Cortés, Hernándo, see Pagden.

Cotgrave, Randle. *A Dictionarie of the French and English Tongues.* London, 1611; reprinted Columbia, S.C., 1950.

Da Civezza, Marcellino. *Saggio di bibliografia geografia storica ethnografica sanfrancescana.* Prato, 1879, pp. 590–4.

De Costa, Benjamin F. *The Northmen in Maine.* Albany, 1870, pp. 63–79.

De Jonghe, Edouard. "Thévet, Mexicaniste." *International Congress of Americanists.* Stuttgart, 1906, pp. 223–40.

Destombes, Marcel. "André Thevet (1504-1592) et sa contribution à la cartographie et à l'océanographie." *Proceedings of the Royal Society of Edinburgh*, sec. B, 72 (1971-2): 123–31.

Dexter, George. "Cortereal, Verrazano, Gomez, Thevet." In *Narrative and Critical History of America,* ed. Justin Winsor. 8 vols. Boston, 1884; reprinted New York, 1967, 4: 1–32.

Dickason, Olive P. *The Myth of the Savage and the Beginnings of French Colonialism in the Americas.* Edmonton, 1984.

Fournier, P-F. "Un collaborateur de Thevet pour la rédaction des *Singularités.*" *Comité des Travaux Historiques et Scientifiques, Bulletin de la Section de Géographie* 25 (1920): 39–42.

Gaffarel, Paul. "André Thevet." *Bulletin de Géographie Historique et Descriptive* (1888): 166–201.

Gagnon, F-M. "Figures dans le texte. A propos de deux gravures dans Thevet." *Etudes Françaises* 14 (1978): 183–98.

– *Jacques Cartier et la découverte du Nouveau Monde.* Quebec, 1984, pp. 16, 39, 42, and 76–7.

Ganong, William F. *Crucial Maps in the Early Cartography and Place-Nomenclature of the Atlantic Coast of Canada,* with an Introduction, Commentary, and Map Notes by Theodore E. Layng. Toronto, 1964.

– "The Identity of the Animals and Plants Mentioned by the Early Voyagers to Eastern Canada and Newfoundland." *Transactions of the Royal Society of Canada*, 3rd ser., 3, sec. 2 (1909): 197–242.

Gentleman of Elvas, see Lewis.

Gómara, Francisco López de. *Historia general de las Indias . . .* Saragossa, 1552; reprinted 2 vols. Barcelona, 1954.

Gusman, P. "Les Singularités de la France antarctique . . . par André Thevet (1558)." *Byblis* 6, fasc. 23 (1927): 92–7.

Hair, P.E.H. "A Note on Thevet's Unpublished Maps of Overseas Islands." *Terrae Incognitae* 14 (1982): 105–16.

Hakluyt, Richard. *The Principal Navigations Voyages Traffiques & Discoveries of the English Nation*. Second ed. 3 vols. London, 1598–1600; reprinted in 12 vols. Glasgow, 1903–5; New York, 1965.

Harrisse, Henry. *Découverte et évolution cartographique de Terre Neuve et de pays circonvoisins 1497-1501-1769*. Paris, 1900.

– *The Discovery of North America: A Critical, Documentary, and Historic Investigation*. London and Paris, 1892; reprinted Amsterdam, 1961.

Hessels, J.H. *Abrahami Ortelii Epistulœ*. Cambridge, Eng., 1887.

Hodge, Frederick W., ed. *The Narrative of Alvar Nuñez Cabeça de Vaca*. In *Spanish Explorers in the Southern United States 1523-1543*, ed. Frederick W. Hodge and Theodore H. Lewis. New York, 1907, pp. 1–126.

Hoffman, Bernard G. "Account of a Voyage Conducted in 1529 to the New World, Africa, Madagascar, and Sumatra, translated from the Italian, with Notes and Comments." *Ethnohistory* 10 (1963): 1–79.

– *Cabot to Cartier. Sources for a Historical Ethnography of Northeastern North America, 1497–1550*. Toronto, 1961.

Huguet, Edmond A. *Dictionnaire de la langue française du seizième siècle*. 7 vols. Paris, 1925–67.

Jaenen, Cornelius J. "Conceptual Frameworks for French Views of America and Amerindians." *French Colonial Studies* 2 (1978): 1–22.

– "France's America and Amerindians: Image and Reality." *History of European Ideas* 6 (1985): 405–20.

– "French Attitudes toward Native Society." In *Old Trails and New Directions: Papers of the Third North American Fur Trade Conference*, ed. Carol Judd and Arthur Ray. Toronto, 1980, pp. 59–72.

Jeanneret, Michael. "Léry et Thevet: comment parler d'un nouveau monde?" In *Mélanges à la mémoire de Franco Simone, IV: Tradition et originalité dans la Création Littéraire*. Geneva, 1983, pp. 227–45.

Joppien, R. "Etude de quelques portraits ethnologiques dans l'oeuvre d'André Thevet." *Gazette des Beaux-Arts* (April, 1978): 125–36.

Lapouge, Gilles. *Equinoxiales*. Paris, 1979, pp. 50–8.

Laudonnière, René de. *L'Histoire notable de la Floride.* Paris, 1586. Reprinted in Hakluyt, *Principal Navigations,* ed. cit., vol. 8; new English translation, Charles E. Bennett, ed. *Three Voyages.* Gainesville, Fla., 1975.

LeClerq, Crestien. *New Relation of Gaspesia.* Ed. and trans. W.F. Ganong. Toronto, 1910.

Le Moyne de Morgues, Jacques. [Illustrations], in *Brevis narratio eorum quae in Florida . . . Gallis acciderunt . . .* by Theodore de Bry. Frankfurt, 1591. See also *The Work of Jacques Le Moyne de Morgues. A Huguenot Artist in France, Florida, and England.* Foreword, Catalogue, and Introductory Studies by Paul Hulton, with contributions by D.B. Quinn, William C. Sturtevant, and William T. Stearn. 2 vols. London, 1977.

Léry, Jean de. *Histoire d'un voyage fait en la terre du Brésil, autrement dit Amerique.* La Rochelle, 1578.

Lestringant, Frank. "André Thevet (1504-1592)." *Publications de l'Académie des Sciences d'Outre-Mer. Travaux et Mémoires. Hommes et Destins (Dictionnaire biographique d'Outre-Mer)* 4 (Paris, n.d.): 668–71.

– "L'Avenir des terres nouvelles." In *La Renaissance et le Nouveau Monde*, ed. Alain Parent et al. Quebec, 1984, pp. 45–51.

– "Champlain, Lescarbot et la 'conférence' des histoires." In *Scritti sulla Nouvelle-France nel seicento, Quaderni del seicento francese*, ed. P.A. Jannini et al. 6 (Bari and Paris, 1984): 83, 85.

– "La Conférence de Saint-Malo (1552-1553)." In *La Renaissance et le Nouveau Monde*, ed. Alain Parent et al. Quebec, 1984, pp. 37–44.

– "La Conférence de Saint-Malo, aujourd'hui." *Etudes Canadiennes/ Canadian Studies* 17 (1984): 53–68.

– "Deux mondes en miroir." In *La Renaissance et le Nouveau Monde*, ed. Alain Parent et al. Quebec, 1984, pp. 3–8.

– "L'Excursion brésilienne: Note sur les trois premières éditions de *l'Histoire d'un voyage* de Jean de Léry (1578-1585)." In *Mélanges sur la littérature de la Renaissance, à la mémoire de V.-L. Saulnier.* Préface de P.-G. Castex. Geneva, 1984, pp. 53–72.

– "Fictions de l'espace brésilien à la Renaissance: l'example de Guanabara." In *Arts et légendes d'espaces: figures du voyage et rhétoriques du monde*, ed. Frank Lestringant and Christian Jacob. Paris, 1981, pp. 205–56.

– "Millénarisme et Age d'Or: Réformation et expériences coloniales au Brésil et en Floride (1555-1565)." In *Les Réformes: Enracinement Socio-Culturel, 25e Colloque d'Etudes Humanistes, Tours 1-13 July 1982*, ed. Bernard Chevalier and Robert Sauzet. N.p. 1985, pp. 25–42.

– "Notes complémentaires sur les séquelles littéraires de la Floride française." *Bibliothèque d'Humanisme et Renaissance* 45 (1983): 331–41.

– "Nouvelle-France et fiction cosmographique dans l'oeuvre d'André Thevet." *Etudes Littéraires* (April-Aug., 1977): 145–73.

– "Les Représentations du Sauvage dans l'iconographie relative aux ouvrages du cosmographe André Thevet." *Bibliothèque d'Humanisme et Renaissance* 40 (1978): 583–95.

– "Les Séquelles littéraires de la Floride française: Laudonnière, Hakluyt, Thevet, Chauveton." *Bibliothèque d'Humanisme et Renaissance* 44 (1982): 7–36.

– "La Ville d'Angoulême et ses métamorphoses dans l'oeuvre du cosmographe André Thevet (1504-1592)." *Société Archéologique et Historique de la Charente. Extrait des Mémoires* (1977-1978): 29–50.

– *Voyages en Egypte 1549-1552: Jean Chesneau, André Thevet.* Coll. *Voyageurs Occidentaux en Egypte* 24 (Cairo, 1984).

–, and Christian Jacob. "Les Iles Menues." In *Arts et légendes d'espaces: figures du voyage et rhétoriques du monde*, ed. Frank Lestringant and Christian Jacob. Paris, 1981, pp. 9–18.

Lewis, Theodore H., ed. *The Narrative of the Expedition of Hernando de Soto, by the Gentleman of Elvas.* In *Spanish Explorers in the Southern United States 1523-1543*, ed. Frederick W. Hodge and Theodore H. Lewis. New York, 1907, pp. 127–272.

Lorant, Stefan. *The New World: The First Pictures of America.* New York, 1946.

Lussagnet, Suzanne. *Les Français en Amérique pendant la deuxième moitié du XVIe siècle: Le Brésil et les Brésiliens par André Thevet.* Introduction par Ch.-A. Julien. Paris, 1953.

Martyr, Peter [Pietro Martire d'Anghiera] *De Orbe novo: The Eight Decades of Peter Martyr d'Anghera.* Translated from the Latin with Notes and Introduction by Francis A. MacNutt. 2 vols. New York, 1912.

Métraux, Alfred. "Un chapitre inédit du cosmographe André Thevet sur la géographie et l'ethnographie du Brésil." *Journal de la Société des Américanistes* 25 (1933): 31–40.

Morison, Samuel Eliot. *The European Discovery of America: The Northern Voyages A.D. 500–1600.* New York, 1971.

Münster, Sebastian. *La Cosmographie universelle.* Basel, 1565. See also Belleforest.

– *Briefe Sebastian Münsters.* Ed. Karl Burmeister. Frankfurt, 1964.

Musset, Georges, see Saintonge.

Nordenskiöld, A.E. *Facsimile Atlas to the Early History of Cartography with Reproductions of the Most Important Maps Printed in the XV and XVI Centuries . . .* Trans. J.A. Ekelof and Clements R. Markham. Stockholm, 1889; reprinted Dover, New York, 1973.

Pagden, A.R., trans. and ed. *Hernán Cortés: Letters from Mexico.* New York, 1971.

Parent, Alain, et al., eds. *La Renaissance et le Nouveau Monde.* Quebec, 1984. Catalogue of the exposition "La Renaissance et le Nouveau Monde" at the Museum of Québec, 6 June-12 August, 1984, plus various articles and descriptive materials.

Parmentier, Jean, see Hoffman.

Pastoureau, Mireille. *Les Atlas français, XVIe–XVIIe siècles: Répertoire bibliographique et étude, avec la collaboration de Frank Lestringant pour* l'Insulaire *d'A. Thevet.* Paris, 1984, pp. 481–95.

Pinto, Estevão. "O Franciscano André Thevet." *Cultura Política* 3 (1943): 118–36.

Porcacchi, Tommaso. *L'isole piv famose del mondo descritte da Thomaso Porcacchi da Castiglione Arretino . . .* Venice, 1572.

Purchas, Samuel. *Hakluytus posthumus, or, Purchas his pilgrimes. Contayning a History of the World in Sea Voyages and Land Travells by Englishmen and others.* 5 vols. London, 1624–6; reprinted in 20 vols. Glasgow, 1905–7.

Quinn, David Beers. *Sources for the Ethnography of Northeastern North America to 1611.* National Museum of Man Mercury Series, Canadian Ethnology Service Paper 76. Ottawa, 1981.

Ramusio, Giovanni Battista. *Terzo volume delle navigationi et viaggi nel quale si contengono le navigationi al mondo nuovo . . .* (Venice, 1556; we have used the 1606 edition). New edition, Torino, 1978-, ed. Marica Milanesi.

Roncière, Charles de la. *Histoire de la marine française.* 3 vols. 3 (Paris, 1923): 362–91.

Ross, Kurt, ed. *Codex Mendoza: Aztec Manuscript.* Fribourg, Switzerland, 1978.

Roy, Jean-L. "Un Français au Brésil au XVIe siècle: André Thevet, cosmographe." *Revue d'Histoire de l'Amérique Française* 21 (1967): 363–96.

Sahagún, Bernardino de. *Historia general de las cosas de Nueva España.* English translation *Florentine Codex: General History of the Things of New Spain.* 12 vols. Ed. A.J.O. Anderson and C.E. Dibble. Santa Fe, N.M., 1950–69.

Saintonge, Jean Fonteneau de [Jean Alfonse de Saintonge]. *La Cosmographie avec l'espère et régime du soleil et du nord par Jean Fonteneau dit Alfonse de Saintonge, Capitaine-pilote de François Ier, publiée et annotée par Georges Musset.* Paris, 1904.

Salwen, Bert. "The Reliability of André Thevet's New England Material." *Ethnohistory* 10 (1963): 183–5.

Sauer, Carl O. *Sixteenth Century North America.* Berkeley, 1971.

Saville, Marshall H., ed. *Narrative of Some Things of New Spain and of the Great City of Temestitan Mexico: Written by the Anonymous Conqueror, A Companion of Hernan Cortes.* New York, 1917.

Schlesinger, Roger. "André Thevet on the Amerindians of New France." *Proceedings of the Tenth Meeting of the French Colonial Historical Society April 12-14, 1984*, ed. Philip Boucher. Lanham, Maryland, 1985, pp. 1–21.

Silveira Cardozo, Manoel da. "Some Remarks Concerning André Thevet." *The Americas* 1 (1944): 15–36.

Stabler, Arthur P. *The Legend of Marguerite de Roberval.* Pullman, Washington, 1972.

– "En Marge des récits de voyage: André Thevet, Hakluyt, Roberval, Jean Alfonse et Jacques Cartier." *Etudes Canadiennes/Canadian Studies* 17 (1984): 69–72.

– "Rabelais, Thevet, l'Ile des Démons et les paroles gelées." *Etudes Rabelaisiennes* 11 (1974): 57–62.

Touzard, Daniel. "André Thevet d'Angoulesme. Géographe et Historien, introducteur du tabac en France (1504-1592)." *Bulletin et Mémoires de la Société Archéologique et Historique de la Charente*, 7th ser., 7 (1907–8): 1–47.

Trudel, Marcel. "André Thevet," *Dictionary of Canadian Biography/ Dictionnaire biographique du Canada* 1: *1000 to 1700*, ed. George W. Brown and Marcel Trudel. Toronto, 1966, pp. 679–80.

– *Histoire de la Nouvelle France.* Montreal, 1963.

Wier, Jean [Johann Weyer]. *Histoires disputes et discours des illusions et impostures des diables . . .* French trans. Paris, 1579.

Winsor, Justin, ed. *Narrative and Critical History of America.* 8 vols. Boston, 1884; reprinted New York, 1967.

Wroth, Lawrence C. *The Voyages of Giovanni da Verrazzano.* New Haven, 1970.

Index

Bold figures refer to illustrations. Items found only in a note (or notes) are indicated by n following the page number.